South Vietnamese Soldiers

South Vietnamese Soldiers

Memories of the Vietnam War and After

Nathalie Huynh Chau Nguyen

BLOOMSBURY ACADEMIC
NEW YORK • LONDON • OXFORD • NEW DELHI • SYDNEY

BLOOMSBURY ACADEMIC
Bloomsbury Publishing Inc
1385 Broadway, New York, NY 10018, USA
50 Bedford Square, London, WC1B 3DP, UK
29 Earlsfort Terrace, Dublin 2, Ireland

BLOOMSBURY, BLOOMSBURY ACADEMIC and the Diana logo
are trademarks of Bloomsbury Publishing Plc

First published in the United States of America by ABC-CLIO 2016
Paperback edition published by Bloomsbury Academic 2024

Copyright © Bloomsbury Publishing Inc, 2024

For legal purposes the Acknowledgments on p. xv constitute
an extension of this copyright page.

Cover photos: SVN Rangers, 1968. (Vietnam Center and Archive); Vietnamese veterans marching
on Anzac Day in Melbourne, Australia, on April 25, 2011. (Photo Courtesy of Keith Broad)
Jacket design by Silverander Communications

All rights reserved. No part of this publication may be reproduced or
transmitted in any form or by any means, electronic or mechanical,
including photocopying, recording, or any information storage or retrieval
system, without prior permission in writing from the publishers.

Bloomsbury Publishing Inc does not have any control over, or responsibility for,
any third-party websites referred to or in this book. All internet addresses given
in this book were correct at the time of going to press. The author and publisher
regret any inconvenience caused if addresses have changed or sites have
ceased to exist, but can accept no responsibility for any such changes.

Library of Congress Cataloging-in-Publication Data
Names: Nguyen, Nathalie Huynh Chau.
Title: South Vietnamese soldiers: memories of the Vietnam War and after /
Nathalie Huynh Chau Nguyen.
Description: Santa Barbara, California: Praeger, [2016] |
Includes bibliographical references and index.
Identifiers: LCCN 2015047118 | ISBN 9781440832413 (alk. paper) |
ISBN 9781440832420 (ebook)
Subjects: LCSH: Vietnam War, 1961–1975—Personal narratives, Vietnamese. |
Veterans—Vietnam (Republic)—Interviews. | Soldiers—Vietnam (Republic)—
Biography. | Vietnam (Republic). Quân lực—Biography. | Vietnam (Republic)—
Armed Forces—Biography. | Vietnamese—Australia—Biography.
Classifi cation: LCC DS559.5 .N584 2016 | DDC 959.704/3409225977—dc23
LC record available at http://lccn.loc.gov/2015047118

ISBN: HB: 978-1-4408-3241-3
PB: 979-8-7651-2384-3
ePDF: 978-1-4408-3242-0
eBook: 979-8-2161-4726-8

To find out more about our authors and books visit www.bloomsbury.com
and sign up for our newsletters.

Copyright Acknowledgments

The author and publisher gratefully acknowledge permission to use the following materials:

Amended sections of the Introduction and Conclusion appeared in "Introduction: New Perceptions of the Vietnam War," in *New Perceptions of the Vietnam War: Essays on the War, the South Vietnamese Experience, the Diaspora and the Continuing Impact*, edited by Nathalie Huynh Chau Nguyen. © 2014 (Jefferson: McFarland, 2015), pp. 1–13. Reprinted here by permission of McFarland & Company, Inc., Box 611, Jefferson NC 28640. www.mcfarlandpub.com.

An amended version of Chapter 3 appeared as "Military Doctors in South Vietnam: Wartime and Post-War Lives," *Oral History* 43, no. 1 (2015): 85–96. Reprinted here by permission of the Oral History Society. www.ohs.org.uk.

An amended version of Chapter 6 appeared as Nathalie Huynh Chau Nguyen, "War and Diaspora: The Memories of South Vietnamese Soldiers," *Journal of Intercultural Studies* 34, no. 6 (2013): 697–713.

An amended version of Chapter 7 appeared as "Recognition of War Service: Vietnamese Veterans and Australian Government Policy," in *New Perceptions of the Vietnam War: Essays on the War, the South Vietnamese Experience, the Diaspora and the Continuing Impact*, edited by Nathalie Huynh Chau Nguyen. © 2014 (Jefferson: McFarland, 2015), pp. 184–202. Reprinted here by permission of McFarland & Company, Inc., Box 611, Jefferson NC 28640. www.mcfarlandpub.com.

An amended version of Chapter 8 appeared as "Fragmented Histories: The Intergenerational Transmission of War Memories in the Vietnamese Diaspora," in *Cultures in Refuge: Seeking Sanctuary in Modern Australia*, edited by Anna Hayes and Robert Mason (Farnham: Ashgate, 2012), pp. 79–94. Reprinted here by permission of the Publishers. Copyright © 2012.

In memory of my father, Nguyen Trieu Dan,
who served his country with distinction and was the last
Republic of Vietnam Ambassador to Japan in 1974–1975

For the men and women who served in
the Republic of Vietnam Armed Forces

CONTENTS

List of Illustrations	xi
Preface and Acknowledgments	xv
Introduction	1
Chapter 1. Generations of Soldiers	19
Chapter 2. In the Field	43
Chapter 3. Army Doctors	67
Chapter 4. Military Women	87
Chapter 5. Friendship and Sacrifice	109
Chapter 6. Aftermaths	139
Chapter 7. Recognition of Service	163
Chapter 8. Children of Veterans	183
Conclusion	207
Notes	213
Bibliography	255
Index	273

ILLUSTRATIONS

Map 1.	South Vietnam, 1966–1967	5
Map 2.	The Ho Chi Minh Trail, 1965–1966	8
Plate 1.	Captain Vu Hoai Duc in Vung Tau in 1954–1956	127
Plate 2.	Saigon circa 1953	127
Plate 3.	Lieutenant Colonel Tran Van Quan in Saigon on November 29, 1972, after a lecture he gave at the Vietnamese-American Association on the role of the 18th Logistics Battalion at the battle of An Loc. He is pictured with Mr. Daniel J. Herget, director of the Vietnamese-American Association	128
Plate 4.	Officer Cadet Nguyen Van Luyen with his best friend Phan Cong Ly at Thu Duc Military Academy in 1972. Ly served in the Airborne Division for a year and then transferred to the 25th Infantry Division. He died in a reeducation camp in Trang Lon in 1977	128
Plate 5.	Warrant Officer Nguyen Van Luyen in front of an M48A1 tank in Long Thanh in 1972. Standing on the tank behind him is his friend Doan Thanh Nghiep, whose life he was to save at the battle of Bau Bang in 1974	129
Plate 6.	Second Lieutenant Nguyen Van Luyen at home in late 1974 after he left the hospital. He was shot in the abdomen at the battle of Bau Bang and had multiple operations in hospital. He returned to the hospital for further treatment in early 1975	129
Plate 7.	Passport photograph of Warrant Officer Vu Van Bao in 1970	130

Plate 8.	Warrant Officer Vu Van Bao inside the side passenger door of a Chinook CH-47 in Fort Rucker, 1970	130
Plate 9.	Class 70-38 B-2 Officer Student Company VNAF U.S. Army Primary Helicopter Center in Fort Wolters. Warrant Officer Vu Van Bao is in the middle row	131
Plate 10.	Officer Cadet Tran Van Giac at Thu Duc Military Academy in 1968. The following year, he attended the Naval Academy in Nha Trang	131
Plate 11.	Lieutenant Tran Van Giac with navy friends in Qui Nhon in 1973 at a celebratory gathering after a successful operation in support of the infantry	132
Plate 12.	First Lieutenant Tran Xuan Dung, MD, in Saigon during the 1968 Tet Offensive	132
Plate 13.	First Lieutenant Nguyen Manh Tien, MD, in Saigon in 1973 just after he joined the Rangers	133
Plate 14.	First Lieutenant Nguyen Hoang Hai, MD, and his surgical team at work in Combat Field Hospital 1 in Quang Ngai in 1968	133
Plate 15.	RVNAF doctors and nurses operating in Combat Field Hospital 1 in Quang Ngai in 1968	134
Plate 16.	Corporal Bui Ngoc Thuy with her parachute pack over her shoulder at the jumping training site in Cu Chi in 1957	134
Plate 17.	Sergeant Nguyen Thi Minh Nguyet on the day of her graduation at the Military Social Services School in Saigon in 1973. She was the top graduate of her course	135
Plate 18.	Second Lieutenant Thuy in Pleiku in II Corps in 1973	135
Plate 19.	Leg bone and rope. Retrieved from mass grave in Cu Chi in 2011	136
Plate 20.	Identification tags of Ly A Sam, born May 19, 1950. Military Number 70/131238. Blood type: A+. Retrieved from mass grave in Cu Chi in 2011	136

Plate 21.	Watch with leather band. Retrieved from mass grave in Cu Chi in 2011	137
Plate 22.	Side by Side (detail). The Vietnam War Memorial in Victoria, Australia	137
Plate 23.	A Vietnamese Navy veteran marching on Anzac Day in Melbourne, Australia, April 25, 2011	138

PREFACE AND ACKNOWLEDGMENTS

The veteran on the cover of the book is a former South Vietnamese Ranger named Pham Van Chuong.[1] He was taking part in the Anzac Day Parade in Melbourne in 2011 when his photograph was taken. He has a gentle and slightly melancholy face, and the composition brings out the colors of the South Vietnamese flag sewn on his shoulder and the maroon of his beret. I found his image striking and used it for the first time at a public lecture I gave on Vietnamese veterans at the National Library of Australia in 2012.[2] I did not know who he was, only that he was a Ranger from the insignia on his uniform and beret. I arrived on his doorstep to interview him in 2013, and the moment he opened the door, I immediately recognized him. He told me that he knew about my 2012 lecture because he had a brother in Canberra who had noticed his image on the library flyers. He introduced me to his wife and we then did the oral history interview in his study.

Born in northern Vietnam to a Buddhist family in 1946, Chuong moved south with his mother after the Geneva Accords of 1954 split Vietnam into two halves north and south of the 17th parallel. As refugees, they formed part of the mass migration of a million Vietnamese who chose to leave the communist North for the noncommunist South. Chuong was not close to his father and was brought up by his mother. After completing high school, he went on to study law at the University of Saigon and worked part time in a bank while he was studying. Upon graduating in 1969, he was mobilized into the armed forces. He did nine weeks of training at Quang Trung and then attended Thu Duc Military Academy. He chose to join the Rangers—an elite corps of the Republic of Vietnam Armed Forces (RVNAF)—because, as he put it, "the war was everywhere, and young people wanted to join famous units like the Rangers and the Airborne." He served in the 7th Ranger Battalion and was sent to IV Corps in the Mekong Delta. He was placed in administration and finance because of his qualifications and work experience. Every month he would go out to the front for three days or maybe a week "to take money and supplies to the soldiers." A difficult memory was that of accompanying the body of his friend Vu Duy Long, a captain in the Rangers, back to his family. He remembers: "There were more than 100 coffins on the flight . . . He was a very close friend and I took him home. He had a wife and young child. It was very sad." A lieutenant at the end of the war, Chuong was interned for four years in communist prison camps. Prisoners were moved from camp to camp, and he was sent to Hoc Mon, Katum, Tay Ninh, Trang Lon, Long Giao, Suoi Mau, Long Khanh, and Suoi Mau again before finally being released in 1979. After a failed escape attempt in 1980, he was able to escape with his son in 1983. Like other former camp inmates, he was denied official registration papers by the postwar authorities. His three children were all born under their mother's name. He and his son reached Malaysia safely and resettled in Australia in 1984. It took Chuong five years to sponsor his wife and daughters to Australia. He remembers that he received "a lot of help from friends and ex-army officers." In 1996, Chuong was recognized as an allied veteran, qualified for an Australian service pension, and joined the Returned and Services League of Australia (RSL). He became president of the Ranger Association in the state of Victoria. He paid tribute to the two most important women in his life: his mother and his wife. Recalling his life in Vietnam and his military service raised strong emotions, and throughout his interview, he wept quietly.

The impetus for this book was the lack of visibility of the RVNAF in the historiography of the Vietnam War. The book forms part of my Australian Research Council Future Fellowship project on Vietnamese veterans. A key outcome of the project was the establishment in 2013–2014 of a new oral history collection at the National Library that contains the oral histories of thirty-six RVNAF veterans. Two generations of service personnel and all branches are represented: the Army, Air Force, Navy, Rangers, Marine Corps, Airborne Division, Regional and Popular Forces, and the Women's Armed Forces Corps. Veterans originate from southern, central and northern Vietnam. Interviews were conducted in English and Vietnamese with French terms used in interviews with older veterans.

Interviews in Vietnamese were then translated into English, which added another layer to the process of interpretation and analysis. In addition to these interviews, the book also draws on sixteen pre-project interviews conducted in Australia in 2010–2011 as well as on interviews conducted in 2005–2010 as part of an earlier project on Vietnamese women. Overall, the book is based on fifty-four oral history interviews. Interviews lasted one to four hours, with repeat interviews in a number of cases. The oldest veteran interviewed was born in 1917 and the youngest in 1955. While the narratives of senior officers are featured, the majority are those of junior officers, and some are from those who were in the ranks. While I was not able to include the oral histories of all the veterans—it would have necessitated a volume many times this size—all have informed my thinking. Vietnamese veterans have endured war, postwar incarceration, and the refugee experience. They have lived hard lives, and many have already died. Whenever younger veterans spoke of a former commanding officer, I would ask them whether they could refer me to him. The answer was often that he had died five or six years earlier. This project is therefore timely.

The purpose of the oral history interviews was to enable the veterans to tell their story. Veterans were not required to fill in questionnaires. Nor were they provided with a detailed list of questions relating to specific aspects of their experiences in the military.[3] The intention was to let them speak of their life from early childhood onwards. Some veterans were comfortable with stating "I was born . . ." and proceed from there to give detailed life histories while others provided a brief outline of their life and then went backward chronologically in order to relate specific incidents. While the veterans' military experiences were obviously a focus of interest, the emphasis was on the veterans telling their perspective of events rather than on the historian extracting answers to pre-prepared research questions.

Gathering material from Vietnamese veterans is a difficult process. Vietnamese are often reluctant to write or tell their life story because it is seen as an individualistic rather than community-oriented activity, and many have experienced censorship or imprisonment in postwar communist Vietnam.[4] Trust is a major issue for veterans, most of whom have experienced years of internment in communist prison camps and then escaped as refugees from Vietnam. Veterans have maintained links with relatives still in Vietnam, and some travel back to provide aid to disabled veterans.

While the majority of interviewees gave their full names, some requested that they only be identified by a single name. The book includes the stories of disabled RVNAF veterans who were interviewed during a brief trip to Australia in 2010. They are only identified by a single name for reasons of confidentiality. In order to gain access to veterans, I was able to draw on the assistance of the Australian Vietnamese Women's Association (AVWA), which has had more than thirty years of welfare experience in the Vietnamese community, RSL Footscray, whose president is a former South Vietnamese naval officer, and Vietnamese veteran associations as well as more informal networks. Personal referrals were essential, and it was important for veterans to be informed of the identity of my parents, and to know that my family had arrived in Australia as political refugees after the end of the war. I was conscious of the gap across age and gender lines in these interviews. I generally addressed veterans as either *chu* (uncle) or *bac* (senior uncle). In the case of female veterans, I addressed them as *co* (aunt). As I was born overseas and my Vietnamese is not fluent, veterans either made an effort to give interviews in English or allowed me to ask questions in English. In some cases, a relative or AVWA staff member would do some interpreting and then leave so that the interview could proceed in Vietnamese. Once the veterans had made up their mind to speak, they did so with generosity, and in the process entrusted difficult events in their lives to the interviewer. Several made a point of stating that they were glad to be given the opportunity to tell their stories. Many gave me additional material such as service magazines, unit histories, photographs, and copies of articles printed in local community newspapers or on websites. It was clear that veterans were conscious of the silencing of their experiences in the wider historiography of the war.

The research and writing of this book were made possible by the award of a generous four-year Future Fellowship from the Australian Research Council. The National Centre for Australian Studies at Monash University provided a welcoming home for the project, and I would like to thank Director Bruce Scates, center staff, and Halina Bluzer for their collegial support. I am grateful to Dean of Arts Rae Frances for supporting my research. At the National Library of Australia, I am indebted to Assistant Director-General Margy Burn and her staff, including Kevin Bradley, Shelly Grant, Rhys Kay, and Emily-Rose Horn in Oral History and Folklore, for their support and for enabling me to conduct several months of research in the Fellows Room in 2012–2014. At the AVWA, grateful thanks are due to Chief Executive Officer Cam Nguyen and her staff for their invaluable assistance in referring me to Vietnamese veterans and veteran organizations, and recommending transcribers and translators. Tania Huynh conducted interviews with eight veterans in 2014. Xuan-Dung Huynh liaised with several transcribers for the project including Hanh Bui, Tania Huynh, Quynh Luc, Long Nguyen, Serena Nguyen, Thuy Nguyen, Quynh Truong, Trinh Phan, John Thuy, and Giang Tran. I am indebted to translators Ngoc Bui, Tuan Bui, Quynh-Du Ton That, Phuong Mai Ung, and So Ung. Tuan Bui, in particular, went above and beyond the call of duty in responding to urgent requests for the translation of material in service magazines and unit histories. I thank RSL Footscray President Long Viet Nguyen for contacting veterans and for allowing interviews to be conducted at the club. My thanks to Cam Nguyen, Hoa Pham, Yen Bui, Andy Nguyen, Tien Kieu, Bao Vu, Xuan-Dung Huynh, Hung Doan, Paul Hawker, Jeanette and Phung Pham, Tien Nguyen, Thanh Le, Giac Tran, Phuc Le, and Minh Nguyen for referring me to veterans. For the pre-project interviews conducted in 2010–2011, I am greatly indebted to the work of Boitran Huynh-Beattie, who went to considerable trouble to conduct detailed interviews in Vietnamese with veterans and relatives of veterans in Sydney and Brisbane. Her unexpected death in 2012 was a loss deeply regretted.

Writing this book has been difficult on a personal level as well as in terms of the subject matter. My father died in 2013 and he was very much in my mind while I was writing this book. Although he was gravely ill in the last few years of his life, he always expressed pride in my work, and I would like to think that somewhere, he approves. At Praeger, I thank Steve Catalano, Military History Editor, for his immediate interest in the project and his patient support. I owe grateful thanks to all those who read draft chapters and provided comments: Gioconda Di Lorenzo, Eve Herring, Peter Hamburger, François Guillemot, and Jay Veith. I am particularly indebted to Peter Hamburger for his thoughtful comments and steady encouragement, and to Jay Veith for responding promptly to material sent to him. I thank Merle Pribbenow for providing detailed information on North Vietnamese troop movements. During the months of research I conducted in Canberra in 2012–2014, Peter and Barbara Hamburger provided wonderful home cooked dinners, and took me to visit Canberra and surrounds. My grateful thanks to Jeffrey Grey and Peter Edwards for putting aside time in their busy schedules in order to write the endorsements for the book. I presented earlier versions of book chapters at the Berkshire Conference on the History of Women in 2011 and 2014; the National Conference of the Oral History Association of Australia in 2011; the State Library of Victoria, the National Library, the 30th Anniversary Conference of the Oxford Refugee Studies Centre in 2012; the Monash School of Journalism, Australian and Indigenous Studies Seminar Series, the Vietnam: International Perspectives on a Long War Conference at the Australian War Memorial, the Vietnam War Symposium at Monash University Prato Centre in 2013; the Melbourne Memory and Commemoration East and West Workshop, and the Vietnamese Community in Australia—Victoria Chapter Dual Identity Leadership Program in 2014. I would like to thank those who invited me to present at these venues: Joy Damousi (with thanks to discussant Sonya Michel), Alistair Thomson, Jill Adams, Elena Fiddian-Qasmiyeh, Heidi El-Megrisi, Ashley Ekins, Kate Darian-Smith, Vivienne Nguyen, Pam Sugiman, and Stacey Zembrzycki. I am indebted to Kate Darian-Smith for her advice, and to Helen MacDonald, Katrena Mitchell, and Jenny Bars for lending a sympathetic ear. My thanks to Sherry Dowdy for the maps. My family and friends in Australia and overseas provided love and encouragement. Finally, this book would not have been possible without all the veterans who gave their time and spoke with such candor about their past, their experiences, and their memories.

INTRODUCTION

> *The Americans took the place of the French.*
> *The Vietminh were called the Vietcong.*
>
> *The Vietcong armed by China and the U.S.S.R.*
> *killed the Vietnamese and the Americans.*
> *The Vietcong prevailed.*
>
> *People fled overseas.*
> —Thuong Vuong-Riddick "History"[1]

My perception of the Vietnam War has been marked by the experiences of my parents and in particular those of my father. He came from a Buddhist family in northern Vietnam, proud of its history and with a long tradition of scholarship. His ancestral lands lie in the Red River Delta, and he has traced the history of his family, the Nguyen of Kim Bai, back to the fifteenth century.[2] Two brothers in the family, Nguyen Tue and Nguyen Huyen, were successful at the doctoral examinations in the imperial capital in 1511.[3] This was a rare achievement as only 1 percent of candidates were successful at these examinations.[4] Both brothers received the doctorate third class.[5] Their names are carved on a stone stele in the Temple of Literature in Hanoi. The older brother, Nguyen Tue, served as a minister under the Mac dynasty and received the title of *ba* or count.[6] He is featured in the *History of Dai Viet*.[7] Nguyen Tue's son, Nguyen Uyen, also achieved academic distinction. He was not only one of thirty-two men to receive the doctoral degree in 1535 but also became an academician and went to China in 1580 as a diplomatic envoy.[8] The fortunes of the Nguyen family rose and fell over the centuries. Over a period of four hundred years, only six men in the family were awarded academic titles.[9]

The last of these was my father's paternal grandfather, who returned to his birthplace at the end of his career as a mandarin and served as the last *Tien Chi* or Head Dignitary of Kim Bai before the ancient system of village administration was dismantled by the communists.[10]

The attachment of the Nguyen family to their ancestral lands was severed by the advent of Ho Chi Minh to power in 1945. Many family members fled south or overseas in the 1950s. It was a family of patriots that perceived communism as a divisive and destructive foreign creed. Tens of thousands of Vietnamese died in the communist purges of 1945–1946.[11] My father left northern Vietnam in 1950 with a copy of the family chronicles written in the Chinese script by his grandfather. His grandfather had taught him Chinese as well as the classics. The many papers detailing the family history and the history of the village of Kim Bai that existed in his grandfather's library were lost when war broke out in 1946. My father carried on the family tradition of scholarly endeavor overseas. He studied at the Institut d'études politiques (known as *Sciences Po*) and Faculté de droit de Paris (Paris Faculty of Law) in France, and obtained a doctorate in law. He served as a diplomat for the Republic of Vietnam. His older brother served in the Republic of Vietnam Armed Forces (RVNAF) and died in 1961. My father held diplomatic postings in England, India, South Vietnam, and France where he was present throughout the negotiations for the 1973 Paris Peace Accords. His last posting was in Japan where he was ambassador in 1974–1975. Our family became political refugees after the fall of Saigon on April 30, 1975. My parents sought asylum in Australia and arrived in Melbourne with their young family on a cold winter day in July 1975. They were able to bring up their children in a stable and prosperous country. My mother became a teacher, and later founder and president of a major community welfare association. My father joined the state public service. While my parents emphasized how fortunate our family was in being spared the final months and the final days of South Vietnam, during which so many died, the hidden injuries of the refugee experience underlay our lives. My father suffered a stroke in 1996, and died in 2013. He never saw his homeland again. Having witnessed communist depredations in northern Vietnam in his youth, he believed that South Vietnam represented the best hope for the future. He loved his country. He felt that with time, South Vietnam would have developed into a truly democratic state and achieved the same prosperity as South Korea or Thailand. I asked him to write a book about his experiences as a high-level diplomat during the war. His perspective as a northerner would have been invaluable. He never did so. He found the topic too painful, and in the end, he became too ill to write such a book. He once confided his belief that his stroke was brought on by the accumulated grief and stress of exile and the refugee state. I remember him sitting in his study listening to the melancholy strains of Trinh Cong Son's *Phoi Pha* (Passage of Time) sung by the great wartime singer Khanh Ly:

> Well, go then.
> What is there to life's journey
> bar the few seasons of youth.
> But sometimes
> from the garden of the night
> your footsteps return, soft and light
> like the soul of those years long ago.[12]

For him as for the million northerners who fled south after partition in 1954, voting with their feet against communism, the collapse of South Vietnam was devastating. Having already left the North, their hopes for a democratic future suffered a terrible blow when the South fell in turn. They had in effect lost their country twice.

My mother's family is Buddhist like my father's, but unlike him, she comes from southern Vietnam. On her mother's side, she is descended from a prince of the Nguyen dynasty who rebelled against the French in the nineteenth century, and fled south. Her father's ancestors, on the other hand, migrated from China to the newly settled lands in southern Vietnam in 1809 and intermarried with Vietnamese. One of my mother's earliest memories is that of witnessing the burning of her grandfather's house in Rach Gia by the communists in 1945. It was a beautiful house with a library and hand-carved columns made of wood imported from Cambodia. My grandmother pleaded with the communists not to burn the house down but to preserve it as part of the country's heritage. Her father-in-law had been a wealthy landowner and died a few years earlier. He had been a just and generous man, and in his memory, local villagers protected his daughter-in-law and her three children, and tried to save as many household items as they could. With their help, my grandmother was able to reach Saigon safely with her daughters. My mother was four years old, and watched as the communists set fire to the house. She remembers being furious as she saw the ashes of her grandfather's books drifting to the ground. She told herself that she would later store all her knowledge in her head and that way no one would be able to burn it out of her. After completing her *Baccalauréat* at the age of sixteen in Saigon, she went to England, where she attended boarding school for a year before sitting the entrance examinations for Oxford and Cambridge. Newnham College in Cambridge and Somerville College in Oxford both offered her a place. She chose Cambridge as she wanted to study economics. She met my father in London. They married after her graduation from Cambridge in 1962 and moved to India at the end of the following year. My siblings and I were all born overseas. My parents' stories are linked by their early exposure to war, their experience of being refugees from communism, and their belief in the importance of scholarship and public service.

It is from this background and family history that I wanted to explore the oral narratives of South Vietnamese veterans. South Vietnam is for the most part absent in the historiography of the Vietnam War. The experiences and aspirations of its people have been silenced, and the service and sacrifice of its soldiers negated. Forty years after the end of the war, it is time to give voice to the former soldiers who fought for the preservation of South Vietnam, and whose stories remain largely unknown. This book is shaped by their memories of and reflections on the war.

SOUTH VIETNAMESE PERSPECTIVES

During its twenty years of existence between 1955 and 1975, South Vietnam embodied an alternative vision of Vietnam to the one-party state that existed north of the 17th parallel. North Vietnam sought to impose communism on the whole of Vietnam. South Vietnam resisted for two decades. With a smaller population than North Vietnam, and containing competing factions and different interest groups, South Vietnam was, for all its faults, a far more open society than North Vietnam. The politicization of the war, the presence of a substantial foreign press corps, and opposition to the war in the West led to every flaw in South Vietnam being magnified while a corresponding silence existed on human rights violations in North Vietnam and communist war crimes. As Anthony James Joes writes, South Vietnam was "a wartime society open to scrutiny by the press, whereas North Viet Nam was not. Very few journalists seemed to appreciate the profound importance of this asymmetry."[13]

Over two decades from the time of the First Republic (1955–1963) under the presidency of Ngo Dinh Diem through the military coups and instability of the Interregnum Period (1963–1967) to the Second Republic (1967–1975) under the presidency of Nguyen Van Thieu, South

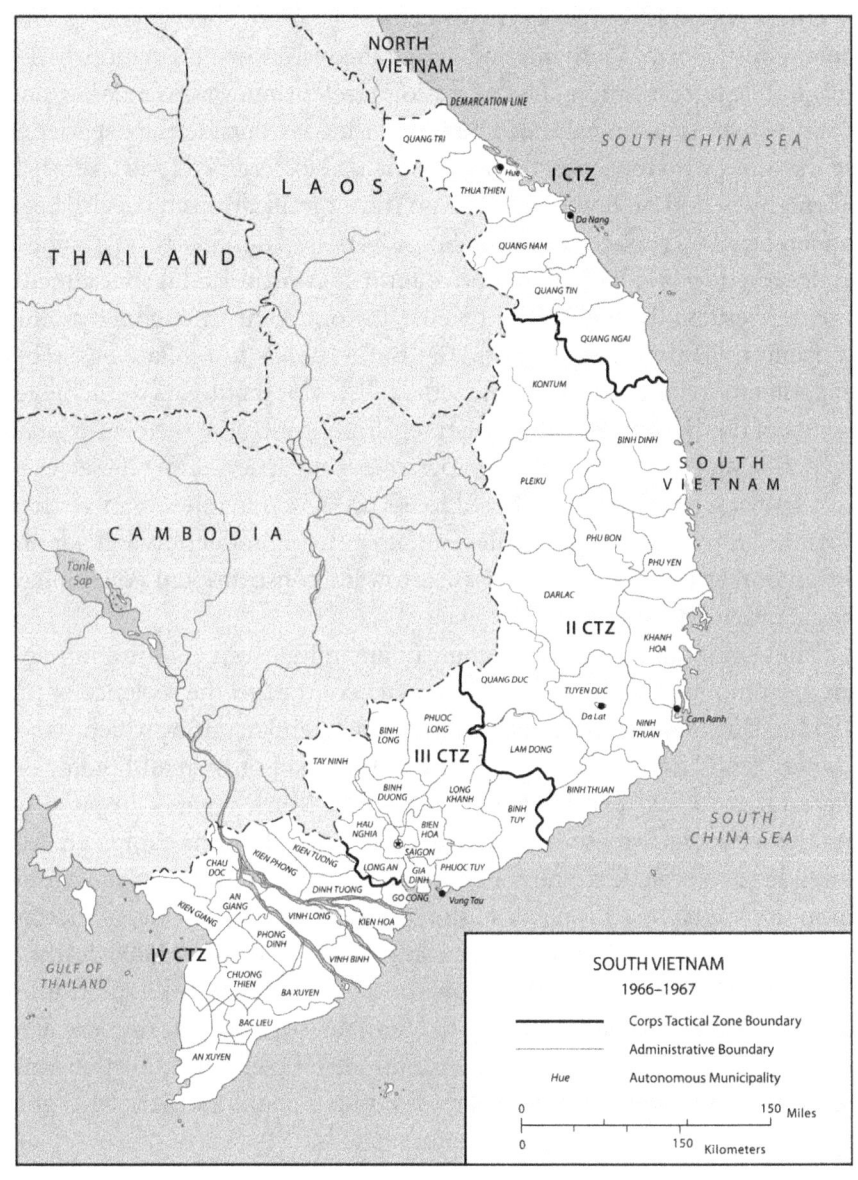

Map 1
South Vietnam, 1966–1967. (U.S. Army Center of Military History)

Vietnam was confronted with two central tasks: to survive war against communist North Vietnam, and simultaneously work on nation building and democratization. The effects of unrelenting war on an army and country over such an extended period of time lay outside the experience of the allies who fought in the war. None had experienced war over such a lengthy period on home soil. The political ramifications have also been underplayed. Through considerable adversity, the South Vietnamese endeavored to build a representative form of constitutional government. South Vietnam, in the words of Keith Taylor, "went through a dynamic wartime trajectory from authoritarianism to chaos to a relatively stable experiment in parliamentary democracy."[14] Taylor highlights the achievements of the Second Republic: first, regaining control of the countryside; second, a successful land reform program during which 2,750,000 acres of rice-growing land were distributed to 900,000 rural families or more than six million people[15]; third, achievements in food production and administrative reform; and fourth, progress toward constitutional government and a relatively independent judiciary.[16]

These gradual reforms in a country emerging from colonization and engaged in protracted war were in marked contrast to the violence of the 1953–1956 Land Reform campaign in North Vietnam during which "landowners" and "rich peasants"—most of whom had only small holdings—were targeted and executed by the Ho Chi Minh regime. Inspired by its Soviet and Chinese antecedents, the Land Reform campaign was intended as a prelude to the collectivization of agriculture. Official figures from the *Vietnamese Economic History* reveal that the majority of victims were unjustly accused, and that the campaign resulted in 172,008 deaths.[17] The attention of the world was on the 1956 Hungarian Revolution in Europe, and the crimes of the North Vietnamese Land Reform campaign passed largely unnoticed, as did later atrocities committed by the communists against the South Vietnamese civilian population, most notably in the former imperial city of Hue in 1968.[18]

South Vietnam was at war throughout most of its twenty-year history. With a small population of approximately eleven million in 1955, it was able to enjoy a brief interlude of peace at the beginning of the Ngo Dinh Diem government. The Diem government defeated the armed gangs of the Binh Xuyen, dealt with the Cao Dai and Hoa Hao religious sects, and successfully resettled a million refugees from North Vietnam. Nguyen Ngoc Phach came from a northern Buddhist family and worked as a journalist for the BBC before joining the RVNAF in 1965. After graduating from Thu Duc Military Academy, he served as press officer for General Cao Van Vien, the chief of the Joint General Staff. In addition to his army duties, Nguyen Ngoc Phach worked freelance for the *Telegraph*, the *Saigon Post*, the *Guardian*, and the *Vietnam Enquirer*, and wrote fortnightly Vietnam Reports for the Vietnam Council on Foreign Relations. He recalls the relative peace of the early years under Diem:

> I remember that period because at the time one of my brothers, my sister and a few of my nephews went to school in Dalat. I would drive to Dalat every Saturday and drive back to Saigon Sunday and I could drive 300 kilometres through the forest at night. Whatever people say, I held President Diem responsible for that peace.
>
> I didn't understand the communists until they killed one of my colleagues. One of my good friends in the press was Mr. Tu Trung Vu Nhat Huy.[19] He was assassinated right in front of his wife. He was the editor of the best newspaper in Saigon at the time, *Chinh Luan* [Opinion]. As far as the communists were concerned, if you are a good man and do your job then it can't be good for the revolution. During President Diem's tenure, the communists killed a lot of teachers, especially in the countryside. In faraway provinces like Ca Mau it was very difficult for the government to recruit teachers, and then those who were recruited had a good chance of being killed.[20]

The communist "campaign of terror" took hold in the southern countryside in 1956, and accounted for the murder or abduction of more than 25,000 South Vietnamese civilians by 1965.[21] Village officials, medical personnel, social workers, and schoolteachers were specially targeted.[22] The Diem government responded by killing 2,000 communists and arresting 65,000 communist sympathizers and suspects.[23] Southern party membership fell and party historians identified 1958–1959 as "the darkest period."[24]

As detailed by Lien-Hang Nguyen in *Hanoi's War*, the main architect and strategist of North Vietnam's war effort was Le Duan, who became the first secretary of the Vietnam Workers' Party in 1960 and held the top position until 1986.[25] Both Le Duan and Le Duc Tho, the head of the Central Organizing Committee, had as their goal a full-scale war for reunification and worked to achieve that objective.[26] Le Duan's Resolution 15 of January 1959 called for the overthrow of the Diem government by political and military means.[27] Group 559 was established later that year in May 1959 to maintain the infiltration of arms, matériel, and

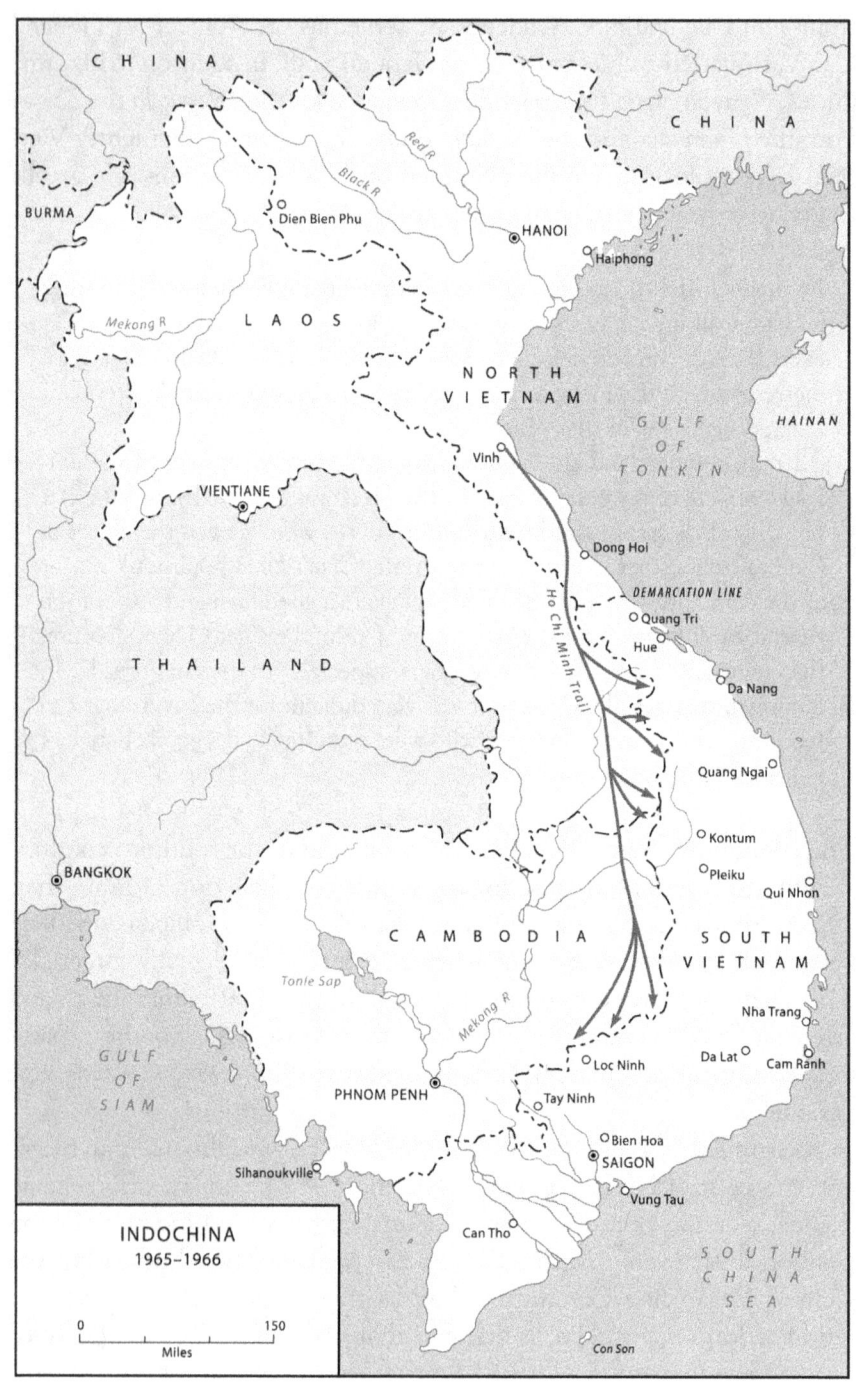

Map 2
The Ho Chi Minh Trail, 1965–1966. (U.S. Army Center of Military History)

troops down the Ho Chi Minh Trail into South Vietnam while the foundation for the National Liberation Front (NLF) was laid at the Third Party Congress in Hanoi in September 1960.[28] At the Ninth Plenum in December 1963, Le Duan advanced the military strategy of General Offensive and General Uprising, a move that would "elevate the Vietnamese civil war to an international Cold War conflict."[29] North Vietnam was fully mobilized behind the campaign for total war by 1964.[30]

Both North and South Vietnam fought the war with the aid of their allies. While North Vietnam was supported by the Soviet Union and the People's Republic of China and their satellite states, South Vietnam had the backing of the United States and its allies. Throughout the war, the North Vietnamese were supplied with more sophisticated weapons by their allies. As Nguyen Ngoc Phach notes,

> North Vietnamese soldiers infiltrating into South Vietnam were equipped with AK47s and rockets as early as 1964. The AK47 was equivalent to a submachine gun. At that time South Vietnamese infantrymen, and even the Marines and the Airborne, were equipped with M1 guns, the standard infantrymen weapon from the Second World War. So there was nothing farfetched about a squad of North Vietnamese overrunning a company of South Vietnamese troops. Equipped as they were with AK47s and B40s, the North Vietnamese had ten times the firepower of South Vietnamese troops. It was only after the 1968 Tet Offensive that the South Vietnamese troops were equipped with something similar to the AK47.

During the battles of the 1968 Tet Offensive, the "sharp automatic bursts of the AK47" on the North Vietnamese side contrasted markedly with the "single shots of the Garand M1 or M1 carbine" on the South Vietnamese side.[31]

It was a sad irony of the war that the precise juncture at which the South Vietnamese population rallied to their government—the 1968 Tet Offensive—was also the point at which the Western allies began to turn away from South Vietnam, and set in train their withdrawal from the country.[32] By the time the Paris Peace Accords were signed, nearly all allied troops had left the country. The RVNAF was thinly strung along the entire length of the country trying to protect it from invasion from several different fronts. When North Vietnam launched a full-scale invasion of South Vietnam in 1972, it threw fourteen divisions supported by armor and artillery against the South but the South prevailed. In 1975, the South collapsed. The collapse, as George Veith argues, did not occur as a result of military incompetence or an unjust dictatorship but because the massive scale of the North Vietnamese invasion, which was in full abrogation of the Paris Peace Accords, struck a country in severe economic straits and weakened by the vast reduction in U.S. aid.[33] President Thieu also made serious military misjudgments in the face of the 1975 Offensive.[34] The steep cutbacks in U.S. aid had had a disastrous effect on RVNAF morale as well as firepower and mobility by 1974:

> [A]rtillery batteries in the Central Highlands that had previously been firing 100 rounds daily were reduced to firing 4. By that summer, each ARVN soldier received only 85 bullets per month. In the Delta, the most populous part of the country and the area where the Communists had always been weakest, cutbacks to the navy forced it to deactivate half of its units, thus uncovering that whole strategic area. The shortage of new batteries cut army radio communications by 50 percent. Aircraft flew fewer missions, and many planes ceased to fly at all because they lacked replacement parts. About half of the ARVN's truck force was put in mothballs for lack of fuel and parts. Even the bandages for the wounded had to be washed and used again.[35]

South Vietnam fought the war at a significant disadvantage and with a gaping wound in its side. North Vietnamese sources reveal that one million troops were infiltrated into South Vietnam between 1959 and 1975.[36] The 1973 Paris Peace Accords left 145,000 North Vietnamese soldiers stationed in South Vietnam. In 1973–1974, 150,000 North Vietnamese troops were transferred south, with an additional 110,000 troops sent in the first four months of 1975 alone.[37] While South Vietnam was crippled by the lack of fuel, munitions, and spare parts, North Vietnam continued to receive aid from its allies. The supply of arms and matériel down the Ho Chi Minh Trail increased to 140,000 tons between January and September 1973, and reached a staggering 823,146 tons between January 1974 and April 1975.[38] As Lewis Sorley writes, "Americans would not have liked hearing it said that two totalitarian states—the Soviet Union and the People's Republic of China—had proven more reliable than the American democracy, but that was indeed the fact."[39]

South Vietnam and its armed forces have been criticized for corruption and factionalism. Former South Vietnamese general Lam Quang Thi acknowledges the extent of both but also argues that corruption is allied with poverty and that this is often a characteristic of emerging nations.[40] He adds that this did not prevent his rise to a generalship, even though he was not part of a political faction, and that many South Vietnamese generals were not from wealthy families but from an undefined middle class consisting of small farmers, teachers and low-ranking civil servants.[41] Another commonly cited problem in the RVNAF was that of desertion. Between 1965 and 1972, "desertions averaged about 120,000 per year, and the average monthly desertion rate was 12 per thousand."[42] Robert Brigham points out, however, that these figures do not take into account three factors: first, the RVNAF had an unusually stringent active-duty classification and many "deserters" were later found to be back in service with their units; second, another 60 percent were subsequently found to be serving in other units; and third, U.S. military advisers estimated that only 20–30 percent of those listed as deserters were actually so.[43] The reasons for desertion were social and economic rather than political, and soldiers did not desert to the other side.[44] Joes finds it instructive to compare these desertion rates to those in another civil war, the American Civil War, during which desertion rates were ten times higher or more.[45]

In spite of the presence of more than a million northern refugees who fled south in 1954, many South Vietnamese were unaware of the extent of repression in a communist state. They found out too late when they experienced the reality of life under a postwar communist regime. When South Vietnam fell to North Vietnamese forces in 1975, and Vietnam was reunified under a postwar communist regime, the ensuing exodus of more than two million people over the following two decades represented a new phenomenon in Vietnamese history. As the following words by Phan Dong Bich convey:

> The Vietnamese people [are] not a migratory people. . . . [I]n 1945, when we had a famine in North Vietnam, two million people died but nobody left the country. We had eighty years under French domination but nobody left the country. We had more than a thousand years of Chinese domination but nobody left the country—because we, as the people of Vietnam, we cling to the soil of our ancestors. We are attached to our villages; we are attached to our cities, our towns; to our friends and relatives. Up until the upheaval of 1975.[46]

The scale of mass departures following the communist takeover of South Vietnam was unprecedented, and this point needs to be emphasized. The postwar exodus followed widespread state repression in the postwar years, including the internment of more than a million former soldiers, civil servants, and teachers in communist reeducation camps,[47] the forced deurbanization of another million to the New Economic Zones,[48] the execution of 65,000 citizens,[49] curtailment of individual and religious liberties, nationalization of commerce and industries,[50] and discrimination against all those associated in any way with the former South Vietnamese government as well as against ethnic Chinese and Amerasians.[51] For many southerners, the reality of the communist state was a shock. As a former law student from the University of Saigon recalls, "I have to admit that the communists were very skillful at spreading propaganda. No one could have foreseen the atrocities that they were capable of committing."[52]

ORAL HISTORY AND MEMORY

"The most distinctive contribution of oral history," suggest Robert Perks and Alistair Thomson, "has been to include within the historical record the experiences and perspectives of groups of people who might otherwise have been 'hidden from history.'"[53] This description is particularly apt in relation to the former soldiers of the Republic of Vietnam. Their histories and perspectives have been "hidden from history" and are only slowly emerging.[54] Histories of the Vietnam War have overwhelmingly privileged the American experience, and those who perceived the war to have been an unjustified enterprise have dominated its historiography. While interest has focused on the smaller allies in the conflict, and more recently on North Vietnamese perspectives and the role of the Soviet Union and the People's Republic of China in the war, the South Vietnamese experience remains elusive.[55] As noted by Jeffrey Grey:

> The Vietnam War impacted primarily and most directly upon the Vietnamese, but the Vietnamese themselves, and especially those former soldiers and citizens of the Republic of Vietnam, are largely invisible in the extensive published literature on the war. The people, the nation, and the cause on whose behalf we fought have yet to be consciously and effectively written into the history of their own war.[56]

In light of the fact that the South Vietnamese were central participants in the war, and the war was largely fought on South Vietnamese soil, this lacuna reflects the partial nature of Vietnam War historiography.

South Vietnam paid a heavy price in the war. More than a quarter of a million South Vietnamese soldiers were killed over the twenty-year period between 1955 and 1975.[57] The RVNAF won significant victories against great odds in battles such as An Loc and Quang Tri in 1972. More than sixteen U.S. Presidential Unit Citations were awarded to South Vietnamese units in recognition of their gallantry in the field.[58] Le Cau, a highly decorated former colonel in South Vietnam, makes an impassioned defense of those who served in the Army of the Republic of Vietnam: "As a man who spent twelve years in combat, I can honestly say that we had many brave, diligent, and patriotic soldiers in our armed forces. They fought valiantly and selflessly against the communists year after year. Many sacrificed in silence and gave their lives [for] their country."[59] RVNAF deaths in the last few years of the war illustrate the extent of losses in the south: 39,587 in 1972; 27,901 in 1973; and 31,219 in 1974.[60] South Vietnam had a population of approximately eighteen million. The number of RVNAF wounded in action was between three and five times the number of dead.[61] As Neil Jamieson writes, "about one of every five soldiers, perhaps one of every twenty adult males, was killed or seriously wounded while fighting for the government. . . . Since virtually every soldier who was killed or wounded had a wife, parents, children, brothers, sisters, and friends who were affected, there were few people in the society whose lives were not blighted by deep personal loss."[62] Despite the scale of these losses, the service of South Vietnamese soldiers has not only been erased from national memory in postwar Vietnam but also suppressed in the wider historiography of the war.[63]

The Vietnamese state pays tribute to the communist soldiers who died in the war in the form of numerous war memorials throughout the country while remaining silent on the military dead of the former South Vietnam. Heonik Kwon notes,

> The postwar Vietnamese state hierarchy put great emphasis on controlling commemorative practices and propagated a genealogy of heroic resistance wars, linking the death of a soldier in the American War to a line stretching back from the French War to the legendary heroes of ancient victories. Every local administrative unit in Vietnam has a war martyrs' cemetery built at the center of the community's public space, and the reminder, "Our Ancestral Land Remembers Your Merit," is inscribed on the gothic memorial placed at the center of this place.[64]

This version of the past removes South Vietnam from the national historical narrative along with all those who fought in its armed forces during the war. The military cemeteries of the south were razed after 1975,[65] or lay abandoned in the postwar years. South Vietnam's war dead remain unacknowledged in the Vietnamese memorial landscape. "[S]outhern dead," writes Hue-Tam Ho Tai, "absent from national commemoration, often go unmentioned in the collective narrative of their extended families. Condemned to the shadows, they refuse, however, to remain unmourned."[66] The war will remain a problematic and contested memory as long as the Vietnamese state refuses to acknowledge the dead and disabled soldiers of the former south. Many severely disabled RVNAF veterans were unable to leave the country after 1975, and have experienced extreme hardship and poverty in postwar Vietnam.[67] Their crippled bodies form loci of memory, and reveal the disjuncture between public or state-sanctioned memories of the war, and private or bodily memory.[68] Denied a service or disability pension by the Vietnamese government, the only help these veterans receive often takes the form of charitable donations from overseas, in particular Vietnamese veteran associations based in North America or Australia.[69]

South Vietnamese servicemen and their families were labeled *nguy* (puppet)[70] by the communist regime, and were subjected to political discrimination in postwar Vietnam and harassment on the part of Vietnamese authorities.[71] Many veterans experienced years of internment and hard labor in postwar reeducation camps while their families were evicted from their homes and forcibly relocated to the New Economic Zones.[72] Those who survived then became refugees or left Vietnam under the Humanitarian Operation Program and resettled overseas. Their avenues for mourning, remembrance and commemoration were to be found away from their homeland, either privately within the context of family and friends or publicly among veteran communities in their new host societies. The firsthand experience of RVNAF veterans is a part of Vietnam's history that for practical reasons can only be recorded at present in the diaspora. The life histories and perspectives of these veterans not only contest state narratives of the war circulating in Vietnam but also interrogate the ways in which the war has been remembered and memorialized internationally. As Katharine Hodgkin and Susannah Radstone note,

> [T]o contest the past is also, of course, to pose questions about the present, and what the past means in the present. Our understanding of the past has strategic, political, and ethical consequences. Contests over the meaning of the past are also contests over the meaning of the present and over ways of taking the past forward.[73]

With their histories silenced and their war dead forgotten in postwar Vietnam, how do South Vietnamese veterans remember the war? What resources of self-reliance or resilience are they able to draw on? How do they commemorate the country and the armed forces that they served?

The oral narratives of these veterans reflect not only on issues of memory and commemoration in the aftermath of war but also on the shaping of stories following state repression and forced migration. Memory, by its very nature, is subjective. As Inga Clendinnen writes, "our stories depend on memory, and memory is unreliable."[74] Oral testimonies are therefore problematic, as they rely on memory. However, as oral historians have argued, memory's very unreliability is also its strength, as it provides "clues not only about the historical experience but also about the relationships between past and present, between memory and personal identity, and between individual and collective memory."[75] The narratives of these veterans strive to make sense of the past in light of their own experiences as well as their current lives and support structures overseas. "In a dynamic way then," suggests Catherine Kohler Riessman, "narrative constitutes past experience at the same time as it provides ways for the individuals to make sense of the past."[76] These former soldiers have had to contend with loss at a personal and communal level. Their individual stories take place amidst the wider tragedy of the collapse of their country. Many have lived hard lives, sustaining injuries in wartime, imprisonment in postwar prison camps, the loss of loved ones, and the stresses of the refugee or migration experience. Their narratives reveal that in spite of successive hardships, tragedies and traumas as well as the considerable challenges posed by the rebuilding of lives in a different country and culture, their loyalty to their former army and country remains steadfast, and their memories and processes of commemoration robust and tenacious.

South Vietnam was a militarized society with several generations in a family serving in the forces. Chapter 1 explores the experiences of three veterans from different generations. The oldest was born in 1917 and is one of the oldest surviving veterans of the Vietnam War. He served in France and North Africa during the Second World War, and in Vietnam during the Indochina War and the Vietnam War. The second veteran was born in 1930 and commanded a logistics battalion from 1972 to 1975 while the youngest was born in 1953, served as a junior officer during the war, and twenty years later joined the Australian Army as a direct entry captain. Their stories illustrate the diversity of ages, backgrounds, and motivations of those who served in the RVNAF. The experiences of soldiers in the field are the topic of Chapter 2, which deals with the combat exposure of junior officers from less well-known branches of the armed forces: armor, air force, and navy. The narratives of these veterans reveal a level of fortitude that sustained them through the unique pressures of combat, witnessing death and injury on the battlefield, enduring internment and separation from loved ones after the war, and escaping their country as refugees. Chapter 3 focuses on the narratives of military doctors who served in elite frontline units during the war: the Vietnamese Marine Corps and the Vietnamese Rangers. Their oral histories elucidate not only the commitment of highly educated officers in the RVNAF during the war but also their capacity to rebuild their lives overseas and honor their service in the aftermath of war. The histories and experiences of women who served in the Women's Armed Forces Corps are examined in Chapter 4. Their narratives illustrate their different motivations for enlisting in the forces, and the importance of military service in the shape and structure of their lives. These women volunteered to serve their country in wartime, and this service exacted a heavy toll in terms of the loss and trauma experienced in the postwar years. All, however, have been sustained by the support provided by veterans and veterans' associations overseas. Chapter 5 explores the notion of friendship and sacrifice in war by focusing on the narrative of a former Ranger, and his retelling of the fate of a friend and fellow Ranger in the last days of the war. His narrative reveals the courage of a group of Rangers who chose to follow their commander and fight "to the last bullet" in the final days of the war. The few survivors, along with their commander, became prisoners of war, and were shot by their captors and buried in a mass grave. The chapter examines the uncovering of this war crime and the excavation of the mass grave in 2011, and reflects on the ways in which these events have been reconstructed and memorialized. Chapter 6 contrasts the experiences of Vietnam-based veterans with those of veterans overseas, in particular the consequences of war for RVNAF soldiers who received disabling injuries during the war. Their narratives reveal that life for these veterans worsened considerably after the war. Despite more than thirty years of oblivion and neglect, the former soldiers still reveal their pride in their service, and the validity of the choices that they made. In Chapter 7, Australia's recognition of the formal status of RVNAF veterans is examined, from the political controversies that arose in the Australian parliament over this issue in 1985–1986, to the official recognition of South Vietnamese veterans as allied veterans and their entitlement to an Australian service pension. Finally, Chapter 8 deals with sequelae of war: the children of RVNAF veterans, from those who watched their fathers serve in the war and then saw them disappear into the gulag only to return years later as gaunt strangers to those who were born after 1975 and have no memories of the war. It explores the intergenerational transmission of war memories and the damage woven into some lives while others have been able to focus on futures overseas.

The oral histories and testimonies gathered here are valuable precisely because history has so far neglected them. The narratives of these former soldiers form a part of Vietnam's history that can be preserved for a time when Vietnam can finally acknowledge them. In the absence of history, as Vieda Skultans suggests in *The Testimony of Lives*,

> memory acquires a central importance for the preservation of authenticity and truth as well as a peculiar poignancy. The role of memory has certain similarities in all totalitarian societies where the state has claimed a monopoly of truth. Under such conditions, individual lives bear witness against the state.[77]

By "bearing witness," these veterans make an essential contribution to the recorded history of the war.

CHAPTER 1

Generations of Soldiers

My family has a long military tradition.
My father also served in the army,
and I was born on an army base.
—Nguyen Viet Huy[1]

These words by Nguyen Viet Huy convey not only a family history of service in the military but also his part in that tradition. His father was a sergeant in the National Army of Vietnam and moved his young family south as part of the mass migration south following partition in 1954. He went on to serve for twenty years in the RVNAF and rose to the rank of major before his discharge from the army just before the end of the war. Huy's older brother served in the Airborne Division, and Huy became an officer cadet in 1972 and joined the Regional Forces. He was taken prisoner in April 1975 when communist forces occupied Phan Thiet in Binh Thuan Province, where his battalion was based. Huy's family had the opportunity to escape from Vietnam, but they all waited for him. He relates: "I never made it so they were caught, and my brother, who was a paratrooper, was sent to a concentration camp. He was released after me, and was treated very badly."[2]

Like other militarized societies, South Vietnam saw several generations in the one family serving in the armed forces. The Republic of Vietnam was divided into four military tactical zones with I Corps covering the northernmost provinces of the country, II Corps covering the Central Highlands, III Corps covering Saigon and surrounding areas, and IV Corps covering the Mekong Delta. Many of those who became senior officers in the RVNAF began their military careers in the National Army of Vietnam (1950–1954). Compulsory military service was established in South Vietnam in 1955 for men aged twenty to twenty-two, and the length of service increased from twelve to eighteen months in 1959.³ In 1964, the age requirement was extended to twenty-five, and military service extended to three years for enlisted men and four years for noncommissioned officers and officers.⁴ The age requirement was further extended to twenty-six in 1965 and thirty-three in 1967.⁵ Following the 1968 Tet Offensive, general mobilization was declared on June 19, 1968, and all males aged between sixteen and fifty were called for military duty.⁶ Those aged between eighteen and thirty-eight were inducted into the RVNAF while those aged below eighteen and between thirty-nine and fifty were incorporated into the People's Self-Defense Forces (PSDF).⁷ In many families, nearly all male adults were in the military. Those who were children in the 1970s remember grandfathers, fathers, and uncles in the forces. As one recollects, "My grandfather was a career soldier, my uncle, my other uncle, cousins of my uncle . . . all the males in the family went to join the war."⁸ In Bui Ngoc Thuy's family, it was not only the sons who were soldiers—two daughters in the family also enlisted in the army in 1955—making it four out of six siblings who were serving in the military.⁹

The war left lasting scars in the lives of those who lost loved ones in the conflict. Kim had four brothers serving in the RVNAF, and of those, two were killed in action, the third lost his leg, and the fourth died of illness after the war.¹⁰ Yung Krall, author of *A Thousand Tears Falling*, worked as an army radio journalist in IV Corps during the war. She remembers donating blood in response to an urgent request from the military hospital in Can Tho in 1964.¹¹ There had been heavy casualties after nearby fighting, and Krall was told that a wounded soldier was awaiting her blood type.¹² She returned to the hospital that evening to see the soldier and describes the scene that confronted her:

> The mother got up and walked to the top of the bed; she lifted the sheet and caressed the hair of her dead son. I didn't have the courage to look at him. I just said, "I want to share your sorrow."
>
> "If my husband were here they would have tried harder to save my son," she wailed. "He had just turned twenty. Oh, God, why my son, my only son?" I didn't have an answer for her.
>
> The mother told me that her husband was still at the front near Chuong Thien. He was heading the operation in which their son had been killed.¹³

Krall herself still mourns the death of a much-loved younger brother, a pilot in the Vietnamese Air Force who was killed in a training accident in Georgia in 1971.¹⁴

Always less populous than North Vietnam, South Vietnam lost more than 254,000 soldiers in the war with wounded in action numbering more than 783,000.[15] It was a country scarred by war. For the older generation of veterans, the war lasted throughout their entire career in the armed forces. As former general Lam Quang Thi writes in his memoir *The Twenty-Five Year Century*:

> If I could borrow from the great French poet [Victor Hugo], I would say that, for a great number of young men of my generation, the twentieth century had only twenty-five years. In fact, in a period of exactly one-quarter of a century, from 1950 to 1975, which covered our entire military careers, we participated in the birth of the Vietnamese National Army in 1950: we grew up and fought with this army that achieved some of the greatest military feats in contemporary history, during the Viet Cong Tet Offensive in 1968 and during North Vietnam's multi-division Great Offensive in 1972. Our careers abruptly ended with its tragic demise in 1975.[16]

Lam Quang Thi formed part of the generation of military men who responded to General de Lattre's call to arms on July 11, 1951: "Be men. This means if you are communists, join the Viet Minh. There, there are people who fought well for a bad cause. But if you are patriots, fight for your country, because this war is yours."[17] Lam Quang Thi believed that "there were no other alternatives."[18] He notes that many young Vietnamese joined the Viet Minh in the mistaken belief that the Viet Minh were genuine nationalists. The story of his distant cousin Lam Quang Phong exemplifies this. Lam Quang Phong joined the Viet Minh in 1945 and distinguished himself as a military leader, rising to the rank of regiment commander. He refused, however, to join the Communist Party. He was sentenced to death by the Viet Minh, and was only "saved from execution by the mothers of the men in his regiment."[19] Lam Quang Phong transferred his allegiance to the National Army of Vietnam after the signing of the Geneva Accords in 1954 and eventually became a colonel in the Special Forces of the RVNAF. Lam Quang Thi, for his part, attained the rank of lieutenant general. He notes that he wrote his memoir at the behest of his son, writer Andrew Lam, and that he did so for two reasons: first, few works by former South Vietnamese soldiers and officials were available in English; and second, enough time had elapsed for him to provide a clear historical perspective of the war.[20]

This chapter deals with the narratives of three RVNAF veterans whose accounts differ widely in terms of generation, service, and experience: the first, Vu Hoai Duc, was born in 1917 and is probably one of the oldest living veterans of the Vietnam War; the second, Tran Van Quan, was born in 1930; and the third, Nguyen Viet Huy, whose story was touched on at the beginning of the chapter, was born in 1953. Their experiences range from service in France and North Africa during the Second World War to Vietnam during the Indochina War and the Vietnam War and Australia in peacetime in the 1990s. The oldest veteran served in the Free French Forces in North Africa in 1940–1943, the National Army of Vietnam from 1950 to 1954, and the RVNAF from 1955 to 1975. In 1975, he was a colonel and the commander of the Psychological Warfare College in Dalat. The second veteran was a career officer with twenty years of service and in 1975 was a lieutenant colonel and commander of the 18th Logistics Battalion. The third and youngest was in the armed forces for three years and in 1975 was a second lieutenant in the Regional Forces. Twenty years later, he joined the Australian Army as a captain, and subsequently served for three years as an army chaplain in Australia. The combined narratives of these three veterans cover five continents, three wars, and a century of history—from Vietnam in the twentieth century to Australia in the twenty-first century. Their experiences convey a diversity of roles in the military ranging across psychological warfare, logistical support, and small-unit combat.

While each account is individual, the veterans reflect on major historical issues in the war: Vu Hoai Duc on concerns relating to the Diem government, Tran Van Quan on the deficiencies of U.S. logistical support for the RVNAF, and Nguyen Viet Huy on the dedication of soldiers in the Regional Forces. Their narratives are connected by a strong underlying sense of conscious patriotism: all three believe that serving their country was the right thing to do at the time, and made an effort to serve and serve actively. In spite of being subjected to mistreatment after the war in the form of incarceration in communist prison camps, all three were able to leave their homeland and build new lives overseas. Their life narratives reveal their ability to not only overcome significant loss but also adapt to altered circumstances.

VETERAN OF THREE WARS

Vu Hoai Duc[21] is the son and grandson of high-ranking court officials from the city of Hue in central Vietnam. He was born in 1917 in Thanh Hoa while his father was stationed in northern Vietnam. After graduating from Hue College, he attended the College of Law and Administration in Hanoi in 1935. He remembers that there were twenty students in his class including two Laotians, three Cambodians and Vietnamese from southern, central and northern Vietnam—referred to respectively as Cochinchine, Annam, and Tonkin in French-administered Indochina. Duc and a number of college friends volunteered for service in the French Army in 1939 when, as he states, "the French government called up all of Indochina to fight against the Fascists."[22] He refers to France recruiting young Vietnamese as ONS or *ouvriers non spécialisés* (nonspecialized workers) for the war effort. As they had academic qualifications, Duc and his friends were recruited as *adjudants* or noncommissioned officers and set off for Marseille from Haiphong harbor. The journey to France took twenty-five days with their ship docking in Singapore, Colombo, and Port Said. After his arrival in France, Duc studied law and journalism at Montpellier University before leaving for North Africa in 1940 where he joined the Free French Forces as a press official. He reported on conditions among the local populations and attended Allied victory celebrations at Tobruk in Libya and El Alamein in Egypt.[23] He left North Africa for France in early 1943, and journeyed back to Vietnam either later that year or in 1944. He refers to friends in Hanoi such as Hoang Dao[24] from the Viet Nam Quoc Dan Dang (National Party of Vietnam), brother of the writer Nhat Linh Nguyen Tuong Tam[25] and "a famous writer" in his own right. Duc was involved in the Tu Ve Thanh (Self-Defense Force), alludes to "political troubles from the Viet Minh," traveled to Laos in 1947, and then fled to France from Thailand. He returned to Vietnam in 1950. He explains:

> The French government agreed to the formation of an independent Vietnamese state with Emperor Bao Dai as chief of state as well as to the formation of a national army. Some 200 of us young men and women from Paris, Lyon, Marseille—most of us were academic people—agreed to come back to Vietnam to support Emperor Bao Dai. TCHYA,[26] Dam Quang Thien, [Nguyen] Buu—the father of General Nguyen Khanh—and I signed on as captains in the new National Army of Vietnam.

Duc was press officer of the Vietnamese General Staff in 1952, and was involved with the army propaganda unit from its inception until he became company commander in 1953: "It was called *Vo Trang Tuyen Truyen* or army propaganda. It started off as a company but a large one. In 1959, it became a battalion." He adds that the National Army of Vietnam had "a lot of different units and a lot of divisions." The National

Army consisted of a diverse mix of regular forces, ethnic minority forces, and paramilitary forces and, as François Guillemot notes, had three weaknesses: first, relations with the former colonizer and the reluctance of the French to fully cede control; second, divergent vested interests of the different groups involved; and third, alliances with local religious sects and armed groups.[27] The National Army was therefore at a disadvantage "fighting the seemingly homogeneous Viet Minh People's Army, which had a single politico-military leadership and the advantage of military experience and Maoist indoctrination since 1950."[28] Duc states that although he supported the Ngo Dinh Diem government, he believes that Diem made significant mistakes in relation to local sects and highland ethnic groups:

> The Cao Dai and Hoa Hao were famously anti-communist. Why destroy them? Why kill Ba Cut, the Hoa Hao leader? It was understandable to destroy the Binh Xuyen but the Cao Dai and Hoa Hao were the most important political parties who were opposed to the communists. Also there were different tribes in southern highland areas and central and northern Vietnam, including a famous division of Nung. The Nung tribe originated from northern Vietnam near the border with China. They spoke their own Chinese language. They were disciplined, and respected the nationalist government. Ngo Dinh Diem ordered Vietnamese officers into the Nung division so as to divide it. Why disperse this Nung division?

Diem took these measures in order to forcibly unify all dissident groups into the National Army and consolidate his power.[29] Duc opines that Diem went too far, and that he could have used these anticommunist groups to better advantage for the South Vietnamese cause. As special aide-de-camp to Diem in 1960, Duc was invited by the president and his brother Ngo Dinh Nhu to accompany them on overseas trips, and traveled to Laos, Cambodia, Morocco, and the United States. He was promoted to major in 1961, had "some problems" after the deaths of Ngo Dinh Diem and Ngo Dinh Nhu in the 1963 coup d'état, and was appointed commander of the Psychological Warfare College in Dalat in 1969. He was based in Dalat from 1969 to 1975. He states:

> To form good officers: the first thing is virtue; the second is experience. The previous commander was Roman Catholic and supported Roman Catholic students. No. No. I believed that we had to integrate students from different backgrounds: Southern, Northern, Catholic, Buddhist, Cham, Nung, Chinese.

In North Africa, the Allied forces knew how to talk to the local people and get them to help allied soldiers. They brought gifts to schools such as books, newspapers, school equipment, and had nurses treat local people. I used my experience from North Africa when I was commander of the Psychological Warfare College.

His assessment of South Vietnam and the nationalist government was that there were "a lot of good plans but not how to put them into practice." In the closing days of the war, the 300 students from his college and 500 students from the nearby National Military Academy were evacuated from Dalat along with thousands of civilians who had asked to join them. The road from Dalat to Phan Rang was so crowded with refugees that "cars could not move." After the war, Duc registered for reeducation with the new authorities. He was to spend ten years in internment:

According to the communist radio, all government officials and employees had to spend a maximum of one month in a reeducation center. I was a group leader. Each group had ten men. We were moved from Go Cong in Russian Molotovas [trucks] from midnight to 3 o'clock in the morning. They drove us around and around so we did not know where we were going. It was a communist tactic. In fact we were taken to Xuan Loc, which was about 14 kilometres from Saigon. After three months, we received orders for another midnight move but this time we were taken to the Saigon harbour. There were 300 people there. The ship took us to Cam Ranh, and then to the north. We were let off one night, we didn't know where, maybe in Thanh Hoa Province, and were taken by train to Hanoi. We were then taken further north and arrived at Nghia Lo camp. We were told: "*Bay gio cac anh la tu binh* [Now you are prisoners]." After five months, we were transferred to a camp under the control of the police. The commander of the camp was an older colonel and had served as a *sous-officer* [non-commissioned officer] with the French forces. He told me, "I ask you to apply discipline in the camp. If you have trouble with any communist cadres, tell me directly." He was a good man. We were moved to a new camp north of Son La. I was able to work for a communist doctor, Doctor Thien, and clean his office. When he had to leave, he left me a certificate which said: "Mr. Vu Hoai Duc, health not good, high blood pressure, cannot work, can only do housework." So the camp commander had me clean the library and help a local nurse. My family came once to visit me. They thought I looked very old. They said: "No, it's not him!" because before, I was a strong man and in good health.

About the communist camps, it depended on the camp commander. If the camp commander was a good man, prisoners had good support.

"The treatment of prisoners," writes Nghia Vo, "varied depending on the location of the camps, proximity of towns or populated areas, and behavior of the staff members and wardens."[30] Duc was released in 1986. His last prison camp was north of Saigon in Xuan Loc, and he said that family and friends were able to visit him and provide him with support and food. He could not return to his former home as it had been taken over by a communist cadre, but he was able to live in the home of friends. He was sponsored by his son and daughter in Australia and arrived in Melbourne in 1991.

Duc's narrative spans the French colonial period, three wars, postwar incarceration, and migration to Australia in the 1990s. While his account overflows with information referring to numerous historical figures and events, there is a detached tone to his reminiscences. This may have been due to a measure of traditional reserve relating to personal matters, but it was difficult to gauge the extent of his personal experiences through these historical markers—volunteering to serve in the French forces during the Second World War; traveling to France and North Africa; traveling to countries in Asia, North Africa, and America; and serving the State of Vietnam (1948–1954) and the Republic of Vietnam (1955–1975). The one point in his narrative that revealed personal engagement and in which the narrative "I" came into prominence was his account of what ensued after 1975. His memories of his ten years of incarceration describe the midnight transfer of prisoners from camp to camp, either in Russian trucks or other forms of transport. Prisoners were left in the dark about their eventual destination, and circuitous routes were taken so as to confuse the prisoners' sense of direction. It is noticeable, however, that Duc has chosen to highlight the positive aspects of his internment: a decent camp commander who had formerly served as a noncommissioned officer in the French forces, a doctor who let him work indoors and made sure that he was taken care of. His narrative of internment displays resilience, and his awareness of how fortunate he was to be spared the hard labor other prisoners were subjected to. This positive attitude may explain his extraordinary longevity. Nearly a centenarian, he still gets up early every morning to exercise.

CAREER OFFICER

Tran Van Quan[31] was born in 1930 in Gia Dinh in southern Vietnam. His family was Buddhist. His father, an engineer who worked for the

French company Eiffel, died following a workplace accident in 1947. Quan attended Tan Thanh Technical College and, in 1951, obtained a job at a *compagnie de réparation d'ensemble* (repair company) that formed part of the French military. He worked there for three years. In 1954, he was mobilized into the army and sent to Thu Duc Reserve Officers School. His company sought to organize a *mobilisation sur place* (on-site mobilization) so that he could continue to work for them but the process took too long. By that stage he had completed nine months of training and was one of the top graduates of Thu Duc. Quan was a founding member of the Ordnance School in 1955, was appointed instructor, and recalls that all the training documents had to be translated from French into Vietnamese. In 1957, he was sent to the United States for further training, and promoted from second lieutenant to lieutenant. He held a number of positions between 1959 and 1966—chief of *Tu Bo Tiep Lieu* (Supply and Maintenance) of the 81st Ordnance Group in I Corps, commanding officer of the Ordnance School, and commander of the 2nd Ordnance Company of the 2nd Infantry Division. The ordnance company's task was to help the division move from Danang to Quang Ngai. He was promoted to captain in 1964, and in 1968 was sent to the United States again, this time to do the advanced course in logistics command at the U.S. Army Ordnance School in Maryland. He was promoted to major and returned to the Ordnance School in 1969 where he served until 1972. He recalls:

> My career was very much in the school. It was getting boring. I asked to serve in an outside unit. At the beginning of 1972, I was promoted to lieutenant colonel, and appointed commander of the 18th Logistics Battalion in support of the 18th Infantry Division. I worked with General Dao [Le Minh Dao] from 1972 until 1975.
>
> My battalion had 600 men. We supported a division of 10,000 men. In the United States, a division would be supported by a logistics group, in other words by several battalions but in Vietnam, we had only the one battalion to support one division.

Quan served at the battle of An Loc in 1972, one of the key battles of the war. He relates:

> We were sent to An Loc to support the 18th Infantry Division. The division was there to defend An Loc and expel all enemy troops. An Loc was one of the biggest battles of the war. The North Vietnamese launched fourteen divisions to invade Vietnam from Quang Tri and Danang to An Loc. They built 1,000 kilometres of highway in Laos and Kampuchea to transfer

supplies and invaded [South] Vietnam from Laos and Kampuchea but they were defeated at Quang Tri and An Loc.

I was in the field at that time. I was there. I will tell you something about the logistics support at the battle of An Loc. We did not use large or heavy equipment, only manpower. All the supplies were dropped by air, and we had to collect these supplies and take them to the combat troops. That was the job of the logistics people. We organized an area for the drop but as the airplanes flew high above, the drop was only accurate within a few hundred metres. We could only collect these supplies by manpower because no car or truck could be used in fields due to North Vietnamese shelling. Many of our soldiers were hit by enemy shells. Each day we would have at least two or three drops. Supplies included everything from rice to ammunition to fuel—at least twenty tons of supplies. Only half my battalion would be in the field at one time, the other half would be in the base camp in Long Khanh. So I had 300 men in the field with an additional forty combat soldiers who were there to help us.

I met with General Dao every day at the operations centre. We would plan and organize the supplies for the combat units in the field. Most people knew that he and I were close friends. He was very good, a good commander, and loved by the men.

When North Vietnam launched a massive offensive against South Vietnam in 1972, most allied troops had left the country. The battle of An Loc pitted 7,500 South Vietnamese troops against an attacking force three times their size: three enemy divisions supported by artillery, armor, antiaircraft, and sapper elements. Consisting of the 3rd Ranger Group, a depleted 5th Division and Binh Long Provincial Forces, the South Vietnamese found themselves confronted with the 9th, 5th, and 7th Divisions, 75th Artillery Division, 11th Anti-Aircraft Regiment, 202nd and 203rd Armored Regiments, and 429th Sapper Group.[32] The An Loc garrison was pounded by 80,000 artillery rounds—three times the number fired into Dien Bien Phu—in April and May 1972.[33] The South Vietnamese defenders had neither tanks nor armored vehicles and had to contend with thousands of civilian refugees. They were supported, however, by the Vietnamese Air Force and U.S. airpower, in particular B52 strikes coordinated by U.S. advisers on the ground. While the 5th Division was the South Vietnamese division primarily involved in the battle, elements of the 18th Division were present from the beginning in that the defense of An Loc involved remnants of Regimental Task Force 52 consisting of single battalions from the 52nd and 48th Regiments of the 18th Division.[34] The garrison at An Loc was reinforced by the 1st Airborne Brigade and the 81st Airborne Ranger Group. The battle has been analyzed in detail in a number of studies including Lam Quang Thi's *Hell in An Loc*.[35] Lam Quang Thi ascribes the successful defense of An Loc to three factors: air support, the determination of South Vietnamese troops, and errors committed by the North Vietnamese side.[36]

While attention on the battle has mostly focused on the siege of An Loc, Tran Van Quan relates the participation of the 18th Division in the broader battle that continued until September 1972. The 18th Division relieved the exhausted 5th Division on July 11–12, 1972.[37] Major problems remained in that the enemy still held high ground southeast of the city as well as the strategic Quan Loi airport.[38] The 18th Division set about recapturing these objectives and on September 23, 1972, forced the withdrawal of the last enemy unit from the city's outer perimeter.[39] Quan singled out the achievements of another commander, Colonel Tran Van Nhut, the Binh Long Province chief, stating that Colonel Nhut had prepared well for the battle by using the territorial forces and People's Self-Defense Forces, implementing the pacification program, and improving relations with the ethnic Montagnards (Highlanders) who provided intelligence information on communist movements and infiltration.

On the loss of South Vietnam, Quan states:

> I will tell you why we lost the war. We won the battle of An Loc. We won the battle of Quang Tri. But we still lost the war because of the ceasefire agreement signed by the North Vietnamese and the Americans in 1973. South Vietnam received 2.8 billion dollars in aid from the United States in 1973. In 1974, it fell to 1.1 billion, and in 1975 to 300 million. The war in Vietnam was fought with outside aid. The Republic of Vietnam was aided by the Americans. The North Vietnamese side was aided by Russia and China. Our aid from America dropped sharply, and that is why we lost the war. That's my opinion.
>
> From the point of view of logistics, the South Vietnamese Army was equipped with Second World War weapons that were not as sophisticated as the weapons supplied to the North Vietnamese. The tanks used by the South Vietnamese were the M24 and M28. They could not be compared with the Russian T52 tanks that were more sophisticated. Our artillery weapons were 105 and 155 howitzers with a range of 11 and 17 kilometres, they could not compare with Chinese 130-mm guns with a range of 27 kilometres. The M1 Garand, the M1 carbine and M16 could not compare with the Chinese AK47 and AK50. And our anti-tank L72 and L74 could not compare with the Chinese B41 and B42, and Russian SR7 missiles. The Russians and Chinese equipped the North Vietnamese with more

sophisticated weapons, and supplies to North Vietnam increased while supplies to South Vietnam decreased so that's the reason we lost the war.

Quan's narrative is measured and understated. He served on the front line in one of the major battles of the war, and with the general who later became famous for leading the defense of Xuan Loc in 1975, when a battered 18th Infantry Division and Long Khanh territorial forces held the town of Xuan Loc for eleven days against a full North Vietnamese Army corps.[40]

After the war, Quan spent five years in a series of internment camps in Long Giao and Suoi Mau in the south, and Son La in the north. Released in 1980, he returned to Saigon, and tried to escape the country. He was caught and sent back to prison. He was finally able to escape Vietnam in 1981. He was briefly at Songkhla and Phanat Nikhom refugee camps in Thailand before arriving in Australia in 1981. Once in Australia, he worked as a motor mechanic before becoming repairman and quality controller at the Holden factory and moving on to Toyota. He retired but proceeded to work in his son's business as a truck driver before obtaining a graduate diploma of civil ceremonies in 1998. He still works as a civil marriage celebrant and has been active in volunteer work for the Vietnamese community, serving as president of the Indochinese Refugee Association since 2000. One of the main achievements of the association was the establishment of a sixty-five-bed Vietnamese high-care nursing home in Melbourne in 2010. He also played a central role in the Vietnamese veteran community. He was a founding member of the Republic of Vietnam sub-branch of the Returned and Services League of Australia (RSL) and served as its president for nearly ten years, first marching on Anzac Day in 1987.

SERVICE IN TWO ARMIES

Nguyen Viet Huy[41] was born in northern Vietnam in 1953 into a military family. They moved south in 1954 and settled in Saigon. There were eight children in the family. The father was in the Medical Corps, while Huy's brother was a paratrooper. Huy studied law at the University of Saigon and was conscripted into the armed forces in 1972. He went on to serve as a second lieutenant and platoon commander in the Regional Forces. He recalls:

> It was just after what we call *Mua He Do Lua* [Red Fire Summer—the 1972 Offensive]. I was trained in Quang Trung for three months and then

posted to Tay Ninh as an officer cadet. We were a big group of fifty, and we were divided into small groups to work with the Regional Forces. We were tasked with winning the minds and hearts of the local people. During our few months there with the local forces, we were attacked many times. These rocket attacks and ambushes did not hurt any of us cadets but they hurt a lot of the local people and militia. For example, we would traverse villages to meet people and a hand grenade would be thrown into our group. We were trained to react quickly and lie flat on the ground whereas local people didn't have that training and they would get badly hurt. Around February 1973, after the Paris ceasefire, we returned to the academy to continue with our training.

We were supposed to be sent to Thu Duc but my unit was sent instead to Nha Trang, where they train non-commissioned officers. We were trained as commissioned officers, and after six months, we all became sub-lieutenants. Our class of 1972 consisted of 1,400 officer cadets, and at the end of the training, I graduated in the top 100, somewhere around 60. I chose to go to Phan Thiet in Binh Thuan, a province about 300 kilometres north of Saigon, where I was posted to an independent battalion of the Regional Forces, Battalion 202, one of eight local battalions.

Our main task was to keep the National Highway secure. We were a mobile unit and engaged in a lot of fighting. I was involved in search-and-destroy missions by helicopter in the area the communists called *mat khu* (secret war zone) Le Hong Phong. I was with Battalion 202 from October 1973 until I was captured eleven days before the communists took over Saigon. During my time with the battalion, we had engagements almost daily. A number of our men were wounded but luckily none of the men under my command were killed. At Christmas time in 1973, I asked for permission to go to Saigon to see my family. I did not receive it but because I missed my family so badly, I just went. While I was away, my company was attacked and a number of men went missing. I met one of them in the prisoner-of-war camp when I was taken there.

Huy was in Class 10/72B and explains that there were so many cadets—15,000—in that one year that each class had to be divided into A and B. Thu Duc Military Academy was so crowded that of his class, 700 went to Thu Duc, and the other 700 to the Non-Commissioned Officer Academy in Nha Trang. He was with a group of six close friends, and although three of them were lucky with the draw and could have attended the more prestigious Thu Duc Military Academy, out of solidarity all seven went to Nha Trang. Of his six friends, two were posted to IV Corps and were killed soon after graduation. At the end of 1973, Huy was twenty years old and had permission from his captain to go on leave locally—just not to Saigon. He states that it was the only time he was able to see his family during his entire time in the army.

The Regional Forces together with the Popular Forces constituted the territorial forces of South Vietnam and made up half of RVNAF strength. Formed in 1960 as the Civil Guard and Self-Defense Corps, the Regional Forces and Popular Forces gained their appellations in 1964, with the Regional Forces serving the province, and the Popular Forces the district.[42] While the Popular Forces remained at platoon level throughout the duration of the war, the Regional Forces expanded from small-unit level to company groups, battalions, and eventually mobile groups.[43] Enlistment into the territorial forces was largely motivated by the desire to serve close to hometowns and families.[44] The Regional Forces expanded from 888 companies in 1967 to thirty-one battalions and 232 company groups in 1970, 360 battalions in 1973, and seven mobile groups in 1975.[45] Ngo Quang Truong notes that:

> Pitted against Communist local force and guerrilla units, the territorial forces fought a low-key warfare of their own at the grassroots level, far removed from the war's limelight. Their exploits were rarely sung, their shortcomings often unjustly criticized. But, without their contribution, pacification could hardly have succeeded as it did.[46]

By the end of the war, the Regional Forces "numbered about 312,000, distributed among 1,810 rifle companies, 24 river boat companies, 51 mechanized platoons (V-100), and logistic and support staff elements."[47]

Huy's platoon in the Regional Forces had twenty to twenty-five men. He notes that in theory a platoon had forty-five men but with the extent of casualties, platoons were understrength and only had twenty-five to thirty men. He relates: "My platoon was divided into two sections. I had three sergeants under my command. One was my second-in-command, and the other two headed the two sections. So I had a medic, a radio man, and my wingman who carried my gear." While all the men were locals, most of the officers, like Huy, were not. Huy relates that even though officers were generally much younger than the men, the men respected them:

> I was twenty or twenty-one at the time. One of my sergeants was in his late thirties but the majority would have been in their late twenties. They respected those who had education, they respected their CO. They used to call us *ong thay*—teacher. We did have some things to teach them, and

they had a lot to teach us. They had more practical experience so it was a learning process—they learnt from us, we learnt from them.

Almost every night, I allowed one or two of my men to go home to visit their family. Even though we were short-staffed, I would allow that. Some cheeky guys would stay home two or three nights but they would always return.

Of the interactions between officers in his company and their social life, he recalls:

We were good friends. We would meet, plan our strategy, how we should move. We would also eat and drink together. It depended on the CO of the company. He would create opportunities for us young officers who mostly came from other parts of the country, to catch up and not feel lonely.

We were young and we had a bit of money so once a week or fortnight, we would go to the city and watch a movie, play billiards, eat at a good restaurant. We were able to make friends with the local families and local students. There were some good families who supported us. One of the wives was extraordinary, a very kind lady. She prayed every night to Buddha. I asked her once, "Why do you pray all the time?" And she said, "I pray for you, I pray for your safety." I spent a lot of my break in their home. Her husband was also religious and they would fast as Buddhists but she would always cook meat for us [soldiers], you see, she was very good.

Huy is proud to have served in the Regional Forces, and states: "In the local forces, we had to be on alert all the time because we had to fight the enemy within our area. We were a brave group of men." He notes that Regional Forces soldiers often lacked proper equipment: "The fighting was constant. It was not on a big scale but we had engagements daily. Men fought very hard and with little support, to the extent that some of our men didn't have proper boots or helmets. We had secondhand stuff from the Americans but most of it was old and broken. We were very ill-equipped."

At the end of the war, Huy's paratrooper brother returned to Saigon, and the entire family waited for Huy so that they could leave Vietnam. They did not know that he had been captured by enemy troops on April 19, 1975. Huy describes his experience as a prisoner of war:

I was imprisoned until 1977, returned home and then went to the New Economic Zone in 1978, where I was recaptured by local communists. They put me in solitary confinement. The prisoner-of-war camp was very hard, and has affected my health to this day. We were forced to work hard, we did not have enough food so we just ate manioc. A lot of my friends died of diabetes as a result. I was in the camp for two years, and we had to bury one or two prisoners every day. We would bury them in shallow graves because we were kept in the jungle at the foot of mountains, and the soil was hard and rocky. A lot of the bodies would disappear, eaten by wild pigs. Twice, I was on the point of death and they carried me to the hut reserved for the dying but twice I crawled my way back out. It was cold at night and I would share the bed and a thin blanket with another prisoner and sometimes in the morning, I would wake and the guy next to me would be dead.

Huy remembers the despair of prisoners in the closing days of the war:

The communists turned on the radio, and let us hear that we were losing. I think it was worse than not knowing, because we could have held on to hope but every day we would hear that another province had fallen, and when we heard that Saigon was going to be captured, we thought that was the end for us.

Huy's attachment to army life is evident in that after escaping from Vietnam in 1980, resettling in Australia, completing ten years of training for the priesthood, being ordained as a Catholic priest, and teaching religious education in high school, he decided to join the Australian Army in 1995. He explains: "The military is in my blood, I have a lot of respect for the army so that's why I joined the Australian Army. I used to be a chaplain and trained at Duntroon. I served in the Australian Army for three years." He was in the unique position of being able to compare the differences in military training between South Vietnam in the 1970s and Australia in the 1990s. He provides the following description of his training at the Royal Military College, Duntroon:

I held the rank of captain by direct entry. We were trained for six weeks, and I must say it was a very different experience from the experience I had in Vietnam. The training there was real but not intense like in Australia because we had to go to war anyway. In Australia, we were not preparing to go to war so the training was very real so as to give us the "real" experience. My first few days, even before I started training at Duntroon, I was taken to the morgue to witness them chopping a body into 100 parts, and a group of us ministers of the church were forced to watch. Oh my god, even in real war, I did not have to see this.

The training was a good experience. I think there were forty-three of us. There was an American guy who had just migrated to Australia a few years before and he had a background in the American Marines. He joined as a journalist so he had the rank of lieutenant. He was the one who was very loud and always made sure they looked after me. See, they were young, the majority were in their early or mid-twenties—a teacher, a dentist, a lawyer. I was forty-two so anytime we had to run or do three days of marching, I was always the last one. The ex-American Marine was always the second last to make sure and he would yell, "Wait for the padre! Wait for the padre!" The spirit of teamwork was really strong through that fellow.

Huy relates that the only activity he refused to participate in during training was live ammunition exercises. He had already fought in war and told his instructor that he had had enough, and the instructor respected his decision. After graduation, he served in the 6th Battalion for a few months before being posted to the 49th Battalion Royal Queensland Regiment (RQR) as an army chaplain. He served two years full time and a year part time before leaving the army, and explains: "I wasn't fit enough and to be honest, it was a bit lonely. I was past the stage of being young and wild, and loving camping. I must say if I were forty years younger, I would love to join the Australian Army." After leaving the army, he went back to being an "ordinary priest" as he terms it.

Huy's narrative is a lively account of life and service in the military. He remembers the camaraderie between officers and the respect between officers, noncommissioned officers, and troopers. He notes that while the Regional Forces are not as well known as other branches of the RVNAF, they fought well, even when poorly equipped and with little support. Although they did not take part in major engagements, they had to deal on a near daily basis with small-scale engagements with the enemy in their local area, and so were involved in regular fighting. He is grateful for the support provided to them by townspeople and families. He describes harsh conditions in the prisoner-of-war camp where he was interned and continued harassment by the postwar authorities after he was released from detention and moved to the New Economic Zone. After fleeing his country and resettling overseas, he again entered the military. He explains:

> I loved the army. There are people who disagree with me, people who think there shouldn't be war. I totally agree that there shouldn't be war but there must be an army because the aim of the army is not to go and attack people or invade other countries but to protect. To me, soldiers, besides the incentive of good money and this and that, they are brave people who are

prepared to die for others, that's my belief, so I have a lot of respect for the army, and that's why I ended up joining the Australian Army.

Clearly, he missed army life and sought to find that sense of camaraderie again in his new country. His affection for that career is evident when he says that if he were "forty years younger" he would join the army again.

SERVICE ACROSS THE GENERATIONS

These three narratives by men originally from central, southern, and northern Vietnam reveal the varied makeup of those who served in the RVNAF. Their life stories reveal different regional origins, socioeconomic backgrounds, and levels of education, as well as different routes to service in the military. Vu Hoai Duc volunteered to serve in the French Army during the Second World War before eventually taking up administrative positions in the National Army of Vietnam and the RVNAF. Tran Van Quan was mobilized into the army in 1954, went twice to the United States for training, and served for many years at the Ordnance School before requesting a field assignment and assuming command of a logistics battalion. Nguyen Viet Huy was conscripted into the forces while he was a university student, and opted to serve in the Regional Forces. While the first veteran, Duc, provides wide-ranging observations through three wars including the errors he believes the Diem government made with respect to the Hoa Hao and Cao Dai sects, the second veteran, Quan, underlines the important contribution that logistics soldiers made to combat operations, and in the process provides a unique perspective of one of the key battles of the Vietnam War. The third veteran, Huy, for his part, defends the service record of those who served in the Regional Forces.

"I don't like war, I don't like military life, but we are at war, and I would not know where else to be. It is not a matter of making a choice between France and Annam. It is only a matter of knowing the place of an Annamite like myself. It is here."[48] These words by Nam Lien, the protagonist of Pham Duy Khiem's novel *La place d'un homme: De Hanoï à La Courtine* (A Man's Place: From Hanoi to La Courtine), justify his decision to volunteer for service in the French Army during the Second World War. The use of the terms "Annam" and "Annamite" to refer to Vietnam and the Vietnamese reveals the novel's colonial context.[49] Set in 1939–1940, *La place d'un homme* begins in Hanoi and ends at the French military encampment at La Courtine. The novel takes the form of a journal, and includes a series of letters in which the narrator seeks to explain his actions to Vietnamese and French correspondents. Nam Lien dies in battle in the Loire in June 1940.[50] The novel's author, Pham Duy Khiem, volunteered for military service in France in 1939, and his novel has autobiographical overtones.[51] He refers to his protagonist Nam Lien as "the only native from Indochina" to go to France as a volunteer recruit in 1939.[52]

Vu Hoai Duc's narrative of service indicates that there were other volunteers from Vietnam who made the journey from Haiphong to Marseille at the beginning of the Second World War, including Duc and his fellow *adjudants*. As he notes, they volunteered "to fight the Fascists." Unlike Pham Duy Khiem's protagonist, Duc did not enlist as a private and did not serve as a combatant in France. Instead, he studied at Montpellier University before joining the Free French Forces in North Africa. Although he refers to France's recruitment of *ouvriers non spécialisés* from Vietnam, his experience differs markedly from that of the majority of the 20,000 Vietnamese workers who were sent to France, many of whom worked essentially as forced labor in French munition factories, and were unable to return to their homeland until well after the end of the war, some as late as 1952.[53] Duc does not elaborate on his decision to volunteer, and his experiences in France and North Africa constitute only one part of a long and eventful career that included extensive travel in four different continents—Asia, Europe, Africa, and America—before he eventually resettled in a fifth continent, Australia.

Duc reveals little about his personal experiences through three major wars of the twentieth century. This may be ascribed to two factors: first, his age and background; and second, his perspective as an observer of events. He was a press official for the Free French Forces during the Second World War, and press officer for Emperor Bai Dai in 1950 and for the Vietnamese General Staff in 1952. He made it clear that when he served the State of Vietnam and the Republic of Vietnam, he did so as an administrator and not as a combatant. He was in position, however, to meet well-known figures and witness pivotal events. Although he is sparing in terms of his experiences during the Second World War and his later work as commander of the Psychological Warfare College in Dalat, he ascribes his recognition of the need to include recruits from all backgrounds to his observation of events in North Africa in 1940–1943 including the support provided to allied troops by the local people. He believed that the college that he commanded—and by extension the armed forces—should not privilege any particular segment of society but instead incorporate personnel from South Vietnam's disparate regional, ethnic, and religious groups. In his eyes, inclusiveness constituted strength, and he was in a position to put his beliefs into practice.

The point at which he revealed strong emotion is his account of his postwar experiences as a prisoner of Vietnam's reeducation camps. Even here though, there are significant silences in his narrative. He was incarcerated for ten years during which he was transferred to several prison camps and then moved to the north of the country. The memoirs of camp survivors and the recollections of Nguyen Viet Huy in this chapter, for example, relate punishing conditions including hard labor, isolation, and prisoner deaths from malnutrition and disease.[54] Duc's only reference to these conditions, however, is indirect and takes the form of his family's shocked exclamations at the way internment had aged and changed him. He presents his years in the Vietnamese gulag in the least negative light possible and highlights the decency of two individuals—a camp commander and doctor—to whom he is indebted for his survival. His physical and emotional resilience in surviving three wars and attendant political troubles—including the downfall of the Ngo brothers—as well as a decade of postwar internment is both heartening and astonishing. It can be ascribed to his generally positive interpretation of past events, and to the fact that he is enjoying life in Australia in the twenty-first century. He remains a hale and fit man at the age of ninety-eight.

The second veteran, Tran Van Quan, relates not only a twenty-year career in the South Vietnamese military—in fact a career that covers the entire history of the RVNAF—but also his participation in one of the key battles of the war where he served under a divisional commander who became one of South Vietnam's most notable generals. Quan provides an unusual perspective of the 1972 battle of An Loc, and focuses on the role played by the logistics battalion in supporting divisional objectives. The task of organizing and coordinating logistics at An Loc was complicated by the fact that supplies could not be collected by mechanized means. Quan's recollections are supplemented by the lecture that he gave on the 18th Logistics Battalion at the Vietnamese-American Association in Saigon on November 29, 1972.[55] He arrived in An Loc with eighty members of his battalion on July 12, 1972, and their first task was to set up their headquarters. The location of the 5th Logistics Battalion was too small so they chose a larger location on the grounds of a school. Quan highlights a central issue in his lecture: the gulf between the level of logistical support provided to U.S. soldiers and that provided to RVNAF soldiers. While in the U.S. Army there were five logistics soldiers to support every combat soldier, in the RVNAF a single logistics soldier had to support eight combat soldiers, a "ratio of 40:1 in favor of U.S. Army logistics."[56] In spite of the vast disparity in resources available to the two armies, he asserts that RVNAF logistics provided effective support to its combat troops on the battlefield. He relates the transport of tons of materials by human labor at An Loc, the construction of storage facilities for petrol, rice and ammunition, the installation of a defense bunker system, additional tasks such as the maintenance and repair of communications equipment and vehicles, and other responsibilities of the logistics unit such as funeral services:

> At An Loc, the funeral service team collected corpses, removed corpses, buried unclaimed dead bodies found here and there among the debris, excavated graves to remove skeletons for their relatives when requested or went to forests to look for corpses of crew-men of crashed airplanes. One of the jobs done by the funeral service team which was worth noting was to keep records on all the graves of soldiers killed at An Loc. . . .
>
> Even when the fighting is taking place, the logistics soldier has to shuttle back and forth to bring to combat soldiers everything needed, ranging from dried cooked rice, munitions, gas to heavy weapons. Logistics activities never end.[57]

The logistics soldier, as he notes, "shares danger and hardship with the combat soldier."[58] Quan's narrative provides not only an account of his experiences in the armed forces, and his role in a key battle of the Vietnam War but also a means of highlighting the tasks undertaken and the dangers faced by his men, the unsung logistics soldiers who may not feature in military histories but whose essential support tasks made the achievements of combat troops possible. His sentiment that logistics soldiers are often perceived through a "prism of false prejudice"[59] illustrates the problems faced by logistics personnel in other armies and other wars. "Demands for economy, and the hostility often felt by fighting soldiers for the men who feed, equip and transport them," suggest John Keegan and Richard Holmes, "should not obscure the real importance of logistics."[60] Quan's leadership and organizational skills have been allied with a strong record of community service in Australia, and he has maintained his friendship with his former commander Le Minh Dao.

The youngest veteran, Nguyen Viet Huy, grew up in a military family and his family's background played an important role in shaping his identity and forming his understanding of and appreciation for the military life. Conditions for military families became increasingly difficult as the war progressed because of the descending value of army salaries.[61] Huy, however, refers to having sufficient means to enjoy outings with his friends on a weekly or fortnightly basis. One aspect of army service that emerges clearly from his account is the intense homesickness and loneliness experienced by young men serving in military units far from home. This explains why he went to Saigon to see his family at Christmas time in 1973 without permission from his captain, and why he sought the companionship of fellow officers. His narrative reveals how grateful he is for the care and comforts provided by local families. From his description, these families became in effect like substitute families for soldiers. By 1970, regular force officers who were transferred into the Regional Forces significantly outnumbered Regional Forces cadres. They originated from all three regions and included a substantial percentage of those who were born in the north.[62] They consisted of officers who graduated from both Thu Duc and Nha Trang. The territorial forces saw their roles expand from territorial security and pacification support to assisting the regular forces in combat missions and search and destroy missions[63]—operations that Huy participated in while he was in the Regional Forces. Huy also underlines the lack of adequate equipment and support. Initially provided with weapons dating back in some cases to the First World War, the territorial forces gradually obtained weapons of Second World War vintage like the regular forces under the U.S. Military Assistance Program. In 1964, these fell well below the standard of weapons supplied to the North Vietnamese by the Soviet Union and the People's Republic of China such as the AK47, RPG7, and B40 and B41 grenade launchers.[64] It was only from 1969 that the Regional Forces were provided with weapons such as the M16, the M60 machine gun, M79 grenade launcher, and LAW rocket launcher.[65] However, as Huy relates, members of the Regional Forces still lacked adequate equipment and support in the 1970s, including proper helmets or boots. He notes that in spite of this, they served bravely and well. His recollections accord with Ngo Quang Truong's assessment of the territorial forces. One of South Vietnam's most respected generals, Ngo Quang Truong was the commander of the 1st Division during the battle for Hue in 1968, and later he commanded IV Corps before being reassigned to command I Corps during the 1972 Offensive. He notes:

> In a deterministic sense, [the Regional Forces and Popular Forces] accepted war as their fate and were resigned to hardship and even death, which

they faced with unequalled impassivity. They fought the war with patience and perseverance.[66]

Ngo Quang Truong adds that in spite of the fact that territorial forces suffered considerably worse losses than the regular forces, they "still accounted for the largest number of volunteers serving in the RVNAF during the entire war."[67] Proximity to home and family was of crucial importance for those who served. Huy is in the unusual position of having served in two different armies on two separate continents two decades apart. The major difference was that his second experience was in peacetime. His narrative reveals that he was able to transpose loyalty to army and country to a new setting. His attachment to the military of both his former and current countries is apparent, and reflects on his ability to adapt to a new life while still maintaining strong links with his past.

Although grief and mourning form part of these men's lives, they have been reticent in expressing these in their narratives. This applies particularly to the accounts of the two older veterans, both of whom would have witnessed death and suffering not only over the course of lengthy careers in the military but also during their postwar incarceration. Their accounts reveal their reluctance to discuss emotive experiences such as personal losses during the war. Another factor that distinguishes the narratives of the two older veterans from that of the youngest veteran is their use of French terms. These linguistic differences denote their experience of growing up in colonial Vietnam, and serving in an army that in its early days still bore the imprint of the former colonizer. Huy, a generation younger, eschews any references to the French. He provides instead a vivid account of his experiences during and after the war, including detailed reconstructions of events and conversations. This gradual progression to greater ease with the narrative "I" reflects the contrast between the reserve of the older generation, and the greater ease in self-expression and communication of the younger generation. For all three, however, their service to their country and their belief in that service occupy a central role in their narrative. All three are survivors—surviving war and the aftermath of war. Duc's service in Vietnam stretched, like Lam Quang Thi's, for twenty-five years—from the formation of the National Army of Vietnam in 1950 to the fall of Saigon in 1975. Quan joined the armed forces at the juncture at which the National Army of Vietnam became the RVNAF and served for twenty years until the end of the war in 1975. Huy served as a young officer from 1972 to 1975, and missed army life to the extent that twenty years later, after becoming a refugee and resettling in another country, he enlisted again, this time as a direct entry captain in the Australian Army. The experiences of all three men reveal both the scope and the extent of service in the RVNAF and the motivations and life circumstances that led men from different social, regional, and religious backgrounds, and from different generations, to serve South Vietnam.

CHAPTER 2

In the Field

Thanh, my signalman, suffered a deep cut from a huge piece of shrapnel . . . I was saturated with blood, but was otherwise unhurt. To this day, I can't explain how Thanh, who had been lying in the middle between me and the orderly, had fallen victim to the shrapnel, whilst I escaped.
—Van Tan Thach[1]

When North Vietnam launched its multidivision offensive against South Vietnam in 1972, Van Tan Thach was serving in the northernmost part of the country in I Corps as a first lieutenant in the 3rd Battalion, 258th Marine Brigade. In his account of his experiences during the 1972 Offensive, he refers to four specific incidents in which he was fortunate to escape injury or death.[2] These provide striking glimpses of the front line. The first incident was the above episode that occurred at My Chanh Base at the beginning of the offensive on March 30, 1972, when the Marines were preparing to head off to Ai Tu and sustained heavy enemy artillery fire. The second occurred when North Vietnamese forces including armored units sought to cross the Dong Ha Bridge. His platoon was deployed to a village northeast of Dong Ha to block the enemy. When he requested Marine artillery support against enemy positions across the river, the rounds fell on the village instead and his platoon was forced to retreat. Some of his men were wounded but luckily none were killed in this "friendly fire" incident. The third occurred after the battalion had successfully halted the enemy advance at Dong Ha. He was sipping coffee away from the line of fire when an 82-mm mortar round landed a meter away. He and the men around him lay flat on the ground knowing that they were too close to the shell to survive. The shell failed to explode. The fourth episode occurred a few weeks later when the Marines were dug into their bunkers. He was observing enemy shelling of 61-mm and 82-mm mortars on Marine positions through the observation slit when his eyes began to ache from the smoke, and he rubbed them and briefly sat down. Another Marine took his place when the following occurred: "Suddenly, he fell down with a terrible cry and died. A piece of shrapnel from a[n] 82mm mortar [round] had somehow flown through the slit and pierced his skull. I held his body in my arms, completely stupefied. I thought of his wife, his children, and his parents, and felt deep sorrow."[3] Van Tan Thach writes that he was lucky to not only have survived the war but also survived "with an intact body."[4]

North Vietnam sent an assault force consisting of two regular divisions plus elements of a third, a sapper regiment, one independent regiment and several independent battalions from the B5 front, two armored regiments, three artillery regiments, two engineer regiments, and an air defense division with a surface-to-air missile (SAM) regiment and a number of antiaircraft artillery (AAA) regiments across the demilitarized zone into I Corps.[5] The 3rd Marine Battalion, along with the 1st and 6th Marine Battalions and the 3rd Marine Artillery Battalion, formed part of the 258th Marine Brigade.[6] The 3rd Battalion was tasked with securing the Dong Ha area, and it succeeded in stopping enemy troops from crossing the Dong Ha Bridge. Significantly outnumbered and subjected to heavy artillery bombardment, the 3rd Battalion held off enemy forces for seven days.[7] The battalion suffered substantial losses.[8] Former brigade commander Ngo Van Dinh writes that the 3rd Battalion "managed to stop the advance of two North Vietnamese Army (NVA) regular divisions (Divisions 304 and 308) and two tank regiments (Regiments 203 and 204) with only the assistance of Naval [gunfire], the Marine's own Artillery and some air support."[9] Ngo Van Dinh adds that many of the battalion's wounded soldiers refused to be evacuated. The battalion's senior American adviser, Captain [John] Ripley, "witnessed . . . a marine who had sustained a serious back injury laboriously assist[ing] a more seriously injured fighter to a safer place [and] recalled that the pair died at dusk the same day."[10]

This chapter explores the narratives of veterans from three different services and their experiences on the front line. The veterans come from less well-known branches of the RVNAF—the Armor Branch, the Vietnamese Air Force, and the Vietnamese Navy. They provide details of service in their respective units, and the different military engagements in which they participated. The three veterans were all junior officers in the 1970s. They were in their early or mid-twenties when South Vietnam collapsed in 1975. Four decades later, they recall the nature of their service, their memories of life in the military, and their experiences in the aftermath of war. Their narratives highlight the importance of resilience in the face of the unique pressures of combat in wartime, and state repression, internment, and forced migration in the aftermath of war. The oral histories of these men reveal the perspectives of former soldiers who assert that the armed forces in which they served were fully the equal of those of their allies, and who believed that the cause they were fighting for was worth the sacrifice and effort.

In his memoir of service as a private soldier in Burma during the Second World War, George MacDonald Fraser refers to the process of remembering the past in the following terms:

> [L]ife is like a piece of string with knots in it, the knots being those moments that live in the mind forever, and the intervals being hazy, half-recalled times when I have a fair idea of what was happening, in a general way, but cannot be sure of dates or places or even the exact order in which events took place. . . . In my case, there are coloured strips of film at each knot of memory, and in between many rather grainy sequences which can be made out only with difficulty, and in some cases the print is spoiled or even underdeveloped.[11]

The recollections of the three veterans reveal a similar pattern in terms of highlighting certain "knots"—in this case battlefield incidents or engagements with the enemy—within a broader life narrative. While some accounts are clear, others contain a mass of detail and are difficult to follow. All three veterans were interned in communist reeducation camps after the war, and escaped their country by boat to eventually resettle in Australia. Their narratives are shaped not only by their family background and the circumstances that led them to enlist in their specific branch of the military but also by the nature of their service and the extent of their combat experiences. All three accounts reveal that in spite of being subjected to a succession of major life stressors such as war, combat, injury, postwar incarceration, and the refugee experience, the men yet managed to survive and endure, and to reconstruct their lives in a different country and culture.

ARMOR OFFICER

Nguyen Van Luyen[12] was born in Saigon in 1952. He was the fifth child in a large Buddhist family of eight children, with four older brothers, two younger brothers, and one younger sister. His father worked as an account manager for a cigarette manufacturer in Saigon. Luyen and his three older brothers all joined the armed forces. Luyen attended the selective Pétrus Truong Vinh Ky school in Saigon. He relates that thousands of children applied for attendance and only 400 were admitted. He was number 303, and completed the Baccaulaureate Parts I and II. He studied law for one year at the University of Saigon, and was mobilized into the armed forces in 1972. He recalls:

> My older brother and I did the army officer course at Thu Duc at the same time but I became a combat soldier while the government transferred him back to high school to teach. The country needed soldiers but also needed teachers. The other three brothers and I were all in combat. My oldest brother joined the army in 1968, and was wounded twice: the first time, he was shot in the leg, and the second time, he was hit by a piece of grenade in the leg, and discharged in 1971. He served in the 25th Infantry Division. My second brother was a captain in the artillery. My other brother was a company commander but he was shot and they sent him to work in the supply battalion because he was no longer strong enough after being wounded. My next brother was the one who went back to teaching, and then there was me. We were all army officers. I served in the tank division.
>
> Normally the training at Thu Duc was from ten months to a year but because of the war, we had only six months of training to become platoon commanders. I became chief warrant officer. After that, I chose to do the test to join the tank division, and did another four months of training at Long Thanh. I qualified to command a company of five tanks—usually about thirty-five soldiers because each M113 had seven soldiers. I became the commander of Company 1, Battalion 2/1, 1st Armored Cavalry Regiment, 5th Infantry Division. Because of the war and the number of deaths, my company only had four tanks so there were about thirty soldiers. I became second lieutenant in July 1974 and four months later I was shot at Bau Bang hamlet. I was in hospital until April 30, 1975.

The conversion of M113 armored personnel carriers into light assault tanks was a South Vietnamese innovation.[13] The M113 was first operated by the RVNAF in the Mekong Delta in 1962.[14] Rather than use the M113 as a means of transporting infantry, the RVNAF added .30 caliber wing machine guns and modified the M113 to perform as a "combat vehicle" or "armored cavalry assault vehicle."[15] The remodeled M113 operated effectively as "a tank with an oversized crew."[16] As Ralph Zumbro notes: "We thought they were infantry, they thought they would rather be cavalry, and by God, they were."¹⁷ Initially met with disapproval by Military Assistance Command Vietnam, these modifications were later adopted by American units arriving in South Vietnam.¹⁸ Luyen refers consistently to the M113 as a "tank," and his vocabulary reflects the South Vietnamese usage of these armored vehicles.

Like other major elements of the RVNAF, the Armor Branch had French antecedents. The National Army of Vietnam received its first armored unit—a reconnaissance platoon—from the French forces in 1950.¹⁹ The platoon commander was a Vietnamese graduate of the Saumur School of Cavalry in France.²⁰ By 1955, the Armor Branch had four regiments and one amphibious group.²¹ The Armor School was opened in May 1955.²² Armor personnel numbered 2,500 by the end of 1955.²³ "After the French handover," writes Ha Ma Viet, "all training was done under Vietnamese officer leadership and administration, with support from their American advisers. The language of instruction was changed from French to Vietnamese."²⁴ The United States provided M113 armored personnel carriers from 1962, M41 light tanks from 1965, and M48 medium tanks from 1970.²⁵ The Armor Branch saw distinguished service: the 3rd Armored Cavalry Squadron was awarded the U.S. Presidential Unit Citation for "extraordinary heroism in military operations against hostile ground forces during the period 1 January 1968 to 30 September 1968."²⁶ The RVNAF had ten armored cavalry squadrons by 1968.²⁷ This was increased to twenty-two squadrons, an M48 squadron, and four armor brigade headquarters in 1973.²⁸ Armor personnel numbered over 20,000 in 1974.²⁹ Ha Ma Viet notes that of the four armored brigades formed between 1968 and 1971, the best was the 3rd Armored Brigade, which performed commendably until the end of the war.³⁰

Interned like other former servicemen in a series of communist prison camps after the war, Luyen recollects the following encounter with another camp inmate in Bao Co that made him recall the battle of Bau Bang hamlet:

> A guy asked me: "Excuse me, were you a lieutenant in the tank division?" I said, "Yes, how do you know me?" He said, "I was a soldier in the tank division, 1st Battalion." I said, "Ah, I remember," because I was in the 2nd Battalion, and we were together in the battlefield at Bau Bang. He said, "I was Lieutenant Nghiep's driver." Nghiep was my friend, we studied together at Thu Duc. I said, "Yes, I remember." My friend's tank was hit. I called him on the radio: "Nghiep, it's Luyen, answer mate." But he was collapsed on top

of the tank. I couldn't leave him there. He was the vice commander of the company, and his company, the first company, had to go back and forth four times. I ordered my soldiers to cover them and shoot . . . the communists, they got the . . . they attacked and they shot . . . three of my tanks, they shot them, and pulled up the cable. . . . And that soldier, Sang, he started the tank. . . . He said, "I know you, Lieutenant, you saved my life." I was in jail but the soldier always looked after me. We loved each other and looked after each other.

Luyen's account reveals the loyalty of the former armor trooper who not only recognized Luyen and remembered that he owed him his life but also proceeded to repay that debt by caring for the former officer in the hard labor camp. Luyen's account of the battle conveys the confusion of the battlefield, and illustrates the difficulty of describing combat experiences, including the role of participants and the sequence of events, to the listener. Luyen later provided further details of this battlefield incident in writing.[31] The events occurred in September 1974. Luyen's battalion was ordered to reinforce the 1st Battalion, and headed along National Route 13 toward Bau Bang hamlet, where it engaged with enemy forces. Luyen's battalion included two companies of ten M41s each. Luyen's company consisted of four M113s. Luyen writes:

Once we found our target, Captain Thuong ordered five M41s to line up. As for my company, we were to line up on the left side behind the M41s to protect them. The 76-mm M41 cannons started firing. The communists opened fire with their own cannons. The crossfire was fierce.

To steer clear of enemy fire, the captain ordered the tanks from Company 1 to roll back. When my tank started to turn around, I saw a motionless M41. I knew that it was Nghiep's tank. On the main body of the cannon, Nghiep and his soldier were collapsed, unconscious. I pressed the radio and roared, hoping to waken my friend, to no avail. I ordered three M113s to approach close to the side of the M41 to protect it. At that moment, the communists started to attack in human waves, a suicidal tactic of theirs. They thought we were withdrawing and did not know how fierce our firepower was. Each tank had three guns, one M50 (12.7 mm) and two M30s (7.62 mm) and one M113 was equipped with a 106-mm cannon.

At that point, Second Lieutenant Trung heard that I was mobilising my company to stay back to rescue Nghiep. Trung also led his company back to a fighting position to destroy the communist attack. I then used cables to pull the M41 back to base, knowing full well that the job was a mammoth one—we had to pull more than 25 tons of steel. But we had to try. There was no way that we could leave Nghiep and his three soldiers there. While I was getting ready to link the cables to the tank, the M41 suddenly started. What a relief! We withdrew 500 to 700 metres.

Once everything was in order, I went to a meeting with Captain Thuong and I also met with Trung. He said, "Thank you. If it wasn't for you, I would have lost the M41, Second Lieutenant Nghiep and three soldiers." The truth was I was really elated and extremely proud. I said, "Anybody would have done the same. Nghiep was my friend from the same year at the academy. I could not give up on him."

We fought the communists all week long. We attacked during the daytime, resting at night, and continued fighting. At midday one day, while advancing on a target, an AK47 bullet pierced my abdomen. I was evacuated to Cong Hoa General Hospital in Saigon.[32]

These two excerpts reveal the difference between oral and written accounts of battlefield events. Luyen's oral narrative conveys the chaos of battle while his written account clarifies his role in the battle as well as the succession of events and their context.

The injuries that Luyen sustained in Bau Bang effectively ended his military career as he was still under medical care when the war ended in April 1975. He recalls his experiences in the military hospital:

I said to the doctor, "I'm going to die, I'm going to die, I can't breathe." I missed my mother, my father, my friends, my brothers, all of them came around and around. I said to myself, "I can't die." I don't know what happened but the day after, the nurse said, "Lieutenant, you were yelling, you were fighting, you were ordering the nurse to shoot here, shoot there." Because in my mind, I was still on the battlefield, I was using coarse language and telling that one to shoot, hurry up, go go go.

There were other soldiers in intensive care. There was a guy next to me linked up to a machine that beeped. A woman came and said, "My son is here." The nurse said, "How do you know?" The woman said, "Last night I dreamt that he was very cold, and he told me to come here to see him." She had brought clothes as in the hospital we were just covered by a thin sheet. It was very sad. The nurse checked the list, and it was the guy next to me. She took the woman to him but the machine was still. He was dead.

One night, I felt something very heavy on my stomach. I told my friend Tham—also a lieutenant—"Tham, turn on the light. I don't feel too good mate." He turned on the light and there was blood all over the bed. He goes to the nurse, she rings the doctor, and they push me back to the operating room and operate on me again. I spent one month in hospital. They gave me three months to recover at home. And then I returned to the hospital for another operation, and they gave me time to recover, and then the war ended.

Luyen provides a vivid portrayal of his distress and delirium in the hospital, and seeing the faces of his loved ones come "around and around." His injuries necessitated further operations. He retells the chilling story of the mother who brought clothes for her son who was "cold" only to find him dead. Luyen was awarded the Gallantry Cross with Gold Star, and the Wounded Soldier Award while lying in his hospital bed.[33] After the war, he was incarcerated in communist prison camps for five years until 1980. He was sent to Hoc Mon, Phu Quoc Island, Tay Ninh, Katum, Camp KK-A, Camp KK-B, Bao Co, and then back to Camp KK-A. He relates that "A" stood for the army and "B" the police. He had limbs that were swollen from the lack of Vitamin B while he was in prison. His brothers were also interned: the teacher for two years, the brother in the artillery for three years (his wife was able to bribe the authorities for his release), another brother for six years. His brother the teacher escaped by boat all the way to Darwin in Australia—Luyen relates that his brother's boat was the second Vietnamese refugee boat to reach Darwin in 1978. Luyen escaped to Songkhla in Thailand, and arrived in Australia on the Queen's Birthday holiday on June 8, 1980. He lived with his brother, and immediately began working at the Chrysler factory in order to earn money to support his family in Vietnam, and a brother who was still interned. He later worked for Mitsubishi. He married, had two children, and ran a clothing business with his wife before he retired. He is a member of the Thu Duc Association, attends commemorations for the battle of Long Tan, and marches on Anzac Day.

CHINOOK PILOT

Vu Van Bao[34] was born in Hanoi in 1948. His family was Catholic, and joined the mass movement of refugees from North to South after the signing of the Geneva Accords in 1954. They stayed in Danang for one year before moving to Saigon, where they lived from 1956 to 1975. Bao's father was a cook and opened a small restaurant where they served *pho* (noodle soup). Bao attended Hung Dao High School and served in the Vietnamese Air Force from 1968 to 1975. He spent his boyhood collecting pictures of the air force and wanted to become an air force pilot but the height requirement was 165 centimeters and he only measured 163 centimeters. He volunteered instead for the National Military Academy at Dalat but one of his friends encouraged him to sit for the entrance examination for the air force. He relates:

> The day they said to go to Tan Son Nhat Air Base for the results, I told my friend, "No, I have no hope, I'm staying home." He came back and said, "Your name is listed with mine." So I did three months of basic training, and another three months to become a platoon commander. I went to Quang Trung and then to Thu Duc but it was too crowded. They told us, "We only have room for army personnel." They kicked sixty-three of us back to Air Force Headquarters. We were then sent to Nha Trang to train. It was a very tough school. I always had to carry the Garand M1 rifle, over 5.5 kilos with two units of ammunition or 120 bullets. It was very heavy. I weighed about 49 or 50 kilos at that time. After that, we went back to Air Force Headquarters. They organized for us to study English in Saigon. I then went to America to undergo training to become a helicopter pilot at the end of 1969. I finished the course after one year but they kept me there for another three months to transition to the Chinook. The basic training was in Texas, the Huey training in Georgia, and Chinook training in Alabama. I then returned to Vietnam and served at Bien Hoa Air Base. I was in Wing 43, Squadron 237. I served until the fall of South Vietnam in 1975.
>
> In Bien Hoa, they had a lot of squadrons. They were divided into two main wings. One was the fixed wing aircraft and the other the rotary wing aircraft. The fixed wing aircraft included fighter aircraft and observation aircraft. The other wing was my wing. When I came back we had twenty-five Chinooks but because of heavy battle, this was increased to thirty-two Chinooks. We were a very good squadron compared with the American squadrons. American squadrons weren't called squadrons but companies. The 205th company in Phu Loi said they were the best American company of Chinooks in Vietnam. They asked us how many aircraft we had available for operations. We said, "75 percent." They didn't believe us. They said, "We are the best and we only have 50 percent available for operations." Because Chinooks are hard to maintain. They came to have a look at our squadron and realized that what we said was true: 75 percent. Our squadron had 10,000 flying hours without accidents, then 20,000 hours, then 30,000, then 40,000 hours. The Americans gave us the A model—the older model. It had almost 4,000 flying hours but we still kept flying it and maintaining it. Our maintenance people had a lot of talent for fixing problems. I served as test pilot and could see them at their

work. After five years in service, eleven aircraft were destroyed. We had five helicopter crews killed in action. That was a heavy loss for us.

Established in 1955 with F8F Bearcats from the French Air Force, the Vietnamese Air Force grew with U.S. assistance to a force of seventeen squadrons and 16,200 personnel in 1968 and sixty-five squadrons and 63,000 personnel in 1975.[35] The Vietnamese Air Force expanded from five fighter squadrons to eleven squadrons of A1, A37, F37, F5A, and F5E aircraft; from five H34 helicopter squadrons to twenty-one squadrons including seventeen UH1 and four CH47 squadrons; and from three C47 transport squadrons to five squadrons of three C7 and two C130A squadrons.[36] The 514th Fighter Squadron was "among the first VNAF units to win a U.S. Presidential Unit Citation 'for extraordinary heroism and outstanding performance of duty in combat against an armed enemy of the Republic of Vietnam throughout the period 1 January 1964 to 28 February 1965.'"[37] The 514th Fighter Squadron lost fifty-three aircraft and thirty-two aircrew between 1962 and 1973.[38] Brian Hukee writes that, "14 aircraft [were] lost in 1972 and during the first six months of 1973 alone, and it would be reasonable to assume that similar, if not greater losses, occurred in the last two years of the war."[39] South Vietnamese pilots were involved in missions over North Vietnam, with pilots from 516th Fighter Squadron flying thirty to forty missions a month in early 1965.[40] First Lieutenant Nguyen Quoc Dat from the 516th Fighter Squadron was shot down on May 14, 1966, while on his twenty-sixth mission over North Vietnam, and spent seven years as a prisoner in Hanoi before being released in March 1973.[41]

Bao's squadron, the 237th Helicopter Squadron, was officially established in September 1970.[42] The squadron supplied munitions to artillery and Airborne units and also transported troops. It flew supply missions to the battle of An Loc in the summer of 1972, and to An Loc, Phuoc Long, and Tay Ninh in 1973 and 1974.[43] The first squadron crewmember to die was Second Lieutenant Trinh Tien Khang, who was hit in the abdomen by antiaircraft fire while on a supply mission to Snoul.[44] Although he was flown directly to Cong Hoa General Hospital, he died on the operating table.[45] After Khang's death, all cockpit side doors were armor-plated.[46] A particularly dangerous mission for which volunteers were requested involved the isolated outpost of Tong Le Chan.[47] When too many flight crews volunteered, the mission was restricted to those who were still single and had few family ties.[48] The aircraft was hit by ground fire within

300 meters of its objective, the flight engineer killed, and the pilot wounded.[49] Between September 1970 and April 1975, the 237th Helicopter Squadron lost five flight crews with eleven pilots and eighteen flight engineers, loadmasters, and gunners killed in action.[50] Another South Vietnamese helicopter squadron, the 219th Helicopter Squadron, was awarded the U.S. Presidential Unit Citation in 2001 for its performance while assigned to the Military Assistance Command Vietnam Studies and Observation Group.[51]

Bao discusses his war service in more detail:

> We had daily resupply missions. We supplied ammunition, food, and in some battles, we transferred soldiers. The missions were normally five hours. The longest that I flew was ten hours and forty-five minutes without shutting down the engine. That day I had to supply the Airborne unit stationed at the border with Cambodia. The Airborne had their own artillery unit, and they wanted 6,000 or 4,000 rounds. That's why I flew back and forth for over ten hours without shutting down the engine. I would drop the supplies, go back, pick up another load, drop the supplies, and it continued.
>
> On the way to the battle of An Loc in 1972, we brought ammunition, medication and food. On our return, we carried civilians as the roads were blocked and they could not get through.
>
> One day, I carried over one hundred people in the Chinook. They were women and children, and had been starving for nearly a week. They were very light. When I went to pick them up, I could not go up. Some women had babies in their arms with two to three kids trailing behind them. I had to wait for them. The flight unit said: "Too many people. Up! Up!" But I said, "Wait! Wait!" When we got to Lai Khe, a guy in the Huey helicopter asked me: "Hey Chinook, how many did you carry?" I counted the number of people getting out of the Chinook: 120, all women and children. We also brought the bodies of the dead back to their families. As it was hot in Vietnam, the bodies would start to smell. They were draped in ponchos. Later on they were put in Conex containers, and the door was closed. It was better for us.

While Bao provides details of the supply and transport missions that he flew, including a ten-hour-long munitions supply run to Airborne troops on the Cambodian border, an undoubted highlight was his successful evacuation of more than 100 emaciated women and children from the battle of An Loc in 1972. Chinooks normally carried up to fifty-five troops. That he was able to lift off with more than double that number of admittedly "light" civilian refugees is still remarkable. He relates that he could not leave while he could still see women and children struggling to reach the Chinook.

He notes the changes that occurred in the service from 1972, and especially after 1973:

> The war intensified and North Vietnam had more anti-aircraft weapons. The worst was the [Soviet] SA7 heat-seeking missile. When fired, it followed the heat and we were very slow. Later a flare box was installed for us, we could release the flare and the missile would follow the flare and not the aircraft. After An Loc, I would take the aircraft out in the morning and wonder if I would come back in the evening. Life and death were so close. We were young, we were scared going into the heat of battle but we still laughed and shared jokes.
>
> After 1973, it was very bad due to the lack of supplies—ammunition, fuel, everything. Before that, if we ran out of fuel, they filled it up for us, and we flew again. But after 1973, they said we could only refuel twice. They only gave us two pieces of paper. If you had a piece of paper, they would open the valve and refuel the aircraft otherwise they refused. We had to work out how to manage and then we had to return to base. We couldn't fly anymore. The fuel from one voucher was used up in less than two hours of flying. Chinooks were very thirsty.
>
> They cut and cut. There was a squadron of A1 Skyraiders that could not fly because they had no spare parts. And Caribou squadron, no spare parts. Squadrons that could no longer fly.

William Momyer writes that between 1973 and 1975, "the magnitude of [North Vietnamese] SAM and AAA defenses constituted a major departure from those of the 1968 and 1972 campaigns. The VNAF, structured for a low scale war, was confronted with an enemy having the most sophisticated air defense weapons of the day."[52] Bao chronicles the damaging effects of cuts in U.S. aid after 1973, in particular the lack of fuel and spare parts, which led to restricted flying hours, and the grounding of fighter planes. One of the grounded squadrons was the 530th Fighter Squadron, which ceased operations because of "shortages of fuel, ordnance and spare parts."[53]

At the end of April 1975, Bao was still flying his Chinook and transporting soldiers and civilians. He took part in the formation that flew the 5th Airborne Battalion from Khanh Duong Pass to Phan Rang Air Base, a nerve-wracking experience that had him landing the Chinook at the base "with almost the last drop of fuel."⁵⁴ Bao also evacuated many civilian refugees from Long Khanh to Long Binh.⁵⁵ A first lieutenant when the war ended, Bao registered for reeducation with the communist authorities in June 1975. Officers were advised to carry enough food for ten days. Like Luyen however, Bao spent a total of five years in internment. Prisoners were moved by truck in the middle of the night, and he was sent to Hoc Mon, about 10 kilometers from Saigon, where he stayed until December 1975. After that the camp inmates were taken to Phu Quoc Island for six months. There was a war between Vietnam and Cambodia at the time, and he relates that the camp authorities were afraid that the Cambodians would come to Phu Quoc to help the prisoners so the prisoners were moved again and transferred to the Tay Ninh area. He stayed in this final location until he was released in May or June 1980. After his release, he had to give a weekly report of his activities to the police. He was not allowed to live in Saigon and was given three months to move to the New Economic Zones. As he had nowhere to go, he became one of many illegal residents in Saigon, moving from place to place to survive. He had married in 1972, and his first son was born in 1973. After his release, his wife became pregnant with their second child. He escaped from Vietnam by boat, and reached Malaysia after a harrowing thirteen-day journey. He arrived in Melbourne in 1982. It was not until 1990 that he was finally reunited with his wife and sons. It took him more than eight years to sponsor his family because his wife did not have an official family certificate in Vietnam. She tried to escape three or four times with their sons but each escape attempt ended in failure. In Australia, Bao has worked for the same transformer company for more than thirty years. He is active in the veteran community and formed the Vietnamese Australian Veteran Friendship Association in Victoria in 1993. He takes part in commemorations for Armed Forces Day, Long Tan Day, and Anzac Day.

NAVAL OFFICER

Tran Van Giac⁵⁶ was born to a Buddhist family in Nha Trang, southern Vietnam, in 1948. His father was a building contractor and the family moved to Saigon in 1950. Giac studied architecture at the University of Saigon because it was his father's wish that he do so. After the 1968 Tet Offensive, Giac's family returned to Nha Trang while he stayed on in

Saigon. He was mobilized into the armed forces and served in the Vietnamese Navy from 1969 to 1975. He recalls:

> I only studied at the university for a year and a half. There was an order for general mobilisation and I joined the navy when I was twenty-one. I was trained at the Naval Academy in Nha Trang. The first course was a three-month foundation course. I then proceeded to a higher level and for six months learnt methods and command strategies. After graduation, I worked in the Second Coastal Zone for a year. I then returned to the Naval Academy for another six months, and became a naval officer. I served on WPBs [Patrol Boat] and PCFs [Patrol Craft Fast]. The WPB was from the U.S. Coast Guard and was a big and powerful ship. It could withstand storms and tidal waves and was practically unsinkable. The PCF was a smaller craft but it was fast so it could hunt and capture vessels that were trespassing in Vietnam.

Founded with the assistance of the French Navy in 1952, the Vietnamese Navy had 2,000 personnel and twenty vessels in 1955.[57] The United States supplied hundreds of additional naval vessels such as escorts, patrol rescue escorts, motor gunboats, large support landing ships, large infantry landing ships, tank landing ships, medium landing ships, and minesweeping launches.[58] By 1966, the Vietnamese Navy had expanded to 16,000 personnel and 560 vessels.[59] After 1968, the U.S. Navy transferred its assets to the Vietnamese Navy through the "Accelerated Turnover to Vietnam" program.[60] By the end of 1972, the Vietnamese Navy had over 40,000 personnel and 1,500 vessels.[61] The Naval Academy was located at Nha Trang, and there were three training centers in Nha Trang, Cam Ranh, and Saigon. The navy had five Coastal Zones covering the four Corps, and two Riverine Zones located in III Corps and IV Corps. In I Corps and II Corps, battleships patrolled the coastline and provided supporting naval gunfire while in III Corps and IV Corps, navy units had the crucial "task of intercepting all enemy movements and infiltration through the interlacing river systems. The task of supporting and supplying military posts along the river was just as essential."[62] Cuts in U.S. aid had crippling effects, and the navy "was compelled to reduce its overall operations by 50 percent and its river combat and patrol activities by 70 percent."[63]

Giac served in the Coastal Surveillance Center in the Second Coastal Zone Headquarters before moving to the 25th Coastal Group as an operations officer, and finally the Coastal Task Forces (Inner Barrier) as commander of PCFs (Patrol Craft Fast) and WPBs (Patrol Boat) from 1973 to 1975. Giac relates details of the following missions in which he took part that involved the transportation of South Korean troops by the navy:

> In 1970, I was in command of two small ships. One was further out at sea for surveillance and support, and the other was transporting troops to the shore. The troops were Korean. There were two Korean divisions at the time and one of them was called *Bach Ma* (White Horse). They fought extremely well. It was in September, the storm season: there were heavy rains, strong winds and high waves so the Korean troops requested that we drop them off closer to land. As the commander, I knew that if we went in any further, the waves would drag us into the shallows and we would be stranded and unable to get back out to deeper water. Only about half the troops disembarked. The rest refused to do so. They wanted the ship to go further in. The Korean troops all disembarked and advanced into the forest. The ship was stuck in the sand and unable to reverse. The communists fired at the stranded ship. It was not clear where the shots were coming from and the ship could not return fire. A male sergeant was shot in the stomach and badly injured—his intestines were exposed. I was in the other ship further out to sea and could not help them because if I came in any closer, I would be stranded as well. The Korean troops heard the call for help and came back out to the rescue. The injured sergeant was taken onshore and we radioed for help and a helicopter arrived to rescue the stranded men. It was fortunate that the sergeant did not die.
>
> The Koreans were very smart. Another time, they appeared to be carrying backpacks but in fact each soldier was carrying a backpack with another soldier hiding inside. The communists only saw one person when in fact there were two. Fifty people got off the ship, completed their mission, and returned to the ship. The communists thought that the area was clear and that all the Korean troops had gone but in fact, unbeknownst to them, fifty Korean soldiers had remained behind. When our ship returned, we turned on the lights and fired shots to get the enemy out of their hiding places. The communists attacked us. The Koreans came out to do battle with them and captured about twenty people.

Giac's narrative conveys two points: first, his inability to directly assist the stricken ship while it was subjected to enemy fire; and second, his admiration of the successful tactics adopted by South Korean troops in their engagements against communist forces. The 9th Infantry Division (White Horse) of the Republic of Korea Armed Forces was stationed in South Vietnam between 1966 and 1973.

Giac provides details of two incidents in 1974 in which he had narrow escapes, including one that involved the horrific death of a friend and fellow naval officer in enemy hands:

> We used to go into areas frequented by the communists and ambush them. At night, we turned off all the lights and stayed quiet. When we heard the sound of a boat or ship approaching we started the chase. After six months, we had captured a lot of communists so they looked for ways to retaliate. They dropped dynamites about 7 or 8 metres deep. When we passed, the dynamite got attached to the propeller. Either that or someone scuba-dived, waited for us to approach and attached it to our ship. Approximately half-an-hour later, it exploded and made a big hole: about 1.5 metres by 3 metres. On board were two officers, myself as captain and my assistant, a sub-lieutenant, as well as five crewmen. We were seven in all and had to jump into a life raft as our ship sank. The communists approached in a boat to capture us. We radioed for help from nearby ships straight after the explosion and one came to help us. When the communists saw the ship, they did not dare attack us. It was lucky that we got rescued otherwise we would all have died. This was in August 1974.
>
> I went on a mission with a friend of mine. The area was full of low trees and swampy. Only small boats could get through. We were in two boats and our objective was to prevent any attempt from the communists to steal food supplies from civilians. I went to Phu Quoc and my friend stayed behind to finish his meal. The next day he vanished without a trace. All of our boats searched for him. We went really deep into the forest and discovered his boat. As the men were eating they did not notice that there was a communist pretending to be a civilian. He came up to the men to ask something, caught then off guard and captured the whole boat with six people onboard. When we found the boat, there were two decapitated bodies. One was my friend the lieutenant, the commander of the boat, the other was just a crewman. Perhaps he tried to stand up for his commander or to protest—his head was also cut off. The remaining four people were captured and taken away. The people who had trained at the same academy, the same class, they all hugged my friend's body and cried. Even to this day, we still hold a yearly memorial for all those who died during the war. His name was Dinh Minh Hung.

Giac relates how fortunate he was to survive not only the sinking of his ship but also to evade capture by enemy troops after he had to jump ship with his crew. The second incident conveys his shock at witnessing the results of communist brutality in the form of the beheading of a young naval officer and crewmember in 1974. The decapitation of his friend Dinh Minh Hung and another navy colleague left a marked imprint on Giac and on Hung's classmates from the Naval Academy. As Giac notes, they still remember and commemorate this loss forty years later.

Giac refers to tensions that could exist between Vietnamese personnel and American advisers:

> At the start of 1972, an American adviser would occasionally accompany us on our ship. He accompanied us to monitor our activities or just to get an understanding of the situation. If we needed help, he could call for assistance. Once there was a lieutenant, we were on operation, he ordered us as if he were my commander. I did not oblige him and told him that I knew where we should go and where we should not go. But the American adviser was adamant that he was correct and that he knew more than us so he ordered us to do as he commanded. We argued at length and I was so mad I felt like kicking him overboard.
>
> There was an existing conflict in the command chain: some advisers were very good but some were not. There were occasional conflicts, but even now, I am truly indebted to the soldiers who lost their lives in Vietnam. Every year, we have a memorial ceremony to remember them. We owe them a deep gratitude.

Giac's narrative illustrates his frustration in dealing with an American adviser who was less knowledgeable about the local waterways and local conditions, and still saw fit to give orders to a fellow officer. While Giac acknowledges "conflicts in the command chain" as he terms it, and disagreements with American advisers, he also underlines the fact that he feels a true sense of indebtedness to all the allied soldiers who gave their lives in South Vietnam. A lieutenant when the war ended, Giac was interned in hard labor camps until 1977. He escaped Vietnam in December 1977 in a boat measuring 15 meters by 4 meters. The refugees left at night from the harbor at Cam Ranh. When they reached Terengganu in Malaysia, they counted 197 people on board. Giac arrived in Australia in February 1978, studied English for two weeks and then looked for a job. He needed to work to support his family in Vietnam. He notes that for twenty years he participated in all the political movements that were anticommunist: "A part of me wanted to strengthen the community in Australia to fight against communism. I left Vietnam because

I wanted to get away from the communists. I didn't want the communists to enter Australia." However, once his children were over ten years old, he realized he needed to devote more time to his family. He had met his wife at the migrant hostel in 1978, and they married in 1982. It was more than twenty years before he returned to Vietnam to visit his family. He did so in 2001 because his mother was severely ill. She died a few months after his visit. Two years later, he returned to visit his father before the latter died. He runs a printing business in Australia, belongs to the Navy Association and has stayed in touch with his classmates from the Naval Academy, many of whom are now in the United States.

WARTIME AND POSTWAR LIVES

"Resilience," write Robert Pietrzak and Steven Southwick, "is defined as the ability to adapt successfully to acute stress and trauma, or more chronic forms of adversity."[64] The life histories of these three veterans all reveal resilience in the face of wartime service and combat exposure. The narrative of the first veteran, Luyen, is dense with information and conveys the combat experience of a junior officer in an armored regiment in the last three years of the war. Luyen's account includes conversational exchanges, anecdotes, and reflection. These narrative devices convey a sense of immediacy to the incidents portrayed. The battle of Bau Bang hamlet occupies a central position in his memory of the war. The sequence of events—seeing his friend collapsed on the tank, attempting to wake him, ordering his other three M113s to provide covering fire, getting the cable attached, and then seeing the other tank unexpectedly start up again—emerges in sharp relief as one of Fraser's "knots of memory." Luong did not make any reference to his medals during his oral history interview. He only provided this information fifteen months later when he was asked for further details about the events at Bau Bang. Unlike many other veterans whose family photographs and documents were either lost or destroyed after the end of the war in 1975, Luyen has surviving photographs of his military service. One depicts him in front of an M48A1 tank in the training field in Long Thanh in 1972 with his friend and classmate Doan Thanh Nghiep—whose life he was to save at the battle of Bau Bang hamlet in 1974—standing on the tank behind him. Another photograph shows Luyen at Thu Duc Military Academy in 1972 with his best friend Phan Cong Ly who later served in the 25th Infantry Division and was to die in the reeducation camp in Trang Lon in 1977.

The second veteran, Bao, provides an orderly account of his enlistment in the Vietnamese Air Force and his service in the 237th Helicopter Squadron. Stationed at the logistics base in Bien Hoa, his missions included the transport of munitions and supplies to the front line—as he did in the case of the Airborne unit on the Cambodian border in 1971, and at the battle of An Loc in 1972—as well as the transport of troops, wounded soldiers and civilian refugees. He holds positive memories of his training in the United States and of his American instructors, and retains copies of his aviator qualifications from the U.S. Army Primary Helicopter School and U.S. Army Aviation School.[65] The postwar years were difficult, with Bao enduring long years of separation from his wife and children. When Bao was first sent to reeducation, his son was two years old. He said that although his son was allowed to visit him once in prison, he looked at his father "like a stranger" when Bao was released in 1980. Bao did not meet his second son until the family was reunited in Australia in 1990. In all he endured thirteen years of separation from his loved ones—five years while he was interned in hard labor camps, and eight years after escaping from Vietnam and resettling in Australia. He is stoic about the hardships that he experienced. One of the surprising pieces of information that he gave was the continued discrimination directed against the children and grandchildren of RVNAF veterans in Vietnam. He has made a number of return trips to Vietnam to visit his mother, the latest in 2012. He states:

> My nephew, around thirteen, was picked as a good soccer player. They said they would put him through school and train him to be a good soccer player for the province first and maybe the nation. But when they looked at his record, they found out that his grandfather was *nguy* [puppet]. That was it. No more future. It happened just last year. His grandfather worked as an interpreter for American soldiers during the war.

He adds that this level of discrimination is extended "three generations" by the Vietnamese government.

The third veteran, Giac, provides a full and detailed reconstruction of his service in the Vietnamese Navy. He holds a positive opinion of South Korean troops stationed in Vietnam. He was responsible for transporting them on mission and was able to see the way in which they operated. While his narrative includes details of narrow escapes from death, and the harrowing fate of friends and colleagues killed by the communists, it also encompasses the lighter side of his military experience. He remembers the banter between crewmembers and moments of mischief and hilarity, as evidenced by the "watermelon incident":

> It was just before Tet in 1971. I was twenty-two years old. At that time we were based approximately 200 kilometres from Saigon. I wanted to return to Saigon to hang out so I declared that our ship was in need of repair and had to go back to port. We were given permission to go. We were keen to reach the port quickly so we were travelling very fast. It was night and there was one boat that was carrying a lot of watermelons. We did not see them and passed by. The waves from our ship caused the boat to sink. It was the last day for them to bring the watermelons to the market to sell. We had to rescue the people but there were lots of watermelons. That whole river seemed to be covered in watermelons. That boat must have held thousands of watermelons. We had to race faster than the current and borrow a boat from folks living downriver to pick up the watermelons. We had to use a net to stop the watermelons from drifting away. It took us a day to pick up all the watermelons and return them to the owner. It was a bit late as they had only one day to sell the watermelons. We missed out on our chance to hang out. We had to return to our area. We had to compensate the people for their lost revenue. We lost two months' worth of pay. Those stories from when we were young, there were a few that were funny but also a bit hard to bear [laughs].

He has a surviving photograph of his time as a young naval officer. Interned for two years after the war, he was able to make his escape by sea and resettle in Australia. He has been active in the veteran community, maintaining links with other veterans, in particular with his classmates from the Naval Academy.

In an article on "Loss, Trauma, and Human Resilience," George Bonnano refers to several pathways to resilience, including hardiness, which he defines as "consist[ing] of three dimensions: being committed to finding meaningful purpose in life, the belief that one can influence one's surroundings and the outcome of events, and the belief that one can learn and grow from both positive and negative life experiences."[66] I would like to explore these dimensions in reference to the life narratives of these three veterans. The first dimension, the notion of meaningful purpose, emerges from all three accounts. While all three had their education interrupted and were mobilized into the armed forces at the age of twenty or twenty-one, their accounts reveal different pathways to service. Luyen relates that he chose to serve in the armored division and successfully completed four additional months of training at the Armor School in

Long Thanh. Bao had always wanted to serve in the air force, and while he believed that he had no chance of being accepted as he did not meet the height requirement, he did sit for the examination (even if it was at the insistence of his friend). Giac, on the other hand, wanted to study information technology. This field of study did not exist in Vietnam at the time, and his father pressured him into studying architecture, a subject that did not interest him. When Giac was mobilized into the armed forces, he selected the navy. All three therefore exerted a measure of control in terms of the unit they ended up serving in.

They believed in the cause they were fighting for, and their perception of South Vietnam and assessment of the war converge on several levels. Luyen relates: "We were fighting in bad conditions, with no help, as the Americans, Australians, South Koreans and Thai all left while North Vietnam had help from Russia, China, East Germany. But I am proud of what we did because we still fought on, we only stopped when we were ordered to do so by President Duong Van Minh." Bao, for his part, makes the following observation:

> We, the South, we just defended ourselves. We did not go up to the North. We were fighting but also building our country. Up North, it was a different story. They were supplied by Russia and China. They did not build the country, they always sent troops down to the South. They set up a third government in the South, saying that it was from the South when it was actually from the North. After 1975, you no longer saw the flag with the two colours and the star in the middle [the flag of the Provisional Revolutionary Government (PRG)]. The war was controlled by the North.
>
> We are all upset because now when people talk about the war, they talk about the American war against North Vietnam. South Vietnam has been forgotten.

These sentiments are echoed by Giac:

> The war left behind a lot of heartache and pain, for the Vietnamese people more so than other nations. The reason being the war lasted a long time. The communist side was supported by the Russians and Chinese. On our side, we had the backing mainly of the Americans, then the Koreans, Australians and New Zealanders. Vietnam was the battlefield for other nations to fight in. When the Americans withdrew, South Vietnam was lost to the communists. The people who suffered the most were the people from the South.

Their comments reflect three main points: first, that South Vietnam sought to defend itself for twenty long years against communist North

Vietnam; second, that while the Soviet Union and China continued to support North Vietnam, the Americans and their allies withdrew from South Vietnam, and withdrew their aid; and third, that the war was not only a civil war between North and South but also a proxy war within the context of the Cold War. All three articulate central concerns relating to the issue of memory, and the ways in which the war, and in particular the role of South Vietnam and its armed forces, have been remembered. When Bao states that, "people talk about the American war against North Vietnam. South Vietnam has been forgotten," he identifies one of the common misapprehensions about the Vietnam War. The three narratives highlight the strong sense of abandonment experienced by the South Vietnamese with respect to their allies—a feeling exacerbated by the crippling consequences of U.S. cutbacks in aid—and relate that South Vietnam fought on alone, and its people were left to suffer in the aftermath of conflict. Oral history enables these veterans to elucidate their personal experience of war, and to assert the centrality of the South Vietnamese experience of the war.

The veterans' portrayals of friendships within the service, and the support extended toward unit members are reflected not only in their wartime memories but also in their lives in the aftermath of war. Luyen recalls the support that he was able to find from a former soldier in his armored regiment at a time when both were prisoners in hard labor camps. He maintains links not only with former classmates from Thu Duc but also with armor veterans. He elaborates:

> About every two months we meet and find out news about friends. If they are sick in hospital we go and visit them, and we collect money to help disabled veterans still in Vietnam. When people go to Vietnam on a visit, we give them the money so that they can help veterans directly. The president of the Thu Duc Association was a second lieutenant during the war as well. He was in Class 5/71 while I was in Class 4/72. We keep in touch with the larger Thu Duc Association in the United States. There are also a lot more of us from the tank family in America. There are twenty of us over here in Melbourne, we meet a couple of times a year. One of the lieutenant colonels was my regimental commander, and I also met one of my soldiers, and a major in Perth.

Bao collaborated with other air force veterans in writing and producing a substantial volume in Vietnamese on the history of the Vietnamese Air Force in 2005.[67] Giac maintains close links with the members of his class at the Naval Academy. In 2000, they produced a large illustrated book containing details of the war service of class members as well as information on the veterans and their families in their current lives overseas.[68] These men all found meaningful purpose in serving their country during the war, and draw comfort in the maintenance of links—local, national, and transnational—with former comrades-in-arms. By sharing their experience either orally or in writing, they participate in a wider project of memorialization among RVNAF veterans now resettled overseas. Their loyalty toward their respective units, and to South Vietnam more broadly, is still evident forty years later.

The second dimension, the ability to influence the outcome of events, is problematic in the context of war. As Bao notes, "life and death were so close." The difference between those who survived and those who were injured or died was arbitrary and a matter of luck, as the account by Van Tan Thach at the beginning of the chapter exemplifies. Luyen refers to the deaths and wounds of other members of the armored regiment. Giac recalls the shock of seeing the decapitated bodies of a fellow officer and crewman after a mission. As he relates: "The memories of seeing my friends injured or killed: these images are etched in my mind until today. After 1975, even after I successfully escaped Vietnam, the memories still haunt me."

While their ability to influence the outcome of events may have been limited during the war and in its immediate aftermath—all three were interned after the war—the decisions that they made after their release reveal them as active agents in the trajectory of their lives in the postwar period. All three chose to escape from their country by boat and proceeded to work toward that goal. Boat journeys entailed a high level of risk and a high mortality rate; however, the men survived the experience and were able to reach a refugee camp where they were accepted for resettlement in Australia. After resettlement, all three focused on working to support families in Vietnam, and to construct new lives in Australia.

The third dimension, the ability to learn from positive and negative experiences, emerges from all three life histories. Each of the experiences that they were confronted with—mobilization and active service in war, combat exposure, witnessing death and injury, experiencing life-threatening injury (in the case of Luyen), seeing the collapse of their army and country, internment, and the stress of becoming refugees—had the potential to result in damaged or ruptured lives. The enmeshing of the servicemen's personal losses and tragedies against the wider backdrop of a nationwide catastrophe, and the ensuing reverberations for the population of the former South in terms of being subjected to years of state violence and postwar repression, emerge from all three narratives. And yet these men were able to not only endure hardship and adversity but also to remake their lives in a new land. John Keegan and Richard Holmes note:

> For some [soldiers], the memory of war is one of unrelieved horror and suffering, but for the majority, war is recalled in tones of light and shade, with the warmth of comradeship, and the pride of achievement and shared endeavour set alongside the anguish of anticipation, the shock of battle and the misery of privation.[69]

While the loss of South Vietnam is felt deeply by these three veterans, they find meaning in having served their country, validation in the process of writing or recording personal or unit histories, and a sense of community by associating with members of their branch of the armed forces as well as with other war veterans. These three factors: their sense of purpose, their determination to be active agents in their own lives in the face of repeated adversity, and their capacity to learn from their experiences have all contributed toward their ability to endure the pressures of repeated exposure to combat during the war, and adapt to vastly changed circumstances in its aftermath.

CHAPTER 3

Army Doctors

> *During those last minutes, the dying combatant only had a medic by his bedside. They left on their final journey in pain and isolation, without their life companion by their side. I was a witness to this on a daily basis.*
> —Pham Viet Tu[1]

Pham Viet Tu recalls in this way his work as an army doctor in one of South Vietnam's largest military hospitals during the 1972 Offensive, relaying the scenes he beheld in triage, and describing hospital wards crowded with wounded and dying soldiers. Assigned to I Corps Headquarters in November 1959, he recollects that the region was relatively calm until 1963.[2] He remembers the beauty of the surrounding countryside, the charms of the city of Danang, and the appeal of nearby attractions such as the cave of Non Nuoc, My Khe beach and the gulf of Tien Sa. He notes his increasing concerns as the war escalated. In 1967, he was assigned to Duy Tan General Hospital. Situated next to Danang Air Base, the hospital was under intense pressure whenever there was heavy fighting, in particular during the 1968 Tet Offensive, the Lam Son 719 campaign of 1971, and the "Red Fire Summer" of 1972.[3] Military casualties were so extensive that the hospital received patients directly from the front line as well as from general reserve forces such as the Marines and the Airborne Division that normally had their own evacuation procedures and medical facilities.[4]

Another military doctor, Tran Duc Tuong, served in the Airborne Division for a decade and recalls: "To ease my wife's grief over my absence, I promised to write her a page every day and to send it on the first connecting flight. I kept this promise throughout my ten years with the paratroopers."⁵ He saw frontline service throughout the length of the war and explains that that he could not remain indifferent to the devastation caused by enemy forces.⁶ His life was devoted to the Airborne Division, and he and his family lived on the modest salary he made as a doctor in the paratroopers.⁷ He is grateful to his wife and children for supporting him and believing in the same ideals.⁸ He did not have a private practice, and their neighbors were the wives and children of military families.⁹ He adds that his contributions and those of so many of his medical colleagues in the armed forces paled in comparison to the sacrifices made by combat soldiers for their country.¹⁰

The war effort dominated the medical profession in South Vietnam and the majority of the country's doctors served in the armed forces. The recollections of these men convey the reality of war for the thousands of medical personnel serving in the forces: dealing with suffering and death as part of their everyday responsibilities, and enduring separation from loved ones. This chapter will explore the narratives of two military doctors who served in frontline units during the war: Tran Xuan Dung and Nguyen Manh Tien. The first was in the Vietnamese Marine Corps and the second in the Vietnamese Rangers. Oral history enables them to, in Robert Perks's and Alistair Thomson's words, "inscrib[e] their experiences on the historical record, and offe[r] their own interpretations of history."¹¹ Such accounts illustrate their unique perspectives as medical professionals in combat situations. While their life trajectories reveal a series of losses and traumas stretching from the 1940s through partition, war and the aftermath of war, they also display a remarkable level of resilience and adaptability, even in the face of major upheavals such as the collapse of their army and country, internment in postwar prison camps, and the refugee experience. Their narratives elucidate the level of commitment of well-educated South Vietnamese officers during the war, the capacity of both men to reconstruct lives in another land, and their means of memorializing the army and country that they had served.

THE MEDICAL CORPS

"At first glance, war and medicine seem contradictory," writes Elizabeth Stewart, "the aim of war is to kill, while medicine, and the professionals who practise it, strive to heal. But the contradiction is only apparent: after all, nations involved in war need fit and healthy soldiers to maintain fighting capability, and the means to repair the effects of the war in order to return men to action as quickly as possible."[12] The Medical Corps was founded in February 1951 under the control of the Ministry of National Defense.[13] Its foundation preceded the establishment of the General Staff of the National Army of Vietnam in May 1952. Following the signing of the Geneva Accords in 1954, and the partitioning of Vietnam into a communist state in the north and a noncommunist state in the south, the Faculty of Medicine and the Military Medical School moved from the University of Hanoi to the University of Saigon.[14] The first Dean of the Faculty of Medicine was Pham Bieu Tam. French professors were among the teaching staff of the Faculty and medical degrees from the University of Saigon were fully recognized in France until 1966.[15] From 1964 to 1965, the faculty shifted to an American-based model.[16] RVNAF medical supplies were largely dependent on the U.S. Army.[17] The Medical Directorate came under the control of Central Logistics Command, and in 1969, four area medical groups were activated, one for each of the four corps in the country.

Hospital facilities grew steadily as the war escalated, with new hospitals being built in 1961, 1963, and 1965, the addition of sector hospitals and district dispensaries in 1967, and two further new hospitals built in 1970.[18] Hospital bed capacity expanded from 2,500 in 1955 to 11,400 in 1965, and 24,547 in 1973 with consistently high occupancy rates of 95–98 percent.[19] Four convalescent centers were built in 1961 and a paraplegic hospital established in Vung Tau in 1972.[20] At the National Rehabilitation Institute in Saigon, 300 new patients were fitted with prosthetic limbs and braces every month.[21] During periods of intense fighting, hospitals overflowed with patients. Pham Viet Tu, for example, served in Duy Tan General Hospital in I Corps—the second largest military hospital in the country after the great Cong Hoa General Hospital in Saigon— and remembers hospital corridors and theaters filled with wounded soldiers during the 1972 Offensive, with numbers reaching 2,000 on some days.[22] The hospital had 1,200 beds.[23] He adds with some bitterness that wounded enemy soldiers were housed separately in individual beds while their own wounded had to share beds or lie in corridors.[24] A tragic incident occurred in 1972, when ambulance trucks attempted to evacuate the last 300 patients from Quang Tri Hospital to Hue. Trapped on National Route 1 amidst military vehicles, retreating troops, and civilian refugees fleeing south, the entire patient cohort died along with hundreds of refugees under enemy artillery fire.[25] This stretch of road came to be known as

Doan Duong Kinh Hoang or Road of Horror. Nguyen Cong Luan describes the sight of the national route two months later:

> There were hundreds of cars, trucks, bikes, and motorbikes riddled with communist bullets and shell fragments, some burned to ashes. Human skeletons lay scattered among the roadbed. . . . The image that sent a wave of compassion through my heart was a tiny skeleton of a child about two years old inside a large aluminum wash basin. A tiny pair of rubber sandals lay beside the mother's remains.[26]

While the RVNAF Medical Corps served throughout the war with distinction, a perennial problem was the constant shortage of personnel and facilities.[27] In 1966, South Vietnam had only 1,000 doctors of whom 700 were serving as medical personnel in the RVNAF.[28] "As a result," notes Dong Van Khuyen, "medical doctors were assigned to hospitals and medical units down to the regimental level only. There were no medical doctors at the district or battalion level, except for the Airborne and Marine Divisions."[29] Most hospitals needed major repairs and improvements, and "running water and sanitation were two permanent problems."[30] By the end of the war, South Vietnam had approximately 2,000 doctors of whom nearly 1,800 served as medical officers in the armed forces.[31] They were still too few, however, considering the scale of RVNAF casualties. RVNAF wounded in action numbered 109,960 in 1972, 131,936 in 1973, and 155,735 in 1974.[32]

Military doctors were assigned to all regions and several served in frontline units. Approximately thirty were killed in action.[33] Hoang Co Lan, for instance, underwent parachute training with the 2è Bataillon étranger de Parachutistes (2nd Foreign Airborne Battalion) in 1955—a unit that had taken part in the battle of Dien Bien Phu in 1954 and was in the process of being reconstituted—while he was still a student in medical school. He needed to complete seven jumps to obtain his parachuting qualifications and describes parachuting from a plane with twenty German legionnaires.[34] After graduation, he served in the Airborne Division, and relates that five doctors in the Airborne were wounded in the field and two killed: Do Vinh in 1965 and Nghiem Sy Tuan in 1968.[35] Vo Thuong served as a military doctor in I Corps between 1965 and 1969, and had to examine the body of his friend Sanh, a doctor in the Marines who was shot along with other wounded soldiers when the battalion headquarters was stormed by enemy troops.[36] Vo relates: "I was reluctant to disturb the body of my friend. For a few minutes, I stared at his poor disfigured face—at the small obscene round hole in the centre of his forehead, surrounded by black flecks of powder. His facial bones and cranium were completely shattered."[37] Le Thanh Y, serving in II Corps, had to remove an unexploded M79 grenade from the leg of a wounded soldier in 1971. He operated successfully on his patient in a border camp at Pleime, and the M79 was then safely detonated in a far corner of the camp.[38]

The cutback of U.S. military aid in 1974 had drastic repercussions for the Medical Corps as with other sections of the armed forces in South Vietnam. The lack of petrol meant flight time was cut by 80 percent, with a direct impact on medical evacuations from the field. Dong Van Khuyen notes:

> Medical evacuation, which depended largely on the VNAF [Vietnamese Air Force] helicopter fleet, suffered accordingly despite the high priority assigned to it by field commanders. The impact was most acutely felt by combat units in the Mekong Delta which depended almost entirely on helicopters for medical evacuation. In remote areas, therefore, units reverted to the old evacuation means of the mid-50s: litters, hammocks, boats, and vehicles, which were slow and unreliable. Troop morale sank perceptibly as a result.[39]

In hospitals, "disposable supplies such as bandages, syringes, needles, surgical gloves and intravenous sets had to be washed, cleaned and sterilized for re-use."[40] After the end of the war, military doctors were interned in communist reeducation camps like other members of the South Vietnamese military as well as civil servants and teachers. The experiences of two RVNAF doctors who served in the Marines and the Rangers, respectively, will now be explored in detail.

EARLY YEARS AND MILITARY SERVICE

The first doctor, Tran Xuan Dung,[41] was born in 1939 in Ha Nam, northern Vietnam. His father worked for the railways, and the family was Buddhist. Dung was the middle child, with an older brother and a younger sister. The life of his family was interrupted and inexorably altered by the events of 1945 when the Viet Minh[42] came to power. He remembers:

> My father was vice station master in Vinh in the middle of Vietnam. After the end of the Second World War, the Viet Minh occupied many parts of the country. They tried to capture everyone who had worked for the government. They arrested my father. They did not feed prisoners so if the

family had enough food, the prisoner would survive but if the family was poor the prisoner died. I was six years old and had to bring meals that my mother prepared twice a day to the prison. My mother had to sell everything. She first sold her clothes then her shoes then the furniture and then the last thing she did was to sell my father's books. It was so sad because my father had a lot of French books and each book was precious. My mother put everything in front of the house in the hope that somebody would pass by, pick up a book and leave some money but nobody dared to touch a French book because doing so meant prison or a death sentence by the Vietnamese communists. . . . My father returned home after three to four months. He told my mother that he had to leave otherwise they would recapture him so he fled north, and left my mother and their three children behind.

The family was forcibly displaced by the Viet Minh, and had to rely on the charity of others to survive. Dung's father returned about a year later and took his family along with other refugees by canoe to Bui Chu in Phat Diem, a Catholic area; however, it was too late for Dung's mother. Dung recounts his mother's suffering:

My mother had dysentery. Daily she had three to six stools and I saw that they were mixed with blood. She would ask my brother to warm a brick and then put it on her abdomen to relieve the pain. She had endured about a year and a half of near starvation. She lay dying in bed. She coughed up blood and after some months she died.

His clinical and understated appraisal of his mother's condition does not detract from the grief of her loss and it is accompanied by his assessment—from his latter day perspective as a physician—that he had kwashiorkor disease at the time: "my abdomen swelled up, I was just skin and bones, and my hair fell out." Dung's father took his children to Hanoi in 1947 and the family moved south following partition in 1954. Dung notes that although his father continued to work for the railways, they had left everything in the north so the family was poor. Dung graduated from Chu Van An High School in 1958, completed his medical studies at the University of Saigon in 1965, and was mobilized into the armed forces. He recalls:

I was in Class 7 for reservist doctors, pharmacists, dentists and veterinarians. We were moved to Quang Trung Training Centre for two nights and then transferred to Thu Duc Military Academy for nine weeks. We were not trained as fighters but as professionals serving the army. After basic training, we had to study another nine weeks in the Military Medical School.

> There were two kinds of graduates, the ones skilled in study who could choose a hospital in the capital or in big towns, and the others who had to choose a fighting unit. The scores that counted were not the ones from the Faculty of Medicine but those from the military academy and medical school. Those who had the highest scores could choose safer positions. Of course, there were exceptions, and if you wanted to choose the most dangerous position, it was always allowed. Honestly, I did not choose the Marines. My scores were not high—I graduated as number 71 out of 73 reserve doctors—and they put me in the Marines.
>
> Once there, I was serious in serving the unit and after a few months I felt very happy. I became chief of the medical platoon in the 4th Marine Battalion. Major Nguyen Thanh Tri[43] was commander and I was his unit doctor. In 1968, I became the doctor of Marine Task Force B, commanded by Lieutenant Colonel Ton That Soan, and this is the task force that rescued Saigon during the Tet Offensive.

Dung's narrative reveals an orderly progression from mobilization through military training to his unexpected assignment to the Marines, one of the elite divisions in the RVNAF. As a general reserve force, the Marines were available for rapid deployment throughout the country, and grew in strength from 1,150 in 1954 to 9,314 in 1969.[44] By 1973, the Marine Division consisted of nine battalions and three brigades with an approved strength of 14,245.[45] Once he was in the Marines, Dung committed himself fully to his new role. He recalls the actions of the task force during the 1968 Tet Offensive as well as his work in providing medical care to civilians in Saigon:

> Forty-four cities in South Vietnam were attacked by North Vietnamese communists. They violated the 36-hour ceasefire. On the morning of New Year at about 8 o'clock the whole task force was mobilised by helicopter to Saigon. The unit was transported to the Joint Chiefs of Staff compound near Tan Son Nhat airbase. That compound was partly occupied the night before by the North Vietnamese. The task force had two battalions. The 2nd Battalion had an interesting name: *Chau Dien* [Crazy Buffaloes]. They were transported first, and then the 1st Battalion. After some hours of fighting, they destroyed all the North Vietnamese who had occupied the gates, and the compound was safe again. After a few days, the area was cleared.
>
> During this time, the military medical team provided aid to locals. One of the worst things I was afraid of was an epidemic—plague, cholera, dysentery, or infectious disease—that could spread through the refugee community. With 1,000 people in a yard or church with no water sources, it would be a disaster but luckily that kind of epidemic did not occur.

> The most frequent conditions I treated among civilians were dysentery and diarrhoea. During my ten days of helping victims of the Tet Offensive in our capital the television team came and filmed us so that was the first time I was on television.

He explains the assignment of doctors in the Marines at battalion level, and speaks of the dangers of serving in frontline units:

> Only two general reserve forces had doctors at battalion level, and those were the Marines and the Airborne Division. The doctor would take care of 600 fighters. General reserve meant jumping in wherever the fighting was hardest. The Marines and the Airborne Division had the highest casualty rates for doctors. Number 72 in my class was a doctor named Nghiem Sy Tuan. He entered the Airborne Division and about a year later, he was killed at Khe Sanh Base. He was twenty-six years old. Another doctor who was one year behind me had multiple injuries to his legs and arms at his first battle. We had to decide whether to cut off both legs but instead sent him to the most famous orthopaedic surgeon in South Vietnam and this surgeon cared for him for eight months, kept him alive, and saved his legs.
>
> My unit was based in Vung Tau. Life for the Marines meant two to three months in the battlefield and then about two weeks' rest in the base, and then two to three months in the battlefield again and so on. Each time the unit returned, there were more women wearing white headbands [mourning headbands] in the family camps next to the unit. From the doctor to the commander to the soldier, everybody had to endure the same dangerous conditions in the battlefield.

Dung's words underline how unusual it was for military doctors to be responsible for a battalion, and therefore 600 men. Most RVNAF doctors were assigned at regimental level and were therefore responsible for 1,200–3,000 men. His account refers to the high mortality rate of soldiers in the Marines and the mounting evidence of mourning in the family camps nearby where the wives and children of soldiers lived.

Nguyen Manh Tien,[46] the second doctor whose narrative is explored here in detail, was born in 1948 in Kien An, northern Vietnam, also to a Buddhist family. His father was acting chief of Kien An Province. Partition proved to be a watershed for the family. Tien remembers:

> In 1954, the whole family moved south during the exodus of about a million people away from the communist occupation of the north. It was a difficult time. Our family had six children close to each other in age. I was about five or six, and the youngest one was a baby. We were not that well

off. I was lucky to be admitted to a famous public school in Vietnam—Chu Van An High School. After finishing high school, I did the competitive examination to be admitted to medical school. The intake every year was about 220, and there were thousands of applicants. I was lucky to be admitted. It was 1966. The medical course was seven years including internship. Saigon at that time was great, especially for young people. We studied hard, played hard, I had my first love there, my first everything there. Saigon is a city close to my heart, that I consider my city, even though I was born in the north.

During my student days, I had friends in the Australian Army and the U.S. Army. Do you know why? I loved music, and they had the PX, and the newest Simon and Garfunkel, Beatles, Searchers, whatever. In exchange for an LP, I would take them around Saigon and do some interpreting for them.

I joined the army as a medical cadet in second year to provide for myself during my studies. The numbers graduating were about 160, and of those about sixty were from the medical cadet school.[47] We were sent to Thu Duc Military Academy where we learnt basic military techniques—shooting, reading maps. During the university holidays, non-military students could enjoy themselves and go to Vung Tau or Dalat but we had to do our training. Upon graduation, I wanted to join the Airborne Division. There were only a couple of places in the Airborne and people above me had already taken them so my next choice was the Rangers. It was a sign of bravado, of *chiu choi*, to join the Rangers.

He provides details of the battlefield conditions that he experienced in the Rangers:

We suffered artillery bombardment every day so we lived and worked in bunkers dug deep into the earth with sandbags on the roof. In the Rangers, only the regiment had a doctor. I had about ten medics with me at the front, with about three or four back in the base. It was half the number of a real platoon. I was the only university-trained doctor. That was the structure. At battalion level, there were sections headed by *si quan tro y* [medical assistants]. They looked after their own sick and injured, and evacuated the more severe cases to me. My job was to treat those people or if they were beyond my ability to treat, to arrange their evacuation to the bigger base hospital.

My unit was the 32nd Ranger Group. We were stationed mainly in An Loc, a hot spot. We were surrounded by jungle, which was heavily infiltrated by the communists, and the only way to get in and out was by helicopter. The communists had heat-sensitive rockets, and to counter them the pilot would drop flares. We always waited for the supplying helicopter because it meant fresh food and vegetables, and especially letters from the family and from my lover: very exciting. Every day, I would look to the horizon to see the flares and special smoke that indicated that a helicopter was coming. Every three to four months, we were allowed about a week's leave to fly back to Saigon to visit our families, and do some work at the base in Bien Hoa, and we would then be back in An Loc. It was a hard time but we accepted that, it was our duty in wartime.

In An Loc, I remember going to the front line and visiting the soldiers in what we called *chot*. *Chot* were like key positions to keep the enemy away. Each had about four or five Ranger soldiers. They all dug a hole and stayed there, they lived there actually, because they could not leave the position. There was a lot of basalt in the area and when it rained, the water couldn't drain away, the mud was like glue, and you have to imagine the soldiers living there with water up to their waist day and night. Quite a few were evacuated to me with terrible gangrene on their feet. So I always feel that the soldiers, the unnamed soldiers, were the real heroes of the war, they suffered a lot, and nobody knows.

Tien's narrative establishes his family's refugee background, and evokes the color and tenor of life as a university student in the 1960s and 1970s as well as his love for his adopted city, Saigon. He provides a practical explanation for his decision to become a Military Medical Cadet and the youthful bravado that led him to join the Rangers. Although the Commando School established by the French in Nha Trang in 1951 was converted into a training facility by the U.S. Military Assistance Advisory Group in 1956, the Vietnamese Rangers were not formally activated until 1960.[48] U.S. Rangers were assigned as advisers, and trained, lived and fought with Vietnamese Ranger units.[49] Rangers were involved in high-risk missions including long-range reconnaissance, espionage, special action, and sabotage.[50] Increasing in size from companies to task forces, battalions and groups, the Rangers evolved from counterinsurgency to light infantry operations.[51] By 1973, there were twenty-one Ranger Battalions, thirty-three Ranger Border Defense Battalions, and seventeen Ranger Groups.[52] An Loc, where the 32nd Ranger Group was stationed, held symbolic meaning as the site of a remarkable feat of arms in which South Vietnamese defenders prevailed against overwhelming force during the 1972 Offensive.[53] Tien's account highlights the isolated location of his regiment and its reliance on helicopter supply runs, as well as the stoicism of Ranger soldiers who had to endure harsh conditions in key forward positions.

For both Dung and Tien, the partition of Vietnam signified a major rupture in their families' lives as their parents left their ancestral lands in northern Vietnam and migrated south as part of a mass movement of population in the wake of the 1954 Geneva Accords. The two families were Buddhist, and the experience that was central to both was that they were refugees from communism. Tien was a young child at the time and does not relate any memories prior to partition. In contrast, Dung's account of his early life is dominated by the events of 1945–1947, a time bracketed by the Viet Minh's seizure of power on one end and his mother's death on the other. The men's narratives reveal a structured sequence of events after displacement: educational achievements, the different paths each took to enter the military, and their positions within their respective units. For both, life on the front line was punctuated by brief periods back at the base. Their memories of battlefield casualties are related in the next section.

COMBAT CASUALTIES

Although Dung served in the Marines, one of his most salient memories of combat casualties involved not the Marines but a group of Rangers in the aftermath of the battle of Vinh Loc in 1966. Dung was to render aid and assistance to the wounded after a nearby nighttime engagement. When he reached the rice field, he was confronted with the following sight:

> Nobody was there. Suddenly one person stood up, he was soaked. He was a lieutenant in the Ranger force that took part in the battle the previous night and his battalion was gone. I said, "Lieutenant, where are the wounded?" We searched the entire rice field row by row. All were cadavers, all were cadavers. At one place, we pulled up a big body, and I saw that the carotid artery was cut and that there was no blood inside. The lieutenant told me that this was the machine gunner of his platoon. When night fell, the communists received the order to go through the field and kill all the wounded on our side. No one was alive, except the lieutenant. My commander asked the American adviser to call the medevac. We counted cadaver after cadaver, and there was no place for the last one, we tried to push the door but it did not close completely and one leg of the eighty-ninth cadaver still protruded. So the helicopter flew away and took the eighty-nine Ranger cadavers, soldiers that had been wounded but were then executed by the soldiers of the other side during the night.

The recurrent use of the word "cadaver" and of the number "eighty-nine" underlines the extent of the atrocity as well as the visual impact of this scene on the narrator. The memory of this battlefield incident is one that has haunted Dung and that he has articulated in written and spoken form. In a published article, he states that, "Around twenty of those would have been killed in combat. The remaining 69 would have been injured, but still alive.... The bodies of these men were quite different [from] those who had been killed in combat."[54]

The second doctor, Tien, also retains compelling recollections of combat casualties, including the death of a personal friend:

> I remember a captain, a friend of mine, who was a company leader stationed out in the front. He was happy because he was about to go on leave. He dropped by the medical section and said, "Let's have some coffee." He asked whether I wanted him to take a letter to my girlfriend. Then he said, "Okay, Doc, I'll see you in two weeks. I'll bring your letter to your family, and before returning, I'll drop by to see if they want to send you some supplies, whisky, or whatever." He got on the jeep that would take him to the helicopter pad. Half an hour later, I heard on the radio, "Doc, provide me with stretchers and personnel. The helicopter was shot down." My men brought back about ten corpses including that friend of mine. It was terrible. He must have been standing when the helicopter crashed. His femur broke the pelvis and moved up into his body. One thing I don't understand even now, every officer had a revolver, and his revolver was twisted. You can imagine the force of that crash, I don't understand the physics of that, his revolver was twisted. His name was Dong and he was a few years older than me, maybe thirty or so.

Tien's narrative underlines the contrast between a routine send-off on the one hand and violent death on the other. He goes on to highlight the impact of cuts in U.S. aid in 1974, especially on combat units like his that were reliant on helicopter supply runs. "I myself witnessed the devastation to the morale of soldiers because of the lack of ammunition and supplies, and the feeling of being abandoned," he notes and adds, "you can't fight with bare hands, whereas the enemy was heavily reinforced and armed with the most modern weapons by Russia and China." The Rangers were ordered to evacuate An Loc in March 1975.[55] The III Corps Ranger commander, Colonel Nguyen Thanh Chuan, "could not imagine abandoning a town that thousands of South Vietnamese soldiers had died to protect," but followed orders.[56]

Tien's most detailed rendering of frontline experiences, however, involves the final days of the war in Go Dau Ha in April 1975. The following excerpt is cited at length because it provides an extraordinarily vivid account of how Tien survived artillery bombardment as the war drew to a close, and the circumstances that forced him to abandon his patients. Surrounded by enemy troops and tanks, the Rangers were dug in and subjected to a daily barrage of artillery fire. At night, Tien could feel his hammock tremble and hear the rumble of heavy tanks. He remembers:

> It was 27 April. As the officers couldn't have meals together, the sergeant chief cook and his staff brought meals to each and every officer. But that morning, there was no artillery fire. We thought, "Maybe peace is coming." They weren't shelling us like usual. I said, "Hey, I have a bottle of whisky. Let's celebrate. Long time no see." We were having some canned meat and saying, "Ah, it's good to eat in the open air like this." Suddenly, we heard "Thup" and then the shell exploded 20 metres away. We all jumped. It was a learnt reflex and we were all back down in the trenches. When I got into the tunnel, another shell exploded right above us. There was a huge "Bang" and I either passed out or was stunned for one or two seconds. When I came to, it was hard to breathe because of the gun smoke and dust, and my glasses had fallen off. Luckily I found them and put them on. I could see out of the tunnel, there was a headless soldier leaning against the trench but there wasn't much blood because the explosion cut off his head but at the same time added a lot of dust and earth. It was one of my patients because it was near where we put our casualties. There were a few people with injuries, including a lieutenant who had lunch with us. He was hard of hearing, that's why he was slow in jumping. We called him "*Tuan diec*" [deaf Tuan], and one of the shrapnel broke his femur. I found the sergeant chief cook lying dead, with his back split open, and his bowel out of his back. I still remember his name, Trung Sy Muc. He had a young wife.
>
> The next day, we had to leave the base. The ammunition ran out. There was no air support because there was no petrol. I had to leave behind all my casualties. Go Dau Ha was a war zone, all the civilians had evacuated elsewhere but there was one inn left. I suspected later that they might have been related to the communists. The old lady who was the owner had a young girl with terrible burns from napalm bombing. I felt sorry for the girl so I treated her and brought medicines, serum and dextrose, and gave her infusions. The old lady was in my debt. When I had to leave six or seven of my patients who couldn't walk, including that deaf lieutenant, I asked her to look after them. She agreed. The poor lieutenant, he was crying and kept on asking me to give him back his revolver. You know what for? You can guess. I said, "No, Tuan, I can't give you that." And he said, "Doc, please, it's mine, give it back to me." I had a nurse, a private, also injured. He had shrapnel in his thigh. It was not serious but he could not walk. He was crying too . . . I know the old lady looked after them because

that private of mine dropped by Saigon two or three weeks later and told me that the lady was very kind and told them that she owed a lot to the doctor.

Dung's and Tien's accounts of battlefield casualties are conveyed in stark and graphic detail. They demonstrate the "intense and absorbing visual imagery"[57] of traumatic memory. The repetition of expressions such as "all were cadavers" and "his revolver was twisted" highlights incidents that both narrators found particularly disturbing and that left permanent imprints. Their detailed recounting of these events constitutes acts of witnessing. Tien became a prisoner of war on April 29, 1975. Released after ten days, he made his way back to his family in Saigon. He states: "I returned home like a ghost walking through the door. Everybody burst out crying because they thought I was dead."

THE AFTERMATH OF WAR

Like many other members of the South Vietnamese military, both men were interned in prison camps after the end of the war. Their narratives convey their memories of detention and hard labor, and the conditions that led them to leave Vietnam. Dung remembers:

In mid-June, I followed the orders of the new government and presented myself at the Institut Taberd where I found a lot of friends from my old unit. On the third night we were transferred in military trucks to Long Giao. We were kept there for nine months without any news from our families, and then they moved us to Suoi Mau concentration camp closer to Saigon. We were then transferred in the night to the border of Vietnam and Cambodia and an area called Bu Gia Map in Phuoc Long Province. I still remember in Long Giao, they gave us one chicken for a 120-person ward. The chicken was cooked until only soup was left and then divided among 120 people. It was the only opportunity we had of eating chicken in nine months.

In December 1977, I was released. My daughter who was nearly three cried when I came home because she did not know who I was. I told my wife that I had to find a way to flee the homeland. In June 1978, I was lucky to find a place in a boat for the whole family. After three nights and three days we reached the island of Tengah in Malaysia. My family was picked by the Australian delegate and given a visa to enter Australia as permanent residents. We were transported to Kuala Lumpur, and then for the first time we boarded a Qantas airplane, and reached Melbourne on 14 August 1978.

We were allocated a room in Midway Hostel in Maribyrnong. From that day, I tried to prepare to restudy [medicine]. My wife would sew throughout the day sometimes until one o'clock in the morning. I saved money to buy the newest medical books, and in 1984, I passed the Australian medical exam. I started to practice again. I have been in this same consulting room for twenty-nine years now. My wife gave birth to a son in 1984 so altogether I have two daughters and one son.

As for Tien, he contends that when the communists released him and his fellow soldiers, it was a propaganda coup. The released war prisoners believed that their captors were honorable and therefore had no qualms about registering for reeducation. He relates:

When they announced that ex-officers would go for ten days of reeducation, 90 to 95 percent fell into that trap. It wasn't ten days but nearly three years for me. For others it was fifteen to seventeen years. We were working in starvation conditions and the only thing we could think about was food, food, food. I saw university professors fighting each other for a piece of corn or some burnt rice. Some people managed to retain their sense of integrity and self-worth but many couldn't. I was moved a few times. At first, we were in Trang Lon for about two months, then they moved us to Long Khanh, and then Bu Gia Map in Phuoc Long Province. We had to clear the forest and build our own accommodation. When I was in Trang Lon—it was a big area so there were many different camps—I heard that a pharmacist who graduated at the same time as me in the Military Medical Academy, his name was Mai Gia Thuoc, he killed himself out of desperation.

Tien's girlfriend was at the Saigon Conservatorium, and stayed true to him throughout his years of internment. He recollects:

She was brilliant and probably the best pianist in the South. She was retained as a teacher by the communists when they took over the Conservatorium. They told her, "You're better off not having anything to do with that *nguy* [puppet]. Forget him." But she didn't. After my release, we got engaged and then we escaped Vietnam together.

It was in June 1980. A nine-day sea voyage. A small boat, 9 metres long, with thirty-three people on board. We encountered pirates seven times. They came close to raping the women but the captain shouted in Thai and slapped the face of one or two of the young men. Paradoxically, we were kept alive by the pirates. The first ones wrecked our engine, the next batch felt sorry for us and gave us some food and water. The final batch towed us until we could see the coastline, and then cut off the rope. It took us two days to row, taking turns, using makeshift oars. It was Malaysia. They took most of the refugees to Bidong but because I was a doctor and I went with my fiancée and her brother, the three of us were taken to Kota Bharu, a nearby refugee camp which had already closed and in which about 1,000 people were waiting for resettlement. It was eighty days from the time I left Vietnam until the day I set foot in Sydney on 19 August 1980.

Like Dung, he was able to requalify as a medical practitioner. He relates how grateful he is to those who helped him:

It took me three years. In September 1980, I was involved in a car accident and broke my hip. I was in Westmead Hospital, immobilized and in pain. One day, there was a newspaper advertisement from the University of New South Wales offering refugee doctors a chance to sit for the final exams of second or third year medicine. Westmead is a teaching hospital of the University of Sydney, and there were medical students. One bloke, I only remember his name was Mark—a redhead with a red beard—came up to me because he was so surprised to see an Asian man in a hospital bed reading a textbook of pathology. I told him my story. He said, "My friend was in third year last year at New South Wales. I'll ask him to lend you his lecture notes." The week after, he brought me five or six stacks of A4 handwritten notes. I had very good experiences with Australian Samaritans. They helped me out of kindness and my only regret is that I failed to keep in contact with them. At the end of 1983, I had the MBBS. I've been working ever since.

Detained without trial in a network of camps in the war's aftermath, and subjected to political discrimination as *nguy* (puppets) after their release, Dung's and Tien's actions in leaving their country not only evince their resistance to Vietnam's postwar communist regime but also echo the choice made by their parents a generation earlier. While the sequence of events conveyed—internment, migration, and resettlement—characterizes the postwar experiences of many veterans, both narratives relate, in addition, the combination of hard work, persistence, and support that enabled the men to regain their professional qualifications in a new country. Their accounts make it clear that after arriving in Australia, both were determined to apply themselves once again to their studies with the goal of reestablishing their medical careers.

POSTWAR REMEMBRANCE

"Memories," suggest Paul Antze and Michael Lambek, "are never simply records of the past, but are interpretive reconstructions that bear the imprint of local narrative conventions, cultural assumptions, discursive formations and practices, and social contexts of recall and commemoration."[58] The narratives of these two former military doctors are set against a background of contested memory regarding the Vietnam War, a context in which South Vietnam, its history, and its war dead have been elided from Vietnam's national historical narrative, and in which the histories of the RVNAF have been largely silenced in the wider historiography of the war. In narrating their stories, Dung and Tien are not only recording their personal histories but also the neglected histories of their units and of those they served with, in the process commemorating an army and country that ceased to exist in 1975.

While the military trajectories of these two men reveal several congruencies, including their service in elite units of the South Vietnamese armed forces, they differ on three levels. The first is agency. Dung explains wryly that he had no say in the unit he was assigned to. Tien, on the other hand, chose his. Dung notes that when he completed his studies, the top graduates among reservist doctors opted for positions in major hospitals while those lower down were assigned to combat units. Graduating eight years later, Tien relates that the Rangers were his second choice. His narrative suggests that in 1973, assignments to elite units such as the Airborne were coveted positions. The previous year, South Vietnam had successfully repulsed a major North Vietnamese offensive—the 1972 Offensive—and confidence in its armed forces was at its peak.[59] The 1972 Offensive saw "young South Vietnamese crowds gather at the gates of recruiting offices to enroll in combat units."[60] While the paths the two men took may have differed, their level of commitment during their service is indubitable, as is the sense of loyalty that, nearly forty years after the end of the war, both still evince toward their respective units.

The second difference is length of service. Dung's career in the Marines covers nine years during which he was assigned different tasks and responsibilities and was promoted twice—first to captain in 1968, and then to major in 1970—before his last posting as chief of training at the Military Medical School. Tien's service in the Rangers, on the other hand, is restricted to two intense years on the front line between 1973 and 1975. Both men, however, provide detailed and vivid accounts of battlefield experiences as well as events away from the front line.

The third area of difference concerns remembrance. Each has sought to memorialize the war in a different way. For Dung, this memorialization has taken the form of recording the histories of the South Vietnamese Marine Corps and Medical Corps, a labor incurred at considerable personal cost.

Dung worked for over twenty years—from 1984 to 2007—to establish an archive of primary and secondary materials on the RVNAF, from his first book commemorating major battles of the Vietnam War to the substantive work of writing and editing volumes of history. In this endeavor, he contacted former commanders and colleagues and gathered written contributions as well as photographs, maps, and documents of service. He was then faced with the major task of translating articles into English or French. He either translated the material himself or requested others to do so. This information was then compiled into four heavy hardcover volumes published at private expense, totaling more than 2,500 pages.[61] Contributors acknowledge that they are doing the best they can in light of the absence of many primary documents.[62] Recording these unit histories has been an obsession for this former military doctor. He explains his motivations for doing so:

> When I was in the concentration camp, I had a dream that if I escaped the country, I would write about the battles of the Vietnam War. And because of that dream, I worked very hard, saved money, and wrote and published [these books].

He achieved his goal over the significant effort involved in reconstructing his life and that of his family as refugees in Australia, and working full time as a medical practitioner. His archival and editorial work reveals his awareness of the lack of visibility of the RVNAF in histories of the Vietnam War as well as his efforts to render the material comprehensible to non-Vietnamese readers. The preserved histories "pla[y] a cultural role in the community to foster memory and understanding of the past."[63] As Joan Schwartz and Terry Cook note:

> Memory, like history, is rooted in archives. Without archives, memory falters, knowledge of accomplishments fades, pride in a shared past dissipates. Archives counter these losses. Archives contain the evidence of what went before.[64]

Dung's self-assigned role in creating and shaping archives on the RVNAF has a threefold purpose: first, to record these histories for future generations; second, to insert the histories of the RVNAF into Vietnam War historiography; and third, to make these histories accessible to a wider public. The monolingual, bilingual, and trilingual volumes that he produced are also his personal means of remembering the armed forces that he served, and those whom he served with.

For Tien on the other hand, remembering South Vietnam and the war has taken the form of community activism. He was at the forefront of efforts to provide practical assistance—material and legal—to the many Vietnamese refugees still languishing in refugee camps in Southeast Asia and Hong Kong in the late 1980s, a time when compassion fatigue had set in on the part of international relief agencies and countries of first and second asylum, screening processes were coming into effect, and refugees were deemed to be "economic migrants."[65] Tien's leadership roles in the Vietnamese Australian community enabled him to lobby on behalf of Vietnamese refugees, as well as for a free and democratic Vietnam. His participation in Anzac Day marches since 1987 and interaction with Australian war veterans attest to his success in integrating into the wider Australian community. Survival proved to be a strong motivating factor. He relates:

> I survived a war in which many people died. I survived the concentration camps, I survived a perilous ocean journey, I survived all those things, and I was lucky enough to regain my qualifications and re-establish myself in such a short time. There must be a reason, there must be a reason. I am so much in debt to life. Life has treated me so well. I consider that as a debt that I have to partly repay by doing something for the community, something unselfish.

The fact that he lived when so many others died has clearly resonated with Tien. As a trauma survivor, he chose to "transform the meaning of [his] personal tragedy by making it the basis for social action."[66]

These two narratives reveal a core of resilience in both men, in spite of the fact that they were exposed to major life stressors throughout their lives, and were refugees twice—in 1954 and again after 1975. The grit and determination that had them excel in their studies saw them serve their combat-hardened units loyally during the war. Both survived punishing conditions in postwar labor camps—the Bamboo Gulag[67]—that destroyed many internees.[68] After their release, they escaped again as refugees, Dung at the age of thirty-nine in 1978, and Tien at the age of thirty-two in 1980. Their experiences are set against a context of mass trauma in the former South that saw the internment of a million people in reeducation camps,[69] and the forced displacement of another million to the New Economic Zones.[70] There was widespread discrimination against former soldiers, civil servants, and teachers as well as against ethnic Chinese and Amerasians.[71] When Dung and Tien escaped their country, they did so as part of a mass movement of population away from Vietnam in the postwar years. By 1979, more than 700,000 people had fled the country.[72]

Their ability to survive these upheavals in their personal lives as well as in the wider contexts of family, society, and country reveals much about the concept of endurance. It may be that part of this resilience is due to the fact that their immediate families did survive the refugee experience. Dung was able to escape with his wife and two daughters by boat in 1978 while Tien escaped with his fiancée in 1980. Both men were also able to regain their professional qualifications instead of experiencing permanent deskilling in Australia. All these factors contributed to their capacity for adaptability. These two men are acutely aware of their good fortune in surviving where many of their compatriots have not. Their medical practices lie at the heart of Vietnamese communities in their respective states. While Dung chooses to remember the country he served and those he served with by recording and publishing histories of the armed forces and medical corps of South Vietnam, Tien has done so by advocating on behalf of Vietnamese refugees and the Vietnamese community in Australia. Their narratives are emblematic not only of a level of personal resilience but also of collective resilience. By "re-creating community structures" through their extracurricular work, they have contributed to "generat[ing] collective resilience."[73] Their actions have the double benefit of not only assisting their community but also of supporting their own process of trauma recovery.[74] Their lives are testimonies to their lost army and homeland as well as a testament to their resolve to insert their histories and the history of their community into the fabric of their new country.

CHAPTER 4

Military Women

I heard that in the armed forces you could go here and there, to lots of places.
I liked to travel, so I joined up. I was like a tomboy.
—Bui Ngoc Thuy

Bui Ngoc Thuy[1] had opened a tailor's shop in Saigon in 1955 when she heard an announcement over the radio that the government was seeking to recruit female army personnel. She volunteered for service in the armed forces and encouraged her older sister and two female friends to do so as well. As she was under twenty-one, she had to ask for her mother's consent. She served in the Airborne Division for seven years and was in the armed forces for a total of sixteen years before she was demobilized in 1971. She obtained parachuting qualifications while in the Airborne. One of her wartime photographs shows her standing at the training site in Cu Chi in 1957 with her parachute pack over her shoulder while in another, she is pictured with a deployed parachute in front of her after she had successfully completed a jump. Nine other women underwent parachute training with her. She notes that they had to complete six successful jumps in order to obtain their qualifications while the men had to complete seven jumps. None of the women were required to undergo this training as part of their military duties—they all volunteered to do so. Thuy elaborates: "There was no compulsion. I liked taking risks, I felt that I had some spare time, and I felt that I could make it."[2] She remembers that one of the women, Chau, broke her leg upon landing and had to be taken to Cong Hoa General Hospital for treatment. While Thuy had her mother's support when she joined the armed forces, the same could not be said of her brothers, both of whom were serving in the army. One of her brothers beat her when he realized that she was undergoing parachute training.³ This did not deter her from completing her course. Thuy then studied nursing for six months and sociology for another six months. Like the majority of women in the RVNAF, she worked in noncombat roles as a nurse and later on as a military social welfare officer. Her assignments took her to Hue, Saigon, and Quang Tri. She reached the rank of second lieutenant, and was promoted to chief of social services in the Medical Corps before retirement.

Thuy's narrative reveals an adventurous, forceful, and resilient personality, and evinces a clear sense of agency. She was nineteen when she opted for a career in the military. She chose to do so over the strong objections of her brothers. The army gave her the opportunity to visit distant locations, and to carry out a range of tasks such as traveling to remote battlefield sites to bring injured soldiers back for treatment, caring for the wounded in military hospitals, and providing support and counseling to soldiers and their families. Thuy was also motivated by her family's history as refugees from communism. She came from a Buddhist family in northern Vietnam. Her father was arrested by the French in 1947, and the family never saw him again. Thuy's mother moved with her six children from Cai Nang to Haiphong in 1949, and the family formed part of the mass migration of refugees south after partition in 1954. By joining up, Thuy believed that she was not only contributing to the war effort but also hastening the possibility of her family being able to return to the north.

Thuy valued her independence and mobility. When she joined the military, she decided she would not marry, however "fate," as she relates, intervened. Her marriage to a fellow soldier in the Airborne Division was unexpected, and motherhood shifted her perceptions and priorities. She gave birth to four children—two boys and two girls—between 1960 and 1965. The assigned travel that she had enjoyed earlier in her career became a fraught issue for her as it meant that she had to spend time away from her children. Her narrative reveals a tension between her evident pride in her career and accomplishments, and the demands of motherhood. Although Thuy articulated her regret that her army duties reduced the amount of time she was able to devote to her family's care, her children honored her for her service to her country. Following her death in Brisbane in 2014, her eldest son sent out a funeral notice that featured three photographs of Thuy during her army days: the first was a 1957 portrait of her in combat uniform wearing a military beret, the second showed her with her parachute pack over her shoulder, and the third was taken in 1968 when she was a military social welfare officer. Later female recruits emulated the example set by Thuy and the women who obtained parachuting qualifications in the 1950s. In 1970, a publication by the Vietnam Council on Foreign Relations referred to several female soldiers who had completed the Airborne School course, "parachuting out of airplanes dressed in jungle fatigues."[4]

Although thousands of women served in the RVNAF and some had military careers stretching for twenty-five years from 1950 to 1975, historians of the war have remained largely silent on their participation.[5] Books on Vietnamese female soldiers have primarily focused on those who fought on the communist side.[6] This chapter will redress this imbalance in the historical record by exploring the service of women in the South Vietnamese military, and illuminate their motivations for volunteering as well as their sense of commitment and patriotism. It will outline the history of the Women's Auxiliary Corps (WAC)—later the Women's Armed Forces Corps (WAFC)—of South Vietnam, and examine the life histories of three RVNAF servicewomen who joined the armed forces between 1966 and 1971, and served until the fall of Saigon in 1975. Their narratives articulate the women's experiences both during and after the war, and reveal the significance of army service in the structure and direction of their lives.

THE WOMEN'S ARMED FORCES CORPS

The Women's Armed Forces Corps (WAFC) was formed on January 1, 1960, from a nucleus of 600 women in the Women's Auxiliary Corps (WAC).[7] By the time the war came to an end in 1975, there were 6,000 women, including 600 officers in the WAFC.[8] Formed over the considerable objections of South Vietnamese military leaders, the WAFC was patterned on the U.S. Women's Army Corps and placed under the command of the Joint General Staff.[9]

While the creation of a female army corps may have signified modernity in the eyes of conservative male military leaders, historical precedents existed in the form of martial female figures in Vietnamese antiquity as well as more recent female revolutionary heroes. During the short-lived rebellion of the Trung sisters against their Chinese overlords in the first century CE, there were female as well as male army leaders.[10] Female sutlers accounted for nearly a third of Le Thai To's army in the fifteenth century, and were called "salvation sisters of the nation."[11] In spite of ten centuries of Chinese domination (from 111 BCE to 939 CE), Vietnam has always had a more liberal attitude toward women than China. In matters of inheritance and marriage, women were on a par with men until the fifteenth century.[12] The Code of the Le Dynasty (1428–1788) was far more liberal toward women than the parallel Chinese Codes of the Ming and Qing Dynasties, with women being entitled to significant property interests and receiving greater protections under criminal law provisions.[13] Although these rights suffered a setback with the promulgation of the Nguyen Code in the nineteenth century, the relative liberalism of the Le Code influenced mores up to and including the status of women in contemporary Vietnamese law. Vietnamese society, however, also internalized Confucian tenets such as the emphasis on male heirs and women's observance of the Three Submissions (to father, husband, and son) and the Four Virtues (right occupation, right speech, right appearance, and right conduct).[14] These conflicting pressures meant that military women in South Vietnam had to negotiate and mediate their disparate roles as daughters, wives, mothers, and soldiers. Military women served their country in an ancillary capacity. In a situation analogous to that of women in other armed forces of the twentieth century who served in a variety of administrative and support roles, "service to the cause was often an extension of what were seen as natural womanly duties."[15]

Female personnel served in the armed forces from 1950 to the fall of Saigon in 1975.[16] Ho Thi Ve, who was to reach the rank of lieutenant colonel by the war's end, published in 2001 the most detailed account of the WAC and WAFC.[17] She began her military career in 1950 in the Viet Binh Doan Trung Viet (Army of the Center). Female personnel in the Viet Binh Doan worked as typists, secretaries, accountants, nurses, and nursing assistants and numbered several hundred in total.[18] Although they were not provided with military uniforms, they held ranks equivalent to first corporal, sergeant, and sergeant major depending on their level of education.

The Viet Binh Doan ceased to exist in 1952, when it was integrated into the National Army of Vietnam. Female personnel who transferred from the Viet Binh Doan to the Nu Phu Ta (Personnel auxiliaire féminin or WAC) had their seniority recognized.[19] Military identity numbers for female personnel were similar to those of male personnel and consisted of the last two digits of their birth year plus twenty, followed by "P" for Personnel auxiliaire féminin, the military zone, and recruitment number. Hence, the first recruit in the Second Military Zone whose birth year was

1927 had the following military identity number: 47P200001.[20] Between 1952 and 1959, the WAC consisted of five specialized branches: Staff, Medical Corps, Communications, Military Supplies, and Social Work. Women working in Military Supplies included those who specialized in folding and repairing parachutes, trained as parachutists, and participated in parachuting exhibitions in the different military zones.[21] Military Social Work initially perceived itself as separate from the rest of the WAC; however, these differences gradually abated over time.[22] In 1959, the Ministry of Defense cut the five WAC branches down to two: the Medical Corps and Military Social Work. Female personnel who wanted to continue in the service had to join one of these two branches after appropriate training otherwise they were demobilized. Women in the WAC were not promoted during this period. Ho Thi Ve notes that, "lieutenants had to mark time during nine years" (the vivid language used was "stamp their feet at the same place" for "mark time").[23] Phung Thi Hanh provides a similar assessment when she writes that, "the Women's Auxiliary Corps continued through the years with little support."[24]

The shift from the WAC to the WAFC in 1965 signified a shift from a French-inspired military model to an American one. The Office of the Chief of the WAFC and the WAFC Training Center were established that same year. The aim was for the WAFC to reach an effective strength of 10,000 or 1 percent of army personnel.[25] The first Chief of the WAFC was Major Tran Cam Huong, who attained the rank of colonel by the time she reached retirement age on April 1, 1975. She was to spend the remaining ten years of her life in reeducation camps after the war. Her successor was Luu Thi Huynh Mai, promoted to lieutenant colonel on January 1, 1975. The WAFC Training Center recruited women aged eighteen and over, who volunteered to join the armed forces. Women served as "typists, supply clerks, switchboard and teletype operators, social workers, nurses, and medics."[26] Their purpose was "to provide 'woman-power' to release men for assignment in combat areas."[27] As to their reasons for joining up:

> Why do women join the WAFC? [In 1969] a questionnaire was distributed to find out. "Half of them said they joined to have a job and make a living," said Colonel Huong. "As for the rest, I think they like military life, and they want to be able, in some way, to help the war effort."[28]

Although they were not tasked with combat duties, female personnel received basic military training including weapons training at Quang

Trung Training Center. They were then dispatched to different army schools to receive further specialized training: General Administration, Medical Corps, Finances, Military Supplies, and Military Social Work. In 1966, WAFC recruitment centers began operating. Women aged between seventeen and thirty with five years of basic schooling were eligible for enlistment while eleven years of schooling were required for officer candidates. Phung Thi Hanh adds that:

> The tour of duty is three years for enlisted personnel and four years for officers. Most women finish their tours. According to Colonel Huong, only one percent quit to marry or have children. After two years of service, WAFCs are permitted to marry and may stay in the corps after they have children if they wish.[29]

In 1967, the Office of the WAFC moved to the Office of the Vice-Chief of the General Staff while the WAFC Training Center became the WAFC School. Ho Thi Ve served as Commander of the WAFC School until April 30, 1975.[30] The number of women in the WAFC had grown to 2,700 by the end of 1967.[31] Dong Van Khuyen refers to 1,025 enrolments in the WAFC School in 1970, out of a programmed input of 1,400.[32] Altogether, seven classes of female officers graduated from the WAFC School.[33] The eighth class was abruptly ended by the fall of Saigon on April 30, 1975.[34] The WAFC School also trained four classes of Air Force nurses at the request of the Vietnamese Air Force and two classes of police officers at the request of the Police Department.[35] The officer training class lasted twenty weeks with enrolments of between sixty and seventy candidates. Future officers learnt "military tactics, leadership, public speaking, and military justice."[36] A small number of female graduates were sent to the United States for training: Army Officer training at Fort McClellan in Alabama, Civil Affairs at Fort Gordon in Georgia, Psychological Warfare at Fort Bragg in North Carolina, and Personnel and General Administration at Fort Benjamin Harrison in Indiana.[37]

In 1968, the WAFC began recruiting female troops. These soldiers received one month of training and worked as security guards and drivers. Priority for these positions was given to the widows of soldiers killed in action. After the 1968 Tet Offensive, larger numbers were required, and "a bill was introduced in the National Assembly to draft women between the ages of 18 and 25."[38] Legislators, however, "quickly vetoed the proposal, feeling that women were needed at home."[39] Resistance to the notion of mobilizing large numbers of women into the RVNAF was reflected in the National Assembly and wider South Vietnamese society as well as in the armed forces. Phung Thi Hanh reports a young WAFC officer observing in 1970: "Some military men still do not accept the idea of a woman in uniform."[40] Yung Krall[41] remembers wanting to join the army as a seventeen-year-old to defend her country against the communists but was told that it was a "no-no" for a girl to be in the military as far as her family was concerned.[42] Frustrated in her efforts, she opted for the closest available alternative and became an army radio journalist instead. In 1964, at the age of eighteen, she joined G5, the propaganda and communications section of IV Corps and worked as a journalist for "The Voice of the ARVN." Her work allowed her to "feel closer every day to the war zone and realize how much [they] owed the soldiers who were fighting, keeping places like Can Tho safe."[43] In light of the general perception that "women were needed at home," the decision of those women who did volunteer for military service is all the more noteworthy. They were not conforming to a widespread movement of their generation, and some overcame considerable opposition on the part of their relatives in order to enlist.

By 1969, there were 4,000 women in the WAFC, 3,000 in the National Police, 365 in Revolutionary Development teams, and more than a million in essentially part-time militia service in the People's Self-Defense Forces.[44] Phung Thi Hanh pays tribute to the women who undertook hazardous service on the ground as Revolutionary Development workers. They included cadres like Nguyen Thi Nam, a twenty-seven-year-old mother of four who distributed medicine and aid in villages and hamlets, mingled with local inhabitants, and in the process effectively hampered communist infiltration.[45] While there were more than 5,000 female Revolutionary Development cadres in 1966–1967, their number was reduced to 365 by 1969 because of the level of hostility directed against female cadres by older village women.[46] Women who assumed these tasks were not only conducting dangerous work but also enduring time away from their families. Nguyen Thi Nam only saw her children once a week. There were, in addition, 130,000 women in combat forces defending hamlets and urban neighborhoods.[47] These volunteers completed sixty hours of course instruction.[48] The wives of soldiers in the Regional and Popular Forces at times provided support to their husbands in fortified defense positions by maintaining weapons and supplying ammunition.[49] Lu Tuan refers to the actions of the wife of a platoon commander of the Popular Forces in a hamlet in the Mekong delta, whose husband was shot dead next to her. She calmly radioed the artillery support unit and gave them directions. They adjusted their fire and inflicted heavy losses on the enemy who subsequently withdrew.[50] In April 1972, in the district of La Vang, the wife of an artillery sergeant hid a dozen South Vietnamese soldiers who had either been injured or had strayed from their units in an underground shelter while her village was under communist control.[51] When South Vietnamese forces counterattacked and reclaimed Quang Tri more than month later, she led the soldiers to friendly units.[52] Her name was Thach Thi Dinh, and she was awarded a medal for outstanding service.[53] Hai Trieu writes of the wife of a Regional Forces soldier in sub-sector Ba To, who was proficient in the use of firearms and insisted on staying beside her husband instead of retiring from the defensive line. She participated in the successful defense of Ba To.[54] The women are referred to as "female soldiers without military numbers."[55] These accounts assert that there were women in South Vietnam who fought as combatants for their country even if they had no formal military status. The narratives of three RVNAF servicewomen, and their experiences during and after the war, will now be explored in detail.

MILITARY SERVICE

Thanh[56] was born in 1947 in southern Vietnam, the third last child in a large family of nine children. Her father was a teacher, "an educator" as she terms it. She joined the armed forces in 1966, and rose from the noncommissioned officer ranks to become a captain in the WAFC. She recalls:

> By joining the military, I could earn a salary immediately. I could look after myself and also help my father. I thought he would not approve of my joining up so I just left home and joined of my own accord. My personality was one that liked freedom, travel, and getting to know places, and I wanted to advance myself academically. It was only in the military that I could simultaneously work and study. After graduating from high school in 1966, I joined the Non-Commissioned Officer Course. I completed it in three months and graduated quite high so I trained at Thu Duc Military Academy. We learnt how to shoot, assemble and disassemble guns, as well as how to manage and train others. I then went to Saigon to study to become a Military Social Officer. There were eighteen of us trainee officers. I studied for another eight months. Our studies covered many fields—education, psychology, law, midwifery, nursing and other matters. Our main task was

to care for military families and help the families of deceased soldiers. The time I was a trainee officer was the best time in my life.

The major event during that time was *Tet Mau Than* [New Year of the Monkey]—the general attack by the communists of the major cities of South Vietnam [the 1968 Tet Offensive]. All trainees had to return to their units. I was assigned to work in the refugee reception centres, schools and other locations where war evacuees who were seeking refuge were assembled. I remember one night a pregnant woman was giving birth and I had to take her to the hospital. There was a 24-hour curfew, not a soul on the road, not a single vehicle. It was very frightening. If the communists had stopped us, we would have been shot.

Upon graduation, I was assigned to I Corps and Regiment 51. Regiment 51 was an independent unit that did not belong to a division but was directly attached to the corps, therefore the social infrastructure was quite large. It was my first unit, so I remember it well. There was a dispensary unit, a small medical clinic stocked full of medication for soldiers' families, a maternity clinic under the responsibility of a female sergeant major, a childcare facility, and most importantly, a primary school for the children of soldiers. There were three officers who were seconded to work with me there. I worked tirelessly and was happy. I knew this social work was right for me and I had a passion for this work. The fighting during those years was fierce. There were many battles and many disabled and deceased soldiers.

The second woman, Nguyen Thi Minh Nguyet,[57] was born to a Buddhist family in northern Vietnam in 1950. When Vietnam was partitioned into two following the Geneva Accords in 1954, her family fled south. Nguyet's father and two brothers were in the military. Her mother was a merchant. Nguyet was the top graduate of her Non-Commissioned Officer Course in 1972, and served as a sergeant in the WAFC. She remembers:

After finishing secondary level one, I stopped studying and worked as a sales assistant in my mother's business. The work was quite easy but I felt I wasn't really suited for it. I wanted to find something that I liked. Each year, on Armed Services Day, there was a military parade in Saigon. Many people went to watch the parade so I followed the crowd. I saw young women around my age wearing sky blue uniforms and marching. I was very proud that the Army of the Republic of Vietnam had a women's corps. I thought to myself: "Could I join the army? Would they accept me?" At that time, my younger sister was seriously injured in an accident and was admitted to hospital for treatment. I brought her a small radio. I heard on the broadcast that the army was recruiting fifty servicewomen for military social work and as non-commissioned officers. I asked my father: "You're a soldier, and my brothers are soldiers. Would you be happy if I joined the army?" My father said, "Which service?" I said, "Military social work." He said, "A career in the military and in social work is very good, child."

I saw how the communists shelled civilians in and around Saigon. It made me see how ruthless they were. The war had gone on too long, and early in 1971, I volunteered for army service. We were taken to the training centre on Nguyen Van Thoai Street for basic training, including judo for self-defence. I graduated after about three months then I was transferred to the Army Social School. I remember my father coming to the training centre to visit me. I was extremely touched. We studied psychology, psychological warfare, politics, philosophy, nursing, how to dispense medication and take care of injured soldiers, as well as how to educate children. I graduated with a degree in Military Social Work. I was retained to work at the military school. We were like the men who served in support roles, in offices. Servicewomen worked in other branches, including the Medical Corps, Communications, and Supplies. Others learnt to be drivers. Sisters who graduated were transferred to all four military zones. I did accounting work, filed books and documents, prepared performing art magazines for the school, and photocopied learning materials for courses. In addition, on major holidays such as Tet or 19 June [Armed Services Day] we organized banquets to entertain dignitaries. We also kept control of military equipment and uniforms.

Servicewomen had green combat uniforms, with green caps and hobnailed boots. Work uniforms consisted of short-sleeved shirts and skirts. Our uniforms were sky blue suits, which we wore with black shoes and black hats, similar to airline attendants. Additionally we raised funds for wounded soldiers being treated in military hospitals such as Cong Hoa General Hospital. As a staff member, I had to set a good example of military discipline. I still remember that in 1973 to 1974 the battleground situation was burning hot. The recruitment centre broadcast urgent calls for servicewomen, and officer courses ran continuously. At the end of 1974, all of us non-commissioned officers were assigned to work at Bien Hoa Military Cemetery. The sounds of helicopters disturbed the cemetery, and the corpses of combat soldiers from battlefields all over South Vietnam were taken to the morgue for cleaning and were kept refrigerated awaiting relatives, or were cleaned, dressed, and put in coffins covered with the yellow flags of justice. When receiving relatives at the army cemetery we served with our best effort, and consoled mothers, fathers, wives and children. They came from distant places to receive the bodies so we had to be really tactful and gentle. The chief of the social department had to take care of the assistance formalities and modes of transport for them. Those were the memories that I have kept in my heart for all these years since the event of 30 April 1975.

The third woman, Thuy,[58] was born in southern Vietnam in 1951. Her father, like Nguyet's, was in the military. She joined up straight from high school and became a second lieutenant in the WAFC. She gives the following account:

> I was walking home from school when I saw a recruitment sign at La Salle Hien Vuong School with a servicewoman in a light sky blue military uniform. I was curious so I went to enquire and found out that I had to be eighteen years old in order to enlist and that my father or mother had to sign the form. I took an application form home. I implored my mum for a whole week before she would sign the form for me. The recruiting lady was a Sergeant First Class and worked for the Joint Chiefs of Staff. She told me to bring a few sets of clothes. I asked my mum for money to buy a bag to carry my clothes and personal effects. A vehicle took us to Recruiting Centre 3 close to Quang Trung. We had a general checkup including chest x-ray and blood tests. There were male military recruits there. They said, "Oh, girl soldiers!" They spoke loudly, laughed and teased us a lot while we were embarrassed but happy inside.
>
> I enlisted on 22 December 1969 and a week later was transferred to the WAFC School on Nguyen Van Thoai Street. There we met Major Ho Thi Ve, Commanding Officer of the School. She was stately and imposing. There were sixty people in my course. I did the Non-Commissioned Officer Course. In the morning, we wore combat fatigues and did basic military training, in the afternoon we wore our suits in class and studied political warfare and other topics. Everyone looked beautiful with the suits on, the tall ones stood at the front, the short ones at the back. I was short so was second last. Male recruits studied all day then had to stand guard at night and sometimes fell asleep while standing. We had it tough but better than the boys. My company of sixty was divided into two platoons. Each time we went to class, the cadre guided us and we walked and sang, you know, "High Mountain Pass":
>
>> High mountain pass, high mountain pass, hey ho,
>> then let it be, hey ho,
>> but love for the country, hey ho,
>> is higher than the mountain pass, hey ho hey ho hey ho.
>
> The course was over after three months. About ten of us went to the Joint Chiefs of Staff while others went to the Personnel Files Centre or worked in the Data Processing Centre. I took night classes for Baccalaureate II,

and took the Officer Course in early 1972. I graduated in April and chose to go to II Corps.

I was in Pleiku at the time of the Red Fire Summer [the 1972 Offensive]. The communists fired 122-mm rockets at the Headquarters of II Corps. The Air Force Headquarters were also close by. We did not fear death. We were only worried about being wounded. One afternoon, I saw that where the booth to the Air Force Headquarters had been, there was a deep hole. There used to be several soldiers guarding the gate. I don't know whether they died, I don't know. Non-combatants were evacuated to Nha Trang but we didn't get there. The communists stopped the convoy and made us get off the coaches, we were so scared we were shaking. Then we heard rifles firing, and a whole troop appeared, a Korean platoon from the Savage Tiger Division stationed high on the hills and mountains, then . . . our military police were there. I was appointed to the Khanh Hoa sector, and my duty was to supervise the servicewomen in the units stationed there. I got married around the middle of 1973. My husband was also in the army, a military ordnance officer stationed in Kontum. I was transferred to the Headquarters of III Corps at Bien Hoa. I gave birth to my son in November 1974.

The first narrative, Thanh's, reveals a strong-willed and independent young woman who left home in order to enlist. Military service not only provided her with a means of improving her personal circumstances by combining academic study with work but also enabled her to fulfill her filial duty toward her father by placing her in a position to assist him financially. She provides a clear rendition of her training, her memory of the 1968 Tet Offensive, and her military assignments. She believes that the army was an ideal career choice for her. The circumstances of the second woman, Nguyet, differ significantly. Nguyet was a refugee from the north and came from a military family. She expresses pride in the fact that the RVNAF had a women's corps, and enlisted with the full support of her father. She paints in vivid detail the tasks assigned to her, the uniforms worn by servicewomen, the escalation of the war in 1973–1974, and the harrowing experience of dealing with the bodies of combat soldiers at the Bien Hoa Military Cemetery. The RVNAF suffered particularly heavy casualties in the 1970s. In 1970–1974, 144,791 soldiers were killed in action and 530,150 wounded in action.[59] The youngest of the three women, Thuy, came, like Nguyet, from a military family, although in her case it was a southern instead of a northern family. She was still in high school when she decided that she wanted to join up. Her narrative reveals a progression from youthful adventure to the violence of war as she witnessed the results of enemy shelling during the 1972 Offensive in Pleiku. All three narratives, like that of Bui Ngoc Thuy which began this chapter, contextualize the women's experiences in terms of their family backgrounds, their motivations for enlisting, and their appraisal of their work in the armed forces.

POSTWAR EXPERIENCES

The women all had difficult postwar experiences and took different routes to leave Vietnam and find refuge overseas. Thanh gives the following account:

> I was on inactive duty and studying at Dalat University when the North Vietnamese attacked Dalat in April 1975. My house was right behind the army housing compound, which was shelled. We had to run with the shelling behind us. I was riding on the Honda with tears streaming down my face to the point that I couldn't see the way to go. After that were the hardest days in my life. The communists mentally terrorized people so everyone was scared. My brothers were interned in reeducation for many years. At night I didn't know whether they were going to knock on my door and arrest me. The hardest was trying to find a way to cross the border. I tried to escape nine, ten times unsuccessfully. The person who helped me in my time of despair was Dat's father. His name was Ha, he was thirty-six years old and a high school teacher. We were together for three years. When Dat was five months old, his father left because there was an opportunity to do so but he went missing at sea. [crying]
>
> Eventually I was able to cross the border to Cambodia. I organized classes and taught there, and saved enough money to build a boat. After living there for five years, we successfully fled across the border. Our boat went straight to Bangkok. There were only twelve people in the boat. We were put in a Bangkok prison and were there for a few months before being transferred to Bangthat camp, a detention centre that held approximately 10,000 people in 1988. A group of military brothers was already there. They invited me to work with them to help the people in the camp. During my two years in the camp, I worked as hard as I did in Regiment 51. I did a lot of social work and was a member of the Judiciary Committee. We were then transferred to Phanat Nikhom camp where we would be interviewed prior to resettlement.
>
> In Australia, I taught Vietnamese children for ten years. What I enjoyed most was to help Vietnamese children to speak Vietnamese. The last

Vietnamese language school that I established was about five, six years ago. I am also involved in the work of taking care of disabled soldiers.

Nguyet, for her part, speaks at length about her experience of forced deurbanization and hard labor after the war.

> We realized that our allies had abandoned us and that we would lose the country. At the Army Social School, Major Nga ordered us to destroy all documents. I said a tearful goodbye to my companions-in-arms. My family was accused by the communists of being *nguy quan, nguy quyen* [puppet army, puppet regime]. My two brothers were ordered to go to reeducation camps. They were told they would only be reeducated for ten days but one spent three years in internment while the other was incarcerated for nine years. The communists assumed power and united the country but people were hungry and lived in poverty. We sold everything that was of any value in order to live. My father's eyesight was poor and my mother fell ill and then died of cancer. There was no democracy, no human rights, no freedom. I lost my youth. Males and females aged eighteen and over were forced to join the Youth Volunteers and sent to the New Economic Zones. We had to clear uninhabited land, cut reeds, and chop down trees in the forest. There was not enough food. It was hard labour, strenuous and heavy work. Then at night, they crammed our heads with political lessons. People disappeared and escaped back to Saigon.
>
> I planned to escape with a friend, and managed to get back to Saigon. However, we no longer had our family registration, they had erased it all. We no longer had proof of identity, we could no longer buy rice or anything. We were living outside the law. I tried to cross the border. I was caught and arrested by Public Security but gave them my gold ring and they let me go. I finally left by boat from Vung Tau. The boat was 19 metres long and carried 249 people. We had no water or food for five days but were lucky because we reached Coconut Island in Indonesia. Then a ship took us to Galang refugee camp. While at Galang, I was a member of the Executive Board of the Army of the Republic of Vietnam to control security in the camp. I completed the English course and was the top student so the teacher gave me the Longman dictionary. I still keep that dictionary as a souvenir of my time in Galang. I helped teach the children, and grew vegetables and bought fish from the locals to distribute to those sisters that did not have relatives overseas. That was the work that I did in the refugee camp. I was very proud that I was a servicewoman, and that I could help educate the younger children so that they knew what the Republic of Vietnam was like, and what the Vietnamese flag with the three red stripes and the yellow background meant. I lived in the camp for two years until

the High Commissioner for Refugees and the Australian, American, and Canadian delegations arrived.

I resettled in Australia in May 1991. I always felt in my heart gratitude to Australia for helping us in our time of need. Australia is a free country, big and wide like Australian hearts. I married a former soldier from the Republic of Vietnam, and gave birth to a daughter in 1993. She is now in her third year at Sydney University. I studied English, sewing, childcare, family care, then hospitality and have been working in a nursing home for nearly ten years. I was introduced to the servicewomen group in 2010. On Anzac Day, we rally to march in the city, and afterwards, we exchange confidences of our time in the army, about the past.

The third account, that of Thuy, reveals a sequence of tragedies and losses in the wake of the war. It is difficult to follow and oscillates between events that were recounted to her as well as those that she witnessed herself:

After 30 April 1975, I had returned to Saigon but my husband came from Kontum. And the North Vietnamese, they came in . . . they didn't let us go by the straight road, people had to follow the trails in the jungle, so many people died . . . I also heard that several servicewomen were hit by bullets and died as there was no medicine, nothing to bandage the wounds. The government put up a very big camp to receive military personnel from the units in I Corps and II Corps that reported in. My house was in Dao Ba Phuoc camp. They fired rockets at the camp . . . next to it was the Medical Corps, that was Trung Vuong Hospital, it was the army hospital for the wives and children of soldiers. They [the North Vietnamese] took everything away. They took the beds, the operating theatres, machines, they took them all back to Hanoi. Nothing was left, only a shell. The same thing happened to Cong Hoa General Hospital. The fighters that were wounded and brought back to Cong Hoa General Hospital, they [the North Vietnamese] cast them all out, those that had their limbs amputated, those still waiting for operations, they cast them all out . . . They [the amputees] didn't have money to go home via vehicle, had to beg for food, and drag themselves . . . They were a pitiful sight. The communist government named the soldiers *nguy quan* [puppet army] and civil servants *nguy quyen* [puppet regime]. Non-commissioned officers were forced to reeducate for three days, as for officers they said to go for a month but there was no return date.

My husband and I went to report for reeducation. I was carrying my baby—he was six months old. They convened for half an hour and asked me, "Don't you have any relatives to take care of your child?" I said: "No."

They convened for another half an hour, then printed a paper with my name, rank, and "deferred reeducation." Every day, they kept on calling . . . they told me to work on irrigation projects. Then they told me to go to the New Economic Zones. I refused to leave. Then they woke me up at 5 a.m. to sweep the streets. They kept on harassing me. I couldn't eat, I couldn't sleep, I went from 50 kilograms down to only 35 kilograms.

In 1978 my husband returned from reeducation, the precinct public security . . . watched us. We began to look for ways to cross the border. The first time was unsuccessful, we lost ten gold leaves. A year later, we lost everything and still didn't get through. The third year, we tried again and were all incarcerated, husband in jail, wife in jail, child also in jail. I was in prison two months short of two years. My boy was by my side. He was only nine years old and suffered with me. Most of the prisoners were "cross the border" prisoners. We worked like animals, and ate only one bowl of rice. It was wretched. They released me on 24 December 1984. My husband drank and fooled around so I applied for a divorce. This child of mine, unfortunately he was very naughty, all the times I went in and out of jail after trying to cross the border, he was with me. The time that I was successful was five years later, in 1989.

I lived in Malaysia for four years . . . two years in Bidong and two years in Sungei Besi. When I went to cross the border, my son went with me. I bought him some food but he said: "Give me the money Mum, I will buy whatever I want to eat." I gave him the money. He used it as fare money and ran all the way back to Saigon. He followed his friends, came home and was sick, then died . . . so I came here on my own, no husband, no child. From the day I arrived in Australia until now I have been living alone. I had constant headaches and chronic insomnia, my head ached unbearably, I was in agony but the doctor couldn't find anything. I qualified as a Vietnamese Australian veteran, and I march every year on Anzac Day.

Thanh was studying at Dalat University when the city fell to North Vietnamese forces in April 1975, and describes the period following the end of the war as "the hardest days" of her life. She gave birth to a son, her partner disappeared at sea, and she was able to make her way to Cambodia and eventually Thailand. At the refugee camp, her military background enabled her to collaborate with other RVNAF veterans in order to make a positive contribution to the structure of camp life. The work that she carried out at the refugee camp was essentially an extension of the social welfare work she had conducted as an army officer. In Australia, she became a teacher, thus continuing her father's legacy. The legacy of her army service is also apparent in her work with disabled veterans.

Nguyet, for her part, worked at the Army Social School until the end of the war. Her family was denounced as *nguy quan, nguy quyen* (puppet army, puppet regime). She relates the repressive nature of the postwar regime, poverty, malnutrition, forced deurbanization, and forced labor, and subsisting "outside the law" as her family was denied formal registration papers. Like Thanh, Nguyet was determined to cross the border and managed to escape to Indonesia by boat. At Galang refugee camp, she was able to use her military background to help others. After resettling in Australia in her forties, Nguyet married a fellow army veteran and gave birth to a daughter. She now works in a nursing home, continuing in this way the social welfare work that she had conducted as a sergeant in the RVNAF. The last account, Thuy's, conveys the chaos that characterized the final days of South Vietnam—the many soldiers and civilians who died under enemy shelling, the North Vietnamese looting of hospitals and the ejection of patients and military amputees. Her account accords with those of disabled RVNAF veterans who were in South Vietnamese hospitals on April 30, 1975, and were cast out by the new authorities.[60] Like Nguyet, she refers to the labeling of *nguy quan, nguy quyen* ascribed to soldiers and civil servants of the South Vietnamese government. She experienced harassment by the communist authorities, and repeated periods of incarceration with her son after unsuccessful escape attempts. She spent four years in Malaysian refugee camps before she was finally resettled in Australia. The fragmented structure of her narrative echoes the emotional breakdown she experienced and the trauma of the postwar years. Postwar state repression and the women's determination to "cross the border" were the motivating factors that enabled them to leave their country and seek resettlement overseas.

THE NARRATIVES

These three former servicewomen came from the same generation born either in the late 1940s or early 1950s. Two were teenagers when they volunteered for service in the military, Thanh at the age of nineteen in 1966 and Thuy at the age of eighteen in 1969, while Nguyet was twenty-one in 1971. All three had high school qualifications—Baccalaureate I—and began their military careers as noncommissioned officers. Nguyet was the top graduate of her course and became a sergeant while Thanh and Thuy completed Baccalaureate II after enlistment and went on to become officers. Thanh's academic interests led her to pursue further studies in the form of a degree at Dalat University. They were all young women still in their twenties when Saigon fell and their country collapsed in 1975. These events ruptured their lives. For all of them, the aftermath of war and the postwar years were bitterly hard, a time that engulfed the remainder of their twenties as well as their thirties. As one said, they "lost their youth." They were only able to reconstruct their lives as refugees in a new land in their early forties. While their narratives are marked by loss and trauma, their service in the military provided a sense of structure and purpose to their lives, and helped them endure harassment by the postwar authorities, internment, the strain of repeated efforts to escape their country, and exile. Thanh relates, "The time spent in the army has forged me, and given me the will and determination to accomplish what I set out to do in spite of any hardship."

All three narratives evince agency in terms of the women joining the armed forces. Thanh knew her father would disapprove of her choice so she did not tell him of her intentions. She simply left home in order to join up. She saw an army career as a means of earning a living as well as pursuing her studies, and her later choices testify to these twin endeavors. Nguyet could have worked in her mother's shop but opted instead for a career in the military like her father and brothers. Thuy was determined to join the army straight from high school, and pressured her mother to sign the papers. Her memories of her training evince youthful idealism, the excitement of enlisting as well as the trepidation of leaving home and adjusting to the regimented nature of military life. All three were noncombatants and did military social work, their duties encompassing a wide range of tasks from accounting, clerical, supervisory, and teaching assignments to caring for the families of deceased soldiers. Their sense of patriotism, and their attachment to the armed forces endured throughout and after their service.

For all three women, the single event that had the greatest adverse impact on their lives and runs like a scar through their narrative is the fall of South Vietnam in 1975. Their individual stories are embedded in the wider mass trauma of the former south in the aftermath of war. Familial and social networks were disrupted as relatives disappeared in reeducation camps, the New Economic Zones, or as escapees. For these three women, 1975 signified the end of their army career and of the life and future they had envisioned for themselves. Thanh speaks of the postwar years as her "time of despair," only alleviated by the companionship of a good man, and the birth of her son. Her partner, however, disappeared at sea in 1979 along with all the people on his boat. She escaped to Cambodia with her son, where she worked patiently for five years in order to cross the border again—this time to a refugee camp in Thailand, and eventually resettlement in Australia in 1990. Nguyet saw her family condemned as *nguy* by the communist regime and her brothers incarcerated in prison camps. She was relocated to the New Economic Zone and forced to do hard labor. Although she was able to escape and return to Saigon, she had to live "outside the law" and sought ways to cross the border. She escaped to Indonesia, and after resettling in Australia in 1991, was able to marry in her forties and have a child. Thuy's account reveals the most damaged life. Her husband was interned in reeducation camps for three years while she coped alone with a small child and was subjected to constant harassment by the authorities. After several unsuccessful escape attempts, she was imprisoned with her son for nearly two years. She was traumatized by this experience, as was her son. She finally managed to escape from Vietnam in 1989 but her son, who was an adolescent at the time, opted to run back to Saigon rather than go with her. She describes a harrowing boat journey, with refugees packed so tightly that she could not put one leg completely down on the deck, and people vomiting repeatedly. She was alone in the refugee camp, and alone when she arrived in Australia in 1993. She does not even know when her son actually died.

While all three accounts follow the same broad narrative framework of explaining the women's reasons for joining the armed forces, their military experiences, and their postwar lives, the first two, those of Thanh and Nguyet, are structured narratives in which the women convey a sense of vocation in terms of their choice of career, and link their former army service with the tasks and responsibilities they assumed in the refugee camps and their later lives and work in Australia. Thanh asserts that she was as committed to the social work she did in the refugee camps as to the work that she had carried out as a young military officer during the war. Her teaching interests and responsibilities encompassed her army career as well as her postwar life in Vietnam and Cambodia, in refugee camps in Thailand, and in Australia. Nguyet, for her part, undertook a range of tasks at the refugee camps in Indonesia just as she had done as an army sergeant, and continues with social work in Australia. Thuy's narrative, on the other hand, is a trauma narrative. The cumulative losses that she experienced—army, country, husband, and son—broke her health. She suffered posttraumatic stress disorder in the form of persistent debilitating headaches and chronic insomnia. Unlike Thanh and Nguyet, she has not been able to work in Australia. She is grateful to veterans and members of the Vietnamese community for their assistance in enabling her to obtain a service pension. While Thuy's narrative is emblematic of loss, the sense of comradeship provided by the servicewomen group connects her story to that of the other two women. All three women gather with other RVNAF veterans and march on Anzac Day in Australia.

As noted by Penny Summerfield, women's narratives "include a dialogue between the present and the past, between what is personal and what is public, between memory and culture."[61] While the narratives of these three former servicewomen entail a dialogue between the present and the past, they are significantly constrained in terms of establishing a dialogue between the personal and public, and between memory and culture. The histories of RVNAF servicewomen have been more effectively silenced than that of RVNAF servicemen. RVNAF servicewomen fail to feature in statistics or "facts" relating to the war, and have no public history against which to contextualize their personal narratives of service. The few books that exist on the RVNAF have either omitted any mention of the WAC and WAFC or relegated them to brief references.[62] "Women's experiences," suggests Summerfield, "are, routinely, omitted from public accounts of the construction of national identity through military activity, and hence from accounts of war, which is reproduced as (inevitably) predominantly masculine."[63] Former servicewomen, however, have maintained links with each other and succeeded in preserving their histories as well as constructing individual discourses of their personal experiences.[64] The first international reunion of RVNAF servicewomen took place in California in 1998, with female veterans from countries as diverse as Australia and Denmark attending.[65] Four issues of the *RVNAF Servicewomen's Magazine* were published in the United States in 1998, 2001, 2004, and 2007. Female veterans remember colleagues lost, including Colonel Tran Cam Huong (1926–1986), the first Chief of the WAFC, who died of illness after ten years in reeducation; Captain Nguyen Thi Van, who died in a communist prison; Lieutenant Nguyen Thi Thinh, who was executed for revolting against the regime; and Major Trinh Thi Tam and Captain Tran Thi Kiem Hue, who died at sea while trying to escape from Vietnam.[66] This list, from such a small segment of South Vietnamese society, points graphically to the scale of the loss of life after the war ended. Female veterans are active in providing assistance to RVNAF veterans in Vietnam. The president of the Disabled Veterans and Widows Relief Association in the United States is Nguyen Hanh Nhon, a former lieutenant colonel in the WAFC. The association organizes fund-raising including a yearly *Cam On An* (Thank You Brother) concert. In 2011, for example, the association raised 893,950 dollars and provided assistance to 7,000 families in Vietnam.[67] RVNAF veterans in Australia have paid tribute to the war service of South Vietnamese female soldiers by producing a special issue of the magazine *Guom Thieng* (Sacred Sword) in 2014 on women of the WAFC.[68] Female veterans have inscribed their histories and experiences into the national narrative of their adopted country by taking part in commemorative marches in their respective countries, such as Memorial Day in the United States and Anzac Day in Australia.[69]

Of the narratives explored in this chapter, Thanh's evinces the strongest sense of mission. One of her principal concerns is the fate of disabled former RVNAF soldiers in Vietnam. She returns to Vietnam each year to help them. She explicitly links her former army experience to her current activities.

> When I received the bodies of soldiers [during the war], they were often not complete [missing body parts]. I had to take the families there to identify the remains. These things sadden me to this day.
>
> That's why, even now, each year, I return to Vietnam to visit invalid soldier brothers that have and are still living in extreme hardship in our home country. These are people who have lost a part of their bodies on the battlefield. They are deserving of receiving aid from us. Community groups here send money directly, and I save money every year and take it to Vietnam to give to these brothers. Each year, we organize money to help them but it hardly makes a dent in terms of their overall needs. There isn't enough. Not enough to give.
>
> Dat said, "Mother, why do you keep wanting to go back to Vietnam? Each time you come back here in pieces, thin. Why do you torment yourself like this?" But I always think of my native land. Many of my comrades, my companions-in-arms are still there, living desolate lives and they need my help. Dat said, "Forget the sad and painful memories." But it is the pain that makes you remember. More than half my life was spent in my native country. So the memories, happy, sad, small, big are all etched into my subconscious, nothing can be forgotten.

Thanh's narrative reflects the gap between memory and commemoration that marks the experiences of many South Vietnamese veterans. For Thanh, as for Nguyet and Thuy, army service was a pivotal experience. The memories of these three women contrast with dominant narratives of the war in Vietnam and in the wider historiography of the war where, in relation to the role of women in particular, the communist side has been given prominence while the service of RVNAF servicewomen has been forgotten. Their stories challenge privileged narratives of the war and in the process evoke "a struggle in the terrain of truth."[70] Thanh's account makes it clear that the process of commemoration is for her a highly personal experience: that of traveling to Vietnam every year, as a private citizen, to bring aid to severely disabled veterans of the former South Vietnam. It is for this reason that she has asked that her full name not be made available in the National Library records. She wishes to avoid any problems with the Vietnamese authorities and would like to continue her self-appointed task as long as she is able to. It is her way of remembering and commemorating the war and those who fought in it.

CHAPTER 5

Friendship and Sacrifice

*Regarding the battle of An Loc, I lost many good friends . . .
I cannot speak of them all.*

—Tran Van Quan[1]

It was the only point in a measured interview in which Tran Van Quan's hands shook. Quan, a former lieutenant colonel and commander of the 18th Logistics Battalion at the battle of An Loc in 1972, was a twenty-year career soldier. A Thu Duc graduate, he served in the army from 1954 until the fall of Saigon in 1975. Quan was born in 1930 and was in his early eighties when he was interviewed. His reticence regarding emotive matters and personal loss may have been a generational issue.[2] A younger veteran, Tran Van Giac,[3] who served in the navy between 1970 and 1975, was less reticent about matters of friendship and spoke at length about a close friend from the Naval Academy, Huynh Kim Buu. Buu did not die during the war—he died many years later in a hospital overseas—but Giac was particularly saddened by the knowledge that his friend lost the girl that he had loved when he was in his twenties, and that it was a loss that Buu never recovered from. Giac remembers that she was a seventeen-year-old student and "very beautiful" while his friend Buu was twenty-four or twenty-five at the time, wore thick glasses and "looked like a professor." The relationship ended after two years not because of the war but because of opposition from Buu's family. Giac relates:

> He was devastated. He was not interested in meeting or marrying anyone else. He was so depressed that he was struck down by illness. When he died, I saw that he still had the photograph of his one true love. He still had her picture in a frame. I felt so sorry for him. I can't imagine how life could have dealt him such an unlucky hand of cards. This was one friend who left an indelible mark on me.

Friendships among soldiers in wartime are poignant not only because of their potentially evanescent dimension but because they are shaped at such a formative time in their lives and in such exceptional circumstances. Tempered as they are by the awareness of loss or impending loss, they can leave a lasting imprint. One of the saddest aspects of war is the "continual forming of real friendships which last for a week or two, or even months, and are then suddenly shattered forever by death or division."[4] Nguyen Manh Tien served as a military doctor in the 32nd Ranger Group in 1973–1975 and remembers the *esprit de corps* forged in combat units:

> I was familiar with war trauma but I remember my time in the army fondly because of the bond that glued the soldiers and the officers on the front line, because you lived together and protected each other, and died together so to speak. That bond has stayed with me until now.[5]

"An effective battalion in being, ready to fight," writes Henry Gullett, "implies a state of mind—I am not sure it is not a state of grace. It implies a giving and a taking, a sharing of almost everything—possessions, comfort, affection, trust, confidence, interest."[6] This "state of grace" endures in the memory of many veterans. It may be for this reason that surviving servicemen often maintain links with former comrades-in-arms through informal networks as well as service associations, and still keep in touch decades after the end of the war. Quan has maintained his friendship with his former commander, Brigadier General Le Minh Dao, who led the valiant defense of Xuan Loc in April 1975, during which the depleted 18th Division and Long Khanh territorial forces held off three North Vietnamese Army divisions supported by armor and artillery.[7] Tien keeps in touch with former Rangers in Australia and the United States, and marches with other Vietnamese veterans on Anzac Day. Giac showed me a large book that contains photographs of his classmates from the Naval Academy, details of their rank and service during the war as well as current news of their families in the diaspora, including pictures of daughters or sons getting married and portraits of round-faced grandchildren. These navy veterans form part of a transnational community of friends and colleagues living on different continents who are linked by their service, and more specifically their class at the Naval Academy. The book included a complete list of all 280 graduates of the class, those who died in the war, and those who had died since the end of the war.

This chapter will explore the account not only of a friendship but also of the ways in which friendship is remembered in the aftermath of war and sacrifice. It will examine the memories of Nguyen Huu An, a former Ranger, and his reconstruction of the events surrounding the fate of a friend and fellow Ranger, Tran Dinh Tu, and of the latter's men in the closing days of the war.[8] In 1975, Tran Dinh Tu was a major and the commander of the 38th Ranger Battalion. The story that Nguyen Huu An relates is that of a war crime that occurred in the district of Cu Chi on or around April 30, 1975. The 38th Battalion formed part of the 32nd Ranger Group retreating from Tay Ninh to Saigon. Tu and his men fought until they ran out of ammunition, at which point they were captured by enemy forces and made prisoners of war. Following an altercation with the enemy commander, Tu was shot. His twelve surviving men were also shot and buried in a mass grave. News of Tu's death reached his widow, and she was able to retrieve his body a few days later. The grave containing the bodies of the twelve soldiers, however, was not excavated until 2011. The execution of Tu and of his men violated Article 13 of the Third Geneva Convention relative to the treatment of prisoners of war.[9] The manner of their deaths went unreported and remains largely unknown. The story of Tu and that of the men of the 38th were circulated within Ranger circles in the United States but did not reach the wider Vietnamese diaspora until more than thirty years later. Nguyen Huu An, a fellow Ranger and boyhood friend of Tran Dinh Tu who resettled in Australia in 1981, only became aware of Tu's death and its details in 2009. An's narrative conveys not only his personal story and his memory of his service in the Rangers but also his interpretation of the circumstances surrounding the executions of Tu and of his men in Cu Chi in 1975.

The exploration of this wartime incident reveals several layers of narration in the form of articles on Tu and the men of the 38th Battalion in Ranger magazines, An's own writings detailing his memory of his boyhood friendship with Tu, An's correspondence with Tu's son in Vietnam, the son's record of the excavation of the mass grave in Cu Chi in 2011, including photographs of human remains, identity tags, and other artifacts recovered at the gravesite, and An's dissemination of this information to the Vietnamese diasporic community. These narratives evince a process of mourning and remembrance on the part of relatives, friends, and former colleagues of the deceased. They counter official silence on the mass shooting, and operate in the following ways: on an individual level, they illustrate the story of a friendship between two boys who later served their country, and the actions of a son to honor his father's memory; on a communal level, they pay tribute to a group of Rangers who chose to follow their commander and fight "to the last bullet" for their country; and on a collective level, they embody contested representations of South Vietnamese soldiers and of their service during the war. These portrayals of life and death in elite Ranger units in the RVNAF convey the value that their members saw in their service as well as the dedication that was often displayed. The uncovering of layers of memory is symbolic of the still buried past and the suppressed histories of the RVNAF in the Vietnamese national memorial landscape. The account of this massacre has strong transitional justice implications. Transitional justice seeks to address the legacies of human rights violations, and involves measures such as criminal prosecutions, reparations and restitution programs, and truth-telling initiatives.[10] For these measures to come into effect, however, authoritarian states need to acknowledge past violations of human rights. The Vietnamese state would therefore have to recognize atrocities carried out by the North Vietnamese army and communist insurgents during the war as well as widespread human rights abuses in the South in the postwar years such as internment without trial in reeducation camps, forced displacement, and forced labor. Nguyen Huu An's narrative of his experiences in the Rangers will be explored in the next section, followed by his reconstruction of Tran Dinh Tu's story. The last section will examine the forms and implications of remembrance.

THE NARRATIVE OF NGUYEN HUU AN

Nguyen Huu An was born in 1946 in Bac Giang in northern Vietnam.[11] His family was Buddhist. His father was a teacher and his mother sold goods for a living. When Vietnam was partitioned into two following the Geneva Accords in 1954, his family joined the one million refugees who fled from the communist north to the noncommunist south. They eventually resettled in Thi Nghe, in an area not far from Saigon. An's father was able to work as a teacher again. An remembers the family's early years in South Vietnam as peaceful before communist insurgents began killing people in the countryside and targeting village officials. He tells of an incident that occurred in 1961 or 1962. The South Vietnamese government had set up a van in the local market and put up a screen in the evening to show films about practical matters such as hygiene and health—washing one's hands before a meal, boiling water before drinking it, taking antimalarial tablets. An was watching one of these films when he heard an explosion and saw "people lying on the ground all bloody." He recalls, "that was the first time I experienced what the communists were doing." An attended Chu Van An High School and completed a law degree at the University of Saigon in 1971. He was mobilized into the RVNAF and graduated from Thu Duc Military Academy in 1972. He then opted to join the Rangers, and went on to serve with the 90th Ranger Battalion in Pleiku. He explains why he chose the Rangers:

> When I was young in 1968, on New Year's Day, the communists started a fierce attack. They wanted to seize the Bien Hoa highway and our troops were sent there to prevent them from doing so. I was with some friends and we wanted to see what was going on. Instead of being scared we were curious so I took my bicycle and we went there. One of the soldiers saw us and said, "Hey people, move back or you'll be killed!" I saw that they were Rangers, they had the sign of the black tiger and I said to myself that they were brave fighters and so if I had to join the army, I would choose this unit. After 1968, everyone from the age of eighteen had to join the army and be trained to protect the country but if you're still at school or university, you can finish your course before joining up so that's why I stayed back. I finished my law degree in 1971 and then I had to join the army. The Thu Duc Military Academy was full so we had to wait until the New Year, and my class was the first of 1972. We were trained to use weapons, ammunition, and explosives, to keep order, and most of all we learned how to obey orders.
>
> When we finished we had to choose the unit we wanted to serve in and of course I wanted to join the Rangers. About thirty of us were selected and we had to undergo training in a special camp called Duc My. In the Rangers, you always have to attack the enemy and you're in a small unit. You're helicoptered somewhere close to the communists, and then have a short fight to capture or kill the communists and run back. Because of this tactic, not many wanted to join the Rangers. Rangers died early—about 60 percent were killed in combat. Girls didn't want to marry you because you'd die soon. We had to do five weeks of *rung nui xinh lay* [jungle, mountain, swamp] training and then I was sent to a battlefield unit to be trained as an officer. We had to do this because you don't feel the atmosphere of the battlefield at Duc My. Some people were good at training but once they were on the battlefield they were scared and froze. The government didn't want us to be killed easily like that so during battlefield training, we heard bullets flying everywhere and felt the atmosphere of a battle. We did the first week with the 42nd Ranger Battalion, a very well-known battalion in Vietnam, and another week with the 44th Ranger unit and after that I was fully trained. I was sent to Pleiku in II Corps, it's a three-nation border area with the North Vietnamese communists sending their troops

along the border from Laos and Cambodia to South Vietnam. There was heavy fighting every day.

The 42nd and 44th Battalions, like several other South Vietnamese Ranger Battalions, were highly decorated. Twenty-three Ranger units received the Gallantry Cross with Palm.[12] A total of eleven U.S. Presidential Unit Citations were awarded to Ranger units: three times to the 37th Battalion, twice to the 39th and 42nd Battalions, and once each to the 1st Ranger Task Force, the 21st, 44th, and 52nd Battalions.[13] Known as "the steel refinery center" of the RVNAF, the Ranger Training Center at Duc My conducted training in jungle and mountain warfare as well as in the techniques of Long Range Reconnaissance Patrolling and Commando and Reconnaissance.[14] The Rangers provided the RVNAF with a quick reaction force, and "intercepted, engaged and delayed main force enemy units."[15] In 1970, the Civilian Irregular Defense Group, formerly under the control of the 5th U.S. Special Forces Group, was reorganized into Ranger units.[16] With the addition of 14,534 troops, the Rangers more than doubled in size and took on the added responsibility of border defense.[17] An was placed in command of a reconnaissance platoon.[18] This is how he remembers his first battle:

> My first battle, I tell you what, your first experience on the battlefield, you still get scared, you still don't know what to do. When I first went to the battlefield, I had my platoon. Normally a platoon has about forty soldiers but in the battlefield you don't expect a full platoon. People got killed so my platoon had just twelve people, twelve soldiers and with me we were thirteen. We had to fight to get back the camp on 30th Hill. We were a reconnaissance platoon so we had to go first to see where the communists were, what sort of guns and ammunition they had and how many units. I was sent first and of course I didn't know what to do. I forgot everything, even the gun, I didn't even know how to hold it, but after a while when I'd calmed down, I thought to myself, "Hey what are you doing, you are strong and you have enough experience, now people are under your control and if you don't do well, they'll get killed because of you, so wake up! Do what you were trained to do." I was an army officer so I had to do my job, I had to do it well because that was the best way to protect my soldiers.
>
> At first when we saw the North Vietnamese communists we radioed back to say we'd seen them and they had seen us and fired at us. If you want to survive, attack them, right? So I checked where their machine gun was and I said, "Okay platoon, go ahead. Attack!" I saw something flashing in my direction but it was very hot at that time, my sweat was coming down

and I had my glasses on. I thought it was sun glare on my glasses so I just ran forward and my soldiers followed and we got to the dugout and we got them. We radioed back to the battalion leader to say we got the place and there was a machine gun as well as a B40, and could we stay there? The battalion commander said, "No, just take the gun and get away because they know where you are and they're going to fire at you now. Run!" So we all ran to the river and we'd just gotten there when the dugout was shelled. I said, "Hey, if we weren't quick enough we would all have gotten killed." When we stopped the soldiers started cooking a meal, they cooked very fast, I don't know how they did it. I was just standing there drinking some water when they brought me a meal. At the battlefield whenever you have food you eat it. So even though I wasn't hungry I ate it, and the soldiers told me, "Officer, you were very brave, they were shooting at you but you didn't care, you just ran ahead." I said, "What did you say? They fired the machine gun at us?" I was lucky that the gunner didn't get me, or he was sick or something, so he couldn't handle his machine gun well because if he'd handled it well, I would have been dead because they were shooting at me and I was running ahead. I didn't know. Now I know the flashing thing was not the reflection from the sun but the machine gun firing. If I knew it, I would not have been running. People thought I was brave, but I wasn't, because I didn't know what was going on.

An's narrative voice conveys a vivid sense of events and illustrates the mixture of curiosity and bravado that characterized his younger self. That sense of curiosity is evident when he describes getting on his bicycle and heading toward instead of away from the sounds of a firefight during the 1968 Tet Offensive. His story also reveals his acceptance of the realities of general mobilization for his generation. Once in the military, An chose to serve in a corps that he admired, even though he knew that assignment to the Rangers was particularly dangerous. His account is leavened with humor when he admits that all his training evaporated the moment he experienced combat for the first time. It was his sense of responsibility toward his men that enabled him to rally and to charge the enemy position.

An later contracted malaria, which required hospitalization. He then returned to fight with his unit. At the end of 1973, he was wounded in the field and was hospitalized for a month. His wounds were assessed as category two injuries,[19] which meant that he could no longer serve on the front line. He was deemed unfit for combat duty. He could either stay in the military and work at a desk job or leave the army. As he had a law degree, he chose to return to civilian life. He was demobilized in 1974 and worked at the Saigon Supreme Court until 1975. In the immediate postwar years between 1975 and 1981 he moved around constantly to hide from the Vietnamese authorities, and avoid imprisonment in communist reeducation camps. He made three failed escape attempts from Vietnam before escaping successfully in 1981. In Australia, An retrained as an accountant. His first task was to sponsor his wife and son over. For twenty years, between 1981 and 2001, his energies were directed toward constructing a new life for himself and his family, and adapting to a new country and culture. In 2001, he joined the Vietnamese Veterans' Association, set up the Ranger Association in Victoria, and marched for the first time on Anzac Day. An was a driving force on the committee that set up the Vietnam War Memorial of Victoria in 2005. He applied for a certificate to be recognized as a South Vietnamese veteran in Australia because "it was a way for [him] to tell [his] children that he had served his country [South Vietnam]." In 2001, he also joined the Ranger Association in the United States and sent out notices to find news of three missing friends from the Rangers. The story of one of these friends is the topic of the next section.

TRAN DINH TU AND THE EVENTS OF APRIL 30, 1975

An provides the following story of his friend Tran Dinh Tu, the commander of the 38th Ranger Battalion, and of his death in the last days of the war:

> When Tu heard the news that President Duong Van Minh had ordered the army to surrender to the North Vietnamese he told his battalion, "I will not surrender, I will fight until the end because Rangers never surrender. Those who want to join me, take this side, and those who want to return to base take that side." About a hundred soldiers joined his group. He told the vice commander, "Take this group back to the base. Give us all your weapons and ammunition. I will fight until the end, I don't want to surrender." So they fought from ten o'clock in the morning until the next day, the first of May, when they ran out of ammunition. They still had their weapons but no more ammunition. By that time there were only ten survivors, no, thirteen, with him, thirteen survived. When he was captured by the North Vietnamese, their leader told him, "I order you to remove your South Vietnamese rank insignia." He refused. He said, "I studied in the training camp, and the South Vietnamese army placed my rank insignia here, they never told me how to remove it. I won't remove it. I am now your prisoner,

a prisoner of war, and I am allowed to keep my rank insignia." The North Vietnamese leader got very angry and said, "In that case, I order you to take off your shirt." Again Tu refused. He said, "No, I am a prisoner of war, and I am allowed to keep my uniform." The North Vietnamese commander stabbed him and then shot him in the head. He then ordered that all of Tu's remaining men be killed. They were shot and left in one big hole.

One of the soldiers who had returned to the base told Tu's wife that he'd heard that Tu was killed somewhere nearby. So on the first of May, in the afternoon, Tu's wife went to the battlefield to look for his body. She could not find it. The next day she returned and still could not find it, until a local guerrilla told her, "Give me some money and I will tell you where I buried them, all the men of the Ranger group." He then took her to the site and Tu's wife took his body back to Saigon and buried him in the Saigon cemetery.

I was very sad when I heard this, but I said to myself that he died a brave death and he died like a soldier. So I spread the news about Tu. Many people admire him, and at ceremonies to remember the sad day of 30 April 1975, people still put up his photo in memory of the past and to remind people that Rangers never surrender. That's Tu my friend.

An's narration is lengthy and detailed. He only learned of Tu's fate many years after the events that he describes. He was clearly moved when he spoke of Tu, the actions of the Rangers who chose to follow their commander, and the manner of their deaths. Theirs was a sacrifice that their fellow soldiers recognized and responded to. Moreover, the actions of Tu and of his men counter many narratives critical of the RVNAF and its performance during the war. There are several aspects about Tu's story that are highlighted: first, his refusal to lay down arms, and the choice he gave his men as to whether to follow him or return to base; second, his refusal to remove his rank insignia and his uniform after he was captured—this relates to Article 18 of the Third Geneva Convention according to which clothes and badges of rank and nationality may not be taken from prisoners of war; and third, the disposition of his body. An relates that Tu's widow could not locate her husband's body on the battlefield and had to pay a communist guerrilla to direct her to the gravesite. She was then able to have Tu's body removed and reburied. An's account reveals his shock at learning of Tu's death more than three decades after the end of the war. The interval of time that elapsed between the events that occurred in Cu Chi in April and May 1975 and An's receipt of the news in Australia in 2009 reveals the fragmented and uneven transmission of information relating to the war in the years after 1975—even for former soldiers like

An who had made a significant effort to reconnect with Vietnamese veteran communities overseas and to seek news of missing friends in the military. An's narrative makes it clear, however, that he was determined to circulate the news about Tu and the men of the 38th Battalion as widely as possible once he was apprised of their story.

MEMORY AND THE RECONSTRUCTION OF WARTIME EVENTS

Although the story of Major Tran Dinh Tu and the men of the 38th Ranger Battalion is largely unknown outside the immediate circles of former Rangers overseas, Vietnamese veterans, and the Vietnamese diaspora, it is a telling incident and far from atypical of the events that took place in the final days of South Vietnam. In his book *Black April: The Fall of South Vietnam 1973–1975*, which is based on a wide range of sources including firsthand reports by South Vietnamese units, American intelligence reports, and North Vietnamese official documents, George Veith makes the following reference to Tran Dinh Tu and the events of April 30, 1975:

> The 32nd Ranger Group, attempting to retreat from Tay Ninh on 29 April, was blocked on Route 1 by the 316th Division. One battalion, the 38th Rangers, refused to surrender, and fought until the end. According to Ranger sources, the battalion commander, Major Tran Dinh Tu, was promptly executed. In a well-publicized example, Colonel Ho Ngoc Can, the province chief of Chuong Thien and Soldier of the Year in 1972, also refused to surrender. He fought until he ran out of ammunition. He was also executed shortly thereafter.[20]

Nguyen Huu An's narrative is predicated on a series of layers. The first is the context of the oral history interview. An knew that his interview formed part of a major oral history project on Vietnamese veterans in Australia, and that it would be preserved in a key national institution. It was important for him that Tu's story be put on record. As Beth Robertson notes, "one of the most important uses of oral history is to record the perspectives of disadvantaged people who traditionally have been either ignored or misrepresented in conventional historical records."[21] Oral history therefore not only gives An the opportunity to tell his own life story and to shed light on the service of South Vietnamese Rangers but also provides him with a vehicle for reconstructing Tu's narrative and the story of the men of the 38th Battalion. Embedded within An's life story is the story of his friend and that of the Rangers.

The second is the fact that the news of Tu's fate had such a powerful effect on An that he wrote a lengthy article on Tu that was published in three installments in the Sydney-based Vietnamese newspaper *Viet Luan* (Vietnamese Herald) on August 14, 21, and 28, 2009.[22] Entitled "No va Toi" (He and I), the article is essentially the account of a friendship. The two boys, An and Tu, had similar backgrounds. Both were from North Vietnamese families and were refugees in 1954. While An's father was a teacher, Tu's father was a public servant. Both families were Buddhist.[23] An relates the series of temporary shelters and centers where northern refugees were housed—usually on school grounds—and the allocations of rice and water each family received from the South Vietnamese government. When these shelters closed, each family received a small amount of money to assist with their resettlement and livelihood. An writes that "all public employees and teachers were re-recruited."[24] An and Tu ended up in the same primary school in Thi Nghe, and were placed in the same class. Both initially experienced prejudice and hostility from southern children because they were from the north and had northern accents. Tu was three years older than An and defended him against bullies. Both boys gradually won over their schoolmates by exerting themselves over the popular game of "can shooting" and foraging energetically for empty cans of condensed milk. The beginning and end of classes at the school were marked by drum rolls, and An writes that his and Tu's friendship was cemented over their drum-beating responsibilities. It was a friendship that endured throughout their school years even though the boys attended different high schools. Tu volunteered for army service after finishing high school and was in Class 14 at Thu Duc Military Academy. He joined the Rangers the following year, in 1964. He confided to An: "We've already left the North, if we cannot defend the South, where are we going to live?"[25] The last time An saw his friend was four years later in 1968, when Tu was a young captain in the 33rd Ranger Battalion and had just returned from an operation. They were asking news about each other's families when Tu told An: "Something has happened. I have to go with my troops now. See you next time. Convey my respects to Teacher [An's father]."[26] Despite the fact that An joined the Rangers in 1972, they lost sight of each other for the rest of the war. An's story and that of his family and their experience of displacement are intertwined with the account of his friendship with Tu. An's portrayal of his family's history after migration to the south is of particular interest because it deals with an aspect of Ngo Dinh Diem's presidency that is seldom acknowledged. In 1954–1955, South Vietnam was a small country with a population of approximately eleven million struggling to establish itself in the aftermath of war and decolonization, and yet it was able to absorb a massive influx of a million refugees from North Vietnam.

A third layer is that An's reconstruction of events is drawn from two other written accounts. One is an article published in *Tap San Biet Dong Quan* (Ranger Magazine) in the United States in 2000,[27] which relates that the story of Major Tran Dinh Tu and the men of the 38th Battalion was derived from two eyewitness accounts: that of Captain Xuong, Second-in-Command of 38th Battalion, who later died in a communist prison in Nghe Tinh in 1979; and that of a Ranger trooper named Duc Troc, who was responsible for carrying communication gear for Tu, and was left for dead when the survivors of the battalion were shot by the North Vietnamese. Duc Troc managed to crawl to a nearby house, where the people dressed his wounds and hid him until he could return to Saigon. The writer of the article states that he heard of Tu's death when he met Captain Xuong in Camp 8 in Yen Bai in 1977. A third eyewitness was of course Tu's wife, who was able to reclaim her husband's body at the site of the executions, but her story did not come to light until after 2009. At the time of publication, An's article stated that he had tried to find news or traces of any surviving members of Tu's family but had been unable to do so.

The information in the *Ranger Magazine* article was superseded by a second account, that of Tu's son Tran Dinh Thai,[28] who writes of his father's death, his mother's recovery of the body in 1975, and the excavation of the mass grave of Rangers in 2011. Thai recounts that his mother recovered his father's body on May 3, 1975, from Trung Lap Ha primary school in Cu Chi. Tu and two other officers were shot at the school and buried on site. The mass grave of twelve soldiers who were also shot lay in a nearby field, now part of a farm. The farmer did not witness the executions but was told by the people who lived in the area about the Rangers retreating from Tay Ninh and the hole in his field that contained the bodies of twelve soldiers. He advised Thai that he did not dare plant any rice at the site and that he made offerings to the dead soldiers every New Year. A former local guerrilla described to Thai the final moments of the 38th Battalion, its surviving men exhausted and out of ammunition, and added: "Altogether, thirteen people were left including the battalion commander, the radio telephone operator, a lieutenant with grey hair, and ten soldiers. They were sitting next to each other smoking the last of the army supply cigarettes."[29] Thai chronicles the exhumation of bodies at the site that occurred in 2011. The first item retrieved was a leg bone in a faded sock with tied nylon rope, which indicated to Thai that the men were bound when they were shot. Next were the dog tag and military identification card of Ly A Sam, listing his date of birth as May 19, 1950, his father as Ly Man Soi and mother as Ho Thi Minh, and the identification card of Trinh Ngoc Thuan, listing his date of birth as March 3, 1957, his father as Trinh Huu Hien and mother as Hua Thi La. Sam was twenty-four and Thuan eighteen. The exhumation was witnessed by approximately forty local people. They advised Thai that the men were shot in the late afternoon, around 4.00 p.m. or 5.00 p.m. More human remains, articles of clothing, and other artifacts were retrieved, including a watch with a black leather wristband and a wallet containing the photograph of a person in uniform with a girl—too faint to be identified. While the watch had rusted, the time displayed was "4 hours 14 minutes day 31."[30] It is unclear whether complete remains were recovered or only partial ones. The article suggests that the burial site was not fully excavated. Thai writes that one set of remains was cremated along with articles of clothing, a belt, and coils of nylon rope, and the remainder placed in a large glazed earthenware jar called a *khap* in the hope that the families of the Rangers would reclaim the remains. An published the correspondence from Thai in 2012, including photographs of the school where Tran Dinh Tu was shot and buried, the field where the bodies of his men were laid, and part of the human remains and artifacts recovered at the site.[31]

A further layer of interpretation is provided by a third account published in May 2013, which provides yet another reconstruction of events.[32] The writer is Nguyen Phan, formerly a captain in the 30th Ranger Battalion, who last heard Tu's voice over the radio at ten o'clock on the evening of April 29, 1975, when Tu asserted that 38th Ranger Battalion would continue operating. Phan writes that Tu and about twenty of his men were captured by local guerrilla forces. Tu spoke to the guerrilla leader and insisted on meeting with a senior officer. The guerrillas conferred among themselves before blindfolding him. Tu tore off his blindfold and shouted that he did not need one before they shot him. He and another officer were shot first, and then ten or more of his men before North Vietnamese regulars arrived on the scene and stopped the executions.

These accounts reveal the difficulty of recreating battlefield events based on eyewitness testimonies decades after the end of the war. There are discrepancies between the oral and written accounts in terms of the details of the events of 1975, those involved, and Tu's final moments. The accounts differ on the number of men who were captured alongside Tu, the nature of the argument between Tu and the enemy commander, whether there were any survivors of the mass shooting, and whether it was North Vietnamese regulars or local communist guerrillas who carried out the executions. All accounts, however, broadly agree on the following sequence of events: Major Tran Dinh Tu and the men of 38th Ranger Battalion continuing to fight, the capture of Tu and a group of survivors by enemy forces, an altercation between Tu and the enemy leader, the execution of Tu and several of his men, and their mass burial at the site of the executions. The accounts not only acknowledge Tu's sacrifice and that of his men but also underline Tu's defiance before he was shot.

Significantly, the exhumation of human remains and the removal of personal effects and other artifacts at the gravesite attest to a desire by surviving relatives to provide a tangible record of the events of 1975. The actions by Tu's son Thai in locating the mass grave, having the site excavated, the soldiers' remains and other identifying items retrieved, and photographing and recording the proceedings, constitute an act of witnessing. Thai writes that it was a notice placed in 2011 by the family of Le Van Tai—a Ranger of the 38th who went missing on the retreat from Tay Ninh—that led him to contact Tai's family and search for the burial site of the men. Le Van Tai had been his father's radio telephone operator. Thirty-six years after the end of the war, Tai's family was still searching for him. Thai's correspondence indicates that he felt a measure of responsibility because his father had commanded the 38th, and his mother was able to recover his father's body and bury it while the bodies of his father's men still lay in a mass grave, and that by acting as he did he sought to give the family of Le Van Tai some form of closure. Tai's relatives, including his younger brother, were present at the burial site throughout the proceedings. An, in turn, recapitulated the events of April 30, 1975, in his 2012 article and published excerpts of Thai's correspondence as well as photographs of the excavation online so that the information they contained would be available to the Vietnamese diasporic community.

The story of Major Tran Dinh Tu and the men of the 38th Ranger Battalion illustrates the disjuncture between public and private memories of the war. While there is neither official acknowledgment of these events from the Vietnamese state nor a formal forensic investigation of the gravesite, the accounts by Tu's family and by surviving Rangers seek to record and flesh out the final hours of Tu and of his men in the closing days of the war. Tu's actions and those of his men are commemorated at Vietnamese veterans' ceremonies overseas, and remembered by family and friends. Thai's account also reveals that the story of Tu and the men of the 38th Battalion endures in the collective memory of local inhabitants. More than forty of them arrived unexpectedly at the burial site as the excavation got underway and Thai notes that onlookers were visibly moved as remains were disinterred. As Selma Leydesdorff, Luisa Passerini, and Paul Thompson note:

> Memories supportive of the maintenance of existing power structures are usually assured a wider social space and easier transmission. But memories of subordinate groups can also show striking resilience, and they can be transmitted ... from the interstices of society, from the boundaries between the public and the private.[33]

The reconstruction of Tu's story is valuable in that: first, it relates a little known episode of the Vietnam War; second, it is a narrative founded upon acts of witnessing, a narrative that has been remembered, recorded, and retold by survivors as well as colleagues, friends, and relatives of the deceased; and third, it is symbolically a matter of pride and grief for former Rangers and soldiers of the RVNAF.

"Testimony," writes Judith Lewis Herman, "has both a private dimension, which is confessional and spiritual, and a public aspect, which is political and judicial."[34] While these individual testimonies articulate loss and pain at a personal level, they also act as counterweights to state-dominated narratives of the war circulating in Vietnam and, moreover, interrogate the wider collective memory of the Vietnam War. An, Thai, and the veterans recalling and recording the past are acting as "agents of remembrance."[35] As Jay Winter suggests, "during and after war, individuals and groups, mostly obscure, come together to do the work of remembrance. This entails their creating a space in which the story of their war, in its local, particular, parochial, familial forms, can be told and retold. The construction of the narrative—in stone, in ceremony, in other works and symbols—is itself the process of remembrance."[36] The scale of the refugee movement from North to South in 1954–1955, the brutality on the North Vietnamese side, and the strength of national identity in South

Vietnam are all aspects of the war that have been subsumed in public consciousness but have remained present in Vietnamese diasporic memory.

In his 2009 article in *Viet Luan*, An expresses his anger that Tu and his men were not protected by prisoner-of-war conventions and that their deaths were neither noted nor recorded. None of the correspondents who had written so negatively about South Vietnam and its soldiers were in the country to report the executions carried out by the North Vietnamese at the war's end or the ensuing fate of many soldiers and civilians of the South in postwar Vietnam. "When memories recall acts of violence against individuals or entire groups," suggest Paul Antze and Michael Lambek, "they carry additional burdens—as indictments or confessions, or as emblems of a victimized identity."[37] In this case, the memories represent not only an indictment of the events in Cu Chi in 1975 but also serve as a reminder of other acts of violence perpetrated in South Vietnam that have received relatively low exposure such as the massacre of several thousand civilians during the North Vietnamese occupation of Hue at the time of the 1968 Tet Offensive. German correspondent Uwe Siemon-Netto covered the war between 1965 and 1969 for the Berlin-based Axel Springer Verlag publishing group, and is highly critical of American apologists for the Hanoi regime who denied that the Hue massacre had taken place.[38] He provides his own eyewitness testimony of events in Hue:

> I saw what the Communists have done in Hue, and I stood at the rim of shallow mass graves where they had buried their victims while many of them were evidently still alive. Some of these sites were discovered because the manicured fingers of dying women had protruded through the surface in a vain effort to escape their fate.[39]

The transitional justice connotations of the mass killings in Hue and other acts of atrocity carried out by the communists during the war are that these war crimes should be formally acknowledged by the Vietnamese state. "Transitional justice," as Roger Duthie notes, "refers to a set of measures that can be implemented to redress the legacies of massive human rights abuses that occur during conflict and under authoritarian regimes, where 'redressing the legacies' means, primarily, giving force to human rights norms that were systematically violated."[40] The excavation of the mass grave in Cu Chi should have been conducted by forensic experts, the human skeletal remains and associated personal objects formally identified, witnesses and surviving relatives interviewed, written records collected,⁴¹ and appropriate transitional justice measures implemented such as "prosecutions, truth-telling, restitution, and reform of abusive state institutions."⁴² In the absence of state recognition, and the continuing silence by Vietnamese communist authorities on human rights violations both during and after the war,⁴³ it was left to the families of the deceased to excavate the gravesite, disinter the remains, record the proceedings, and cremate a set of remains and artifacts as a symbolic gesture of acknowledgment and mourning.

For An, the discovery of what occurred in that field in Cu Chi in 1975 had a profound impact, not only because Tu was a personal friend but because Tu's death held particular symbolism and meaning. An was spurred into revisiting memories of their joint childhood and youth, and to reflect on these memories in writing. An also felt compelled to seek news of Tu's family. The process of honoring Tu's memory occurs within a context of displacement and diaspora, exile and resettlement. Many former soldiers took part in the mass exodus of refugees from communist Vietnam after 1975. After twenty years spent rebuilding his life in Australia, An made the decision to reconnect with his military past and to search for missing friends from the war. This search led to the uncovering of Tu's story and the eventual unearthing of the mass grave in Cu Chi. Joan Schwartz and Terry Cook write that, "the archive remains a foundation of historical understanding. Archives validate our experiences, our perceptions, our narratives, our stories."⁴⁴ In the absence of state archives, the records kept by Tu's son Thai, An's written and oral narratives, and the articles published by former Rangers strive to counter the weight of official silence and oblivion, shape an archive of events, and foster an understanding of the past. In endeavoring to preserve the histories of the South and of South Vietnamese soldiers, they represent a vital need for recognition and validation.

Geoffrey Price, the last Australian Ambassador to South Vietnam, recognized the staggering cost of the war for the South Vietnamese. In a dispatch dated August 15, 1974, he refers to 18,000 South Vietnamese casualties over an eighteen-month period.⁴⁵ To compare this to Australian casualty figures in wartime, Price pointed out that Australia lost 27,073 men in the Second World War, and that this figure included deaths in prisoner-of-war camps and in all theaters of the war.⁴⁶ In fact, South Vietnamese combat deaths exceeded Price's figures. In 1974 alone, they numbered 31,219.⁴⁷ The scale of this loss is now scarcely remembered.

Veith writes of the last days of the war,

> The fighting during the final days destroyed many units; very few did not sustain heavy losses. . . . In reality, very few regular Army or Marine officers commanding troops during the final days left their soldiers. While some younger officers deserted, most mid- and upper-level commanders stayed with their men. . . .
>
> Many of them demonstrated incredible courage, even in hopeless situations such as the battles of Tan Son Nhut, Ho Nai, and many others.[48]

An's tribute to Tu is the retelling of a close relationship between two boys who shared a similar background and history as refugees from North Vietnam. Both transferred their loyalty and allegiance to South Vietnam, their new country and their new home. They maintained their friendship despite different life trajectories until the escalation of the war in 1968. Although they lost sight of each other, both served not only in the armed forces of South Vietnam but also in one of its elite corps. Their story is at heart one of friendship, service, and sacrifice. An's reconstruction of Tu's story and that of the men of the 38th Ranger Battalion both orally and in writing attests to a desire to bear witness, and to communicate and make known this specific incident of the war beyond the closed circles of former Rangers and veterans to the Vietnamese diaspora and the wider community.

Plate 1
Captain Vu Hoai Duc in Vung Tau in 1954–1956. (Photograph courtesy of Vu Hoai Duc)

Plate 2
Saigon circa 1953. (Photograph courtesy of Vu Hoai Duc)

Plate 3
Lieutenant Colonel Tran Van Quan (center left) in Saigon on November 29, 1972, after a lecture he gave at the Vietnamese-American Association on the role of the 18th Logistics Battalion at the battle of An Loc. He is pictured with Mr. Daniel J. Herget, director of the Vietnamese-American Association. (Photograph courtesy of Tran Van Quan)

Plate 4
Officer Cadet Nguyen Van Luyen (left) with his best friend Phan Cong Ly at Thu Duc Military Academy in 1972. Ly served in the Airborne Division for a year and then transferred to the 25th Infantry Division. He died in a reeducation camp in Trang Lon in 1977. (Photograph courtesy of Nguyen Van Luyen)

Plate 5
Warrant Officer Nguyen Van Luyen (foreground) in front of an M48A1 tank in Long Thanh in 1972. Standing on the tank behind him is his friend Doan Thanh Nghiep, whose life he was to save at the battle of Bau Bang in 1974. (Photograph courtesy of Nguyen Van Luyen)

Plate 6
Second Lieutenant Nguyen Van Luyen at home in late 1974 after he left the hospital. He was shot in the abdomen at the battle of Bau Bang and had multiple operations in hospital. He returned to the hospital for further treatment in early 1975. (Photograph courtesy of Nguyen Van Luyen)

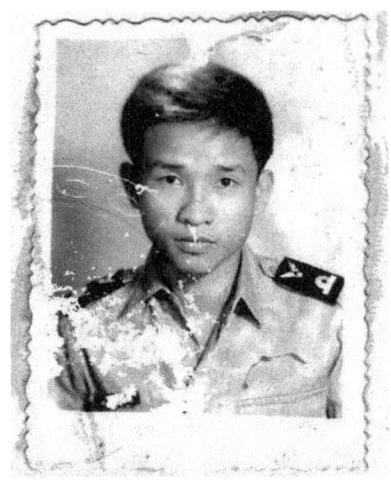

Plate 7
Passport photograph of Warrant Officer Vu Van Bao in 1970. (Photograph courtesy of Vu Van Bao)

Plate 8
Warrant Officer Vu Van Bao inside the side passenger door of a Chinook CH-47 in Fort Rucker, 1970. (Photograph courtesy of Vu Van Bao)

Plate 9
Class 70-38 B-2 Officer Student Company VNAF U.S. Army Primary Helicopter Center in Fort Wolters. Warrant Officer Vu Van Bao is in the middle row (fourth from left). (Photograph courtesy of Vu Van Bao)

Plate 10
Officer Cadet Tran Van Giac at Thu Duc Military Academy in 1968. The following year, he attended the Naval Academy in Nha Trang. (Photograph courtesy of Tran Van Giac)

Plate 11
Lieutenant Tran Van Giac (standing far right) with navy friends in Qui Nhon in 1973 at a celebratory gathering after a successful operation in support of the infantry. (Photograph courtesy of Tran Van Giac)

Plate 12
First Lieutenant Tran Xuan Dung, MD, in Saigon during the 1968 Tet Offensive. (Photograph courtesy of Tran Xuan Dung)

Plate 13
First Lieutenant Nguyen Manh Tien, MD, in Saigon in 1973 just after he joined the Rangers. (Photograph courtesy of Nguyen Manh Tien)

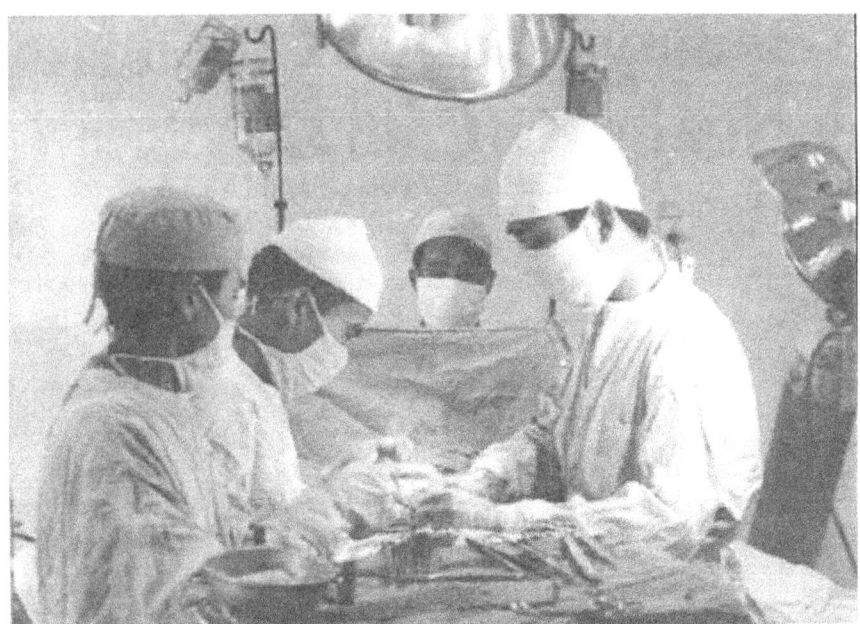

Plate 14
First Lieutenant Nguyen Hoang Hai, MD (right) and his surgical team at work in Combat Field Hospital 1 in Quang Ngai in 1968. (Photograph courtesy of Tran Xuan Dung and Nguyen Hoang Hai)

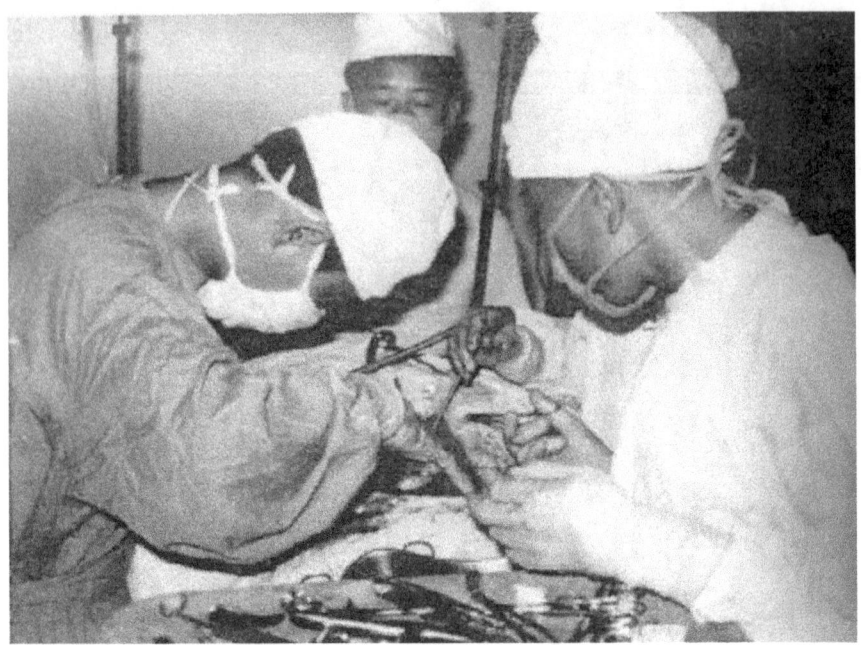

Plate 15
RVNAF doctors and nurses operating in Combat Field Hospital 1 in Quang Ngai in 1968. (Photograph courtesy of Tran Xuan Dung and Nguyen Hoang Hai)

Plate 16
Corporal Bui Ngoc Thuy with her parachute pack over her shoulder at the jumping training site in Cu Chi in 1957. (Photograph courtesy of Bui Ngoc Thuy's son Kieu Tien Dung)

Plate 17
Sergeant Nguyen Thi Minh Nguyet (foreground, left corner) on the day of her graduation at the Military Social Services School in Saigon in 1973. She was the top graduate of her course. (Photograph courtesy of Nguyen Thi Minh Nguyet)

Plate 18
Second Lieutenant Thuy in Pleiku in II Corps in 1973. (Photograph courtesy of Thuy)

Plate 19
Leg bone and rope. Retrieved from mass grave in Cu Chi in 2011. (Photograph courtesy of Tran Dinh Thai)

Plate 20
Identification tags of Ly A Sam, born May 19, 1950. Military Number 70/131238. Blood type: A+. Retrieved from mass grave in Cu Chi in 2011. (Photograph courtesy of Tran Dinh Thai)

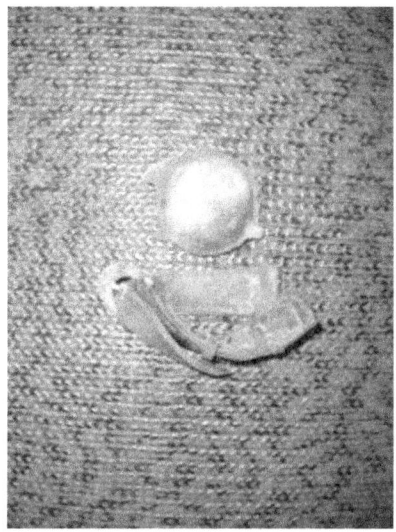

Plate 21
Watch with leather band. Retrieved from mass grave in Cu Chi in 2011.
(Photograph courtesy of Tran Dinh Thai)

Plate 22
Side by Side (detail). The Vietnam War Memorial in Victoria, Australia.
(Photograph courtesy of Steve Lowe)

Plate 23
A Vietnamese Navy veteran marching on Anzac Day in Melbourne, Australia, April 25, 2011. (Photograph courtesy of Keith Broad)

CHAPTER 6

Aftermaths

> *A life worn out, but still a life.*
> *Crushed, smothered, life persists in me.*
> *Let despair sound the knell.*
> *Let Death stalk all around and toll.*
> —Nguyen Chi Thien[1]

These lines by dissident poet Nguyen Chi Thien from his prison collection *Flowers from Hell* encapsulate the stoicism and will to endure of many veterans and others who were internees in Vietnam's reeducation camp system after 1975. Born in Hanoi in 1939 and the most famous detainee of Vietnam's gulag, Nguyen Chi Thien spent a total of twenty-seven years in internment. He first became a political prisoner in North Vietnam in 1961 under "Reeducation Act No. 49."[2] Voted into law in 1961, this act allowed for the internment of "bad, dangerous elements" for up to three years without trial, although in reality detainees were often held in prison indefinitely.[3] Nguyen Chi Thien had queried a history textbook, *The History of the August Revolution*, which stated that the Japanese surrender at the end of the Second World War was due to the Soviet victory over Japanese forces in Manchuria.[4] This was reported to the communist authorities. As he writes, "My country was becoming a land of snitches."[5] He was arrested and accused of "anti-propaganda," and did three years of hard labor in camps in Phu Tho and Yen Bai Provinces.[6] He began writing poems in prison and continued to do so after his release in 1964. He had "made up his mind . . . that no self-respecting person could bear to see or suffer such injustices in silence."[7] His writing forms part of a tradition of prison poetry in modern Vietnam.[8] His poems were circulated by word of mouth in Haiphong and Hanoi, and in 1966, he was interrogated by the authorities and imprisoned again, this time for twelve years.[9]

Nguyen Chi Thien's poetry received international recognition after he managed to smuggle a handwritten collection of 400 poems into the British Embassy in Hanoi during a brief period of liberty in 1979.[10] He had composed the majority of these poems in prison and memorized them. Arrested by Vietnamese security agents as he left the embassy, he was incarcerated for a further twelve years.[11] *Flowers from Hell* was awarded the International Poetry Prize in 1985. Adopted as one of six "prisoners of conscience" by Amnesty International in 1986, Nguyen Chi Thien was finally released in October 1991.[12] He was able to leave Vietnam for the United States under the Humanitarian Operation program in 1995.[13] In his testimony before the U.S. Congress on November 8, 1995, he gave a strong indictment of human rights violations after the communists came to power in Vietnam, referring to the 1953–1956 Land Reform campaign, the corralling of political prisoners in hard labor camps in 1961, the millions who died in the struggle to impose communism on the whole of Vietnam, and the hundreds of thousands who filled up the Vietnamese gulag after the fall of South Vietnam in 1975.[14]

This chapter will deal with the aftermath of war for the soldiers of the South and their families. For many, it signified internment in reeducation camps while for others it meant imprisonment of another kind in that they were living under a repressive regime, and unable to leave either because of disabling injury or acute poverty after the war. While war may cause lasting physical and emotional damage, once it is over, soldiers would in the normal course of events expect to be able to return to their homes and families, and begin the process of readjusting to life in peacetime. They would assume that the end of the war would give them the opportunity to rebuild their lives and communities. Then there are those casualties of war who, in the words of John Keegan and Richard Holmes, "live on, crippled in body or in mind, dependent for their livelihood upon the support of their family and friends and the gratitude of the state they served."[15] For many soldiers of the South, however, the end of war provided no such avenues for reconstruction or recovery but led instead to even greater loss and trauma. Vietnam's "reunification" under a postwar communist regime did not bring relief or consolation to many of the citizens of the former Republic of Vietnam. Rather, their wartime trauma was compounded by the extent of mass trauma in the aftermath of war. "Traumatic events in general and situations of mass trauma in particular," notes Nancy Boyd Webb, "create extreme stress for the individuals involved."[16] In the case of South Vietnam, it was the war's aftermath that was responsible for engendering profound traumatic stress, with mass internment, forced deurbanization, and forced labor.[17] The level of political repression following the war was such that it led to years of destabilization in the South and the breakdown of social and familial networks as relatives disappeared in reeducation camps, the New Economic Zones, or as escapees.

Former South Vietnamese military and civilian subjects registered for reeducation believing the new government's assurances that they would only be away from their families for a short time. They were also lulled by the fact that most noncommissioned officers and privates who registered for reeducation were released after three days.[18] It was not only former military personnel and civil servants who were required to register but also teachers.[19] In this way, in the words of Tiziano Terzani, "some 250,000 people disappeared into the remote jungle concentration camps that [were] distributed over the whole country."[20] Actual numbers of those interned are difficult to gauge, since the regime released contradictory information about the number of detainees held in its prison camps.[21] The reeducation camp system first came into operation in northern Vietnam during the Indochina War (1946–1954).[22] Nguyen Van Canh writes:

> All political prisoners in communist North Vietnam had to undergo *cai tao tu tuong*, or thought reform. In official documents it was always referred to as *cai tao* ("thought reform" or "re-education") or simply *hoc tap* ("education" or "study").[23]

After Vietnam was reunified in 1975, the Bamboo Gulag became an extensive network of camps spread throughout the country. Nguyen refers to more than 100 camps containing an average of 3,000 prisoners each,[24] but a more recent study by Nghia Vo posits the existence of more than 1,000 camps of varying sizes in postwar Vietnam, holding between a few hundred to more than 20,000 prisoners.[25] One of the most notorious, Katum Camp, was located in Tay Ninh, close to the Cambodian border, and housed 10,000 prisoners.[26] Camps not only took in detainees at the end of the war but also continued to receive new prisoners over the next two decades. The practice of illegal arrest and detention was still common in 1988.[27] There were not only camps for political prisoners but also camps for escapees—those who attempted to escape the country either as boat or land refugees after 1975—as well as camps for women and children.[28] In his 2001 memoir, Vietnamese Amerasian Kien Nguyen describes being interned at the age of thirteen in "Re-education Camp No. PK 34" after a failed escape attempt.[29] He spent two months doing hard labor before his mother was able to bribe authorities for his release. He stresses that his was "a specific camp for women and children."[30] Several memoirs of camp life by former male detainees have been published in English and in French.[31] Although women were also subjected to internment in the postwar years, they have rarely spoken about their experience of incarceration and their accounts are only beginning to emerge.[32] Their numbers include not only those who served in the armed forces as either soldiers or civilians, or who worked as civil servants under the former Saigon government, but also those who were caught attempting to escape the country after 1975. Many were interned in prison camps with their children. Vietnamese authorities did not appear to have a uniform policy in relation to escapees. Those who were caught were either fined if they were lucky, or imprisoned for lengths of time varying from a few weeks to more than a year after failed escape attempts.[33]

Life, in consequence, became worst for most former soldiers in the postwar period. Veterans found themselves incarcerated in prison camps and subjected to hard labor while their families experienced harassment on the part of the authorities. After their release, many sought to leave Vietnam and escape so that they and their families would have a chance at rebuilding their lives overseas. While the choice to escape from Vietnam brought with it the risk of death at sea, it also offered hope of a new life. These options, however, were not available to soldiers who received disabling wounds during the war. Their bodily injuries were too severe for them to be in a position to contemplate "crossing the border." Other former soldiers were too poor or had to give up on escape plans after repeated failed attempts and further periods of incarceration. They were trapped in a postwar country that ignored their war wounds and erased their service.

The surviving soldiers of the South are ghosts of the war—unseen, unheard, and unacknowledged by the Vietnamese government. The narratives explored here reveal a tension between the continued existence of these former soldiers and their omission from Vietnam's national landscape and history. Veterans carry the mental and physical scars of their service, with their traumatized minds and bodies forming loci of memory. Their stories underline the contrast between individual or corporeal memory and the political and historical amnesia relating to their war service. The use of oral history in this context is of particular relevance, as "oral history has influenced and overlapped with some of the most important contemporary uses of historical memory."[34] The oral histories of RVNAF veterans are valuable because: first, they record the "the stories of those who are rarely heard"[35]; second, they redress the dearth of official histories relating to the RVNAF; and third, they have the capacity to shift and alter perceptions of the war. Memory can be transformative and constitute "an agent of transition."[36] As Aleida Assmann and Linda Shortt note, "Accredited with the power of transforming our relationship to the past and the ability to revise former values and attitudes, memory can create new frames of action."[37] Indeed, South Vietnamese veterans are symbols and sites of contestation, embodying contested interpretations of the past, of history, and of the war. Their stories underline the divide between public and private memories of the Vietnam War. This chapter will contrast the narratives of veterans who were able to leave Vietnam with those of veterans who were unable to do so. While the life trajectories of the first three veterans encompass their military service, postwar internment, and forced migration, those of the last three highlight the nature of their injuries and the hardships they and their families were subjected to in postwar Vietnam.

WARTIME AND POSTWAR LIVES

The first veteran, Nguyen Minh Tran,[38] was born in 1945 in Ben Tre, southern Vietnam. His family was poor and he could not therefore continue with his education after primary school. He went to Saigon to take up an apprenticeship in mechanics. He remembers the communist terror as a child in Ben Tre and, later on, the casualties of the 1968 Tet Offensive in Saigon. Tran recounts the following details of his early life and enlistment:

> When I was twelve or thirteen, the war in the countryside was devastating. The acts of terrorism by the communists were ruthless: decapitation, stabbings, slashings. The entire countryside was like that, not just Ben Tre. From 1960 to 1968, life was normal. Until the Tet Offensive in 1968, when I witnessed many deaths. Everywhere there were corpses, the injured, weapons and ammunition. I was a mechanic working for Vinatexco. Because I was a skilled mechanic when I enlisted in 1970, I joined the Airborne Engineer Corps. I joined the paratroopers because they had a nice uniform and I was interested in airplanes and parachuting. Moreover, joining an engineering battalion meant that I didn't have to go into combat but

I could still feel proud. We still had to go out to the battlefield, but we did much lighter work. For example, if the division went to Hue, we also had to go to Hue. We then set up the base, dug shelter tunnels, and built the command centre for headquarters to use during the operation.

The support staff lived behind where the division was stationed. We were shelled regularly—at least ten to fifteen shells a week. People were injured and people were killed. As for carrying a gun in battle I have not had that honour. That was for the combatants. I was a corporal. In 1975, I should have been promoted to first corporal but we lost our country before that happened.

Tran recounts his experiences in 1975 and the difficult years that followed, and explains his motivation for leaving Vietnam:

In [March] 1975, the Airborne Division handed over the responsibility for I Corps to the Marines. The Airborne Division moved back to Danang, the combatants left first, the engineers were left to find their own transportation such as rollers or bulldozers. Many places were lost in Hue and there was no facility to receive orders from Saigon, so we made our own way there. After arriving in Danang, it took us another half a month before we reached Saigon. I was the last soldier in the Airborne Engineer battalion to leave.

I was reeducated for a short period of about three months. When they [the communists] took over Saigon, they ordered people to go back to their hometown, so I went back to the countryside. But I led a very difficult life. People who were close to me in the old days did not dare to contact me, as I was labelled "*nguy*" [puppet].[39] Not only was I *nguy*, I was a *nguy* thug because I was in the Airborne. Thus life was hard and we were looking for ways to cross the border. I was worried about how I would affect my family, so I left them.

In 1981, I boarded the boat to cross the border. We went straight to Indonesia. We arrived at Buru Island and were transferred to Pulau Galang, an island for refugees. We were there for about five months. I arrived in Australia in early 1982.

The Airborne Division was ordered back to Saigon on March 12, 1975, over the strong objections of I Corps commander Lieutenant General Ngo Quang Truong, and began to withdraw on March 17, 1975.[40] Tran relates that support staff were left to their own devices in the closing days of the war. He makes it clear that although he was not a combatant, he was proud to have served as an engineer in the Airborne. After experiencing a relatively brief period of reeducation, he tried to readjust to civilian life but the level of ostracism he was subjected to because of his service background spurred him to leave the country.

The second veteran, Truong Cong Hai,[41] was born in 1943 in My Tho, southern Vietnam. His father worked on the land and his mother looked after a large family. Hai completed his primary and secondary schooling and went to university in 1962 to study mathematics, physics, and chemistry. He remembers a peaceful life until he began his university education:

> It was not until 1964 that I joined the armed forces. I was still young but during that time the South was very peaceful, there were no problems. My mother was worried and said, "I don't like you becoming a soldier, why don't you stay at the university?" I said, "I can't continue to study now that all my school friends have gone." I did the *concours*—the competitive examination to join the navy.
>
> I enlisted because first, the state of affairs of the country was such that all my brothers had joined the military and second, my mother was getting old. The navy was a branch of the service that she liked. It was considered safer—not as much fighting. But to tell you the truth, my brothers and I had always dreamt of joining the navy. I did the officer course—deck training and command. I graduated in 1966 and was selected to join the U.S. Seventh Fleet in Yokohama, Japan, for three months of work experience. Fleet Higher Command then assigned me to the ship HQ228. Its purpose was to travel on rivers and patrol the My Tho and Vinh Long areas. Our ships supplied supporting fire to the ground forces. My highest rank was lieutenant commander in the navy.

Hai remembers the events of 1975 and the following details of his years of internment in communist prison camps:

> I was the manager of the Maritime Checkpoint in Vung Tau. At the time I was recently married with a three-month-old child. I thought that if our countrymen arrested us, they would let us out after a while, it wouldn't be a problem.
>
> I was in prison altogether ten years, two years in the South then eight years in the North. I was treated like a convict. I was beaten, I was also shackled. Many [camp inmates] died of starvation and hard labour. Out in the North the climate is really harsh. There was nothing to eat other than cassava and sweet potatoes, and if you wanted some meat you had to catch frogs.
>
> I came out in 1985. There was nothing to live on, they [the communist authorities] used the term *"nguy"* [puppet], they would not let the children

go to school, they would check everything, and I had to report to the local public security station. When I returned, I was subjected to probation for two years. You understand, I had to find a way to escape. In 1986, we were lucky crossing the border, I was in the navy so we could travel pretty quickly [laughs]. We went straight to Singapore so I was in Singapore for two months and a few days and I came over here [to Australia].

Hai's narrative illustrates his belief in 1975 that any reeducation he would have to undergo would be brief and that he would soon be reunited with his young family. He had no premonition that he would be incarcerated not only for a decade but also in the north of the country. Subjected to monitoring by the authorities after his release, he sought ways to cross the border.

The third veteran, Tran Nhu Hung,[42] was born in 1951 in Hanoi. His father served in the National Army of Vietnam and the family moved south after partition in 1954. He joined the Vietnamese Marine Corps and relates:

My family migrated to the South because we chose not to live under the communist regime. My father continued to serve in the army. After primary and secondary school, I studied Physics and Chemistry for two years at the university. The war reached the stage where the government ordered general mobilization, and I was called to service in 1972. I joined the armed forces in July 1972, and graduated as a warrant officer in December 1972. I chose to serve in the Vietnamese Marine Corps. I served in the 8th Marine Battalion. The Marines and the Airborne were the two general reserve units of the armed forces, and were used for heavy fighting. During the whole of my time in the Marines, my unit was always engaged in battle. We fought in Quang Tri in 1972, and stayed there until March 1975. My last rank was that of first lieutenant and my function that of company executive officer.

Like Tran and Hai, Hung was incarcerated by the postwar government and provides a detailed account of what happened after April 1975 as well as the conditions that he experienced after his release from detention:

We were ordered to go south so we went back to Vung Tau and were assigned to fight in the perimeter of Saigon in Long Binh. On the 30th of April the war ended by order of the last president, Mr. Duong Van Minh. Like other Vietnamese army officers and officials, both myself and my father, at that time a major, were sent to communist reeducation camps. We considered them prisons. All the camps were in remote areas in the mountains or jungle. I spent nearly seven years in reeducation. The Marines and paratroopers were the striking force of the army and the communists considered these two divisions as their worst enemies. That is why we spent a longer time in prison than officers in other units.

After my release, I only had a temporary residence permit. So every month, I had to report to the local police. I had to submit a diary stating clearly what I did, who I met with. I was put under strict observation and monitored by the government. After three months, I had to resubmit for an extension to my temporary permit. I had to ask for permission to stay in my own family home. I couldn't find a job because I didn't have permanent residence, and I could only apply for a residence permit if I had a proper job. Like millions of others, I became an illegal resident of Saigon. At night, you could see that in every corner, there were homeless people on the street. Each family had a registration card, and only people with permanent permits could be registered on the card. Without your name on the card, you could be arrested anytime, and sent to a reeducation camp, a hard labour camp or the New Economic Zones.

So thousands of people kept leaving the country. If you wanted to escape from Vietnam at that time, you had to have either money or gold, or know how to escape. I tried to escape a few times, I didn't have any money, I was caught in Ba Ria in 1983, and they locked me up in a remote village with other people. I decided to escape with another former officer. We ended up lost in a mangrove. After two nights, we saw an old man in a small boat rowing in the mangrove to collect wood. My friend made up some story but the old man told him straightaway, "You two tried to escape from Vietnam, you were caught, and now you're trying to escape from where you were kept. If you tell me the truth, I will help you." I said that we were former officers. He laughed and said that he would row us to the nearest spot where we could get out to the main road. He was from Bien Hoa, and had been sent to live in the New Economic Zone. He considered himself a former citizen of the nationalist government instead of the communist government.

Former reeducation camp prisoners were classified as *thanh phan tap trung* ("concentration elements") and blacklisted by the authorities, and could be arrested and sent back to the camps at any time.[43] Hung made another escape attempt in 1984 and was caught again. He managed to run away to Vung Tau where he received help from former Marines. He says:

> There were some former soldiers in my unit and I went and stayed with them, and asked them to inform my family. I was there for two months. There was one person who was under my direct command before [during the war].

So I trusted him. He took me to his place, fed me and allowed me to live there. I had to hide from the local police. He introduced me to a group of people who wanted to leave the country. They thought that a former officer who knew how to read maps and a compass and had some English could be useful. I asked my friend to go to Saigon, tell my parents, and bring one of my younger brothers back with him.

My brother was sixteen. Children of former army officers were called for labour service. Those who did not have a clean background—in other words whose families had a connection with the former regime—had to sign up for *Thanh Nien Xung Phong*, that is the program to use youth for labour.

Hung's narrative reveals the fate of thousands of former camp detainees who found themselves to be without official permits and homeless after their release from internment. Nearly ten years after the end of the war, Hung was still able to rely on the loyalty of the men from his former unit in the Marines. They helped him even though he was an "illegal resident" who had already spent seven years in internment and had escaped arrest after yet another attempt to leave the country. Hung and his brother fled from Vietnam in a boat measuring 15 meters in length with 175 people on board. The refugees reached Singapore but were escorted back out to sea. Eventually, they made landfall at Pulau Galang in Indonesia. Hung worked as a volunteer for the U.N. High Commissioner for Refugees in the camp and was accepted for resettlement in Australia. He and his younger brother arrived in Melbourne in 1985.

These narratives reveal the circumstances in which the men enlisted ranging from the two older veterans reflecting on a growing awareness of the worsening state of the war and a practical recognition that most of their contemporaries were in the armed forces to the younger veteran being mobilized in 1972. The first veteran Tran's memories of atrocities in the countryside refer to the communist "reign of terror" in rural South Vietnam between 1956 and 1965.[44] Tran joined the armed forces two years after witnessing the dead and injured of the 1968 Tet Offensive. He recalls the contributions that he and other support personnel made to the Airborne Division. The second veteran Hai, for his part, states that all his friends had left and joined the military so he decided to enlist as well instead of completing his university studies. He candidly admits to choosing what was considered a safer branch of the services but also avers that he and his brothers had always wanted to join the Vietnamese Navy.

It was also a matter of pride that he was successful in the competitive examinations to enter this service and was one of the navy's top graduates. Of the three veterans, he served the longest and achieved the highest military rank. The third veteran, Hung, was born in a military family and was three years old when his family left communist North Vietnam to resettle in South Vietnam. His science studies at the University of Saigon were interrupted by his mobilization into the armed forces. He states that it was his choice to serve in the Marine Corps, and that his unit was engaged in continuous fighting until 1975.

Although all three men had to undergo "reeducation," their experiences of incarceration diverged sharply. Tran spent three months in detention while Hai was imprisoned for a total of ten years in different parts of the country and Hung did hard labor for seven years. The much harsher treatment that Hai and Hung were subjected to reflects their greater "crimes" in the eyes of communist authorities. While Tran had been a noncommissioned officer in a support unit, Hai had served for ten years in the Vietnamese Navy and Hung in one of South Vietnam's elite corps. All three, however, refer to their sense of isolation and alienation from postwar Vietnamese society. They were singled out by Vietnamese authorities and denied access to residential permits and employment opportunities because they were former soldiers and therefore *nguy*. They were keen to escape and reconstruct their lives elsewhere.

DIASPORA LIVES

Tran married in Australia in 1984. He ran a restaurant for a number of years and also did some farming. In 1994, he began philanthropic work to help disabled children and veterans in Vietnam. When he returned to Vietnam in 1999 to help build two medical clinics, he was interrogated for his actions by the Vietnamese Department of Public Security and Political Protection. He relates:

> I got married in 1984 and have two children. I am very satisfied. The reason being, there is neither persecution nor terrorism here. Second, Australians are good people. Third, my family now have a house to live in, transportation, and a normal life like many others. I am very content.
>
> In 1994, when I felt that my life was settled, I started philanthropic work by cooperating with the Royal Hospital in Brisbane to bring children without an anus from Vietnam to be treated here. The other thing

I did was to cooperate with an Australian wheelchair company. I asked for wheelchairs and sent them to the disabled people in Vietnam, ex-soldiers, or children, or elderly people injured in accidents. I have sent nearly 3,000 wheelchairs.

The day after I arrived [in Vietnam], I received a letter of invitation to meet two weeks later with the Department of Public Security and Political Protection. I'd planned to stay for three months but upon receiving the letter of "invitation," I immediately booked a return flight to Australia. There were no available seats until four weeks later. When I saw them [the Department], they said, "You gather the legless people of the old regime to do what?" I said to them that I was just helping those who were less fortunate. "Look at me," I told them, "one, you can see I am old, two, I am uneducated, I couldn't be involved in politics. I only wanted to help the unfortunate, share whatever I have, or ask others to help these ill-fated people, I'm not involved in politics at all." I have not had the nerve to go back [to Vietnam] to visit my family since then.

As for Hai, he did factory work in Australia but suffered from chronic lung ailments. His ill health is a legacy of his ten years of internment in reeducation camps after the war. He receives an Australian service pension, identifies himself as a Vietnamese Australian war veteran, and is honored to wave the Republic of Vietnam flag and march alongside other veterans on Anzac Day. His two sons have done well with their education: the older is an engineer and the younger an accountant. Hai states:

> I am proud that our flag is once again flying. I have shared with Australians how I feel as a war veteran. I said to them, "You left behind your wife and children, and brought with you a fighting spirit to serve the cause of freedom in my country. We treasure you guys. We are grateful. Not only that but when the war ended, you let us come here. Your good deeds are something that cannot be expressed in words."
>
> I am still Vietnamese but Australia is my second country. Australia is an ideal place.

Hung, for his part, had to pay back the people who had helped him to escape from Vietnam. After arriving in Australia, he immediately began working at the Ford factory. He also studied English, and applied to do a postgraduate degree in social work. He recalls his interview:

> I said, "I want to work as a social worker." She said, "Why?" I said it was because of my life experience: I was in war, I was in prison. More importantly,

I was a refugee. She tasked me with finding work in a related field for a year and return for another assessment. So I worked at the Ministry of Housing as a housing officer, and as a volunteer with Lifeline—the telephone counselling service. Before I enlisted in the army, I was a Scout leader in Vietnam, so I joined the Scout movement again, and worked as a volunteer for the Vietnamese community. When La Trobe University accepted me, I gave up my job as housing officer and studied full time. I worked any job that I could find at night. In 1988, things changed for Vietnamese boat people. They were no longer granted refugee status automatically. They became asylum seekers and had to go undergo a screening procedure. The situation in Hong Kong was terrible, I heard that they needed people with language and professional skills to help Vietnamese boat people. I applied and was accepted straightaway. I went to Hong Kong in December 1988.

Hung married in 1989 but continued working in Hong Kong until 1991, when he and his wife returned to Australia for the birth of their child. He then worked in the Child Protection Unit and continued volunteering for a number of organizations. For twenty years, he was in charge of the Vietnamese program for the Special Broadcasting Service (SBS) radio. He belongs to the Vietnamese Marine Corps Association, marches on Anzac Day, and participates in activities on Long Tan Day and Armed Forces Day as well as the yearly anniversary of the Vietnamese Marine Corps on October 1. Of his work in public broadcasting, he says:

> I see the radio program in Vietnamese as an ideal medium for me to continue my work with the Vietnamese community and help them to understand a new culture, and bridge the gap between their former culture, their former life, and here. SBS is here to serve people and to help them have a better life after resettlement. I see it as another aspect of social work.

Although he has since left SBS, Hung is still involved in independent radio programming.

The narratives of Tran, Hai, and Hung register their gratitude for new lives built in Australia. They have not forgotten their previous lives, however, and identify themselves as army veterans. Tran is active in his philanthropic endeavors and seeks to help ill and disabled people in Vietnam, in particular disabled RVNAF veterans. Hai is proud to carry the South Vietnamese flag and march alongside other Vietnam veterans—whether Vietnamese, Australian, or New Zealander—on Anzac Day. Hung not only worked as a volunteer for the Vietnamese community but also applied his skills in social work to aid Vietnamese refugees in Hong Kong between 1988 and 1991, and links his work as a radio journalist to servicing the needs of the Vietnamese community in Australia.

DISABLING INJURY AND LIFE IN POSTWAR VIETNAM

The narratives of the Vietnam-based veterans reveal life trajectories that differ significantly from those of Tran, Hai, and Hung. Lap[45] was born in 1952 in Thuy Phu in central Vietnam, the eldest in a blended family. He remembers conflicts between his parents because the children were from different relationships. He left school after grade six, and helped with the farming. He volunteered for service at the age of eighteen and recalls:

> I volunteered for the Rangers in May 1970. I was primarily encouraged to join by my peers. The training was for three months and I was transferred to the 37th Battalion based in Phu Luc, Hoa Khanh and Danang.
>
> The battle that was most memorable was in 1972 when I got injured. The night that we arrived in Quang Tri, I wrote a letter to my family telling them that I had been transferred there. At that time I was already married, my child was only four months old. . . . On April 4, 1972, we received our wages and food supplies. After that we went back to the national highway. I was in the commanding unit. All the people who went ahead did so without any mishaps. I was unfortunately the one who stepped on a mine. I was injured along with three teammates and one officer. When I looked down, my right leg was severed below the knee and my left leg was still there but half the left foot was broken. I yelled, "both legs gone, both legs gone" but the male nurses did not come because they were worried about stepping on another mine. Then the major started to yell, "Nurse, please help him. See why he is screaming." Only then did the nurse come and console me. I said to him, "Huy, I'm dead, it cannot be fixed now." He told me to stop screaming and continued to calm me down. I tried to compose myself. Two people carried me in a hammock. I heard my mates exclaiming, "Oh no, Lap, I saw you just then and now you're the victim." We got to the Red Cross vehicles. . . . When I regained consciousness, I realized that I was in Quang Tri Hospital. I could not bring myself to look at my legs anymore but I realized that they were both gone.
>
> After two or three days, I was transferred to Nguyen Tri Phuong Hospital. When my family finally found me, they all cried. As there were so many injured soldiers there, I was transferred to Duy Tan General Hospital in Danang by air. I stayed there until my wounds were completely healed and then I was transferred to Physiotherapy Centre 1 in Phuoc Tuong, where I spent six months in recovery. I left the military in October 1974.

Life was extremely hard and very sad, but with the encouragement from my family, the social assistance I received, and the benefits for war invalids, life became more stable.

Lap was in Hue in the closing days of the war in March 1975, and explains that he was evacuated to Danang before his family:

My mother told me I should go first. I was evacuated to Danang and then my army unit picked up the rest of my family.

After 1975, with my disability, I could not do anything strenuous at all. My wife returned to farming. With the introduction of collective enterprise, we did not have much rice and life was quite hard. The years between 1975 and 1980 were very tough. There was widespread famine, and we had to mix cassava with rice.

My job at home was to cook the meals and do the washing for the family. In short, I was in charge of the housework. That was my part of helping out. I have six children, the youngest was born in 1989.

Lap provides a graphic description of the circumstances surrounding his injury, and relates the treatment and post-operative care that he received, the grief of his family, and the importance of service and disability benefits. He recalls the difficulty of the postwar years, and the fact that his disability prevented him from doing any work outside of home.

Another veteran, Lua,[46] was born in 1953 in Saigon. His family was poor—his father was a street sweeper and his mother carried water for the fishmongers—and he went straight to work after finishing primary school. To help support his family, he found a job as an assistant mason and then became a mortar mixer. He enlisted in the armed forces in 1972, and like Lap, was seriously wounded in the field. He relates the following account:

I didn't join the military until I was nineteen years old but before that I was already a core cadre of the People's Self-Defense Forces. At home, the uniform of the paratroopers was seen as proud and powerful [laughs]. To describe it accurately, it was then every young man's dream to join a military service that was proud and strong. On 2 April 1972, I was formally enlisted into the paratroopers.

After completing my training at the end of August, I participated in the Lam Son Eagle 72 campaign out in Hue. It was a heated battlefield. The fighting started in the summer of 1972 and people called it the "Red Fire Summer." I lost both of my legs. I caught fragments of a mortar causing the injury at 3 a.m. The fragments hit my right leg and severed it in two sections. As for the left leg, the fragment went right through chipping a bit of the bone and leading to the loss of soft tissue. I got to Nguyen Tri Phuong Hospital in Hue. I was in there for a month and some days and the right leg was so infected it caused a high temperature so the emergency doctor had to cut it off immediately. They cut the leg above the kneecap. After the amputation I was not well enough to get on a plane.

I was transferred to the Do Vinh Hospital in Hoang Hoa Tham. Then realizing my critical condition Do Vinh Hospital transferred me to Cong Hoa General Hospital for treatment. It took five months to recover then I went to Rehabilitation Centre 3 to rehabilitate and to learn how to walk again. After that I was officially discharged from the military on 5 October 1974.

Lua was readmitted to hospital as a war veteran on April 26, 1975, and was still hospitalized when the war ended:

On 30 April, I was still in hospital. We were not allowed to stay there anymore. They [the new authorities] cast us all out. I had to look for a crutch and find my way home. Mr. Duong Van Minh had ordered the troops in Saigon to give up their arms and surrender. I was stunned. No feeling. Walked like a zombie without a soul. After the turmoil of 30 April, it was hard to subsist. My family and I carried what little we had to the New Economic Zone. Back then I was still strong so I also carried my prosthesis. But there was no more government to look after us, so we went hungry many times. I had to work to find food each day for my children.

My first daughter, she was seven years old and healthy, one afternoon she had a fever, she was screaming, and my wife carried her and ran to the clinic but she did not make it, she died ... along the way [he is emotional] ... yes, she tried to run all the way but ... red spots appeared all over her body. The hospital said it was acute petechial fever.

My boy who was born in 1979, just after we returned to Saigon from the New Economic Zone, also had chronic petechial fever but we didn't know. We had no money to go to the hospital. We had to give him traditional medicinal herbs. After two weeks, he wasn't better and we had tried, our neighbours knew this, so when we asked to borrow some money, they lent us the money. Having ... the money but the child was lost ... [he sobs]. He was nine years old. We got the money, carried him to the hospital ... but it was too late.

Lua's narrative conveys his sense of accomplishment in joining the Airborne Division after previous paramilitary service in the People's Self-Defense Forces. Like Lap, his account of his battlefield injuries is graphic.

He reveals his shock at the collapse of South Vietnam, the eviction of hospital patients by the communist authorities, his family's forced relocation to one of the New Economic Zones, and the grinding poverty they experienced after the war. Life was unbearable, and he sold blood to support his family. His account reveals that his sharpest grief was for the loss of two of his children to illness.

The last and youngest veteran, Ngoc,[47] was born in 1955 in Saigon and came from a service family. He lost his father to the war at the age of nine. His mother was a small trader and relied on a widow and orphan allowance from the South Vietnamese government to support her three children. Like Lap and Lua, he lost his legs on the battlefield. He remembers:

> As a Southerner, with my dad being a Ranger it was natural for me to follow in my father's footsteps. When I was seventeen, I enlisted in the Marines and was posted to Battalion 5 *Hac Long* [Black Dragons]. I loved my arm of the army. I chose it. The Marines were the topnotch fighting unit of the Army of the Republic of Vietnam. We were not restricted to any area. We shouldn't praise ourselves too much but in over three years, I had a fair bit of battle experience.
>
> I lost both of my legs, I left my legs at the battlefield. In my last battle at the Cu Bi steel bridge in Hien Si. At the time, I was at my highest rank, squad leader. I led a squad and my platoon had four squads. My unit overran the post. The opposition fled, and I went searching. I followed them, I tracked the blood trail of their injured, but unfortunately for me, I stepped on a mine and from then on I was a person no more . . . nothing left. Finished since then.
>
> I was taken to the Nguyen Tri Phuong Hospital in Hue, and stayed there for eight days and after that the order came down to take me to Duy Tan General Hospital in Danang for seven days. Then finally a C130 took me to the Cong Hoa General Hospital where I stayed for one month and two days then came 30 April '75.

Ngoc would have been entitled to a disability pension from the South Vietnamese government but Saigon fell on April 30, 1975. His wife was the daughter of an officer and life became extremely difficult for them in postwar Vietnam as he did not receive any government pension as a former RVNAF soldier:

> After '75, even those with all four limbs intact found it hard, let alone those like me who lost their legs and were not entitled to any benefit from the government, because my government had collapsed. You can imagine

how hard our life was. I can't say that I've done this or I've done that, but at the time I thought that for people like me, of my generation . . . What have they been able to achieve let alone us, as disabled people, without any government benefit? That's all I can say, I can't say any more than that, I hope you understand.

They [his wife's family] also suffered a great deal of hardship, that's all I can say, it was difficult. I don't want to talk much. In reality, as far as my life is concerned, I think things were normal, but as to the life of others, I don't know anything. I can't say much.

We have three children. The oldest was born in '76, the next in '78 and the youngest in '80. All three are sons. To bring them up was a lucky feat in itself, but without an education they can't make as much money as the others and their life is quite bad.

Ngoc's narrative reveals his pride in his wartime service in the Marines. Having enlisted as a seventeen-year-old, he was a combat veteran by the time he turned twenty. For him, all ended when he stepped on a mine and lost his legs, and he speaks sparingly about the difficulties experienced in the postwar years.

These accounts relate that all three men not only volunteered for military service as teenagers but also served in elite units in the RVNAF: the Rangers, the Airborne Division, and the Marine Corps. Lap's statement that he was encouraged to do so by his peers suggests that he was part of a cohort of volunteer youth in the spring of 1972. The number of those who volunteered for combat units was more than double the planned intake of draftees.[48] The narratives of both Lua and Ngoc convey the youthful idealism and patriotic fervor that accompanied their actions at the time of enlistment. All three received horrific injuries on the battlefield and would have been entitled to disability benefits from the Saigon government. Nguyen Cong Luan was a member of the Standing Committee of the Interministerial Committee for Disabled Veterans in 1970, and notes that there were widespread protests by disabled veterans throughout South Vietnam for better living conditions.[49] Following demonstrations in front of the Veteran Affairs Ministry and the Presidential Palace, a new law was passed involving higher levels of supplementary payments to be made to disabled veterans than those proposed in President Thieu's legislation bill.[50] Nguyen Cong Luan adds that benefits to disabled veterans, widows, and orphans would have placed a considerable financial burden on South Vietnam for years to come.[51] These concerns became moot when Saigon fell in 1975. While the extent of their injuries meant that Lap, Lua, and Ngoc were spared incarceration in Vietnam's gulag, they were denied a war or disability pension, and they and their families suffered under the discriminatory policies of the postwar government. Ngoc's sons were refused access to educational and employment opportunities while Lua's daughter and son died of childhood fevers due to lack of money for medical care.

POSTWAR LIVES, POSTWAR MEMORIES

The six veterans whose oral narratives feature here differ in their family backgrounds and levels of education, and their war service varied both in its nature and duration. All six, however, enlisted in the military while their country was at war. Despite the loss of the war and the collapse of their country, they identify strongly with their past identities as soldiers and with their branch of the armed forces whether it be the Airborne Division, the Navy, the Marines, or the Rangers. All six experienced loss and trauma during as well as after the war. Their accounts reveal that the men were exposed to a combination of life stressors including war, debilitating injury (for three of them), and state repression. Despite these experiences, their life stories demonstrate a core of resilience and a will to survive, even in the case of the most damaged among them. Their accounts provide insights not only into the lives of former RVNAF soldiers during the war but also in its aftermath.

The first three veterans, Tran, Hai, and Hung, experienced internment followed by social ostracism in postwar society. They were *nguy* and therefore undesirable in the eyes of the new regime. This ideological label set them apart from their countrymen and contributed to their marginalization and sense of exclusion in postwar society. It not only singled them out but also targeted, by association, their loved ones. Tran distanced himself from his parents and siblings so that they would not suffer through association with him. After a decade of internment, Hai was put on probation for two years, had to report to the local authorities, and saw his children being denied access to education. Hung only had temporary residence in his own home, could not obtain work, and ended up living illegally like many others who were "not of a clean background." All three men reacted to this form of discrimination by "crossing the border" and constructing new lives overseas. Hung sought not only to change his own circumstances but also those of a younger brother who would otherwise have been called for "labor service" by the authorities. Tran and Hai saw no future for themselves or for their children in Vietnam. To the wartime service and postwar experiences of these veterans were added the challenges of escaping from Vietnam by boat and resettling in a new land. As refugees from communism and migrants to a new land, they form part of a wider international Vietnamese diaspora that stretches across borders and continents. The narratives of the three men evince a clear recognition of their good fortune and the debt they owe their less fortunate compatriots still in Vietnam.

A common emotion among survivors of trauma is a feeling of guilt—they survived and were able to rebuild their lives while others could not. For Tran, this guilt is twofold, emerging from his experiences as a former soldier and former refugee. As Judith Lewis Herman notes,

> Most survivors seek the resolution of their traumatic experience within the confines of their personal lives. But a significant minority, as a result of the trauma, feel called upon to engage in a wider world. These survivors recognize a political or religious dimension in their misfortune and discover they can transform the meaning of their personal tragedy by making it the basis for social action.[52]

Tran uses his background as a veteran and refugee to engage in social action and provide practical help to others in need. His actions serve to maintain ongoing links with Vietnam and with veterans in Vietnam, and he persists in his endeavors even though he believes he can no longer return to Vietnam. While Tran has chosen to take an active role in aiding and assisting the sick and the disabled in Vietnam, in particular the "brothers" who served with him in the RVNAF, Hai has sought validation and emotional sustenance from fellow veterans by engaging with the Australian Vietnam veteran community and taking part in commemorative practices such as the Anzac Day march. Hai has never returned to Vietnam, largely because he believes that he would be arrested by the Vietnamese authorities were he to do so. His reaction is understandable in view of his ten years of incarceration after the war. His narrative reveals how grateful he is to have his war service and that of his compatriots recognized in his adopted country. He notes that Australian Vietnam veterans have finally been publicly recognized in their own country. The "Welcome Home" parade for Australian Vietnam veterans took place in Sydney on October 3, 1987, and its "greatest permanent legacy was the decision to erect a national monument in Canberra, in memory of Australia's Vietnam veterans."[53] For Hai, marching "every year" on Anzac Day is not only an acknowledgment of his status as a Vietnamese Australian veteran but also a public tribute to his lost country, its flag, and its armed forces. Hung, for his part, volunteered in a range of roles—counselor, Scout leader, interpreter, and translator—to assist the Vietnamese community in Australia. He used his degree in social work—obtained at considerable personal and financial cost—to alleviate the plight of Vietnamese refugees in Hong Kong camps in the late 1980s and early 1990s. His two decades in radio journalism were another means of providing service to his community. All three men have succeeded in transforming the memories of their individual tragedies into meaningful action.

The experiences of the three Vietnam-based veterans differ markedly from those of veterans in Australia. Lap, Lua, and Ngoc suffered massive physical trauma during the war and bear the visible and enduring scars of their service. They relate in detail the extent of their injuries, and the months of treatment in a series of military hospitals and ongoing postoperational complications. As former soldiers whose wartime service has never been recognized in their own country, their war trauma was intensified in the postwar years. The army and the country they had served and fought for were obliterated from the national consciousness and expunged from history. Handicapped by their disability and subjected as they were to the discriminatory policies visited upon all those who were associated with the former South Vietnamese government, they experienced acute poverty and hardship after 1975. As Ngoc points out, this would have been hard enough for former soldiers who were whole of body. For disabled veterans, it proved doubly difficult. Lap referred to the support provided to him by the South Vietnamese government before 1975 in the form of social assistance and benefits for invalids. He is silent on these issues after 1975 but makes a revealing comment:

> In life, everyone must have a dream. My dream, although big, is small. For the remaining years of my life, I wish: first, that I could receive encouragement from my countrymen; and second, that my family would be happy. That's all I wish for.

These few words are unexpectedly moving and reveal the two elements that he seeks and that have been missing from his life in Vietnam: recognition of his status as a war veteran and his family's happiness. Lua, for his part, does not refer to the policies of the postwar government. He does, however, describe the consequences of these policies and their damaging impact upon his family and the lives of his children. Ngoc's narrative reveals that while he is grateful for the help provided by Vietnamese veterans and philanthropic organizations overseas, he is also unwilling to disclose details of his postwar situation. Thirty-five years after the end of the war, he still fears possible repercussions on the part of the authorities in Vietnam. He stresses repeatedly, "That's all I can say" and "I can't say much." His guarded comments suggest that his memories are potentially dangerous and cannot be relayed publicly. Lap echoes this when he states at the end of his interview, "I have to be very subtle for fear of when I return to Vietnam . . . It may not be wise [to speak]." The reticence of the men relating to their postwar experiences contrasts with their detailed rendition of the military engagements that they took part in during the war. Their narratives reveal in this way as much in their silences and lacunae regarding their postwar lives as in the details they do provide of their war service, their experience of combat, and the nature of their horrific injuries.

War and its aftermath may have damaged these men but it is also clear from their accounts that they were sustained through years of adversity by their past identities as soldiers and their memories of military service. Lap refers to the sense of comradeship among the Rangers. Lua and Ngoc express pride in their service and in particular the elite units that they belonged to. All three were young amputees. In spite of more than three decades of suffering and grief following the collapse of their army and the loss of South Vietnam, they still assert their agency in joining the RVNAF and their desire to serve their country in the midst of war. Their crippled bodies in this way symbolize not only the destruction and suffering of the South in the aftermath of war but also its stoicism and endurance. Partial and incomplete as these accounts are, they serve as counternarratives to official versions of the war in Vietnam.

The structure of the oral narratives reflects the divergent experiences of the six veterans. Tran, Hai, and Hung were in their twenties when they joined the armed forces and after the war remade their lives overseas. Their oral histories provide details of familial and social backgrounds prior to their enlistment as well as their reflections on postwar Vietnam and their resettlement experiences in Australia. Their military service in the RVNAF features prominently in their life stories but it is contextualized within a wider life trajectory that includes memories of childhood and youth, as well as their experiences as migrants overseas. While their accounts reveal the traumas that both men suffered, the enduring psychological and physical scars of war, and the aftermath of war, they also illustrate the men's resilience and their capacity to adjust to lives in a vastly different country and culture. The oral histories of Lap, Lua, and Ngoc are trauma narratives, and differ in structure and focus from the first three. Lap and Lua's accounts linger in detail on their years of service, the nature of their wounds, and ensuing complications. Lap's life after the war is conveyed sparingly while Lua relates the pain of seeing his family suffer in the postwar years. Ngoc's account focuses on those three years between the ages of seventeen and twenty when he found validation and purpose as a soldier and combatant. While he does provide glimpses of his life before he joined the Marines, his military experience dominates his life story. His vivid and detailed account of combat reflects the intensity of his experiences. The shock of becoming a double amputee is conflated with a series of losses: the abrupt end of his life as a soldier, and the loss of his army and his country.

The individual traumas that the six men experienced as soldiers were echoed by the mass trauma of South Vietnamese society around them as Saigon fell, the war was lost, and the country collapsed in 1975. The harrowing grief of losing comrades in the war or of sustaining crippling injuries was then exacerbated by the erosion of South Vietnamese society after the war. As Selma Leydesdorff, Graham Dawson, Natasha Burchardt, and T. G. Ashplant note, "Traumatic experiences and their consequences often constitute the core of life stories told by those who have survived natural disasters or war, or other kinds of social, state, or interpersonal violence."[54] Trauma for these men is "the outcome of a constellation of life experiences."[55] They report the classic symptoms of posttraumatic stress disorder in the form of obsessive and recurring dreams and nightmares of their war service or postwar arrest and internment. Tran, for example, relates:

> I will probably be haunted by dreams for the rest of my life. I have terrifying flashbacks—just in the afternoon, people were walking here and there when all of a sudden we heard the sound of a mortar and then I heard that the friend that I was talking to in the afternoon had died or was injured. I saw artillery [shells] cut the bodies of my friends and comrades. These are hard to forget. I was a soldier in the Engineer Corps and this was how people were killed, not from gunshots. The shells that the communists used to call 130 mm or 122 mm, those shells were big and if they fell on your shelter, you were dead. War was horrible. Weapons and ammunitions, they don't spare anybody and nobody can dodge them. Occasionally I dream of the war and wake up screaming. It is ingrained in my head and I could never forget it.

Hai's nightmares relate mostly to his imprisonment in the Vietnamese gulag. He says, "The dreams are imprinted in my mind. At night, I still see. I am in Australia and the communists could still arrest me. I still see it. Even now it's still not over. Even now it still obsesses me." Ngoc, who was a seasoned soldier by the time he was twenty, states:

> I often have dreams in which I am a soldier of the Republic of Vietnam, in battle, being surrounded, being shot at. All these, and these nightmares often come to me. They are regular nightmares still. My wife often hears me when I scream in my sleep, she would shake me to wake me up.

"[I]ntrusions of traumatic memory," note Bessel van der Kolk and Alexander McFarlane, "can take many different shapes: flashbacks; intense emotions, such as panic or rage; somatic sensations; nightmares; interpersonal reenactments; character styles; and pervasive life themes."[56] For these veterans, memories of their wartime and postwar experiences still generate intense emotions. Although the factors that contributed to high levels of traumatic stress and grief for these veterans were numerous, a major factor was the erasure of their military past and history by the postwar Vietnamese government. For these veterans, speaking their stories is a means of reasserting the histories and experiences of RVNAF soldiers. As Sandra Soon-Jin Lee observes, "Where memory is constantly under attack or under threat of being erased, living, breathing witnesses are often instrumental in establishing the credibility of contested versions of the past."[57] These oral narratives are the forms through which these veterans bear witness to the events of the past. Their accounts not only counter dominant state interpretations of the war but also reinforce the validity of oral history as a key means with which to convey the memories of those whose participation in larger events has been forgotten, and of reinserting them into the historical record.

"In truth," writes Elie Wiesel, "memory can be stifled but not erased."[58] While RVNAF veterans have been neglected by the Vietnamese government and forgotten in their own country, they are remembered by their comrades overseas and the wider Vietnamese diaspora. The narratives reveal the close links that continue to exist between veterans in Vietnam and veterans overseas. Recreating these veterans' histories in the diaspora is not only a means of validating their existence and their service but also, fundamentally, to counter their absence within Vietnam itself.

CHAPTER 7

Recognition of Service

South Vietnamese veterans who served their country during the time that Australian troops were in Vietnam are recognized as allied veterans and can apply for an Australian army pension.
—Nguyen Huu An[1]

Having served in the RVNAF from 1972 to 1974, escaped from Vietnam in 1981, and resettled in Australia, Nguyen Huu An applied to be formally recognized as an allied veteran in 2001.[2] He did so not in order to obtain a service pension—he works full time as an accountant and runs a successful practice, and, as he notes, the war pension should go to those who are in need of it—but as a way of demonstrating to his children that he had served his country during the war, and that he was proud of that service. Like many other veterans who left as refugees from Vietnam, An has no photographs or documents of service. The certificate from the Australian Department of Veterans' Affairs is a government document attesting that An was a member of the Armed Forces of the Republic of Vietnam. It is a document that he can show his children. Australia's recognition of his former military status and that of other Vietnamese veterans is not only a means of validating their service as allied veterans of the Vietnam War but also of acknowledging their place in Australian war and migration history, and of incorporating them into the Australian veteran community. An points out that this degree of recognition is not extended to Vietnamese veterans in the United States.

As generous as this measure is on the part of the Australian government toward ex-members of the forces of their former South Vietnamese ally, its application was not without controversy. This chapter will explore this largely unknown aspect of Australian policy toward a significant component of the Vietnamese refugee and migrant community in Australia—namely RVNAF veterans—and examine the recognition of their war service by the Australian government as well as the political controversies that surrounded this issue in the Australian Parliament in 1985–1986. Drawing on archives at the National Library of Australia and the National Archives of Australia, government documents including Australian House of Representatives and Senate parliamentary debates of the 1970s and 1980s as well as oral history interviews with Vietnamese veterans and the children of veterans, it will illustrate the veterans' reactions to this level of acknowledgment on the part of the Australian government, and reveal that the respective policies of the Liberal and Labor governments toward Vietnamese veterans and issues of entitlement were closely aligned with their positions on the Vietnam War.

VIETNAMESE REFUGEES AND AUSTRALIA

Prior to 1975, there were approximately 1,000 Vietnamese in Australia, consisting mostly of students, war orphans, and spouses of Australian diplomats and service personnel.[3] There were three main waves of Vietnamese immigration to Australia. A small group of 539 highly educated Vietnamese refugees was admitted in 1975–1976[4] but numbers remained modest until 1979–1980 when the second wave of Vietnamese arrivals peaked at 12,915.[5] These included many ethnic Chinese fleeing Vietnam after the closure of private businesses in 1978 and the border war between China and Vietnam in 1979. By 1981, 49,000 Vietnamese refugees had been admitted for resettlement in Australia.[6] The third wave consisted of so-called "economic refugees"—largely small traders, rural and urban workers, and the unemployed.[7] The number of Vietnamese refugees peaked at 13,248 in 1990–1991.[8] Although migration from Vietnam has been largely through the Family Reunion program since the mid-1990s, the Vietnamese community in Australia is essentially a refugee community. As Mandy Thomas writes, "the struggle against communism in their homeland has often fused Vietnamese in Australia of disparate religious, regional and class backgrounds into a political and unified force."[9] The Vietnamese community now numbers 233,000 people or just over 1 percent of the Australian population.[10] Vietnamese migrants have an unusually high rate of Australian citizenship among overseas-born at 95 percent.[11] War veterans form an essential component of this community, although now an aging one.

Australia's involvement in the Vietnam War left a lasting impact on national consciousness. A majority of Australians supported their country's participation in the war initially; however, public opinion shifted in the later stages of the war.[12] Of the more than 50,000 Australian soldiers who served in Vietnam between 1962 and 1973, 17,000 were conscripts, and this was a central factor in the mass protest movements of the late 1960s and early 1970s. The Vietnamese community in Australia is a legacy of the war and its aftermath. Vietnamese refugees constituted not only "the first and most difficult test case of the abolition of the White Australia Policy"[13] but were also a visible reminder of a controversial war that had divided public opinion in Australia and in which more than 500 Australians had died. The war highlighted divisions between the political Left and Right in Australia. In the closing days of the war in April 1975, the Whitlam Labor government refused to grant asylum to the Vietnamese staff of the Australian Embassy in Saigon, and took measures to minimize the number of refugees Australia would have to contend with.[14] Geoffrey Price, the last Australian Ambassador to South Vietnam cabled Canberra urgently on April 20, 1975, regarding his concerns for the embassy's locally engaged staff and their families.[15] Canberra cabled back on April 21, 1975, that, "Locally engaged Embassy Staff are not to be regarded as endangered by their Australian Embassy associations and therefore should not repeat should not be granted entry into Australia"[16] (emphasis in the original cable). Ambassador Price left Saigon on the last Australian plane on April 25, 1975, five days before the city fell. Veteran war correspondent Denis Warner was on the same flight and recalls in his memoir:

> I left with tears in my eyes late in the afternoon on ANZAC Day in the RAAF Hercules that had been waiting to evacuate Geoffrey Price and his staff. Keith Hyland, who spent almost a year in a cage as a guest of the Viet Cong, was a fellow passenger, as was Michael Richardson, of the Age ... The Australian Embassy had a list of a hundred and twenty-four Vietnamese who had been approved for entry into Australia, and whose safety was believed to have been at risk. At Canberra's insistence, none was aboard, although there was space for many of them.[17]

Although Price obeyed his government's instructions by not evacuating the embassy's fifty-five Vietnamese staff, this decision was to haunt him for the rest of his life. Price's son Christopher published a letter in *The Australian* newspaper in 2005 that stated that his father had disputed the

Australian government's orders bitterly but unsuccessfully in the final days of the war.[18] He added that his father's "enduring sense of shame at Australia's petty betrayal of Vietnamese colleagues who had worked alongside him . . . did remain with him until the day he died."[19]

The 1976 Report of the Senate Standing Committee on Foreign Affairs and Defence on the issue of Vietnamese refugees was highly critical of the Whitlam administration, and recorded the following findings: first, the admission criteria for Vietnamese refugees were announced too late on April 22, 1975; second, every decision was centralized in Canberra, which impeded the work of the Australian Embassy in Saigon; third, only one Vietnamese member of staff was evacuated (with his wife and child) and; fourth, the Australian government had a moral obligation to assist in the evacuation of Vietnamese but had deliberately delayed so that Australia would have the least number of refugees to deal with.[20] Confidential documents in the National Archives that were released after their thirty-year embargo reveal that in 1975 Prime Minister Gough Whitlam personally rejected Vietnamese refugee applications that had already been approved by his Foreign Minister, Don Willesee, and that a number of Vietnamese refugees, including members of the diplomatic corps, journalists, and editors, were required to sign an undertaking not to engage in politics in Australia.[21] When the Fraser Liberal government came to power in 1976, Michael MacKellar, Minister for Immigration, sent a letter of apology to the Vietnamese refugees which states that, "the government considers it inappropriate for you to be required to sign that undertaking and . . . has decided that the undertaking will no longer be binding upon you. The document will be cancelled and your continued residency in Australia will be entirely unconditional in respect of its contents."[22]

In his R. G. Neale lecture on the fall of Saigon, Peter Edwards notes that,

> We see the irony of a Labor Prime Minister taking a hard line against asylum seekers, while a Liberal opposition leader proclaims his attitude to be hard-hearted and shameful. . . . The Vietnam War in particular had allowed Labor to present itself as the party that best understood world, and especially Asian, affairs. But the refugee issue, and other controversies surrounding the fall of Saigon, removed much of that authority. Now it was the Liberals, led by Malcolm Fraser, a former Minister for the Army and Minister for Defence during the war, who were claiming the moral high ground, while Labor appeared to be politically, diplomatically and morally inept.[23]

Although the Liberal government sympathized on a political level with the refugees from Vietnam, few were admitted to Australia in the first years of the Fraser Liberal government. The arrival of a small number of refugee boats on Australia's northern shores and the rapidly escalating scale of departures from Vietnam in the late 1970s were to change this state of affairs, and it was under Prime Minister Malcolm Fraser that Australia responded generously to international pressure during the Indochinese refugee crisis of 1978–1979 by accepting "the largest number of refugees per head of population of all nations."[24]

In 1980, under the *Repatriation Acts Amendment Act (No. 2) 1979*, the service pension entitlement in Australia was extended to allied war veterans. The veterans concerned were largely allied veterans from the Second World War; however, the policy included allied veterans of later conflicts including the Vietnam War. The subject of repatriation in Australia, the extension of the service pension entitlement to allied war veterans—under which Vietnamese veterans were included—and the responses of Vietnamese veterans to this entitlement and recognition are explored in the next section.

AUSTRALIAN GOVERNMENT POLICY AND VIETNAMESE VETERANS

In *The Last Shilling: A History of Repatriation in Australia*, Clem Lloyd and Jacqui Rees note that repatriation, "in the sense of a comprehensive war veterans' policy is a distinctively Australian usage, one applied by no other country."[25] The word became the official Australian term for veterans' benefits because at the time the Australian benefits system was established in 1919, the most pressing issue was the need to repatriate the large number of veterans who had served overseas during the First World War. Repatriation involves a wide range of policies and welfare services in order to assist war veterans to reintegrate into society following the end of their service. Australia has, arguably, one of the most generous and costly repatriation systems in the world, and it is a system that has benefited from widespread support by the Australian community.[26] The repatriation system that came into being at the end of the First World War covered the aftermaths of subsequent wars and conflicts including Korea and Malaya in the 1950s and Vietnam in the 1960s and 1970s. In 1980, under the Fraser Liberal government, the *Repatriation Acts Amendment Act (No. 2) 1979* came into effect, which, for the first time, extended the service pension entitlement to "Members of the Forces of an Allied Country."[27]

The Bill that became the *Repatriation Acts Amendment Act (No. 2) 1979* was presented in the House of Representatives on October 11, 1979, by Evan Adermann,[28] then Minister for Veterans' Affairs, who stated that by referring to allied veterans the bill honored an election promise made by the Government in 1977.[29] The bill proposed that eligible veterans of allied countries be entitled to receive a service pension as long as the following conditions were fulfilled: first, they had served in a formally raised force; second, they had served in a theater of war; third, they had resided for a minimum of ten years in Australia; fourth, they had satisfied the income test applicable to Australian and British Commonwealth veterans; and fifth, they had reached the age of sixty for men or fifty-five for women.[30] A person would be excluded from entitlement, however, if they had served in the forces of a country that was, at that time, at war with Australia or in forces engaged in war-like operations against Australian forces.[31] Allied veterans, however, would not be eligible for other significant repatriation benefits such as "income tax concessions, a defence service home loan, or repatriation medical treatment benefits."[32] As veterans of the forces of the British Commonwealth were already entitled to service pensions, the change extended to Second World War veterans from Europe who had fought with Allied forces. The Labor Opposition expressed some concerns regarding definitions but in essence the bill passed both Houses with relatively little fanfare.

The *Repatriation Acts Amendment Act (No. 2) 1979* encompassed war veterans among newly arrived refugees from Vietnam. Australia had fought in the Vietnam War as an ally of the Republic of Vietnam, and RVNAF veterans were eligible for the service pension as "Members of the Forces of an Allied Country," providing they fulfilled the residence prerequisite and other criteria. Since the residence requirement was ten years and Vietnamese refugees only began arriving in Australia in large numbers from the late 1970s onwards, Vietnamese veterans would not be eligible for this benefit before the late 1980s and the 1990s. The numbers of allied veterans from the First World War, Second World War, and the Korean War receiving the service pension in Australia were modest. A confidential Cabinet Submission from 1985 refers to 3,279 allied veterans and mariners receiving the service pension at that time.[33] The same document acknowledges that only approximately ten allied veterans from the Vietnam War were receiving the service pension but that it was expected that numbers would escalate "upwards of 10,000" over the next five to ten years as these veterans reached the age of sixty and gained ten years of residence in Australia.[34]

For Vietnamese veterans in Australia, their entitlement to an Australian war pension signifies the public recognition of their war service, the official acknowledgment of their status as allied veterans, and their acceptance as members of the Australian community. By extending the service pension to RVNAF veterans, Australia is not only "repatriating" former soldiers who have lost their own army and country in the Australian sense of providing supporting payments but also symbolically welcoming them into their new *patria*. The perspectives of Vietnamese veterans are provided in the following narratives. The first veteran, Truong Cong Hai,[35] was born in My Tho in southern Vietnam in 1943, and served for twelve years in the Vietnamese Navy. He was assigned to the U.S. Seventh Fleet in Yokohama, Japan, for three months, and then to Fleet Higher Command and river patrols in the My Tho and Vinh Long areas. By 1975, he had attained the rank of lieutenant commander and was the manager of the Maritime Checkpoint at Vung Tau. After the war, he experienced ten years of internment in communist prison camps. Released in 1985, he became a boat refugee in 1986, and resettled in Australia. He suffers from chronic ill health as a result of his years of internment in postwar Vietnam. He states,

> Doctors examined me, and after a while they considered my situation as if I was disabled. The truth is, the worst one is asthma. I've suffered from asthma since I went out to the North [prison camps in northern Vietnam]. It destroyed my lungs and made me very morose. After a period of examination, they let me stop work permanently. I am a Vietnamese Australian war veteran. Now I receive a pension from the Department of Veterans' Affairs. I've had it since July 1994.
>
> Just recently the Governor-General of Australia paid tribute to the soldiers who died in the war and they built a statue in Canberra. I also attended that event, and they invited us to participate in the ceremony as honoured guests. I was very honoured to receive such treatment. I went waving the Republic of Vietnam flag with Australian and New Zealand veterans. We were all brothers. They have been recognized because of us, because of our war so I am very happy. The brothers are now very happy. And I am also very proud that our flag is once again flying.
>
> I march on Anzac Day every year.

For Hai, an Australian war pension acknowledges not only his military service but also his postwar incarceration and the subsequent damage to his health. He expresses his gratitude for this formal recognition and reveals the pride he takes in marching alongside his Vietnamese, Australian, and New Zealand "brothers" on Anzac Day.

The second veteran, Tran Dang Vinh,[36] was born in Nha Trang in southern Vietnam in 1945, and served in the Vietnamese Air Force for ten years, reaching the rank of major by the end of the war. He was sent to Lackland, Texas, in the United States, where he did a course on aerial photography and photo interpretation, and continued with further specialized training in Colorado. He spent several years in detention after the war before escaping from Vietnam as a boat refugee in 1983. Vinh contends that Australia is unique in its recognition of the service of RVNAF veterans. He notes,

> Our brothers have joined the RSL [Returned and Services League of Australia]. We endorse a policy of working closely with our brothers in the RSL. These days they don't regard us as the ARVN [Army of the Republic of Vietnam], as an ally anymore, instead they regard us as a sub-branch of the RSL, which means we have the right to vote and to stand for office within the RSL. They regard us as Australians, as former members of the Australian Armed Forces and we enjoy the same statutory rights and the same benefits as other Australians. That's an honour for all Vietnamese veterans living in Australia. Those resettled in the United States and elsewhere, they all say that those of us in Australia are very lucky. And I say, "Yes, it's the lucky country." They regard us as equals, not as second-class citizens like in America.

Vinh stresses that by incorporating Vietnamese veterans into the RSL, Australia regards Vietnamese veterans as more than former allies—it puts them on a par with former Australian servicemen. He notes that this honor has not been extended to Vietnamese veterans in the United States. In spite of Vinh's assertions, however, Vietnamese veterans do not have access to all the benefits that Australian veterans are entitled to. Vietnamese veterans cannot seek counseling or health care, for example, from the Vietnam Veterans' and Veterans' Family Counselling Service or the Department of Veterans' Affairs for service-related conditions such as anxiety or posttraumatic stress disorder.[37]

The third veteran, Nguyen Viet Long,[38] was born in 1946 in southern Vietnam. He volunteered for service in the Navy in 1968, and was assigned to a number of units including the naval logistics base in Thuan

An, a river assault unit in the Mekong Delta, and a large LST (Landing Ship Tank) in 1974. He was incarcerated for four years by the communist authorities after the war. He escaped from Vietnam in 1982, and arrived in Australia in 1983. Long joined the Vietnamese Veterans' Association of Victoria the year he arrived and RSL Footscray in 2008. It is noticeable that the South Vietnamese flag flies in front of the building alongside the Australian flag. The then president of the club, Clem David, allowed the display of the South Vietnamese flag. Long became president of RSL Footscray in 2011, and explains:

> Mr. Clem was in the Australian Navy in World War II. He passed away in 2011 at the age of eighty-five. Anzac House, the headquarters of the RSL, asked me to take over as President of RSL Footscray. Now in 2013, we have ninety fee-paying Vietnamese veterans and twenty-five Australian veterans still left. The World War II veterans are now very old and many have passed away while the Vietnam War generation is still young.
>
> To get a pension from the DVA [Department of Veterans' Affairs] you have to qualify as an allied veteran. If the DVA accepts you as an allied veteran, they give you a number and when you turn sixty, you can apply for the DVA pension. They ask for many papers—for example, you have to provide your service number, your rank, whether you were in any danger when you served in Vietnam—and you need to have two witnesses sign the form.
>
> On Anzac Day most Vietnamese veterans join the parade in the city. I started to march on Anzac Day in 1984. Every year, I join the parade, and about 150 members of the Vietnamese Veterans' Association join the march. Veterans from the Army, Navy, Air Force, Airborne, Marines—we gather under the umbrella of the Vietnamese Veterans' Association of Victoria and we walk together. The biggest march was in 1987 when we had the Welcome Home parade, 300 members marched that year.

Long's account links Vietnamese veterans to the earlier generation of Australian veterans of the Second World War. As the older generation of veterans age and disappear, a younger generation of veterans—Vietnamese veterans—inject new life and purpose into RSL Footscray. Long relates that the Vietnamese Veterans' Association of Victoria has approximately 800 members with around 200 joining activities on a regular basis. RSL Footscray organizes social events as well as commemorative marches and fund-raising activities. Veterans from different services in the RVNAF gather to march together on major national events such as the Anzac Day parade each year. The accounts of the three veterans are characterized by their shared experience of service to their country during the war, incarceration in postwar prison camps, and their sense of being fully accepted as members of the veteran community in Australia.

A fourth perspective is provided by Thien,[39] a second-generation Vietnamese Australian whose father served in the RVNAF during the war. Thien's parents arrived in Australia as refugees in 1983, and Thien was born in Hobart, Tasmania, in 1985. She suggests that while Vietnamese veterans may be entitled to a service pension in Australia, the process of applying for and obtaining a pension can be problematic. She relates:

> My father was a second lieutenant in Intelligence in . . . I think it was the 7th Battalion . . .
>
> He receives a DVA [Department of Veterans' Affairs] pension here. I did his application for him and found that it was very difficult to get one. For example, they ask you to recount the number of times that you have been under siege or in grave danger. That's fairly easy for someone to recount but when you have to write it down, it's hard to write things in a way that really conveys what you've gone through, so I think that whole process is totally flawed. You also have to prove what battalion you were in and my dad found that challenging because he threw all his papers away. He wrote a love letter to my mother every day that he was away and she also wrote to him but in '75 he got everything—his ID, badges, papers, letters, anything that had to do with him as a person, as an identity in Vietnam—he tied it all to a rock and threw it in the river, never to be seen again. He knew that the new government was going to take over and so he did as much as he could to erase his documented identity. And so when he applied for a DVA pension, he had no documentation. And then—and this is uncanny—his second nephew found a photo of him in his soldier's uniform and that was obviously strong evidence. He wasn't sure how that photo even came about, it was a gift from God but . . . I think a lot of veterans wouldn't even have that and so they would struggle to get a war pension.

In the closing days of the war, many South Vietnamese soldiers and civilians, like Thien's father, destroyed identity papers, family photographs, records of service, and qualifications—anything that would identify them to the incoming communist regime.[40] Thien's account reveals how difficult it can be for Vietnamese veterans to apply for a service pension in Australia. Her unfamiliarity with military terms and the details of her father's army experience also complicated the process. Although she was born in Australia and is a university graduate, Thien found the procedure of applying for a pension difficult and challenging. These challenges would be multiplied for veterans who have to contend with the language barrier and the difficulty of producing original documents of their service. Although veterans can request fellow ex-service personnel to vouch for them in the witness questionnaire, this needs to be someone who served in the same unit with them and took part in the same engagements against enemy forces, or at the least knew them well during their service, again a difficult proposition for many veterans whose surviving colleagues are members of an internationally scattered Vietnamese diaspora. While Thien is forthright in articulating her concerns regarding the application process, Vietnamese veterans register a range of responses. Some recall the procedure as being relatively straightforward while others state that they are thankful for the help and support provided by relatives and friends—the latter may relate to language issues and the difficulty of providing proof of service as asserted by Thien. A number of veterans also refer to cases in which fraudulent claims were made while others state that many more veterans are entitled to the service pension than actually apply for it.

The Department of Veterans' Affairs "Service Details Questionnaire: (Pension or Qualify Service Claim) Service with Forces in Vietnam" is where the balance has to be achieved between the veteran providing proof of service and the state providing an entitlement. The form includes questions on veterans' training and service in the Republic of Vietnam, whether they were conscripted or enlisted voluntarily, the units they served with, the names of their commanding officers, their military duties, their combat experiences between July 31, 1962, and January 11, 1973, as well as details of imprisonment in internment camps or reeducation camps after the end of the war.[41] A map of South Vietnam during the war depicting the four military zones is included at the end of the form, and veterans are asked to provide original documents or authorized translations of identity papers, service papers, and other documents relating to their military service.[42] The issue of documentation is problematic for many of the veterans, as only a few have retained documents or photographs of their service. The Department of Veterans' Affairs acknowledges this difficulty by providing a "Witness Questionnaire: Service with Forces in South Vietnam," which enables those who do not have supporting documentation of their war service to ask a fellow veteran who either served with them or who knew them during their military service to certify that they are RVNAF veterans.

In spite of the practical difficulties highlighted in the story of Thien's father, it is clear from the narratives of Hai, Vinh, and Long that Australia's official recognition of their military past and their service means a great deal. They draw connections between this acceptance and their membership of the RSL, the relations they have forged with Australian veterans, and their participation in national commemorative marches. This formal acknowledgment on the part of their adopted country is all the more symbolic in light of the absence of the RVNAF from much of the historiography of the Vietnam War.[43] Postwar communist Vietnam has erased the histories of these former soldiers. It recognizes neither the service nor the sacrifice of the RVNAF during the war.[44] Official recognition in Australia therefore signifies that: first, they have not been forgotten; second, their military service has been recognized; third, they have been identified as former allies; and fourth, this acknowledgment has taken practical shape in the form of entitlement to the service pension and membership of the RSL. As veterans, as refugees, and as members of a minority community, the veterans are particularly sensitive to the implications of this public acknowledgment. While the process of applying for a service pension in Australia may be challenging and problematic (as evidenced in Thien's account and the instructions from the Department of Veterans' Affairs), it remains nevertheless a generous and tangible recognition of this new refugee and migrant community as well as the veterans who form such a significant group within this community. By enabling Vietnamese veterans to apply for an Australian war pension, the *Repatriation Acts Amendment Act (No. 2) 1979* confirmed their place in their new country.

Few are aware, however, that this entitlement was nearly revoked under the Hawke Labor Government in 1985, five years after the implementation of the *Repatriation Acts Amendment Act (No. 2) 1979*. Extensive political debates arose in the Australian Parliament over this issue and reveal perspectives from different sides of politics regarding the Vietnam War, Vietnamese refugees in Australia, and the war veterans in their midst.

THE HAWKE LABOR GOVERNMENT SEEKS TO CHANGE POLICY

In 1985, two initiatives of the Hawke Labor Government combined in a way that led to a proposal to remove the recognition of Vietnamese veterans in the repatriation system. First, the Veterans' Entitlements Bill 1985 was presented in the House of Representatives on October 16, 1985. The purpose of this Bill was to "consolidate, rationalise and simplify the entitlements available to members of the veteran community."[45] With this new bill, the term "repatriation" passed out of usage. The bill represented "the most important and comprehensive overhaul of the repatriation system since its establishment over 60 years ago."[46] Second, as the new system of Veterans' Entitlements was being developed, the government was seeking to find expenditure savings from the national budget and it found some of these in the area of veterans' entitlements. Cabinet files reveal that the Minister for Veterans' Affairs, Senator Arthur Gietzelt, opposed the main savings proposals first advanced by the Minister of Finance, Senator Peter Walsh, but then undertook to find alternative savings possibilities.[47] A proposal emerged to limit recognition of allied veteran status to those who had served in wars and conflicts that ended before September 1, 1957. This proposal found its way into the Veterans' Entitlements Bill.

The cabinet documents reveal that Gietzelt initially proposed the exclusion of service pension eligibility for allied veterans of the Vietnam War as an alternative to a series of measures to cut expenditure favored by Walsh in the months leading up to the Hawke Labor Government's May Economic Statement of 1985. The May Economic Statement of 1985 included savings in the Veterans' Affairs portfolio totaling 274 million Australian dollars over the following three fiscal years as part of a much larger amount of savings from across the government. Gietzelt's proposal on allied veterans was estimated to provide negligible savings over the period, although possible savings of 21 million Australian dollars four years later were flagged.[48] In any case, it was not included in the Statement but was deferred to the proposed rationalization of veterans' entitlements to be undertaken through the Veterans' Entitlements Bill.[49] In his proposal to the Cabinet on that Bill, Gietzelt stated:

> I do not see any justification for continuing eligibility to members of Allied Forces serving in Vietnam. The Repatriation Commission has advised me that it believes it is impossible to administer the service pension provisions for such forces when records are not available. In particular, it is impossible to ascertain whether such applicants have served in a theatre of war or served in, or assisted, the forces of the enemy. Australia is the only country with provisions of this kind. They have applied only since 1980. In terms of priorities for expenditure, there is no doubt that payment or equivalent of the age pension five years earlier than the age of 65 for males, to people who did not serve in the Australian forces, must rank very far down the scale. To remove this potential liability, I propose that the eligibility of

Commonwealth and allied Veterans be limited to participation in wars and conflicts that ended before 1 September 1957. The proposed change has the support of the Advisory Committee of the R.S.L.[50]

The submission makes it clear that Gietzelt's proposal was aimed at excluding Vietnamese veterans from the service pension. The support of the RSL appears to have been in the context of the overall package of changes to veterans' entitlements embodied in the bill. Cabinet agreed to the proposals in Submission 2596 on May 13, 1985, including limiting the service pension to allied veterans in service before September 1, 1957.[51] There is no indication in the cabinet files of any government consideration of implications of the allied veterans' proposal other than the financial or of any attention to the measure apart from its minor place in a much larger package. The nonfinancial implications, as events developed, would become an issue when the parliament considered the proposal.

THE CONTROVERSIES IN THE AUSTRALIAN SENATE

When the Veterans' Entitlements Bill was first considered in the Parliament in the House of Representatives, Tim Fisher, the Deputy Opposition Leader, himself a Vietnam Veteran, noted concern for "different levels of entitlement and categories for allied veterans" that he considered a "discriminatory approach" but he also acknowledged that the Department of Veterans' Affairs had finite resources.[52] The Senate, however, requested a total of forty-one amendments to this bill, and it was at that stage that the issue of discrimination was raised.

One of the most heated debates in the Senate regarding the bill took place on November 28, 1985, when Australian Democrat Senator Michael Macklin moved: "That the House of Representatives be requested to make the following amendment: Sub-clause 35 (1), definition of 'allied veteran', leave out ', before 1 September 1957.'"[53] This sub-clause in the bill defined "allied veteran" as a veteran who served "before 1 September 1957." This definition therefore excised from the bill all allied veterans who served in the Vietnam War. As Senator Macklin noted:

> Inclusion of "before 1 September 1957" in a definition of allied veterans removes service pension rights from Allies whose service was post-Korean war. Of course we are talking mainly about veterans who are American, Korean, Thai or Vietnamese. That is a major group of people involved. No logical reason seems to have been given for discriminating against

one particular group of allied veterans—that is, veterans who fought in the Vietnam War.[54]

Senator Macklin observed possible reasons circulating in the Australian community for this exclusion including cost, the difficulty of finding out who these veterans are, and racial discrimination. The main point of his argument was that a group of Australian citizens who had fought as allies in wars up to and including the Korean War would be entitled to service pensions, while another group of Australians, who had fought as allies during the Vietnam War, would be denied this entitlement. He considered this practice discriminatory and at variance with the spirit of the Australian constitution "under which all citizens, if they have equal basis for claim, are treated equally."[55] He was referring to Vietnamese veterans in Australia since—references to American, Thai, and Korean veterans aside—the Vietnamese were the major group to be affected by this new proposed legislation. As Macklin underlines:

> So we are going to have a group of people who came from South Vietnam and who are Australian citizens being treated differently from the way in which other people—for example, people from Britain who fought with Australians and who are now Australian citizens—are being treated. I abhor that situation. I do not think it is fair. It is not acceptable in Australia that we should make that arbitrary distinction between two groups of Australian citizens.[56]

Senator Arthur Gietzelt, as Minister for Veterans' Affairs, responded that the Vietnamese community in Australia numbered approximately 80,000 and that some 15 percent of that group or 4,000 were war veterans. He claimed that since Vietnamese veterans had arrived in Australia as refugees, it would not be possible to provide proof from the current Vietnamese government that they had served in the armed forces or in an operational area.[57]

Senator Gietzelt's argument was vigorously refuted by Liberal Senator Austin Lewis and Senator Macklin, both of whom stated (in relation to Vietnamese veterans in Australia): "They are Australians."[58] Senator Macklin had pointed out, "If we know that there are 3,000 or 4,000 veterans, presumably we know who they are."[59] Senator Lewis went on:

> We are talking about Australian citizens... The Minister kept saying that the Democrats are trying to extend this benefit to these Vietnamese; he kept calling them Vietnamese. In fact, they are Australians... The

Minister kept saying that the amendment will extend the benefit to Australian citizens of Vietnamese origin. The truth of the matter is that under the present legislation they are entitled to it already . . . So the Minister will have two classes of allied veterans in Australia. He will have allied veterans who served in Australian forces anywhere, so long as it was not Vietnam . . . this was a Fraser initiative. This was introduced in 1979.[60]

On the issue of eligibility, Senator Lewis suggested:

As an old country lawyer . . . I would say to my Australian citizen of Vietnamese origin: "Do you know any Australian servicemen? Can you find an Australian serviceman?" Then I would produce that Australian serviceman and he would say: "I know this fellow, I remember fighting alongside him in such and such a theatre of war." To my mind that would be pretty substantial evidence.[61]

Senator Lewis's speech was impassioned and emotive, and linked these veterans' war experiences to later traumas including postwar repression and the dangers they faced as refugees. He underlines repeatedly that he is referring to Australian citizens:

. . . these are our own citizens. These people are Australians . . . These people have had to survive the Vietnam war, a war in which some of them were fighting for many years. . . . Somehow or other they had to survive that war. Then they had to survive the debacle when the surrender took place. Then, having been members of the South Vietnamese armed forces, they had to survive the executions that took place in 1973. Then they somehow or other had to escape and survive the camps. They had to survive the extortionists, the pirates, the rapists, in order to get on to a boat or get away somehow or other into a camp. Those left had to survive living in camps until finally they either escaped by boat to Australia or were brought to this country as part of a scheme. After all of that, they live in Australia for many years and they become Australian citizens . . . They must go through all of that . . . and at the end this Government says: "The Vietnam war was not worth fighting. You should not have been involved in the Vietnam war. We are not going to treat you as allied veterans." I am appalled.[62]

Senator Macklin acknowledged the support from Senator Lewis: "I think he [Senator Lewis] has put them cogently and very well, to the point where he has answered all the problems I had enumerated."[63] Senator Macklin finished with: "Let us treat equally every Australian citizen who was an ally of ours and who fought with Australians in an operational area. Let us not say that those who served before 1 September 1957 are fine but that those who served afterwards are not."⁶⁴ Senator Lewis added that:

> The truth of the matter is that it is this Government's detestation of the Vietnam war that is the problem. It is that detestation that makes the Government say: "Look, that war is different, and we will not provide for people even if they are United States citizens, or Thais, or Koreans, or Vietnamese. It does not matter where they came from, if they fought with our troops in Vietnam, Vietnam is out."⁶⁵

Senator Macklin's motion was passed by the Senate (33 to 29) on November 28, 1985.⁶⁶

The matter was not over however. On November 29, 1985, the House of Representatives advised the Senate that it had not made the requested amendments to the bill. Senator Lewis said that the Opposition would press its requests and Senator Macklin reiterated that they would stand by the amendments and requests that they had moved.⁶⁷ The Senate therefore advised the House of Representatives that it "presses its requests for amendments to the Bill."⁶⁸ The Senate stood firm on this issue and in April 1986, the Government caved in. On April 11, 1986, it agreed to all but two of the forty-one requested amendments from the Senate. In "Schedule A, Requests by the Senate for amendments," the first amendment agreed referred to allied veterans: "No. 1—Page 40, sub-clause 35(1), definition of 'allied veteran', line 22, leave out ', before 1 September 1957.'"⁶⁹ The Australian Parliament thus passed the amended Veterans' Entitlements Bill 1986 and Veterans' Entitlements Amendment Bill 1986 on May 20, 1986.

The interesting aspect of this debate in the Australian Parliament is that it referred to the contentious issue of Australia's involvement in the Vietnam War and the political divide between the Left and Right on this matter. Senator Lewis linked the government's attempt to discriminate against Vietnamese veterans in Australia to Labor's objections to Australian involvement in the war. Vietnamese refugees arrived in Australia as a direct result of the aftermath of the Vietnam War. The main points made by the Opposition were that: first, these Vietnamese veterans were now Australian citizens and should therefore be treated equally to other Australian citizens; second, they had experienced enough hardship as war veterans, camp internees, and refugees and; third, the government's actions were rooted in Labor's opposition to Australian participation in the Vietnam War and subsequent antipathy toward refugees from Vietnam.

Lewis's comments hark back to Labor's opposition to the Vietnam War, the Whitlam government's refusal to grant asylum to Vietnamese staff of the Australian Embassy in Saigon in 1975, and the measures it took to minimize refugee arrivals.

These political disputes and divisions relating to the Vietnam War and Australia's role in the war had therefore reemerged ten years after the end of the war in these arguments regarding service pension entitlements for Vietnamese veterans—former RVNAF soldiers who had since become refugees, resettled in Australia, and become Australian citizens. Political divides however, are not always clear-cut. Although opinion on the war was linked to party allegiances, there was also a wide diversity of opinion within political parties.[70] Australian Democrats Senator Macklin, for example, had opposed Australia's involvement in the war[71] but he was the one who moved the motion for the removal of discriminatory measures against Vietnamese veterans in the Veterans' Entitlements Bill 1985. He was staunchly supported in this motion by the Liberals in the Senate, who felt that this removal of an entitlement that already existed since the passage of the former *Repatriation Acts Amendment Act (No. 2) 1979*—an act that had been supported by both sides of parliament—was deeply unfair. The government backed down on this issue, accepted this amendment, and Vietnamese veterans in Australia were therefore entitled to apply for the service pension once they fulfilled the ten years' residence requirement.

Service pension entitlements also raise issues of identity and belonging for members of minority communities in migrant countries. Fiona Jenkins, Mark Nolan, and Kim Rubenstein suggest that, "true examples of biculturalism are becoming a reality for the many generations who draw their sense of self from post-migration experience."[72] The identities of Vietnamese veterans are strongly anchored in their military past as members of the RVNAF. The fact that their army and country ceased to exist on April 30, 1975, has not lessened their sense of loyalty toward South Vietnam. This identification with the past is now coupled with an allegiance to their new country, Australia. By extending the service pension eligibility to these veterans, Australia has enabled them to embrace their previous histories and identities as South Vietnamese ex-service personnel and concurrently adopt new identities as Vietnamese Australian veterans. Because of the veterans' experiences as refugees from Vietnam, and the particular nature of the postwar Vietnamese diaspora, these allegiances do not entail complications such as bifurcated transnational loyalties. The veterans' attachment to Vietnamese values and Vietnamese culture is divorced from the postwar Vietnamese state and government. They can therefore assert their pride in being Vietnamese and in having served in the RVNAF while affirming their sense of belonging to a new homeland—Australia.

When the Fraser Liberal government extended service pension entitlements to allied veterans in Australia (including Vietnamese veterans) in the *Repatriation Acts Amendment Act (No. 2) 1979*, it was approved by both sides of the Australian Parliament. However, the overhaul of the repatriation system by the Hawke Labor government five years later in the form of the Veterans' Entitlements Bill 1985 and the government's attempt to block access to service pension entitlements to allied veterans of the Vietnam War reignited political divisions and differences over Australia's involvement in the war and led to heated debates in the Senate. Notwithstanding the small numbers of American, Thai, and Korean veterans of the Vietnam War in Australia, this aspect of the new bill targeted veterans in the newly arrived Vietnamese refugee community, and raised issues of discrimination and national identity. This bill was vigorously contested, especially in the Senate, by the Australian Democrats and the Liberals, and the government did eventually accede to the Senate's requests for amendments and amend the proposed bill.

Australia fulfilled its international obligations by taking in tens of thousands of Vietnamese refugees in response to the Indochinese refugee crisis of 1978–1979. This government policy under Liberal prime minister Fraser was not without controversy but overall the Vietnamese community has settled well and been accepted by the wider Australian society. Amidst this group of refugees that were traumatized by war, the aftermath of war, political repression, and the dangers of escape by sea or land, there were significant numbers of war veterans, many of whom had experienced further traumas in the form of internment in prison camps after the war. While the country and the army these former soldiers served have disappeared, and despite the historical and political amnesia relating to their history, these veterans have been recognized on a formal level by Australia. Australia has given them a public forum in which to register their presence and their service, and in which they can make their own contributions to public life and to official Australian commemorations of the Vietnam War.

CHAPTER 8

Children of Veterans

His image in my mind has always been that of a paratrooper in the Airborne uniform, tall and handsome . . . On the 29th my family was in Saigon. We had lost contact with my father. He stayed back in Tay Ninh to hold the police station there. He rang my mother to say that he had to stay to hold the fort and the soldiers together, he could not abandon his post.

—Oanh

Oanh[1] was only twelve when Saigon fell on April 30, 1975. Her family lived in Bien Hoa, and she remembers taking refuge in the bomb shelter every second night throughout the first four months of 1975: "When the siren wailed, everyone shouted 'Go to the shelter, rocket attack.' Half asleep, I would grab two of my younger siblings and we would scurry into the shelter. In the last days of April, we were in our shelter almost twenty-four hours a day. With the electricity cut off, sirens wailing all the time, and loud rocket explosions, we did not dare go outside." Oanh has a vivid recollection of the chaos of the final months and days of the war. The fear and uncertainty were compounded by not knowing the fate of her father, and by the family receiving conflicting news about him—that he had killed himself, that he had been shot dead, that he had led his troops into the jungle or been evacuated by the Americans. Oanh relates that it was a month later that her mother heard that he had been captured and imprisoned in Tay Ninh. Like many other children whose fathers were soldiers, the postwar years were characterized by adversity and privation. The families of those in the military and in the civil service were subjected to political discrimination by the authorities because of their association with the previous South Vietnamese government, and experienced a range of repressive measures such as harassment, eviction from their homes, forced displacement to the New Economic Zones, and forced labor.²

Oanh saw her father only once at the prison camp in Tay Ninh in 1976 before her escape from Vietnam by boat in 1979 with her younger brother and sister. The three siblings—aged between twelve and sixteen—spent eight months on Kuku Island in Indonesia and two months at the Galang refugee camp before leaving for America. The next time Oanh saw her father was thirteen years later on her first return trip to Vietnam in 1989, after his release from detention. She remembers: "When I saw him I nearly fainted. When he was captured, he was only in his thirties. In jail, I could still recognize him. But this time, he was an old man, his teeth were falling out, his back was stooped, his hair white, his face haggard." The changes wrought in Oanh's father after years of internment echo those of other detainees of Vietnam's reeducation camp system. Survivors returned to their families emaciated and prematurely aged.³ The grief that Oanh experienced, the escape from Vietnam, the separation from her family, and the shock of reuniting with her parents after the hardship of the postwar years reflect the experiences of many others whose parents had been service personnel or worked in the public sector during the war. As Robert McKelvey writes, families "never knew when, or even if, their husbands or fathers would return. There was no due process or sentencing. Prisoners served until they died, were killed, or were released, 'forgiven' at last by the Communist government."⁴

The children of veterans, whether they were born during the war, after the war, or for that matter after their parents fled Vietnam and resettled overseas, have in many cases been profoundly affected by their family's military past, whether they understood the nature of that service or not. This chapter will examine the ways in which the Vietnamese experience of diaspora has affected the intergenerational transmission of war memories and narratives, and how the younger generation of Vietnamese "remember" and formulate the wartime experiences and stories of the previous generation. It will explore the narratives of six members of the younger generation—three men and three women—ranging from those who were born in the 1960s and have childhood recollections of life in wartime to those who were born in the late 1970s and in the 1980s and have no personal memory of the war. The older generations of Vietnamese lived through decades of conflict and widespread internal displacement within Vietnam, most notably following partition in 1954, and have memories stretching from the Second World War through to the collapse of South Vietnam in 1975 and life under state repression in postwar communist Vietnam. Their experience of war encompassed their formative years as well as adulthood. The loss of homeland, exodus, and resettlement in a new country then followed. Younger Vietnamese, on the other hand, may not have experienced the war directly; however, their narratives reveal that their lives have also been shaped by war and the "memory" of war.

While these six narratives relate either early recollections of war or memories transmitted by the older generation, they demonstrate different forms of telling and hearing stories within families as well as distinct interpretations of the past and the shadow cast by the past. The life stories of these individuals reveal that "memories" of the war and of the past are linked not only to the diasporic experience but also to issues of identity and belonging in contemporary Australia. The concept of Australia as a place of refuge and sanctuary is mediated through these accounts of postwar hardship and at times difficult post-migration experiences. I will explore these narratives in detail before expanding on the differences as well as the commonalities in their accounts.

DIFFICULT LIVES

The first narrative is that of Hai,[5] born in Long Xuyen in 1960, the oldest of four children. He relates that his father worked for the South Vietnamese government but remains unclear about what his father actually did. He recalls:

> I rarely saw him in his military uniform. One day, when I was about nine or ten, my father said, "Today, I'll take you to have breakfast and coffee." So I climbed on his Honda motorbike and put my arms around his waist. He had a gun on one side and a pair of handcuffs on the other. I didn't think of asking him what he did, all I knew was that I was going to have a bowl of *hu tieu* [noodle soup] with him. It was a wonderful memory of my father.
>
> He worked hard but when he came home, he would get changed and instead of sitting down and waiting for dinner to be served, if my mum was busy he would go to the kitchen without being asked and cook for her and for us children so we could all eat together. He was a good man and I loved him a great deal.
>
> After [April] 1975, the Public Security police came, cuffed him up and took him away. They said, "A blood debt has to be paid in blood."

From Hai's description, his father may have worked for the Special Branch of the police. Hai states that his father was beaten and tortured in prison, transferred to a larger prison camp, and interned for seven years. He notes:

> The events from 1975 onwards changed the life of my family completely. It wasn't just my family—the majority of people in the south suffered in similar ways. My mother sold off her jewellery and valuables, and then the crockery so that she could feed us and still feed my father in the reeducation camp. It was a terrible time.
>
> I was not allowed to continue with my schooling because I was related to someone who worked for the old regime. They let my sister go to school because she was a girl but stopped her from doing the high school exam. My brother also gave up school.

Hai's mother tried to arrange for her children to escape the country but her efforts were unsuccessful. Hai went to a work camp in 1978 and contracted malaria. When the team leader refused to let him return home for treatment, he ran away and lived a peripatetic and precarious existence "outside the law," hiding from the communist authorities, and moving from place to place until he was finally able to escape from Vietnam by boat in 1981. He relates a traumatic journey during which Thai pirates wielding machetes and knives attacked their boat, and he witnessed the ensuing rape of the women and girls:

> One particular sound has stayed with me ever since, and every time someone talks to me about escaping from Vietnam, that sound returns to my mind. It was a thirteen-year-old girl, her wailing coming from the Thai boat, 'Daddy, Daddy, I'd rather die.' Every time anyone talks about escaping the country, that wailing comes flooding back to me.
>
> They returned the women, took our engine and let us drift in the sea.

The refugees reached Thailand, and Hai spent one month in a transit camp in Songkhla and then three years at the Sikhiu refugee camp in northern Thailand, a place he describes as "terrifying." He was rejected by the American delegation because he did not have any papers, and subsequently rejected by the other delegations. He said that he even applied to go to Israel but was rejected by that delegation as well. He was finally able to leave the camp when a member of a Vietnamese organization in Brisbane sponsored him to Australia in 1985. He was twenty-five years old. He stayed in a migrant center for six months, and tried to live with his sponsor for a few months but that arrangement failed. He moved to

Sydney, worked in a factory, and was involved in a serious car accident as a passenger. He had to have eight inches of his small intestine removed. He has never recovered his health, and has lived on a disability pension since the accident. He says: "I lost half my strength. Two years after the accident, I was practically half-dead. All my energy was gone. I was overwhelmed with sadness." The book that changed the direction of his thoughts was Krishnamurti's *The First and Last Freedom*. He recalls:

> The ideas in there saved my soul, despite the fact that my body had deteriorated. With that book, I revisited my childhood and my past. I could better relate to my fate. First, I didn't have to face war directly as a combatant. Second, I wasn't imprisoned the way my father was. I saw how the victorious Northerners treated the Southerners: they were cruel because within themselves, they had no sense of humanity.
>
> Finally, I realized that the fate of a human being is insignificant. I understood the pain of that fate but I needed to do something directed at beauty. From aesthetics, I could rise above pain. I studied photography.

Hai returned to Vietnam for the first time in 1999. He had not seen his family for eighteen years. He relates that his father was "mentally disturbed" and suffered from "obsessive fears" after he was released from internment. Hai's interactions with his parents and a surviving sister were initially fraught and strained, and then gradually eased over time. He made return trips to Vietnam to visit his family in 2001 and 2010. He believes, however, that he has never fully adjusted to life in Australia:

> I've never felt I have truly integrated. I always feel there's a distance. I am very conscious of this. I came here too late in my life. I didn't go back to high school. I tend to be introverted, and the state of my health affects my emotions. Living in Australia, I don't feel at ease. I feel a sense of gratitude towards them for providing us with a place to live, and I am especially grateful for their social welfare—I would be in dire straits otherwise. I can't live over there, where I was born and grew up, I cannot live in my own country, and I can't feel at peace in the place where I live so I'm always torn.

Hai chronicles the hardship that characterized his life after 1975—the years of struggle, the harrowing boat journey, the grim refugee camp, difficulties with resettlement, and a serious injury that wrecked him physically and emotionally. The collapse of South Vietnam in 1975 not only altered his family's circumstances but also caused lasting damage on a personal level.

The second narrative is that of Nghiem,[6] born in Saigon in 1964, the fourth child in a family of five. Like Hai, Nghiem does not have a clear concept of what his father did during the war; however, he does identify him as a major in the Bureau of Purchasing. The family lived in Doan Thi Diem Street next to the Presidential Palace and Nghiem's mother had a tailor's shop. He relates:

> Talking about memories of my dad, every afternoon he would pick me up after school and take me somewhere to eat. He enjoyed his food. I would ride pillion on his Vespa, and he would take me to the streets where they sold food. He said not to tell my mum, she'd tell him off [laughs]. Later on, my younger brother went to the same school, and my dad collected both of us from school and we went to eat together. He was in uniform. If he finished work late, we had to wait for him, sometimes for an hour.
>
> Several days before 30 April, I saw planes flying over the Presidential Palace and dropping bombs, and on the 30th, soldiers were fighting diagonally across from our home. I was scared that day because there was a lot of gunfire and dead bodies. I saw a soldier who was shot and died, it was a soldier of the Republic, and he must have known he was going to die because he wore a crisp new uniform. I witnessed this.
>
> My parents argued over what to do. My mum wanted to leave but my dad didn't want to go. A few months later, officers had to report in [for reeducation]. My dad went to report in. It was as if he was going away for work. He seemed normal. At the time I paid little attention. I was too young to notice details.... My dad was in prison for six years, from 1975 to 1981. At the beginning he was at Suoi Mau, then he was transferred to the frontier at Bui Gia Map. When he was at Suoi Mau, my mum visited him every month, and took me with her. When he was transferred near the border with Kampuchea, the trip was dangerous, and it took two or three days just to get there. We only got to see my father for half an hour or an hour. It was very difficult.

Nghiem recalls several failed attempts to escape from Vietnam. His older sister was barred from attending university because of their father's background. Nghiem notes: "I felt like a second-class citizen. Only those who followed the Communist Party were first-class citizens." His older and younger sisters both sought to leave the country by boat, and died at sea. After his father's release in 1981, the family again tried to escape but were caught by the authorities and imprisoned in Ben Tre. Nghiem was kept in a small cell with four adults. There was not enough space for inmates to lie down to sleep so they had to take turns sleeping sitting up. After seven days, they were sent to Dong Phu for hard labor. Nghiem specifies that he should have been sent to Dong Phu I, a prison reserved for escapees but that instead he was sent to Dong Phu II, which was reserved for criminals and orphans. Children aged twelve or thirteen were doing hard labor and he notes that, "every day some died." Detainees had to go into the jungle to cut down bamboos and tie them in bunches of five. Conditions were terrible, and Nghiem had hands, legs, and feet swollen with beriberi. He was interned for nearly a year. He says of the prison camp: "I remember its horror."

Nghiem escaped from Vietnam in 1983 and arrived in Australia in 1984. His father was released in 1987 or 1988. Nghiem was able to sponsor his parents to Australia but relates: "My dad was in a wheelchair. He could not talk. He was alive but already dead." Nghiem had a difficult experience of resettlement in Australia. He wanted to study but was dependent on an uncle and pressured to work. He reflects on a gradual loss of confidence: "So much hope when I first came here, and when my hopes were shattered, I didn't know what to do. Once your spirit goes down, you can't do anything. If I fall down and I can't walk then I'd crawl. There are many ways to crawl. I tried all kind of ways but in the end, nothing amounted to anything." He is married and has traveled to America but has never returned to Vietnam. His narrative relates the successive tragedies that his family experienced in the postwar years, the strain of failed escape attempts, the deaths of his sisters at sea, the terrible conditions surviving family members experienced in labor camps. Although he was able to escape from Vietnam and resettle overseas, he was unable to fully rebuild his life.

SIBLINGS

The third and fourth narratives are those of a sister and brother, Ngoc[7] and Tuan,[8] born in Saigon in 1969 and 1970, respectively. Their father was a civil engineer, their mother a teacher, and there were three other children in the family. Ngoc remembers her childhood during the war and visits to the mountain town of Dalat, where their grandfather, a highly ranked officer in the RVNAF, was based, as well as the closing days of the war.

> During the school holidays, we went to Dalat to visit my grandfather. I enjoyed living in the house reserved for military officers. We had the jeep and drivers to drive us around and I remember visiting the soldiers'

camp. When the communists approached Saigon, my first thought was "we are going to be encountering the enemy." I was scared that we would be shot. My mum was really worried and prepared bags of clothing for all of us labelled with our name, address and phone number just in case we ever got separated.

Ngoc's strongest memories of Vietnam, however, are of the postwar years.[9] Her family escaped the country in 1980. Their boat measured 12 meters and held 140 people. Ngoc was marked by the memory of this escape and the high levels of anxiety that accompanied this experience. She remembers:

> It took a long time for my parents to plan our escape, I think it took a few years, it seemed like ages, and we had to keep that information secret. I remember getting very agitated because the plan took a long time to eventuate. It was a long time before we actually made the final journey. When we left, I was worried about being starved to death, of not having enough food or water, but obviously my parents were a lot more worried, about the pirates, the weather conditions and things like that. When we left the country, it was July, it was the roughest time of year for the sea, it was a really rough journey.

This is how she describes the impact of the postwar years on her family:

> We thought that my dad would have to go to reeducation camp since he had had some sort of involvement with the military. He presented himself but he only had to do a few weeks. He didn't have to go for long because I think his involvement in the war was not considered material enough. So that was quite a relief for us.
>
> On the other hand, my grandfather and uncle were considered the "Number One Enemy" by the communists because they were involved in the political arm of the former government. Both were highly ranked soldiers. My grandfather was a colonel and my uncle was . . . of lower rank. They had to go to the reeducation camp and we thought that they would be away at most two or three months. But do you know what happened? They were relocated to North Vietnam and imprisoned in a hard labour concentration camp from 1975 to . . . I think it was 1983. Throughout that time they were allowed some visits from the family but it was expensive and difficult for my aunty to travel to the north to visit them, and she had young children as well. It was hard for her because her children were only one or two years old when they were robbed of their father. I think that the aim of the reeducation camp system is to break down the spirit of prisoners

so that they are no longer a threat to the government. My grandfather was finally released because all his children had gone overseas by that time and he was the only person remaining in Vietnam. As for my uncle, he was released after he was severely injured in an accident in the camp. When he returned home, he was a stranger to his children. Being from a military background, he felt that his children were very undisciplined. I think that for a long time there was . . . a battle between the different generations. He found it hard to fit into society.

Ngoc's narrative conveys not only the stories transmitted by the older generations but also her own memories of wartime and postwar Vietnam. Her father is not central to her account of the war; however, she does relate in some detail the experiences of her grandfather and uncle, both of whom served in the military. She recollects her experience in primary school and the impact of postwar propaganda:

At school, we were brainwashed from a young age. There were pictures of Ho Chi Minh everywhere, we were told how brave northern soldiers were and all that they had done to bring peace to South Vietnam. I joined a youth group, wore the red scarf and sang songs to Ho Chi Minh. It was all propaganda.

I'm not really interested in war. To me, war is the past. I'm only interested in the future; I don't want to look back at the past. I prefer not to remember unpleasant memories. Why do we need to look back at the past? I think it is so that we can learn and take stock and somehow improve our destiny. Maybe that's the reason why our children are taught history but I was never much into history. I thought that talking to my grandfather and uncle and letting them recount their experiences might be too painful for them but thinking back . . . I think it might be good for them to be able to tell me their stories.

Ngoc's narrative interweaves her memories as a child with stories of the internment of male relatives in prison camps in northern Vietnam after the war and her family's escape from the country. Her account also reveals, however, her ambivalence about recalling the war and retelling the past. She shies away from the topic a number of times before reluctantly conceding that it is important that this history be remembered.

Ngoc's brother Tuan was not yet five when the war ended on April 30, 1975. He relates:

My dad was not involved in the war other than when bridges got pulled down and roads got blown up, he had to go and sort that out. We were connected to the war through our extended family. My grandfather was a career soldier and was some big shot in Dalat, and my uncle, my mum's brother, was in the navy. My grandfather was a lieutenant colonel, and he was made a colonel just before the war ended, and my uncle was a captain on a ship, and had we wanted to go, we could all have jumped on the ship and fled but we didn't want to leave our country.

I distinctly remember an occasion when a bomb was dropped on a primary school, so many kids died, that was on TV, day after day. A few months or a year after the war ended, there was a place up the road from our house where there was a lot of ammunition. One day, there was a huge explosion, it shook our house. Out of curiosity I ran out to see what had happened and there was a little kid lying on the road, with his guts blown up. A young man tried to push the intestines back in and took him to the hospital.

As kids, we adapted very quickly. We had to wear the Red Scarf, which I think was an idea stolen from the Scouts, and we had to remember the five commandments of Uncle Ho. I still remember the communist national anthem but not the five commandments. And early in the morning, they'd put up loudspeakers everywhere on the streets and make announcements. They'd play music at an ungodly hour and you had to turn up and march around.

Tuan provides a different angle of the same family story and recalls violent events that were either reported on the news or that he witnessed. In March 1974, the communist shelling of an elementary school in the Cai Lay district killed twenty-three children and wounded forty others.[10] "Photos of the incident," writes Nguyen Ngoc Bich, "showed the school yard spattered with blood and the mangled bodies of the children."[11] It was a major news item in South Vietnam and one that Tuan recalls even though he was only a young child at the time. The other incident that he refers to, the explosion of the Bien Hoa ammunition depot, occurred in early 1977 and is related in other refugee memoirs.[12] One aspect that differentiated Tuan's experience from that of his older sister Ngoc was that his parents took him on a memorable journey to the north of the country to visit his uncle and grandfather in internment. Tuan's father was from a Buddhist family in northern Vietnam, and this was his first time back north. Tuan recalls:

I was born under a lucky sign, and my parents took me to visit my uncle and my grandfather who were both in the North. The term for visiting prisoners in reeducation was *di tham nuoi*. I've never been able to translate it into English properly but it literally means "visit and nurture." Without the supplements brought by the family, they [reeducation camp prisoners] would die of malnutrition. My uncle was somewhere in Vinh, and my grandfather further north. We went by train, the name of the train was *Tau Thong Nhat*—United Train—and the trip was very exciting for a little kid, I was, what, seven or eight years old. It was an eye opener, I got to see the whole country, and it was my dad's first time back in the north since 1954. We were dropped off at the train station, and then had to walk all the way to the camp. For a kid like me it felt like forever, I mean hours and hours of walking. My mum and dad were carrying food, and when we got there, we could only spend half an hour with my uncle. The whole trip took a month back and forth, all for a half-hour visit. And then we went from there further north to Hanoi, where my dad had relatives and friends. My grandfather was too far away so I was left with one of my dad's friends while my mum and dad went to visit my grandfather.

I have two memories of Hanoi. One was a lady selling sweet black bean dessert—*che dau den*—it smelled of jasmine, and was the best thing. The other wasn't so pleasant. We went to visit one of dad's relatives, the family lived in a small apartment and there was no toilet in the apartment, only a communal toilet for the building and that is an experience you don't want to know. It was on returning from that trip that my parents made the decision to leave Vietnam.

The term was *di chui*, which literally means going into hiding, burrowing into holes so that people don't see you. I remember that at school, every so often someone in class would disappear, and you'd think, "Oh, they're gone." Now they could have *di vuot bien*—crossed the border, escaped by boat—but then again they could have been sent to the New Economic Zones. Another memory from when the communists first took over, there was a public burning of books, a big fire. I was pretty upset because I was a keen reader and had many storybooks and comics—the Smurfs, Lucky Luke—and they were all taken out and chucked into the fire.

Tuan's narrative reveals that he found the train journey fascinating as a boy even though he realized that it was difficult for his parents, and in particular his mother. He remembers that she was "tight-lipped and sad," and that he "could see the exhaustion on her face" after she had visited her brother and father in prison camps. His account also alludes to the isolated location of the prison camps, and relatives traveling long distances and walking for kilometers for a brief half-hour reunion with a loved one. Another event that left a vivid memory in Tuan's mind was the burning of books after the communist takeover. One of the first significant acts of repression, as noted by Jacqueline Desbarats, was the burning of works at the Khai Tri publishing house in Saigon, and the arrest of its general manager.[13] She adds that:

> University professors, doctors, judges, poets, writers, journalists, publishers, actors, and producers were either sent to re-education camps or thrown in jail. Simultaneously, a campaign to "exterminate decadent literature" was set in motion.[14]

Tuan's account relates to broader events such as the "disappearance" of those who had either escaped or had been forcibly displaced to the New Economic Zones as well as to specific incidents such as the burning of books that not only affected the adults around him but also had an impact on him on a personal level.

In Australia, Tuan recalls that the five children were all aware of how hard things were so they learnt early on to not ask their parents for money and to work as soon as they could so that they could pay for their own school uniforms and other expenses. Tuan studied engineering and then spent six years working in Hong Kong to assist Vietnamese refugees there. He belonged to a Vietnamese youth group in Melbourne called *Hoa Nien* (Flower of Youth). Many members of the group went overseas to help Vietnamese refugees in 1988–1989—the point at which screening procedures first came into effect in Southeast Asia and Hong Kong. These young Vietnamese in Australia remembered their own experiences as boat people and wanted to help compatriots who now found themselves stranded in camps. Tuan's trip to Hong Kong in 1993 was funded by the organization Australian Lawyers for Refugees. He was supposed to work in Hong Kong for three months but stayed on until 1999. While Tuan's memories of the war intersperses his own recollections with stories transmitted in his family, a common thread with his sister's narrative is the importance he assigns to his grandfather and uncle's roles in the military during the war, and their effect on his immediate family.

STORIES OVERHEARD

The fifth narrative is that of Thy,[15] who was one year old when her family escaped from Vietnam by boat in 1980. A hundred and sixty people were crammed together aboard a boat measuring 10 meters. Thy has no memory of these events but she relates: "We drifted on the ocean for five nights and five days. I was there, I shared in that story." These recurrent and haunting phrases in her narrative not only anchor her part in her family story but also set it within the wider framework of the Vietnamese diaspora. Her narrative reveals the secondary trauma that she was subjected to as a result of her parents' harrowing experiences in the postwar years, their flight from Vietnam, and the difficulties and stresses of resettlement in Australia. Much of the poignancy of Thy's account stems from the fact that she lost her mother to leukemia when she was seventeen and was diagnosed with depression at the age of twenty.

Thy has had no direct communication from her father regarding his memories of the war and can only relate the stories that she "overheard" as a child. Despite this, her narrative includes a moving rendition of her father's experiences. She recounts:

> My dad fought in the war and he was in hiding [after the war] because people were trying to find him to lock him up in reeducation camp and so it was not a good time. And I think in his head, he has never let go of Vietnam. I grew up with stories about Vietnam. I don't remember Vietnam at all. I don't have a personal image of Vietnam or a personal recollection of anything that ever happened to me in Vietnam. The only ties that I have with Vietnam are my parents and the stories they told, not that they told me stories, but the stories that I would overhear. My dad used to talk a lot about the war. He spoke of it with pride because I think it was a time in his life when he had purpose, he was worth something, his life had value.
>
> I was about six or seven when I heard these stories. My older sister had to look after the younger kids but I was free to run around the house and eavesdrop on people. When my father had his mates over, they would sit on the floor and *nhac* [remind, recall] the war. It was always in the lounge room where the TV was, and as a child, if you're not in front of the TV, then there's nothing else to do so I always wanted to listen in.
>
> My father was a funny, funny man. Apparently he and his best mate in Vietnam, one of the soldiers who did the fighting with him, were the two most troublesome and mischievous guys in the village. My grandmother had a little coffee shop and, before her wedding, my mum worked at the coffee shop with my grandmother and her assistant. One day my father came in with his best mate. They ordered tea, pulled out a grenade, and chucked it in the tea, and then just sat there. Everyone went a bit nuts and ran out of the coffee shop, and my father and his mate just cracked up because they knew it was a faulty grenade. They thought they'd scare everyone. My father was a good soldier, apparently, everyone looked up to him, he commanded a lot of people. I don't know [his rank], but I know he led people.

Thy's portrayal of her father reveals the physical and mental scars of war:

> I know that he has bullet scars [indicates the location of scars] in his arms, his legs and around his belly area. When we were growing up and it was hot, he'd wear shorts around the house, and you could see these bullet wounds in his body. They're quite big, like fifty-cent coins, and the bullet has a spider type effect on the wound. He never spoke to us about the war, or how he fought or anything, and I think it's because . . . we were just so removed, as his children, from that time, that he couldn't find a connection. So that's why he never shared his stories with us. I didn't feel like I wasn't loved or think "why doesn't my dad smile at me?" or "why doesn't my dad hug me?" I never questioned that, 'cause I knew that my dad, he had bullet wounds on his body, his life must have been hard, it was the war that did that to him, being in it, seeing his friends die, that's why he's like that, and I've always accepted it.

Thy's gestures indicate that her father's embodied memory of combat injuries has in some measure transferred to her.[16] She describes her curiosity and interest as a child in obtaining indirect knowledge of her father's experiences. Her narrative reveals that the intergenerational transmission of war memories in her family was not only indirect but also partial and fragmented. Her consciousness of the precarious nature of this history is driven by her grief at her mother's premature death and the difficulty of communicating with her father. She is aware of the many silences and lacunae in this family history. Her narrative reveals what Marianne Hirsch and Leo Spitzer, writing about the children of Holocaust survivors, refer to as a "postmemory, a secondary, belated memory mediated by stories, images and behaviours among which [they] grew up, but which never added up to a complete or linear tale."[17] Although Thy states that she understands why her father is undemonstrative, her words reveal the pain caused by his physical and emotional distance from his children. Her rendition of the war appears in the guise of glimpses and vignettes, as striking and as elusive as the bullet scars that she saw on her father's body when she was a child.

STORIES TOLD DIRECTLY

The last narrative is that of Thien,[18] the youngest of the six. Thien was born in 1985 in Hobart, Tasmania. As there were few Vietnamese refugees living in Tasmania, Thien and her parents mostly associated with

Australians rather than with other Vietnamese. It may have been because of this relative isolation from the Vietnamese Australian community that Thien's father was able to speak openly about his experiences and convey his memories directly to his daughter. Thien's father receives an Australian service pension and Thien pointed out that it was difficult to secure this for him because in 1975, he disposed of all his documents, including love letters to Thien's mother, in order to erase his documented identity before the communist government took over. She relates:

> I know that my father fought for the South Vietnamese military and, after the war, he was sent to a reeducation camp for seven years. During that time, my mother tried to escape from Vietnam. It was under my father's instructions—he'd said that he wasn't sure when he would come out. My mother tried to escape with my brother, who was then about eight or nine years old but they were caught and put in some kind of cage in the town square for a week. When my dad was released, they were able to escape from Vietnam but people died on the way. Thai pirates boarded the boat and raped many of the women. When my parents arrived at the refugee camp, everyone had to be quarantined and several women had to have abortions. It was a horrible time. My mother was one of the very few women who found a hiding place on the boat and stayed safe.

Of her father's military experience, she states:

> My father was a second lieutenant in Intelligence in . . . I think it was the 7th Battalion. He was about to start university but decided to join the army instead. I know that he went to cadet school. I've seen photos of him in uniform. He looks really happy. He was really excited to be, you know, fighting for something. He still firmly believes that what he did was the right thing. War is a terrible thing but he was fighting for his country's independence. He recounts his time in training as quite fun. He and his friends were out in the fields practicing shooting and somehow his friend hit a stick and the stick hit a bird and the bird died but there was no bullet to be found. And then the war got worse. At first he was able to come home every week and visit Mum and his family. Then he got posted further away and came home less and less. I've often heard Dad say that he can't cry. He's often talked about having to pick up his fellow soldiers' remains and put them in a bag and send them home.
>
> As for my brother, he grew up with women only: my mother, her sisters and my grandmother. I remember when Dad, well, I wasn't there, but Mum told me that when Dad came home from prison, my brother didn't know him and wasn't interested in hanging out with him. They didn't know each

other. Now that my brother has children of his own, things have changed. I think they have a really good relationship now.

Thien's account reveals the direct transmission of war memories between the generations. Her retelling of the past is vivid and illustrates the extent to which she has absorbed her parents' experiences. She often relates them as if they were "her" memories. Several times throughout the course of her narrative she states "I remember" and then qualifies it with a "well, I wasn't there." Thien transmits information that she not only heard as a child but that was confirmed when she grew older and that she then formalized in writing. These different layers of transmission provide for a richly textured recounting of her parents' war and postwar memories.

MEMORIES AND NARRATIVES BETWEEN GENERATIONS

In an essay on loss, Eva Hoffman writes that, "Loss leaves a long trail in its wake. Sometimes, if the loss is large enough, the trail sweeps and winds like invisible psychic ink through individual lives, decades, and generations."[19] War and loss have left a psychic imprint in the lives of these six individuals. Their stories reveal multiple narrative layers. The memories of the older generation, whether conveyed directly or indirectly, constitute one layer. The collective history of the Vietnamese diaspora and the wider context of the refugee experience constitute a second layer, while the narrators' own perceptions, memories, and reinterpretations constitute a third layer. Their accounts reveal different modes of telling and hearing stories between the generations. The intergenerational transmission of war memories is further complicated by the ruptures of the diasporic experience. All six witnessed the suffering of loved ones and experienced the difficulties of life in the aftermath of war and forced migration. The challenge, in the words of Hoffman, is "[h]ow to acknowledge another's grief without being swallowed up by it oneself; how to gain one's own autonomy without abandoning those who need us."[20]

The narratives of Hai and Nghiem, both of whom were born in the 1960s, reveal the most difficult postwar and post-migration experiences. Before 1975, they recall ordinary concerns such as going to school, taking part in festivities with their families, and outings such as riding pillion on their father's motorbike. The end of the war in 1975 was a watershed in their lives, and signaled a downward spiral into years of insecurity and deprivation. The arrest of Hai's father was followed by Hai's expulsion from school, and the interrupted education of his siblings. He remembers: "I lived in a state of confused anxiety. I did not know what the next day would bring. Life was very dark." Hai refers to his "personal history" as problematic in the eyes of the postwar authorities. He and his siblings were barred from leading normal lives because their father was a former serviceman. Nghiem, for his part, recalls dangerous trips to the Cambodian border to visit his father in the reeducation camp, food shortages after the war, the disappearance of siblings at sea, internment, and hard labor. From their accounts, it is clear that both Hai and Nghiem were scarred by the cumulative stresses and losses of the postwar years. They were then separated from their parents and siblings when they escaped from Vietnam and resettled overseas. Their early years in Australia were marked by isolation, loneliness, and grief. Hai states that he was "too old" when he arrived in Australia—too old to return to school, to seek the education that he had been deprived of in Vietnam, to reconstruct his life. He was only twenty-five but the accumulated traumas that he endured and his crippling car accident seem to have shattered his life. Nghiem gave up on the dreams and hopes he had entertained regarding a new life in Australia. Both men remain haunted by the scenes of violence and death that they witnessed, whether it was the sight of a soldier shot to death in front of them, children dying in postwar labor camps, or the rape of refugee women and girls by pirates. The events of 1975 caused an abrupt sundering in their family's history. Their lives are characterized by a discontinuity between past and present, a discontinuity that further alienated them from their own sense of family and history, and made the process of rebuilding their lives in a different country and culture even more challenging. The tragedies of the postwar years eroded the secure foundations on which they had hoped to build new lives. Even if they had wanted to fully reconnect with their fathers, reclaim their family history, and seek more details about the role their fathers may have played during the war, they would not have been able to, as the fathers of both suffered permanent damage to their physical and mental health as a result of internment. Although Hai and Nghiem were only children during the war and have scant knowledge of their fathers' military pasts, they suffered by association in the postwar years. War and the political aftermath of war have cast a long shadow over the lives of both men.

Ngoc's account, on the other hand, reveals a mixture of remembered experiences as well as memories of war and exodus transmitted by her parents and other family members. While she is strongly marked by the diasporic experience, her main concern is how to deal with this past and this history in terms of the future, in particular the future of her Australian-born children. How can she inform them of their history and heritage when she is ambivalent about the act of remembering? She avers that she is not interested in history or in remembering the past and yet each negative statement is followed by the admission that it is important to do so. She relates:

> I have never thought of going back to Vietnam because I left the country as a refugee and it was a very treacherous journey and I felt that by going back I'd be betraying all the people who have lost their lives and all the soldiers who have risked their life to defend our country, so that's why I haven't returned.
>
> Now that I have children of my own, I want them to know about Vietnam and they have been asking me questions. I find that I don't know much so that's why I need to read up on things so as to be able to tell them. One day I will need to take my children to Vietnam.

Her account stresses her loyalty to the memory of the dead—civilian as well as military—of wartime and postwar Vietnam. Her narrative attests to a conflicted embrace of the past coupled with a difficult admission that she needs to acknowledge this past if she and her family are to move forward with their lives in Australia. Her brother Tuan, for his part, acknowledges that a busy life involving family and career leaves him with little time for reflection. He admits, "As adults reflecting on the war, to be honest, we don't have time to think about these things, which is very sad, as the war is part of our history. However, it does interest me to hear about the war, and to see it from the perspectives of different individuals." His narrative includes vivid depictions of specific events that he either witnessed or that would have been recounted to him by family members. He demonstrates the same sense of loyalty as his sister toward relatives who served in the South Vietnamese military, and the refugees who fled Vietnam in the postwar years. This loyalty had its practical application in the six years that he spent providing aid and assistance to Vietnamese refugees in Hong Kong in the 1990s. He remembers that he had a passion for the work that he did. In spite of the difficulties experienced in the postwar years, Ngoc and Tuan have both been sustained by the fact that their family unit remained intact through adversity and hardship—their father was only in reeducation for a brief period, and the parents and children were able to escape the country together, survive the boat journey, stay together at the refugee camp, and rebuild their lives in Australia.

Thy was born after the end of the war, and was too young to remember her family's experience of exodus from Vietnam. Her narrative reveals, however, that both events have had an enduring emotional impact on her life. Her account conveys her father's former identity and status in South Vietnam: he was a soldier, he was proud to serve his country, and he bore visible scars of this service. The successive losses that he sustained—of friends, family, country, profession, and freedom—and the stresses of the refugee experience eroded this identity. It may be for this reason that he needs to, in Thy's words quoted earlier, "*nhac*"—remind, recall—the war and his role in the war with his contemporaries. While this process of recall is important to him, it is an aspect of his life that he has not been able to share with his children. Thy's narrative reveals the continuing shadow cast by the past. Grief-ridden and painful as it is, this past is also, however, a link to her mother and father. Thy underlines the importance of history and heritage for the second generation of Vietnamese overseas. She makes the following plea for the transmission of stories between the generations:

> I think that parents should be encouraged to talk about their story and their history, 'cause for children, it's their only connection to Vietnam, it's through their stories. And if they're not sharing them, then their children are basically cut off. If you don't share stories of what happened in Vietnam, then, you know, you've lost it. You can't expect your child to understand. And if you don't have a history, if you don't know your history, you can't know yourself. In terms of cultural identity, I think a lot of us [second generation] are lost, because we lack that history, because the first generation has not shared that story with us. And because the second generation hasn't asked the first generation to share that story.

Her narrative reveals the difficulty of communicating traumatic history across the generations, especially when this process occurs within the context of forced migration. She believes that without these shared histories and stories from the previous generation, however, the second generation will be cut adrift and "lost." Her words also allude to communication between the generations being a matter of will and intent: the first generation needs to transmit its stories to the second generation while the second generation should also want to hear the accounts of the first generation.

Thien, for her part, was able to obtain stories directly from her parents, in particular her father. Her father, like Thy's, had an identity and status as a soldier in South Vietnam before 1975. He volunteered to join the army, he fought for his country's independence and he believed his cause to be worthy. Thien relates that, like many others in the closing days of the war, he destroyed all evidence of his former life.[21] This destruction, however, is counterbalanced by his later willingness to speak to his daughter and to others about his experiences. Thien's narrative illustrates an interesting paradox. While she was marked by her parents' experiences and has in some measure appropriated their stories, her understanding and empathy were accompanied by an early disassociation from her Asian or Vietnamese identity. This disassociation may have been a defense mechanism to insulate her from the traumatic nature of her parents' experiences. Her narrative reveals in this way a more robust and resilient personality than Thy's. She recounts:

> I'm not sure if this is a product of my upbringing, but when I was growing up I didn't really associate myself as being, one, Asian or, two, Vietnamese. I was disassociated from my heritage. I knew what my parents had been through and I thought that was an important part of who I was but I never recognized myself as Asian, none of my friends were Asian so when I actually moved from Tasmania to [Melbourne], it was a huge culture shock for me.
>
> My parents took me to Springvale [an area full of Vietnamese shops] and I saw all these Vietnamese people around and the market atmosphere and I was like "Wow," I was so freaked out. I remember writing a letter home and saying to my friends in Tassie [Tasmania], "I can't handle this, there are Asian people everywhere" and in the middle of writing that I thought, "Oh, I'm Asian and I look exactly the same." I had an identity crisis. I remember having an argument with my parents about this and saying, "You've brought me up in this way and now you expect me to embrace Vietnamese culture. How am I supposed to do so?" I would refuse to go to Victoria Street [another area full of Vietnamese shops] with my mum. It was almost like reverse racism. I couldn't deal with it. I think my parents really sensed that so they kept on trying. Now that I am associated with a Vietnamese women's organisation in Australia, I think they're really happy about it.

Thien was able to reconcile her Australian identity with her Vietnamese heritage and this reconciliation is symbolized by her work for a Vietnamese Australian welfare organization.

While these narratives reveal different modes of transmission as well as individual reinterpretations of their family stories, common threads do emerge. The first is that the stories are not only mediated by memories of war but also by the experience of forced migration. The second is that many families were splintered during and after the war, with negative consequences in terms of familial relationships. The third is the need of the older generation to remember their homeland and their lives before 1975.

In many families, the father (or other male relative) was away fighting during the war and was then either in hiding from the communist authorities or interned in reeducation camps after the war. Children often grew up without their father while their mother struggled to manage the household and earn a living as a single parent. Fathers who were incarcerated for lengthy periods in remote prison camps were essentially "lost" to their children in the postwar years. When the father returned after years of internment, he was a stranger to his children and they were strangers to him. This was the case with Hai and Nghiem. Ngoc retells the story of her uncle and aunt and their children, and the fact that this separation led to difficulties and clashes between the father and his children in terms of discipline. Thien relates similar problems between her father and her brother in postwar Vietnam, but tempers this history with the assertion that father and son were able to rebuild their relationship once the family had migrated to Australia and her brother had children of his own. Hai and Nghiem escaped from Vietnam and did not see their fathers for many years. The cost of this separation has left enduring scars in the lives of many Vietnamese immigrants and placed an added strain on intergenerational tensions. The narratives reveal that the fathers had difficulty in readjusting not only to family life but also to civilian life. The situation in southern Vietnam was exacerbated by the fact that all those associated in any way with the former regime, whether military or civilian, were discriminated against by the postwar communist authorities.[22] Children were prevented from furthering their education, and expelled from schools, colleges, or universities. Families who attempted to cross the border and were caught by the authorities were fined if they were lucky, or imprisoned and sent to labor camps.[23]

The narrators' knowledge of the war experiences of their fathers, uncles, or grandfathers is partial and incomplete. Many details remain unclear: the rank that the male relatives held in the army, the unit or units in which they served, where and when they served. This lack of knowledge cannot be remedied or supplemented by documents because there are few or no surviving documents. The refugee experience further complicated the relationship between parent and child by adding linguistic and cultural barriers.

As these accounts illustrate, the legacy of war extends not only across generations but also across national boundaries. Nicolas Argenti and Katharina Schramm ask:

> How does violence affect remembering? How are the large-scale cataclysms, crises, disasters and dispersals that befall communities entrusted by one generation of witnesses to the next? If bearing witness to violence cannot be a disinterested act, and if memory—despite its relationship to the past—is always deployed in the present, a question arises regarding the mediation of memory, or the relationship of remembering to forgetting.[24]

Memories of violence and loss, and the stories of internment and separation of Vietnamese families are shaped by their experience of displacement and resettlement in another country. The Australian context of these narratives needs to be examined. The Vietnam War is remembered as a controversial war in which over 500 Australians lost their lives. Although Australian soldiers were denied the status accorded to previous generations of Anzacs when they returned home from the war,[25] they left a positive imprint in South Vietnam. The Australian Task Force in Phuoc Tuy Province established relations with the local Vietnamese population that were described by veteran war correspondent Denis Warner as "exemplary."[26] The people of the province erected a memorial to Australian soldiers outside the provincial capital of Ba Ria and plans were underway for an Australian Vietnamese library and museum next to the memorial when Saigon fell.[27] The Vietnamese who sought refuge in Australia after the end of the war form an extension to the history of Australian involvement in the Vietnam War. The shared Vietnamese and Australian experience of war is acknowledged in Australia. The service of RVNAF veterans is recognized at a national level by their entitlement to Australian war pensions and their participation in commemorative marches.[28] In 2005, the opening of the Vietnam War Memorial in Dandenong in the state of Victoria, by then Governor-General Michael Jeffery, represented the outcome of collaborative fund-raising by Vietnamese veterans, Vietnamese community associations, and RSL Dandenong, and was a visible symbol of cross-cultural remembrance and commemoration of military losses in the war. The memorial includes the bronze statues of two soldiers—an Australian soldier and a South Vietnamese soldier—standing side by side under a Huey helicopter donated by the U.S. Army and flown over to Australia by the RSL. The memorial is an eloquent reminder that South Vietnamese and Australian soldiers fought as allies during the war.[29]

These narratives deal not only with postwar discourses within the Vietnamese community and the wider Australian context but also with underlying issues of identity and belonging for the different generations. "Identities, individual and collective," suggest Susannah Radstone and Bill Schwartz, "are formed and re-formed through narrative, in history and through adversity."[30] For the older generation of Vietnamese, the formation and reformation of identity occurred through war, exodus, and resettlement. Their stories describe identities transformed by loss: loss of country, citizenship, and status. For many veterans, past identities were closely interwoven with their service to South Vietnam. More than three decades after the end of the war, these men remain loyal to the memory of their former homeland. They have transmitted this loyalty to the younger generation.

The narratives of Hai, Nghiem, Ngoc, Tuan, Thy, and Thien acknowledge this enduring loyalty to the Vietnamese past. While Australia signifies home—even if the sense of place in Australia is problematic as is the case with Hai—Vietnam and the shadow cast by the war continue to exert a formative influence on their lives. In the final analysis, while there may be a dearth of public knowledge about the histories of soldiers who served in the RVNAF, these children and grandchildren of veterans privilege the experiences of their fathers, grandfathers, or uncles. Their transmission of war stories and memories reveals a tension between private and public history, and between the reluctance to record the past and the imperative to do so. While Australia represents the present and the future, the narratives of these six individuals are shaped by the lives of the previous generation, and bear the imprint of the past.

CONCLUSION

Le pays d'avant
Il n'existe plus
Il est perdu
On n'a jamais su
On l'a jamais vu

(The country from before
Is no more
It is lost
We never knew it
We never saw it)

—Thanh-Vân Tôn-Thât[1]

South Vietnam represents "the country from before" for all those who believed in and fought for it, and for the younger generations of the diaspora for whom it remains a country they never knew. The narratives of these former soldiers convey unforgettable images of their homeland through decades of war. Their recollections of combat and of the hardships and dangers of life on the front line are interspersed with memories of their childhood and youth, the faces of loved ones, and scenes of daily life in South Vietnam. Their military service in wartime was followed by internment, forced labor, and forced migration after the war. The life histories of these veterans have been shaped not only by war but also by postwar incarceration and the refugee experience. Their narratives highlight the scale of the mass migration from north to south in 1954, including the departure of many northern Buddhists opposed to communism, the extent of North Vietnamese military buildup and infiltration into South Vietnam during the war, and the strength of southern patriotism. The level of communist brutality during and after the war, the strong sense of abandonment felt by the people and soldiers of South Vietnam, and the enduring loyalty to the southern cause are also elucidated in these accounts.

There were scenes of terrible suffering and despair in the last days of South Vietnam. As the northernmost cities fell following the 1975 North Vietnamese invasion, South Vietnam's few arterial roads were clogged with thousands of civilian refugees fleeing south. These impeded the ability of the army to maneuver and roads became sites of carnage as civilians and soldiers died under enemy shelling. Armor was a key factor in the North Vietnamese victory.[2] Columns of Soviet-built T54 tanks rolled south as I Corps and II Corps collapsed. The memoir of former Marine Cao Xuan Huy relates that many Marines who found themselves stranded on the coast near Hue at the end of March committed suicide rather than surrender:

> Without prompting or urging, without making arrangements, and most of them didn't seem to know, or were unable to recognize each other in the moments before their death. One person would peel himself away from the stream of runners and sit down on the sand, another peeled off and sat down next to him, then another and another joined in. They sat in a tight huddle, and a grenade blew up in the middle.[3]

Nguyen Viet Long[4] took part in the naval evacuation of soldiers and civilians from Danang in March 1975. His ship was able to take on 5,000 people but he remembers the plight of 4,000 or 5,000 refugees who made their way onto a pontoon towed by a smaller ship. The journey from Danang to Vung Tau took three to four days and during that time, a third of those on the pontoon died of exposure. Long's brother, a twenty-three-year-old officer in the Marines, was killed in action in Hue, "in the 25th hour of the war" as Long relates.

"War," writes Michael Humphrey, "involves the destruction of people and their worlds. It involves laying waste life and property. And when the war is over its legacies live on in personal memories, bodily scars and destroyed cultural landscapes. People and landscapes remain contaminated by war for the long term."[5] The following lines by Trinh Cong Son of a young woman grieving a dead soldier epitomize the mourning of the people of the south:

> You walk over the bridge
> Gunfire echoes after you

> Villages in the country
> Are tinged with sorrow
>
> You walk over the bridge
> A gentle breeze blows
> Carrying your heart
> To an unknown place.[6]

Anh[7] was a pharmacy student at the University of Saigon in the 1960s, and remembers that, "there were a lot of songs, sad songs about the love of a soldier, the life of a soldier, the loss of a soldier. Some of these songs are still popular now."[8]

At the town of Xuan Loc northeast of Saigon between April 9 and 21, 1975, the 18th Infantry Division and Long Khanh provincial forces, under the command of Brigadier General Le Minh Dao, held off massive combined-arms attacks by an entire North Vietnamese army corps comprising three divisions supported by armor and artillery.[9] The gallant defense of Xuan Loc was one of the fiercest battles of the war and one of its least known. The 18th Division succeeded in halting the communist offensive against vastly superior odds.[10] When the division was ordered to retreat on April 20, it did so in good order the following day. Its commander, Le Minh Dao, was to spend seventeen years in the gulag after the war.[11] Acts of bravery in the final days of the war include that of Lieutenant Vu Dinh Long, who ordered his crew to bail out of their armed cargo aircraft AC119K while he steered the stricken plane out to sea so as to avoid civilian casualties on the ground.[12] Their plane had attacked an enemy convoy of T54 tanks, armored vehicles, and Molotova trucks heading south before it was hit by antiaircraft fire. All nine of the crew survived but the pilot was never seen again. They knew that he had parachuted out of the plane into the sea and that local fishermen had tried to rescue him before coming under enemy fire themselves. Thirty-seven years later, the men of his former crew still mourn his loss.[13] Among the accounts of resistance to advancing communist forces was that of cadets from the Junior Military Academy in Vung Tau. More than 100 boys aged between twelve and fifteen put up a stiff resistance for a few hours.[14] "At last, after accepting a truce," writes Nguyen Cong Luan, "the young boys stood at attention to strike the national colors. Then they snuck out the back gates and into the nearby neighborhood. Communist forces had no choice but to let them go."[15]

The Vietnamese who sought refuge overseas after the war brought with them South Vietnam's aspirations to become a free and democratic state. Their country may have been lost to them but in seeking to reconstruct lives for themselves and their families in a new land, refugees carried with them the hopes that South Vietnam had embodied. In the early years following resettlement, refugees focused on working several jobs to support their families overseas and adapting to different countries and cultures. While the plight of boat people received international recognition, few comprehended the reasons why refugees were leaving their homeland in such unprecedented numbers. The experiences of Vietnamese refugees in the wake of the Vietnam War echo those of East European refugees in the wake of the Second World War. Both groups were confronted with a similar lack of understanding on the part of their host communities as to their reasons for fleeing communism.[16]

The diaspora and resettlement overseas have enabled Vietnamese veterans to remember and record their experiences of the war. In Australia, Vietnamese veterans have marched on Anzac Day since 1981.[17] The large numbers marching in the 1980s were notable for such a new refugee community. They revealed the veterans' pride in their service and their gratitude that they were given the opportunity to remember their country and their cause at a public commemorative event. The presence of the Vietnamese community and the role of its members in the war are making an impact on wider Australian society, and leading to altered perceptions of the war and gradual shifts in understanding. In his 2006 R.G. Neale Lecture on the fall of Saigon, Peter Edwards noted:

> A year ago many newspapers devoted extensive space to articles marking the 30th anniversary of the fall of Saigon. What was strikingly different in this coverage, compared with similar exercises in the immediate aftermath of the war, was the impact made by Australians of Vietnamese origin. Individuals, including former diplomats and officers of the former South Vietnamese regime, and their families told their stories, and in the process wove a new strand into the fabric of the Australian national narrative.[18]

In the absence of a public space in which to remember and commemorate the war in their own country, Vietnamese veterans' only avenues for commemoration lie overseas—among veterans of the war, the Vietnamese diasporic community, and their new host societies. As members of refugee and migrant communities in their new countries, Vietnamese veterans have a unique double lens on the war. Veterans have shown a determination to keep their history, and their individual stories, alive. While many of their publications remain "in-house" in that they are generally available only in Vietnamese and have a limited circulation outside the Vietnamese community, the existence of these writings nevertheless attests to a strong desire by the veterans themselves to remember and record their unit histories, their personal experiences of service, and the stories of friends and compatriots who died in the war, in postwar internment camps or as refugees. The veterans' persistence in continuing to honor their service in the face of negative representations of their country and armed forces underlines the value they accord to their military past. Their stories and memories raise "questions," in the words of Selma Leydesdorff, Luisa Passerini, and Paul Thompson, "on the historical past, but also questions about how contemporary society deals with the historical past."[19] The reception of their stories by their host communities relates not only to shifts in the understanding of the war but also to the ways in which resettlement countries contend with experiences of loss, grief, and trauma among minority communities.

In telling their stories, veterans have provided personal testimonies of their service. As Nancy Miller and Jason Tougaw note, "Testimony records a movement from individual experience to the collective archive, from personal trauma to public memory."[20] In the midst of the grief and mourning associated with the loss of their army and country, these narratives have also enabled veterans to record positive elements—loyalty to their cause, courage and resilience in the midst of adversity, affection for those who served beside them, pride in their service, and their determination to weave their history and experiences into the fabric of their adopted country.

NOTES

PREFACE AND ACKNOWLEDGMENTS

1. Pham Van Chuong, interview by author, June 26, 2013, Melbourne. NLA ORAL TRC 6525/8.

2. Photographer Keith Broad kindly gave permission for the use of the photograph.

3. Veterans were provided with broad questions such as "What are your memories of your childhood/youth/family?" These questions were not prescriptive and were only there to suggest possible topics for discussion.

4. John C. Schafer, *Vietnamese Perspectives on the War in Vietnam: Annotated Bibliography of Works in English* (New Haven: Yale University Council on Southeast Asian Studies, 1996), 1. http://www.yale.edu/seas/bibliography/home.html

INTRODUCTION

1. Thuong Vuong-Riddick, *Two Shores/Deux rives* (Vancouver: Ronsdale Press, 1995), 40. Reprinted here by permission.

2. Nguyen Trieu Dan, *A Vietnamese Family Chronicle: Twelve Generations on the Banks of the Hat River* (Jefferson, NC: McFarland, 1991).

3. Nguyen, *Vietnamese Family Chronicle*, 162.

4. Nguyen, *Vietnamese Family Chronicle*, 162.

5. Nguyen, *Vietnamese Family Chronicle*, 165.

6. Nguyen, *Vietnamese Family Chronicle*, 168.

7. Nguyen, *Vietnamese Family Chronicle*, 168.

8. Nguyen, *Vietnamese Family Chronicle*, 187 and 193–194. "The Academy had a right to remonstrate against governmental wrongdoings, but mainly

its work was in the fields of education and research, away from the pressure of day to day government." Nguyen, *Vietnamese Family Chronicle*, 193.

9. Nguyen, *Vietnamese Family Chronicle*, 60.

10. Nguyen, *Vietnamese Family Chronicle*, 8.

11. François Guillemot writes that up to 50,000 Vietnamese may have died between 1945 and 1947. He notes that although violence did occur on both sides of politics, it was much more systematic on the part of the Viet Minh. See François Guillemot, "Au cœur de la fracture vietnamienne: L'élimination de l'opposition nationaliste et anticolonialiste dans le Nord du Vietnam (1945–1946) (At the Heart of the Vietnamese Fracture: The Elimination of Nationalist and Anticolonial Opposition in Northern Vietnam (1945–1946))." In Christopher E. Goscha and Benoît De Tréglodé, eds. *Naissance d'un Etat-Parti: Le Viêt Nam depuis 1945 / The Birth of a Party-State: Vietnam since 1945* (Paris: Les Indes Savantes, 2004), 208–209.

12. From *Phoi Pha* (1960) by Trinh Cong Son. Translation by Quynh-Du Ton That reprinted here by permission. Additional line break inserted at the request of Quynh-Du Ton That in email correspondence to the author on September 7, 2015. http://damau.org/archives/11356

13. Anthony James Joes, *The War for South Viet Nam 1954–1975*. Rev. Ed. (Westport: Praeger, 2001), 102.

14. K. W. Taylor, "Introduction: Voices from the South." In K. W. Taylor, ed. *Voices from the Second Republic of South Vietnam (1967–1975)* (Ithaca, NY: Cornell Southeast Asia Program Publications, 2015), 1.

15. See Tran Quang Minh, "A Decade of Public Service: Nation Building during the Interregnum and Second Republic (1964–75)." In Taylor, *Voices*, 39–87.

16. Taylor, "Introduction," 4–5.

17. Dang Phong, ed. *Lich Su Kinh Te Viet Nam 1945–2000* (Vietnamese Economic History 1945–2000), Vol II: 1955–1975 (Hanoi: Social Sciences Publishing House, 2005), 85. My thanks to Nguyen Ngoc Phach and Phuong Mai Ung for the Vietnamese translation.

18. During the 1968 Tet Offensive, thousands of civilians in Hue were massacred during the communist occupation of the city. See Neil L. Jamieson, *Understanding Vietnam* (Berkeley: University of California Press, 1995), 320–321.

"Among the reports concerning the number of victims, the most reliable came from the police department of Hue-Thua Thien, which compiled information from the authorities of the village level and records of every mass grave. According to Major Lien Thanh, chief of Hue-Thua Thien Police

Department in 1968, in his book, there were 5,327 bodies found in twenty-six mass graves; about 1,200 were reported as missing. There has been no information about the fate of the missing. Civilians were executed by communist units all around the country, but only in Hue were they done so systematically and in so great a number." Nguyen Cong Luan, *Nationalist in the Viet Nam Wars: Memoirs of a Victim Turned Soldier* (Bloomington: Indiana University Press, 2012), 334.

19. "Tu Trung" was the pen name and "Vu Nhat Huy" the full name. The pen name is affixed in front of the actual name.

20. Nguyen Ngoc Phach, interview by author, March 18, 2013, Melbourne. NLA ORAL TRC 6525/3.

21. "Communist guerrillas . . . were killing off the very cream of South Viet Nam's middle class: officials, medical personnel, social workers, schoolteachers. Teachers were a special target of Viet Cong assassination; many of them were nationalists, and all of them knew enough about politics to become opinion leaders in villages. This 'campaign of terror in the countryside' took the lives of 20 percent of the village chiefs in South Viet Nam by the end of 1958. In 1960 alone, terrorists killed 1,400 local officials and civilians. By 1965, the total number of civilians killed (excluding battle deaths) or abducted had reached 25,000." Joes, *War for South Viet Nam*, 49.

Between 1965 and 1972, 33,052 civilians were killed and 57,970 kidnapped in communist terror incidents. Thomas C. Thayer, *War without Fronts: The American Experience in Vietnam* (Boulder: Westview Press, 1985), 51. Table 5.6. Thayer's figures are from Southeast Asia Statistical Summary, Office of the Assistant Secretary of Defense (Comptroller), April 11, 1973, 1–9. Thayer adds that, "the figures showing persons killed do not include the entire toll exacted by the communists. Many additional civilians were killed in communist attacks and other actions not included in the terrorism report." Thayer, *War without Fronts*, 50.

22. Joes, *War for South Viet Nam*, 49.

23. Joes, *War for South Viet Nam*, 49–50, 59.

24. Joes, *War for South Viet Nam*, 50.

25. Lien-Hang T. Nguyen, *Hanoi's War: An International History of the War for Peace in Vietnam* (Chapel Hill: The University of North Carolina Press, 2012), 2. Lien-Hang Nguyen's book is based on more than ten years of research in the Vietnam National Archives and libraries and academic centers in Vietnam as well as unprecedented access to the Archives of the Vietnam Ministry of Foreign Affairs.

26. Nguyen, *Hanoi's War*, 47.

27. Nguyen, *Hanoi's War*, 44–47.

28. Nguyen, *Hanoi's War*, 45–52.

29. Nguyen, *Hanoi's War*, 64–65.

30. "The VWP first secretary could either negotiate with the new southern regime and consolidate the insurgency's military victories or he could accelerate the war to attempt a total military victory before the Americans, whose presence now numbered 16,000 advisors, could further intervene. With the upcoming Ninth Plenum in late 1963, Le Duan set his sights on the latter option, just as his American counterparts would do during the 'long 1964.' His success meant that the militant hawks achieved the categorical response in 1963 that they wanted in 1959: mobilization of the entire country behind the war effort through a marked increase in the rate of infiltration of arms, matériel, and troops to the South . . . Attempting total victory over the RVN before the Americans could intervene, Le Duan was essentially 'going for broke' in 1964." Nguyen, *Hanoi's War*, 63–65.

31. Dong Van Khuyen, *The RVNAF* (Washington D.C.: U.S. Army Center of Military History, 1980), 276.

32. "The Communist Tet general offensive actually caused the armed forces and people of South Vietnam to strengthen their determination and become more closely united. The number of youths volunteering to serve in the armed forces increased remarkably." Dong, *RVNAF*, 17.

"[R]ight after the enemy general offensive started, the number of male Vietnamese under the age of twenty who enlisted as volunteers to serve ARVN combat units was more than double the planned intake of draftees." Nguyen, *Nationalist in the Viet Nam Wars*, 330.

Lam Quang Thi refers to the high number of volunteers for the National Military Academy in the fall of 1968: "For the 400 slots for the freshman class, there were about 4,000 applicants. This high turnout was due to the fact that many young men—quite a few of them university students—had witnessed VC terror tactics in urban centers during the Tet Offensive and decided to serve in the Army to fight against the Communists." Lam Quang Thi, *The Twenty-Five Year Century: A South Vietnamese General Remembers the Indochina War to the Fall of Saigon* (Denton: University of North Texas Press, 2001), 225–226.

33. See George J. Veith, *Black April: The Fall of South Vietnam 1973–1975* (New York: Encounter Books, 2012), 6–7.

34. See Veith, *Black April*, 6.

35. Joes, *War for South Viet Nam*, 135.

36. My thanks to Merle Pribbenow, the translator of the *Official History of the People's Army of Vietnam: 1945–1975*, published in English as *Victory in Vietnam* by the University Press of Kansas in 2002, for providing me with this overall figure and for sending me his detailed file on North Vietnamese troop infiltration into South Vietnam between 1959 and 1975.

Pribbenow's figures are compiled from North Vietnamese histories including: *Victory in Vietnam*; *Lich Su Bo Doi Truong Son Duong Ho Chi Minh* (History of the Annamite Mountain Troops on the Ho Chi Minh Trail) (Hanoi: People's Army Publishing House, 1994); *Lich Su Cong Tac Dang, Cong Tac Chinh Tri Chien Dich Trong Khang Chien Chong Phap va Chong My, 1945–1975* (History of Party and Political Operations in the Campaigns Conducted During the Resistance Wars Against France and the United States, 1945–1975) (Hanoi: People's Army Publishing House, 1998); *Lich Su Khang Chien Chong My, Cuu Nuoc 1954–1975, Tap VII: Thang Loi Quyet Dinh Nam 1972* (History of the Resistance War Against the Americans to Save the Nation, 1954–1975, Vol VII: The Decisive Victory in 1972) (Hanoi: National Political Publishing House, 2007); *Lich su Quan y Doan 559 bo doi Truong Son-Duong Ho Chi Minh (luu hanh noi bo)* (Group 559 Annamite Mountain-Ho Chi Minh Trail Troops Medical History (for internal distribution only)) (Hanoi: People's Army Publishing House, 2004); *Tong Ket Cuoc Khang Chien Chong My Cuu Nuoc: Thang Loi va Bai Hoc* (Review of the Resistance War Against the Americans to Save the Nation: Victory and Lessons) (Hanoi: National Political Publishing House, 1995); and *Tran Quyet Chien Lich Su Xuan 1975* (The Historic Decisive Battle of Spring 1975) (Hanoi: Ministry of Defense, 1990). Pribbenow notes that the figures in *Tran Quyet Chien Lich Su Xuan 1975* add up to 930,000 troops sent south in 1965–1975, and that when added to the 50,000 sent south in 1959–1964, the overall total comes to at least 980,000 North Vietnamese troops.

37. Pribbenow draws these figures from *Tran Quyet Chien Lich Su Xuan 1975*, 162 and 164.

38. Lewis Sorley, "Could the War Have Been Won?" In John Norton Moore and Robert F. Turner, eds. *The Real Lessons of the Vietnam War: Reflections Twenty-Five Years after the Fall of Saigon* (Durham, NC: Carolina Academic Press, 2003), 417–418.

39. Sorley, "Could the War Have Been Won?," 418.

40. Lam, *Twenty-Five Year Century*, 257. See Dong Van Khuyen for a detailed analysis of the forms and causes of corruption as well as RVNAF anticorruption efforts. Dong, *RVNAF*, 341–378.

41. Lam, *Twenty-Five Year Century*, 257.

42. Dong, *RVNAF*, 139.

43. Robert Brigham, *ARVN: Life and Death in the South Vietnamese Army* (Lawrence: University Press of Kansas, 2006), 49.

44. Dong, *RVNAF*, 139–143. "Five causes were cited by deserters to justify their actions: (1) homesickness brought about by separation from their families; (2) dislike of units to which assigned; (3) dislike of military service, abhorrence of killings; (4) discontent with commanders; (5) poverty and inadequacy of military pay to support families." Dong, *RVNAF*, 139.

On the other hand, nearly 160,000 communist troops defected to the South Vietnamese government between 1962 and 1975. See a detailed examination of the Chieu Hoi program in Nguyen, *Nationalist in the Viet Nam Wars*, 342–356.

45. Joes, *War for South Viet Nam*, 92–93.

46. Phan Dong Bich, interview by Judith Winternitz, May 25, 1986, Sydney. NLA ORAL TRC 2010 S/86, 20.

47. United Nations High Commissioner for Refugees, *The State of the World's Refugees: Fifty Years of Humanitarian Action* (Oxford: Oxford University Press, 2000), 82.

48. Jacqueline Desbarats, "Human Rights: Two Steps Forward, One Step Backward?" In Thai Quang Trung, ed. *Vietnam Today: Assessing the New Trends* (New York: Crane Russak, a member of the Taylor & Francis Group, 1990), 60.

49. Desbarats, "Human Rights," 63; Nguyen Van Canh, *Vietnam under Communism, 1975–1982* (Stanford: Hoover Institution Press, 1982), 123–128.

50. Desbarats, "Human Rights," 49–53; Linda Hitchcox, *Vietnamese Refugees in Southeast Asian Camps* (Basingstoke: Macmillan in association with St Antony's College, 1990), 36–68; James M. Freeman and Nguyen Dinh Huu, *Voices from the Camps: Vietnamese Children Seeking Asylum* (Seattle: University of Washington Press, 2003), 7–8.

51. See Desbarats, "Human Rights," 47–66; Kieu-Linh Caroline Valverde, "From Dust to Gold: the Vietnamese Amerasian Experience." In P. P. Maria Root, ed. *Racially Mixed People in America* (Newbury Park: Sage Publications, 1992), 144–161; Steven DeBonis, *Children of the Enemy: Oral Histories of Vietnamese Amerasians and their Mothers* (Jefferson, NC: McFarland, 1995); and Robert S. McKelvey, *The Dust of Life: America's Children Abandoned in Vietnam* (Seattle: University of Washington Press, 1999).

52. Tran Van Khuyen, interview by author, September 10 and 11, 2013, Melbourne. NLA ORAL TRC 6525/16. Tran Van Khuyen studied law at the University of Saigon in 1967–1968 and was mobilized into the armed forces in 1969.

53. Robert Perks and Alistair Thomson, "Introduction to Second Edition." In Robert Perks and Alistair Thomson, eds. *The Oral History Reader: Second Edition* (London: Routledge, 1998), ix.

54. There exist few English-language works on the Republic of Vietnam Armed Forces (RVNAF). See Dong, *RVNAF*; Brigham, *ARVN*. See Lam, *Twenty-Five Year Century*; Andrew Wiest, *Vietnam's Forgotten Army: Heroism and Betrayal in the ARVN* (New York: New York University Press, 2008); and Veith, *Black April*. Dong's *RVNAF* forms part of the Indochina Monographs Series produced by the U.S. Army Center of Military History between 1979 and 1983. Lewis Sorley edited and introduced extracts of these monographs in one volume in order to make them more accessible to scholars. See Lewis Sorley, ed., *The Vietnam War: An Assessment by South Vietnam's Generals* (Lubbock: Texas Tech University Press, 2010).

Studies of the Vietnam War that have provided a more positive assessment of South Vietnam have been in the minority. They include, for example, Guenter Lewy, *America in Vietnam* (New York: Oxford University Press, 1978); Lewis Sorley, *A Better War: The Unexamined Victories and Final Tragedies of America's Last Years in Vietnam* (Orlando: Harcourt, 1999); Joes, *War for South Viet Nam*; Mark Moyar, *Triumph Forsaken: The Vietnam War, 1954–1965* (Cambridge: Cambridge University Press, 2006); and Veith, *Black April*.

55. See, for example, Nguyen, *Hanoi's War*; Pierre Asselin, *Hanoi's Road to the Vietnam War, 1954–1965* (Berkeley: University of California Press, 2013); Qiang Zhai, *China and the Vietnam Wars, 1950–1975* (Chapel Hill: University of North Carolina Press, 2000); Chen Guang Ang, *Ending the Vietnam War: The Vietnamese Communists' Perspective* (London: Routledge Curzon, 2004); Ilya V. Gaiduk, *The Soviet Union and the Vietnam War* (Chicago: Ivan R. Dee, 1996); and Ilya V. Gaiduk, *Confronting Vietnam: Soviet Policy toward the Indochina Conflict, 1954–1963* (Stanford: Stanford University Press, 2003).

56. Jeffrey Grey, "Review of Lam Quang Thi, *The Twenty-Five Year Century: A South Vietnamese General Remembers the Indochina War to the Fall of Saigon*," H-War, H-Net Reviews in the Humanities and Social Sciences, 1–2. http://www.h-net.org/reviews/showrev.php?id=9193

Van Nguyen-Marshall refers to "the most underrepresented in English-language historiography, the non-communist South Vietnamese perspective." Van Nguyen-Marshall, "Oral History and Popular Memory in the Historiography of the Vietnam War." In Paul Budra and Michael Zeitlin, eds. *Soldier Talk: The Vietnam War in Oral Narrative* (Bloomington: Indiana University Press, 2004), 159.

Brigham writes, "According to historian George C. Herring, the South Vietnamese have been conspicuously absent from most histories of the war. Indeed, in our collective rush to find explanations for the US failure in Vietnam, we may have accepted negative stereotypes of the ARVN that do not fully explain the conduct and outcome of the war." Robert K. Brigham, "Dreaming Different Dreams: the United States and the Army of the Republic of Vietnam." In Marilyn B. Young and Robert Buzzanco, eds. *A Companion to the Vietnam War* (Malden: Blackwell, 2002), 146.

Joes refers to "the much-neglected South Vietnamese military and militia." Joes, *War for South Viet Nam*, xiv.

57. Jeffrey J. Clarke, *Advice and Support: The Final Years, 1965–1973* (Washington D.C.: Center of Military History, United States Army, 1988), 275.

58. "Eleven U.S. Presidential Unit Citations (PUC) were awarded to Vietnamese Ranger units." McDonald Valentine, "Advisors to ARVN Rangers (Biet Dong Quan)." http://www.soft-vision.com/ranger/index2.html?http%3A//www.soft-vision.com/ranger/home.html

The 514th Fighter Squadron was "among the first VNAF units to win a U.S. Presidential Unit Citation." Byron E. Hukee, *USAF and VNAF A-1 Skyraider Units of the Vietnam War* (Oxford: Osprey Publishing, 2013), 22.

The 219th Helicopter Squadron was awarded the U.S. Presidential Unit Citation in 2001. U.S. Department of the Army Headquarters, General Orders No. 25, Washington D.C., June 8, 2001, 19.

The 2nd and 5th Marine Battalions were each awarded the U.S. Presidential Unit Citation. James F. Dunnigan and Albert A. Nofi, *Dirty Little Secrets of the Vietnam War: Military Information You're Not Supposed to Know* (New York: Thomas Dunne Books, 2000), 88.

The 3rd Armored Cavalry Squadron was awarded the U.S. Presidential Unit Citation. U.S. Department of the Army Headquarters, General Orders No. 24, Washington D.C., April 27, 1971, 1.

59. Cau Le quoted in Gil Dorland, *Legacy of Discord: Voices of the Vietnam War Era* (Dulles: Brassey's, 2001), 143.

60. Clarke, *Advice and Support*, 275.

61. RVNAF Wounded in Action numbered 109,960 in 1972, 131,936 in 1973, and 155,735 in 1974. Clarke, *Advice and Support*, 275.

62. Jamieson, *Understanding Vietnam*, 296.

63. See Hue-Tam Ho Tai, "Faces of Remembrance and Forgetting." In Hue-Tam Ho Tai, ed. *The Country of Memory: Remaking the Past in Late Socialist Vietnam* (Berkeley: University of California Press, 2001), 182.

64. Heonik Kwon, *Ghosts of War in Vietnam* (Cambridge: Cambridge University Press, 2008), 48.

65. Tai, "Faces of Remembrance," 191.

"A few days after April 30, communist authorities destroyed monuments honoring RVN war dead (front gates, memorials) in many ARVN cemeteries around the country. In some places, they even destroyed their graves. In Sai Gon, they vandalized the Go Vap ARVN Cemetery and displayed a signboard that read, 'Here lie the Americans' puppet soldiers after they have paid for their crimes.' Not long after that, they bulldozed the entire cemetery for their government building construction. The large ARVN National Cemetery near Sai Gon-Bien Hoa Highway was still there, but many graves were vandalized. The famous statue 'Thuong Tiec' (The Mourning Soldier) at the front of the cemetery was destroyed." (Nguyen, *Nationalist in the Viet Nam Wars*, 462).

An encouraging sign is that the Vietnamese American Foundation has been able to begin restoration work on graves in the Bien Hoa Military Cemetery. A 2015 concert organized by the Vietnamese community in Melbourne to commemorate forty years since the end of the war was able to raise 13,510 Australian dollars for the Vietnamese American Foundation, and 10,710 Australian dollars for the Tinh Thuong Foundation to assist disabled RVNAF veterans in Vietnam. See *Viet Luan*, April 24, 2015, 75.

66. Tai, "Faces of Remembrance," 191.

67. See Nathalie Huynh Chau Nguyen, "War and Diaspora: The Memories of South Vietnamese Soldiers," *Journal of Intercultural Studies* 34, no. 6 (2013): 697–713.

68. See Nguyen, "War and Diaspora," 700.

69. The head of the Disabled Veterans and Widows Relief Association of the Republic of Vietnam in the United States is Nguyen Thi Hanh Nhon, a former lieutenant colonel in the Women's Armed Forces Corps. The association organizes fund-raising for disabled veterans and the widows and families of veterans in Vietnam including a yearly *Cam On An* (Thank You Brother) concert. In 2011, for example, the association raised 893,950 dollars

and provided assistance to 7,000 families in Vietnam. See Hoi H.O. Cuu Tro Thuong Phe Binh va Qua Phu VNCH (Disabled Veterans and Widows Relief Association of the Republic of Vietnam), *Cam On Anh* (Thank You Brother), July 28, 2013, 31.

70. The term *"nguy"* originally meant "false, spurious, rebel, renegade, bogus" as well as "puppet." The North Vietnamese paired *"nguy"* with *"quan"* (army) and *"quyen"* (government) to label the former South Vietnamese army and government as *nguy quan, nguy quyen* (puppet army, puppet regime).

71. See Nguyen, "War and Diaspora," 707–711; Nathalie Huynh Chau Nguyen, *Voyage of Hope: Vietnamese Australian Women's Narratives* (Altona: Common Ground Publishing, 2005), 97–115; W. Courtland Robinson, *Terms of Refuge: The Indochinese Exodus and the International Response* (London: Zed Books Ltd, 1998), 26–27.

72. "In June 1976, when North and South were officially reunified as the Socialist Republic of Vietnam, relocation efforts shifted into higher gear. Earlier that year, in April, the Fourth Party Congress had approved the development of New Economic Zones (NEZs) as the keystone of a new five-year development plan . . . One government directive listed some of the groups slated for rural resettlement: 'The unemployed or semi-employed; traders; those who have capital; students who cannot pursue their studies; officers, officials and personnel of the old regime; members of religious minorities; and skilled machinery workers.' . . . The family members of re-education camp prisoners not only waited out the years in the same uncertainty [as the prisoners] but generally were blacklisted by the communist authorities, which led to confiscation of property, denial of citizenship rights as well as education and employment opportunities, and removal to NEZs." Robinson, *Refuge*, 26–27. See also Freeman and Nguyen, *Voices*, 7.

73. Katharine Hodgkin and Susannah Radstone, "Introduction: Contested Pasts." In Katharine Hodgkin and Susannah Radstone, eds. *Contested Pasts: The Politics of Memory* (London: Routledge, 2003), 1.

74. Inga Clendinnen, "The History Question: Who Owns the Past?" *Quarterly Essay* 23 (2006): 38.

75. Robert Perks and Alistair Thomson, "Critical Developments: Introduction." In Perks and Thomson, *Oral History Reader*, 3.

76. Catherine Kohler Riessman, *Narrative Methods for the Human Sciences* (Thousand Oaks, CA: Sage Publications, 2008), 8.

77. Vieda Skultans, *The Testimony of Lives: Narrative and Memory in Post-Soviet Latvia* (London: Routledge, 1998), 28.

CHAPTER 1

1. Nguyen Viet Huy, interview by author, June 28, 2013, Melbourne. NLA ORAL TRC 6525/9.

2. Nguyen Viet Huy.

3. Dong, *RVNAF*, 34–35.

4. Dong, *RVNAF*, 36.

5. Dong, *RVNAF*, 36.

6. Dong, *RVNAF*, 37.

7. Dong, *RVNAF*, 37.

8. Tuan, interview by author, December 4, 2014, Melbourne.

9. For further details, see Thuy's narrative in Nathalie Huynh Chau Nguyen, *Memory Is Another Country: Women of the Vietnamese Diaspora* (Santa Barbara: Praeger, 2009), 57–88, and Nathalie Huynh Chau Nguyen, "South Vietnamese Women in Uniform: Wartime and Post War Lives," *The Minerva Journal of Women and War* 3, no. 2 (2009): 8–33.

10. For further details, see Kim's story in Nguyen, *Memory Is Another Country*, 101–119.

11. Yung Krall, *A Thousand Tears Falling: The True Story of a Vietnamese Family Torn Apart by War, Communism, and the CIA* (Atlanta: Longstreet Press, 1995), 137.

12. Krall, *Thousand Tears*, 138.

13. Krall, *Thousand Tears*, 138.

14. Yung Krall, interview by author, November 27, 2000, Atlanta. See also Krall, *Thousand Tears*, 203, and Elizabeth Kurylo, "Honored Patriot Learned of Liberty the Hard Way," *The Atlanta Journal—Constitution*, July 4, 1998, D10.

15. Clarke, *Advice and Support*, 275. Actual numbers of RVNAF Killed in Action and Wounded in Action are higher as Clarke's figures only cover military casualties between 1960 and 1974.

16. Lam, *Twenty-Five Year Century*, 1.

17. Lam, *Twenty-Five Year Century*, 26.

See also François Guillemot, "'Be Men!': Fighting and Dying for the State of Vietnam (1951–54)," *War & Society* 31, no. 2 (2012): 184.

18. Lam, *Twenty-Five Year Century*, 26.

19. Lam, *Twenty-Five Year Century*, 22.

20. Lam, *Twenty-Five Year Century*, 1–3.

21. Vu Hoai Duc, interview by author, February 14, 2003, Melbourne. NLA ORAL TRC 6525/1.

22. Vu Hoai Duc.

23. Email from Vu Hoai Duc's grandson Tuan Bui to the author, May 22, 2015.

24. Nguyen Tuong Long (1907–1948), *Tu Luc Van Doan* (Self Reliance Literary Group) writer and theorist.

25. "Nhat Linh" was the pen name of Nguyen Tuong Tam (1906–1963), well-known writer and founder of *Tu Luc Van Doan*. The pen name is affixed in front of the full name.

26. Acronym pseudonym *Toi Chang Yeu Ai* (I Love No One) for Dai Duc Tuan (1908–1969), a well-known writer affiliated with the *Dai Viet Quoc Dan Dang* party. See François Guillemot, *Dai Viêt, indépendance et révolution au Viêt-Nam: L'échec de la troisième voie (1938–1955)* (Dai Viet, Independence and Revolution in Vietnam: The Failure of the Third Path) (Paris: Les Indes savantes, 2012), 78–79.

27. Guillemot, "Be Men!," 190.

28. Guillemot, "Be Men!," 190.

29. See, for example, Moyar, *Triumph Forsaken*, 51–55; Philip E. Catton, *Diem's Final Failure: Prelude to America's War in Vietnam* (Lawrence: University Press of Kansas, 2002), 9; Seth Jacobs, *Cold War Mandarin: Ngo Dinh Diem and the Origins of America's War in Vietnam, 1950–1963* (Lanham: Rowman & Littlefield, 2006), 70–71, 84–85. While Ba Cut was executed, other Hoa Hao leaders and the Cao Dai were able to come to an accommodation with the Diem government.

30. Nghia M. Vo, *The Bamboo Gulag: Political Imprisonment in Communist Vietnam* (Jefferson: McFarland, 2004), 65.

31. Tran Van Quan, interview by author, April 22 and 29, 2013, Melbourne. NLA ORAL TRC 6525/5.

32. These were the 9th, 5th, and 7th Divisions supported by the 75th Artillery Division, the 11th Anti-Aircraft Regiment, the 202nd and 203rd Armored Regiments, and the 429th Sapper Group. Lam Quang Thi, *Hell in An Loc: The 1972 Easter Invasion and the Battle that Saved South Viet Nam* (Denton: University of North Texas Press, 2009), 80–81.

33. Lam, *Hell in An Loc*, 209.

34. Lam, *Hell in An Loc*, 42.

35. See G. H. Turley, *The Easter Offensive, Vietnam, 1972* (Novato: Presidio Press, 1985); Dale Andradé, *Trial by Fire: The 1972 Easter Offensive, America's Last Vietnam Battle* (New York: Hippocrene Books, 1995); James H. Willbanks, *The Battle of An Loc* (Bloomington: Indiana University Press, 2005); and Wiest, *Vietnam's Forgotten Army*.

36. Lam, *Hell in An Loc*, 208–212.
37. Lam, *Hell in An Loc*, 186.
38. Lam, *Hell in An Loc*, 194.
39. Lam, *Hell in An Loc*, 193–203.
40. See George J. Veith and Merle L. Pribbenow II, "'Fighting is an Art': The Army of the Republic of Vietnam's Defense of Xuan Loc, 9–21 April 1975," *The Journal of Military History* 68, no. 1 (2004): 163–213.
41. Nguyen Viet Huy.
42. Ngo Quang Truong, "Territorial Forces." In Lewis Sorley, ed. *The Vietnam War: An Assessment by South Vietnam's Generals* (Lubbock: Texas Tech University Press, 2010), 187.
43. Ngo, "Territorial Forces," 191.
44. Ngo, "Territorial Forces," 192.
45. Ngo, "Territorial Forces," 190–191.
46. Ngo, "Territorial Forces," 178.
47. Ngo, "Territorial Forces," 191.
48. Pham Duy Khiem, *La place d'un homme : De Hanoï à la Courtine* (A Man's Place: From Hanoi to La Courtine) (Paris: Librairie Plon, 1958), 120. Author's translation.
49. "Annam" meant "Pacified South" and was the term given to Vietnam by China. In French-administered Indochina, "Annam" referred to central Vietnam but the term "Annamite" was used to refer to all Vietnamese. See, for example, Virginia Thompson, *French Indo-China* (London: George Allen and Unwin, 1937).
50. For a detailed analysis of this novel, see Nathalie Huynh Chau Nguyen, *Vietnamese Voices: Gender and Cultural Identity in the Vietnamese Francophone Novel* (DeKalb: Southeast Asia Publications, Center for Southeast Asian Studies, Northern Illinois University, 2003), 130–151.
51. Jack A. Yeager, *The Vietnamese Novel in French: A Literary Response to Colonialism* (Hanover: University Press of New England, 1987), 177.
52. Nguyen, *Vietnamese Voices*, 137.
53. See, for example, Liêm-Khê Luguern, "Ni civil ni militaire: le travailleur indochinois inconnu de la Second Guerre mondiale (Neither civilian nor military: Unknown Indochinese Workers of the Second World War)." *Le Mouvement Social* 2, nos. 219–220 (2007): 185–199; Pierre Daum, *Immigrés de force: Les travailleurs indochinois en France (1939–1952)* (Forced Migrants: Indochinese Workers in France (1939–1952)) (Arles: Actes Sud, 2009).
54. See, for example, Lucien Trong, *Enfer rouge mon amour* (Red Hell My Love) (Paris: Editions du Seuil, 1980), and Tran Tri Vu, *Lost Years: My 1,*

632 Days in Vietnamese Reeducation Camps (Berkeley: Institute of East Asian Studies, University of California, 1988).

55. Tran Van Quan, "Hinh Anh Nguoi Linh Tiep-Van tai Chien Truong truoc Co-Quan Bao-Tro HOI VIET-MY (Image of the Logistics Soldier on the Battlefield for Sponsorship of the Vietnamese-American Association)." Vietnamese-American Association Auditorium, November 29, 1972. Bilingual copy. Tran Van Quan advised the author that only 100 copies of the lecture were printed. One of his men kept a copy and held on to it after the end of the war.

56. Tran, "Hinh," 12.
57. Tran, "Hinh," 16.
58. Tran, "Hinh," 16.
59. Tran, "Hinh," 16.
60. John Keegan and Richard Holmes with John Gau, *Soldiers: A History of Men in Battle* (London: Hamish Hamilton, 1985), 239.
61. "[M]onthly salary payments, the only source of income for the majority of servicemen, rapidly decreased in purchasing power beginning in 1963 to the point that ten years later no serviceman was able to subsist on his salary alone . . . In 1964, a colonel, for example, made approximately US $400 a month (at the official exchange rate of 1 US dollar to 35 VN piasters); in 1972, he only made US $82 (rate: 1 US dollar=465 VN piasters). During the same period, an army captain found his monthly salary shrinking from US $287 to US $61, and a private, from US $77 to US $30. If we compared a private's pay with that of a minimum-wage earner, we found that he made only about half as much as a laborer in 1969 (VN $4,594 versus 9,113)." Dong, *RVNAF*, 252–253.
62. Ngo, "Territorial Forces," 194.
63. Ngo, "Territorial Forces," 197.
64. Ngo, "Territorial Forces," 202. The RPG7 and B41 are the same weapon—the first was built by the Soviets and the second by the Chinese. "The Soviet RPG7 (Chinese Type 69 or Vietnamese B41) appeared in 1962 and represented an improved version of the RPG2 with a rocket assist motor that fired 10 meters from the muzzle of the launcher. Effective range was increased to 500 meters and armor penetration up to 330 mm." Robert J. Bunker, "Grenades, Launched: Allied and Democratic Republic of Vietnam." In Spencer C. Tucker, ed. *Encyclopedia of the Vietnam War: A Political, Social and Military History*. Vol. I (Santa Barbara: ABC-CLIO, 1998), 252.
65. Ngo, "Territorial Forces," 202.

66. Ngo, "Territorial Forces," 207.
67. Ngo, "Territorial Forces," 207.

CHAPTER 2

1. Van Tan Thach, "Miracles." In Tran Xuan Dung, ed. *History of the South Vietnamese Marine Corps Army of the Republic of Vietnam / Chien Su Thuy Quan Luc Chien Quan Luc Viet Nam Cong Hoa* (South Melbourne: Tran Xuan Dung, 2007), 832.
2. See Van, "Miracles," 832–834.
3. Van, "Miracles," 834.
4. Van, "Miracles," 832.
5. My thanks to Merle Pribbenow for clarifying the details of the North Vietnamese units involved in the initial attack across the demilitarized zone on March 30, 1972, and for providing his translation of a segment of *Chien Dich Tien Cong Quang Tri 1972, Mat* (The 1972 Quang Tri Offensive Campaign, Secret) (Hanoi: Military Art Faculty of the Military Science Institute, 1976), that includes a detailed list of the units involved.
6. Ngo Van Dinh, "Marine Brigade 258's Victory at Quang Tri." In Tran, *South Vietnamese Marine Corps*, 898.
7. Ngo, "Marine Brigade 258," 900.

Ngo Van Dinh notes that, "Having stopped the VC troops from crossing Dong Ha Bridge and taking Quang Tri, the bridge was subsequently destroyed through the valiant efforts of Captain Ripley and the marines of the 3rd Battalion." Ngo, "Marine Brigade 258," 900.

Captain John Ripley and Major James Smock, adviser to the 20th Armor Battalion, were decorated for blowing up the Dong Ha Bridge on April 2, 1972. See Charles D. Melson, "Ripley at the Bridge: Dong Ha, South Vietnam, 2 April 1972." http://kbc3337design.tripod.com/ripley.htm

Victory in Vietnam relates: "The 2nd Infantry Battalion (36th Regiment, 308th Division) crossed the Cam Lo River through a curtain of enemy air and artillery bombardment and pursued the puppet 5th Regiment all the way to the northern outskirts of Dong Ha. The regiment's mechanized infantry battalion quickly made a deep penetration attack to the east of the town but was struck by enemy aircraft while they were on the move. Eight armored personnel carriers were knocked out and 29 cadre and soldiers were killed or wounded, forcing the battalion to stop to regroup. Although enemy troops in Dong Ha were terrified, we did not bring our reserves forward quickly enough and missed a chance to capture Dong Ha." The Military Institute of Vietnam, *Victory in Vietnam: The Official History of the People's Army of Vietnam, 1954–1975*. Merle L. Pribbenow, trans. (Lawrence: University Press of Kansas, 2002), 291.

8. Ngo, "Marine Brigade 258," 900.

9. Ngo, "Marine Brigade 258," 900.

10. Ngo, "Marine Brigade 258," 900.

Ngo Van Dinh writes that, "On 22 April 1972, Brigade 258 was ordered to leave Ai Tu to be replaced there by Marine Brigade 147. The 3rd and 6th Battalions, the 3rd Marine Artillery Battalion, and my Brigade Headquarters moved to Hue for R & R. The 1st Marine Battalion remained with Brigade 147 and a number of other Battalions: the 7th, the 8th, and the 2nd Artillery Battalion." Ngo, "Marine Brigade 258," 900.

11. George MacDonald Fraser, *Quartered Safe out Here: A Recollection of the War in Burma* (London: Harvill, 1993), xiii.

12. Nguyen Van Luyen, interview by author, April 26, 2013, Melbourne. NLA ORAL TRC 6525/6.

13. See Ralph Zumbro, *The Iron Cavalry* (New York: Pocket Books, 1998), 467–482; and Simon Dunstan, *The M113 Series* (London: Osprey Publishing, 1983), 9–11. Zumbro writes, "The ACAV [Armor Cavalry Assault Vehicle] version of the then-new M-113 was basically a Vietnamese invention, not an American design." Zumbro, *Iron Cavalry*, 469.

14. See Dunstan, *M113*, 9–11.

15. See Zumbro, *Iron Cavalry*, 468–470.

16. Zumbro, *Iron Cavalry*, 470.

17. Zumbro, *Iron Cavalry*, 468.

18. Dunstan, *M113*, 10–11.

19. Ha Mai Viet, *Steel and Blood: South Vietnamese Armor and the War for Southeast Asia* (Annapolis: Naval Institute Press, 2008), 281.

20. Ha, *Steel and Blood*, 281.

21. Ha, *Steel and Blood*, 273.

22. Ha, *Steel and Blood*, 273.

23. Ha, *Steel and Blood*, 291.

24. Ha, *Steel and Blood*, 289.

25. See Ha, *Steel and Blood*, 292–300.

26. U.S. Department of the Army Headquarters, General Orders No. 24, Washington D.C., April 27, 1971, 1.

27. Ha, *Steel and Blood*, 289.

28. See Ha, *Steel and Blood*, 298–300.
29. Ha, *Steel and Blood*, 306.
30. See Ha, *Steel and Blood*, 302–303.
31. I was interested in this particular account of battle because Luyen spoke of saving the life of his friend Nghiep. He returned to the subject of the battle during his interview but the sequence of events remained unclear. I contacted him a year after the original interview and asked him whether he would mind providing further details of this battle and of his role in it. He emailed a written account of his experiences on November 1, 2014. A slightly edited version of his account is reproduced.
32. Email from Nguyen Van Luyen to the author, November 1, 2014.
33. Email from Nguyen Van Luyen.
34. Vu Van Bao, interview by author, July 27, 2013, Melbourne. NLA ORAL TRC 6525/11.
35. See William W. Momyer, "The Vietnamese Air Force, 1951–1975: An Analysis of Its Role in Combat." In Major A.J.C. Lavalle, gen. ed. *The Vietnamese Air Force, 1951–1975: An Analysis of Its Role in Combat* and *Fourteen Hours at Koh Tang* (Washington, D.C.: Office of Air Force History, United States Air Force, 1985), 61.

See also Dong, *RVNAF*, 20–22.
36. Dong, *RVNAF*, 18.
37. Hukee, *Skyraider Units*, 22.
38. Hukee, *Skyraider Units*, 22.
39. Hukee, *Skyraider Units*, 22.
40. Hukee, *Skyraider Units*, 60.
41. Hukee, *Skyraider Units*, 60. "The 516th FS had 14 pilots killed or listed as MIA during the five years it flew the A-1—a total of 23 Skyraiders were lost. The unit's heaviest year for attrition was 1965, when it lost seven A-1s and had five pilots killed or listed as MIA. 1965 was also the highest Skyraider loss year for the VNAF, which had no fewer than 43 A-1s destroyed." Hukee, *Skyraider Units*, 61.
42. Vu Van Bao, "Phi Doan 237 Truc Thang Chinook CH 47-A (237th Helicopter Squadron Chinook CH-47A)." In Lien Hoi Ai Huu Khong Quan Australia (Republic of Vietnam Air Force Veteran Association in Australia), *Quan Su Khong Quan Viet Nam Cong Hoa* (Military History of the Republic of Vietnam Air Force) (Melbourne: Van Luong, 2005), 272.
43. Vu, "Phi Doan 237," 272–276.
44. Vu, "Phi Doan 237," 274.

45. Vu, "Phi Doan 237," 274.
46. Vu, "Phi Doan 237," 274.
47. Vu, "Phi Doan 237," 276.
48. Vu, "Phi Doan 237," 276.
49. Vu, "Phi Doan 237," 276.
50. Vu, "Phi Doan 237," 276–277.
51. U.S. Department of the Army Headquarters, General Orders No. 25, Washington D.C., June 8, 2001, 19.
52. Momyer, "The Vietnamese Air Force," xii.
53. Hukee, *Skyraider Units*, 20.
54. Email from Vu Van Bao to the author, July 27, 2015. Bao explained that the formation consisted of two Chinooks, four "Slicks" (Hueys) and two gunships. The Hueys were supposed to land first but the Chinooks flew faster and arrived at the landing zone first. Control and Command wanted the Chinooks to circle above but the Chinooks could not do so because otherwise they would not have enough fuel to fly back to Phan Rang Air Base. The battalion commander, Lieutenant Colonel Bui Quyen was picked up by a Huey.
55. Email from Vu Van Bao to the author, June 19, 2015.
56. Tran Van Giac, interview by author, September 25, 2013, Sydney. NLA ORAL TRC 6525/21.
57. Thong Ba Le, "Organizations and Progressive Activities of the Republic of Vietnam Navy." Mobile Riverine Force Association Website.
   http://www.mrfa.org/VNN.ThongLe.htm.
58. Edward J. Marolda, "Vietnam, Republic of: Navy (VNN)." In Spencer C. Tucker, ed. *Encyclopedia of the Vietnam War: A Political, Social, and Military History*. Vol. II (Santa Barbara: ABC-CLIO, 1998), 782.
59. Le, "Republic of Vietnam Navy."
60. Le, "Republic of Vietnam Navy."
61. Le, "Republic of Vietnam Navy."
62. Tran Do Cam, "Giang Doan 26 Xung Phong tai Chien Truong Tan Chau—Hong Ngu (River Assault Group 26 at the Battle of Tan Chau—Hong Ngu)." *Ra Khoi* (Head to Open Sea) *Giai Pham Xuan Quy Ty* 2013 (Spring Year of the Snake 2013), 62.
63. Marolda, "Navy," 784.
64. Robert H. Pietrzak and Steven M. Southwick, "Psychological Resilience in OEF-OIF Veterans: Application of a novel classification approach

and examination of demographic and psychosocial correlates." *Journal of Affective Disorders* 133 (2011): 560.

65. Vu Van Bao holds certificates from: the U.S. Army Primary Helicopter School, July 11, 1970; Officer Rotary Wing Aviator Course (UH-1) (VNAF), October 27, 1970; and CH-47 Aviator Qualification Course, December 11, 1970.

66. George Bonnano, "Loss, Trauma, and Human Resilience: Have We Underestimated the Human Capacity to Thrive After Extremely Aversive Events?" *American Psychologist* 59, no. 1 (2004): 25.

67. *Quan Su Khong Quan Viet Nam Cong Hoa* (Military History of the Republic of Vietnam Air Force) has numerous contributing authors and includes photographs, illustrations, and an organizational chart.

68. *Luu Day Ky Yeu* (Exile Record) was printed specifically for members of the Naval Academy Class of 1970.

69. Keegan and Holmes with Gau, *Soldiers*, 259.

CHAPTER 3

1. Médecin Lieutenant-Colonel Pham Viet Tu, "Le Grand Hôpital Militaire Duy Tân dans la Guerre Contre l'Invasion Communiste (The Great Duy Tan Military Hospital in the War against the Communist Invasion)." In Tran Xuan Dung, Tran Quoc Dong, Vu Van Tung, Bui Khiet, eds. *Quan Y Quan Luc Viet Nam Cong Hoa: Le Corps de Santé des Forces Armées de la République du Viet Nam* (The Medical Corps of the Republic of Vietnam Armed Forces) (South Melbourne, Victoria: Tran Xuan Dung, 2000), 312. Author's translation.

2. Pham, "Duy Tân," 308.

3. Pham, "Duy Tân," 310.

4. Pham, "Duy Tân," 310.

5. Médecin Commandant Tran Duc Tuong, "Le Médecin Parachutiste (Paratrooper Doctor)." In Tran et al., *Quan Y Quan Luc*, 116. Author's translation.

6. Tran, "Médecin Parachutiste," 138.

7. Tran, "Médecin Parachutiste," 138.

8. Tran, "Médecin Parachutiste," 138.

9. Tran, "Médecin Parachutiste," 138.

10. Tran, "Médecin Parachutiste," 138.

11. Perks and Thomson, "Introduction to Second Edition," ix.

12. Elizabeth Stewart, "Introduction." In Ashley Ekins and Elizabeth Stewart, eds. *War Wounds: Medicine and the Trauma of Conflict* (Wollombi, NSW: Exisle Publishing, 2011), 18.

13. This brief history of the South Vietnamese Medical Corps is drawn from Dong's *RVNAF* and supplemented by information on military units and hospitals as well as vignettes of service provided by former RVNAF doctors and pharmacists in the trilingual volume *Quan Y Quan Luc*. See Dong, *RVNAF*; and Tran et al., *Quan Y Quan Luc*.

14. Médecin Colonel Hoang Co Lan, "Etudiant et Médecin au Viet Nam (Student and Doctor in Vietnam)." In Tran et al., *Quan Y Quan Luc*, 81.

15. Hoang, "Etudiant et Médecin," 80–82.

16. Hoang, "Etudiant et Médecin," 84.

17. Dong, *RNVAF*, 268.

18. See Dong, *RVNAF*, 256–262.

19. Dong, *RVNAF*, 259.

20. Dong, *RVNAF*, 261–262.

21. Alistair Brass writes that the National Rehabilitation Institute was established in May 1966 by Dr. Nguyen Huu Vi, formerly an army doctor at Cong Hoa General Hospital, and that it was popularly known as "Dr Vi's Limb Factory." 500 new military and civilian patients were referred to the institute from all over South Vietnam every month, and each month approximately 300 patients were fitted—free of charge—with artificial limbs and braces. "The institute comes under the control of the War Veterans Department, and is financed jointly from the national budget, donations and foreign aid, while USAID runs a weekly plane to carry patients to and from their home towns." Alistair Brass, *Medicine in South Vietnam Today* (Sydney: Australasian Medical Publishing, 1967), 32.

A different account is provided by C. H. William Ruhe, Norman W. Hoover and Ira Singer in their book *Saigon Medical School*. They note that the National Rehabilitation Center was a government agency within the Ministry of Social Welfare, Division of Veterans Affairs, that it was initially organized by Colonel Le Van Thung, MD, and provided service to wounded veterans before expanding to serve civilians. See C. H. William Ruhe, Norman W. Hoover and Ira Singer, *Saigon Medical School: An Experiment in International Medical Education: An Account of the American Medical Association's Medical Education Project in South Viet Nam 1966–1975* (Chicago: American Medical Association, 1988), 211–212.

22. Pham, "Duy Tân," 312.

23. Pham, "Duy Tân," 312.
24. Pham, "Duy Tân," 314.
25. Dong, *RVNAF*, 266.

Lam Quang Thi writes: "On May 2 [1972], the remnants of the 3rd Division, the 1st Armored Brigade, the 5th Ranger Group, and the two Marine brigades had to fight their way back against pursuing NVA [North Vietnamese Army] units along that fateful portion of RN1 located between Quang Tri and My Chanh. The withdrawal was rendered more difficult by thousands of refugees from Quang Tri who fled south to escape the war. Many perished under artillery and missile concentrations along this section of RN1, which was subsequently littered with charred corpses and burned vehicles. That section of RN1 was later known as 'The Freeway of Horror.'" Lam, *Twenty-Five Year Century*, 271.

26. Nguyen, *Nationalist in the Viet Nam Wars*, 406.
27. Dong, *RVNAF*, 274.
28. Dong, *RVNAF*, 274.
29. Dong, *RVNAF*, 274.
30. Dong, *RVNAF*, 275.
31. Email from Tran Xuan Dung to the author, July 28, 2014.

There is some fluctuation in the estimates of the number of medical doctors in South Vietnam by 1975. However, the figure of approximately 2,000 doctors by 1975 accords with Dong's figure of 1,000 doctors in 1966. With 160 doctors graduating per year in South Vietnam, there would have been approximately 2,200 doctors by 1975. Pham Huu Trac writes that there were 1,715 doctors serving in the RVNAF in 1974. See Médecin Lieutenant-Colonel Pham Huu Trac, "Quelques Propos sur les Activités du Corps Médical Militaire (Some Reflections on the Activities of the Army Medical Corps)." In Tran et al., *Quan Y Quan Luc*, 38.

32. Clarke, *Advice and Support*, 275.
33. Pham, "Quelques Propos," 38.
34. Hoang, "Etudiant et Médecin," 84.
35. Hoang, "Etudiant et Médecin," 86.
36. Major Vo Thuong, "The Coup de Grâce." In Tran et al., *Quan Y Quan Luc*, 290–294.
37. Vo Thuong, "Coup de Grâce," 292.
38. Médecin Lieutenant Le Thanh Y, "Pleime, Été 71 (Pleime, Summer 71)." In Tran et al., *Quan Y Quan Luc*, 362–366. Le Thanh Y notes that an American surgeon named Humphreys successfully removed an M79 grenade

from a patient at Cho Ray hospital while Le was still a medical student. Le, "Pleime," 364. Pham Huu Trac writes that while Humphreys's achievement in 1967 is well known, few are aware that five South Vietnamese doctors successfully performed the same operation, and were decorated for it. Pham, "Quelques Propos," 44.

39. Dong, *RVNAF*, 265.

40. Dong, *RVNAF*, 269.

41. Tran Xuan Dung, interview by author, December 18, 2013, Melbourne. NLA ORAL TRC 6525/26.

42. "Viet Minh" is a condensation of Viet Nam Doc Lap Dong Minh Hoi or League for the Independence of Vietnam.

43. Nguyen Thanh Tri later became a colonel and the deputy commander of the Marine Division.

44. Peter Brush, "The Vietnamese Marine Corps." *Viet Nam Generation: A Journal of Recent History and Contemporary Culture* 7, nos. 1–2 (1996): 73; and Dong, *RVNAF*, 22.

45. Dong, *RVNAF*, 19 and 22.

46. Nguyen Manh Tien, interview by author, September 23, 2013, Sydney. NLA ORAL TRC 6525/18.

47. Regarding the student composition in the medical school: "The number of women was slightly over 10% as a rule. There were also usually a few foreign students, chiefly French, Chinese, or Cambodian nationals, and about one-third of the students were in the Army Medical Career Officers Student Program." Ruhe, Hoover and Singer, *Saigon Medical School*, 20–21.

48. Valentine, "Advisors to ARVN Rangers."

49. Martin, "Introduction." In Michael N. Martin and McDonald Valentine Jr., eds. *The Black Tigers: Elite South Vietnamese Rangers and their American Advisors* (Louisville: Harmony House Publishers, 1993), 13.

50. Martin, "Introduction," 13.

51. Valentine, "Advisors to ARVN Rangers."

52. Dong, *RVNAF*, 19.

53. See Lam, *Hell in An Loc*.

54. Dr. Tran Xuan Dung, Major, MC, "A Bloody Battle, Albeit None Wounded." In Tran et al., *Quan Y Quan Luc*, 171.

55. See Veith, *Black April*, 256–260.

56. Veith, *Black April*, 257.

57. Daniel L. Schachter, *Searching for Memory: The Brain, the Mind, and the Past* (New York: Basic Books, 1996), 216.

58. Paul Antze and Michael Lambek, "Preface." In Paul Antze and Michael Lambek, eds. *Tense Past: Essays in Trauma and Memory* (New York: Routledge, 1996), vii.

59. "The triple victory of An Loc, Kontum, and Quang Tri clearly demonstrated that ARVN, with U.S. air support, could beat NVA's finest divisions, supported and supplied by Russia and China. . . . The entire country was proud of its Army: people realized for the first time that a well-trained, motivated, and properly equipped National Army with adequate logistical and fire support could gain the upper hand." Lam, *Twenty-Five Year Century*, 289.

60. Nguyen, *Nationalist in the Viet Nam Wars*, 413.

61. Tran Xuan Dung edited three volumes on the *History of the South Vietnamese Marine Corps*, a first edition in one volume in 1997, and a second edition in two volumes in 2007. He was also editor-in-chief of *Quan Y Quan Luc*.

62. Pham, "Quelques Propos," 32.

63. Terry Eastwood, "Reflections on the Goal of Archival Appraisal in Democratic Societies," *Archivaria* 54 (2002): 61.

64. Joan M. Schwartz and Terry Cook, "Archives, Records, and Power: The Making of Modern Memory," *Archival Science* 2 (2002): 18.

65. See Nguyen, *Voyage of Hope*, 2–5.

66. Judith Lewis Herman, *Trauma and Recovery* (New York: BasicBooks, 1992), 207.

67. See Vo, *Bamboo Gulag*, 2004.

68. Nguyen Huu Hiep, a military doctor who was also interned after the war, witnessed the death of prisoners from a combination of malnutrition and depression. See Médecin Capitaine Nguyen Huu Hiep, "Souvenirs d'après Guerre (Postwar Memories)." In Tran et al., *Quan Y Quan Luc*, 448.

69. United Nations High Commissioner for Refugees, *Refugees*, 82.

70. Desbarats, "Human Rights," 60.

71. See Desbarats, "Human Rights," 47–66; Valverde, "From Dust to Gold," 144–161; DeBonis, *Children of the Enemy*; and McKelvey, *Dust of Life*.

72. Robinson, *Terms of Refuge*, 50.

73. Angela Fielding and Judi Anderson, "Working with Refugee Communities to Build Collective Resilience." AseTTS Occasional Paper 2008 (Perth, WA: Association for Services to Torture and Trauma Survivors Inc., 2008), 7.

74. See Fielding and Anderson, "Refugee Communities," 7.

CHAPTER 4

1. For further details on Bui Ngoc Thuy (1936–2014), see Thuy's narrative in Nguyen, *Memory Is Another Country*, 57–88. Bui Ngoc Thuy's full name is used here by permission of her son, Kieu Tien Dung.

2. Nguyen, *Memory Is Another Country*, 64.

3. For full details of this incident, please refer to Nguyen, *Memory Is Another Country*, 62–67.

4. Phung Thi Hanh, "South Vietnam's Women in Uniform." Saigon: The Vietnam Council on Foreign Relations, c. 1970, 9. My thanks to Mary McLain Saffell from the Vietnam Center and Archive at Texas Tech University for informing me about this article on South Vietnamese servicewomen. The Vietnam Center and Archive has two versions of the same article, one published by the Vietnam Council on Foreign Relations, illustrated with photographs, and undated, and the other published by the Vietnam Feature Service, without photographs, and dated April 1970. Page references refer to the illustrated version.

5. See my earlier work on women who served in the RVNAF: Nguyen, "Women in Uniform," 8–33; Nguyen, *Memory Is Another Country*, 57–88.

   A recent book by François Guillemot explores the experiences of women on both sides of the war. See François Guillemot, *Des Vietnamiennes dans la guerre civile: L'autre moitié de la guerre 1945–1975* (Vietnamese Women in the Civil War: The Other Half of the War 1945–1975) (Paris: Les Indes Savantes, 2014).

6. An exception is Guillemot, *Vietnamiennes*. For histories and accounts of women who fought on the communist side, see Karen Gottschang Turner, *Even the Women Must Fight: Memories of War from North Vietnam* (New York: John Wiley and Sons, 1998); Sandra C. Taylor, *Vietnamese Women at War: Fighting for Ho Chi Minh and the Revolution* (Lawrence: University Press of Kansas, 1999); and Dang Thuy Tram, *Last Night I Dreamed of Peace: The Diary of Dang Thuy Tram*. Andrew X. Pham, trans. (New York: Harmony Books, 2007).

7. Phung, "Women in Uniform," 5.

8. See Ho Thi Ve, "Nu Quan Nhan (Servicewomen)." *Dac San Cuu Nu Quan Nhan QLVNCH: Ky Niem Ngay Hoi Ngo NQN 12 Thang 8 Nam 2001* (Magazine of the Servicewomen of the Republic of Vietnam Armed Forces: Special Bulletin of the Reunion of Servicewomen on August 12, 2001). 18. Translation by Phuong Mai Ung.

9. Phung, "Women in Uniform," 5.

10. Nguyen, *Vietnamese Family Chronicle*, 142.

11. See Brigham, *ARVN*, 112–113.

12. Nguyen, *Vietnamese Family Chronicle*, 122.

13. Ta Van Tai, "The Status of Women in Traditional Vietnam: A Comparison of the Code of the Lê Dynasty (1428–1788) with the Chinese Code." *Journal of Asian History* 15 (1981): 136.

14. See, for example, Cam Nguyen, "East, West, and Vietnamese Women," *Journal of Vietnamese Studies* 5 (1992): 46.

15. Gerard J. DeGroot, "Introduction to Part 1: Arms and the Woman." In Gerard J. DeGroot and Corinna Peniston-Bird, eds. *A Soldier and a Woman: Sexual Integration in the Military* (Harlow: Longman, 2000), 6.

16. This brief history of the Women's Auxiliary Corps and the Women's Armed Forces Corps of South Vietnam is drawn from Ho's "Nu Quan Nhan" and Phung's "Women in Uniform." It is supplemented by information provided in RVNAF veterans' magazines, and brief references in Dong Van Khuyen's *RVNAF*. See Ho, "Nu Quan Nhan," 7–18; Phung, "Women in Uniform," 1–18; and Dong, *RVNAF*.

17. See Ho, "Nu Quan Nhan," 7–18.

18. Ho, "Nu Quan Nhan," 7.

19. Ho Thi Ve writes that that was the case for her and a small number of other servicewomen. By 1975, they had accrued twenty-five years of service and were entitled to full retirement benefits. Ho, "Nu Quan Nhan," 8.

A French officer on the General Staff of the National Army of Vietnam, Arlette Arnaud, guided Nguyen Thi Hang in laying the foundation for the *Nu Phu Ta*. See Ho, "Nu Quan Nhan," 8.

20. Ho, "Nu Quan Nhan," 9.

21. Ho, "Nu Quan Nhan," 10.

22. Ho, "Nu Quan Nhan," 11.

23. Ho, "Nu Quan Nhan," 13.

24. Phung, "Women in Uniform," 5.

25. Ho, "Nu Quan Nhan," 18.

26. Phung, "Women in Uniform," 7.

27. Phung, "Women in Uniform," 7.

28. Phung, "Women in Uniform," 7.

29. Phung, "Women in Uniform," 7.

30. Ho, "Nu Quan Nhan," 18.

31. Phung, "Women in Uniform," 5.

32. Dong, *RVNAF*, 208.
33. Ho, "Nu Quan Nhan," 15.
34. Ho, "Nu Quan Nhan," 15–16.
35. Ho, "Nu Quan Nhan," 16.
36. Phung, "Women in Uniform," 9.
37. Ho, "Nu Quan Nhan," 17.
38. Phung, "Women in Uniform," 5.
39. Phung, "Women in Uniform," 5.
40. Phung, "Women in Uniform," 10–11.
41. See Krall, *Thousand Tears*, 1995.
42. Yung Krall, interview by author, November 27, 2000, Atlanta.
43. Krall, *Thousand Tears*, 170.
44. Phung, "Women in Uniform," 5.
45. Phung, "Women in Uniform," 3.
46. Phung, "Women in Uniform," 11.
47. Phung, "Women in Uniform," 17.
48. Phung, "Women in Uniform," 17.
49. See Lu Tuan, "Nhung Phu Nu Dung Cam (The Brave Women)." *Dac San Cuu Nu Quan Nhan QLVNCH: Ky Niem Hoi Ngo NQN Ky IV 25–26 Thang 8 Nam 2007* (Magazine of the Servicewomen of the Republic of Vietnam Armed Forces: Special Bulletin of the 4th Reunion of Servicewomen on August 25–26, 2007), 28. Translation by Tuan Bui.
50. Lu Tuan, "Phu Nu," 28.
51. See Nguyen, *Nationalist in the Viet Nam Wars*, 409.
52. Nguyen, *Nationalist in the Viet Nam Wars*, 409.
53. Nguyen, *Nationalist in the Viet Nam Wars*, 409–410.
54. Hai Trieu, "Nguoi Nu Binh khong co So Quan tren khang tuyen Ba To (The Female Soldier without Military Number in Resistance Line Ba To)." *Guom Thieng* 2014, 86–88. Translation by Tuan Bui.
55. Title of article by Hai Trieu, "Nguoi Nu Binh khong co So Quan."
56. Thanh, interview by author, September 25, 2013, Sydney. NLA ORAL TRC 6525/20.
57. Nguyen Thi Minh Nguyet, interview by author, December 11, 2013, Sydney. NLA ORAL TRC 6525/25.
58. Thuy, interview by author, December 10, 2013, Sydney. NLA ORAL TRC 6525/24.
59. See Clarke, *Advice and Support*, 275. RVNAF Killed in Action: 23,346 in 1970; 22,738 in 1971; 39,587 in 1972; 27,901 in 1973; 31,219 in 1974.

RVNAF Wounded in Action: 71,582 in 1970; 60,939 in 1971; 109,960 in 1972; 131,936 in 1973; 155,735 in 1974.

60. See Nguyen, "War and Diaspora," 697–713.

61. Penny Summerfield, *Reconstructing Women's Wartime Lives: Discourse and Subjectivity in Oral Histories of the Second World War* (Manchester: Manchester University Press, 1998), 2.

62. Dong's *RVNAF* is a detailed study of the RVNAF from its formation through to its demise in 1975, but it contains only brief references to the WAC and WAFC. In the preface to his monograph, Dong thanks Pham Thi Bong, "a former Captain in the Republic of Vietnam Armed Forces" for her work on the manuscript but she is the only servicewoman he refers to by name in the study. Brigham's *ARVN* refers to North Vietnamese women who served in the People's Army of Vietnam (PAVN). South Vietnamese women, however, only feature as Army of the Republic of Vietnam (ARVN) "wives and companions." See Dong, *RVNAF*, vi; and Brigham, *ARVN*, 112–118.

63. Summerfield, *Women's Wartime Lives*, 28.

64. See Nguyen, *Memory Is Another Country*, 82–88.

65. Nguyen Thi Hanh Nhon, "Thu Moi Hop Mat Nu Quan Nhan Hai Ngoai (Letter of Invitation to a Meeting of Overseas Servicewomen)." *Dac San Cuu Nu Quan Nhan QLVNCH: Ky Niem Ngay Hoi Ngo NQN 12 Thang 8 Nam 2001* (Magazine of the Servicewomen of the Republic of Vietnam Armed Forces: Special Bulletin of the Reunion of Servicewomen on August 21, 2001), 5. Translation by Phuong Mai Ung.

66. Nguyen Thi Hanh Nhon, "Phat bieu cua Dai dien Ban To Chuc Hoi Ngo Nu Quan Nhan Hai Ngoai Ky IV (Speech of the WAFC Committee Representative delivered at the Fourth Overseas Reunion)." *Dac San Cuu Nu Quan Nha QLVNCH: Ky Niem Hoi Ngo NQN Ky IV 25–26 Thang 8 Nam 2007 Tai Nam California* (Magazine of the Servicewomen of the Republic of Vietnam Armed Forces: Special Bulletin to commemorate the Fourth Reunion of Servicewomen on August 25–26, 2007, Southern California), 5. Translation by Ngoc Bui.

67. See Hoi H.O. Cuu Tro Thuong Phe Binh va Qua Phu VNCH (Disabled Veterans and Widows Relief Association of the Republic of Vietnam), *Cam On Anh* (Thank You Brother), 28 July 2013, 31.

68. See *Guom Thieng: Vinh Danh Nu Quan Nhan QLVNCH* (Sacred Sword: Special Issue Glorifying the Women's Armed Forces Corps of the RVNAF, 2014), the voice of The General Association of the Veterans of the Army of the Republic of Vietnam—Australia.

69. For further detailed life narratives of WAFC veterans, including one who resettled in the United States, see Nguyen, *Memory Is Another Country*, 57–88; and Nguyen, "Women in Uniform," 8–33.

70. Hodgkin and Radstone, "Introduction: Contested Pasts," 1.

CHAPTER 5

1. Tran Van Quan, interview by author, April 22 and 29, 2013, Melbourne. NLA ORAL TRC 6525/5.

2. I had conducted two interviews with Tran Van Quan and asked him whether I could interview him a third time and whether he would be willing to speak of friendships throughout his army career. He did not grant me another interview and I inferred from this that he found the topic too personal and painful.

3. Tran Van Giac, interview by author, September 25, 2013, Sydney. NLA ORAL TRC 6525/21.

4. Lieutenant Vaughan as quoted in Keegan and Holmes with Gau, *Soldiers*, 265.

5. Nguyen Manh Tien, interview by author, September 23, 2013, Sydney. NLA ORAL TRC 6525/18.

6. Henry ('Jo') Gullett, *Not as a Duty Only: An Infantryman's War* (Melbourne: Melbourne University Press, 1976), 1.

7. See Veith and Pribbenow II, "'Fighting Is an Art,'" 163–213.

8. The material in this chapter was first presented at the "Vietnam: International Perspectives on a Long War" conference at the Australian War Memorial on August 15–16, 2013.

9. The Democratic Republic of Vietnam ratified the Third Geneva Convention relative to the Treatment of Prisoners of War on June 28, 1957.

"ART. 13.—Prisoners of war must at all times be humanely treated. Any unlawful act or omission by the Detaining Power causing death or seriously endangering the health of a prisoner of war in its custody is prohibited, and will be regarded as a serious breach of the present Convention. In particular, no prisoner of war may be subjected to physical mutilation or to medical or scientific experiments of any kind which are not justified by the medical, dental or hospital treatment of the prisoner concerned and carried out in his interest. Likewise, prisoners of war must at all times be protected, particularly against acts of violence or intimidation and against insults and public curiosity. Measures of reprisal against prisoners of war are prohibited." *III Geneva Convention relative to the Treatment of Prisoners of War of 12 August 1949.* 97.

10. See, for example, Paige Arthur, "How 'Transitions' Reshaped Human Rights: A Conceptual History of Transitional Justice," *Human Rights Quarterly* 31 (2009): 321–327; Roger Duthie, "Transitional Justice and Displacement," *The International Journal of Transitional Justice* 5 (2011): 243.

11. Nguyen Huu An, interview by author, March 4, 2013, Melbourne. NLA ORAL TRC 6525/4.

12. Martin, "Introduction," 18.

13. Valentine, "Advisors to ARVN Rangers." See also Martin, "Introduction," 18. Martin cites fewer PUCs but the book that he and McDonald Valentine edited predates Valentine's later article that contains updated information.

14. McDonald Valentine, "The Vietnamese Rangers: An Overview." In Martin and Valentine, *Black Tigers*, 21–22.

15. Valentine, "Vietnamese Rangers," 21. Valentine, "Advisors to ARVN Rangers."

16. Martin, "Introduction," 13; Valentine, "Advisors to ARVN Rangers"; Francis John Kelly, *U.S. Army Special Forces 1961–1971* (Washington, D.C.: Department of the Army, 1989), 156–158.

17. Valentine, "Vietnamese Rangers," 22; Valentine, "Advisors to ARVN Rangers"; Kelly, *Special Forces*, 158.

18. When I interviewed Nguyen Huu An, he was wearing his Ranger pin on his lapel.

19. An relates that there were three categories of injury: category one meant that the soldier was fit for combat duty; category two meant that the soldier was unfit for combat duty but could either serve on an army base or leave the military; category three meant that the soldier was disabled and was entitled to a disability pension.

20. Veith, *Black April*, 495.

21. Beth M. Robertson, *Oral History Handbook: Fourth Edition* (Adelaide: Oral History Association of Australia, 2000), 3.

22. Nguyen Huu An, "No va Toi (He and I)," *Viet Luan* (Vietnamese Herald), August 14, 2009, 54–55; August 21, 2009, 54–55; and August 28, 2009, 54–55. Translation by So Ung.

23. Email from Nguyen Huu An to the author, August 13, 2015.

24. Nguyen, "No va Toi," *Viet Luan*, August 14, 2009, 54.

25. Nguyen, "No va Toi," *Viet Luan*, August 14, 2009, 55.

26. Nguyen, "No va Toi," *Viet Luan*, August 21, 2009, 54.

27. Thien Loi, "Su Tra Thu De Hen va Da Man (Despicable and Savage Reprisals)." *Tap San Biet Dong Quan So 2* (Ranger Magazine No. 2), 2000, 37–50. Translation by Tuan Bui.

28. Pseudonym.

29. Thai is quoting the words of the former local guerrilla who took him to the site of the mass grave. Thai's account is reproduced in Nguyen Huu An, "Con Cop Den Co 13 Cai Rang (The Black Tiger Has Thirteen Teeth)," *Nguyen Khap Noi* (Nguyen Everywhere), May 2, 2012. Translation by Tuan Bui. http://www.nguyenkhapnoi.com/2012/05/02/con-cop-den-co-13-cai-rang/

30. Thai's account in Nguyen, "Con Cop Den."

31. Thai's account in Nguyen, "Con Cop Den."

32. Nguyen Phan, "Nhung Gio Phut Cuoi Cua Nhung Manh Ho (The Final Minutes of the Tigers)," *Que Huong Ngay Mai* (Homeland Tomorrow), May 9, 2013. Translation by Tuan Bui. My thanks to Nguyen Huu An for referring me to this article. http://www.uminhcoc.com/forums/showthread.php?t=191931

33. Selma Leydesdorff, Luisa Passerini, and Paul Thompson, "Introduction." In Selma Leydesdorff, Luisa Passerini and Paul Thompson, eds. *Gender and Memory* (New Brunswick: Transaction Publishers, 2006), 8.

34. Herman, *Trauma and Recovery*, 181.

35. Jay Winter, "Forms of Kinship and Remembrance in the Aftermath of the Great War." In Jay Winter and Emmanuel Sivan, eds. *War and Remembrance in the Twentieth Century* (Cambridge: Cambridge University Press, 1999), 40.

36. Winter, "Forms of Kinship," 40.

37. Antze and Lambek, "Preface," vii.

38. Uwe Siemon-Netto, *Duc: A reporter's love for the wounded people of Vietnam*. Uwe Siemon-Netto, 2013, 2.

39. Siemon-Netto, *Duc*, 2.

40. Duthie, "Transitional Justice," 243.

41. See, for example, Luis Ríos, José Ignacio Casado Ovejero, Jorge Puente Prieto, "Identification Process in Mass Graves from the Spanish Civil War I," *Forensic Science International* 199 (2010): e27–e36; Luis Ríos, Almudena García-Rubio, Berta Martínez, Andrea Alonso, Jorge Puente, "Identification Process in Mass Graves from the Spanish Civil War II," *Forensic Science International* 219 (2012): e4–e9; Claudia Garrido Varas, Marisol Intriago Leiva, "Managing Commingled Remains from Mass Graves: Considerations,

Implications and Recommendations from a Human Rights Case in Chile," *Forensic Science International* 219 (2012): e19–e24. Ríos, Overjero and Prieto note: "The identification of human remains in massive contexts is a complex process whose success depends on different factors, as it has been described by professionals working in mass graves resulting from human rights violations in Croatia, Kosovo and Serbia, or in natural disasters such as the Asian tsunami. Besides time and infrastructure constraints, the most important factors are the number of victims; the preservation of the remains and associated personal objects; the availability of appropriate methods and reference samples for the anthropological study and for an adequate presentation of the results; the quantity and quality of the antemortem information from relatives, witnesses and diverse documentary sources; the availability of financial support, living relatives and adequate statistical methods to conduct DNA analyses when possible." Ríos, Ovejero, Prieto, "Identification process," e27.

42. Arthur, "Human Rights," 326.

43. This situation may slowly change. The remains of twelve individuals were recovered at the formal archeological excavation of a gravesite at the former Lang Da reeducation camp in northern Vietnam in July 2010 as part of "The Returning Casualty" initiative by the Vietnamese American Foundation, and DNA analysis was conducted by the University of North Texas Center for Human Identification in 2011. Eleven remains provided viable mtDNA. See Julie Martin, "Excavations of Burial Sites at Vietnamese Re-Education Camps by The Returning Casualty," *The Southeast Asian Archeology Newsblog*. March 1, 2012.

http://www.southeastasianarchaeology.com/2012/03/01/excavations-of-burial-sites-at-vietnamese-re-education-camps-by-the-returning-casualty/

The Returning Casualty Blog contains entries between 2009 and 2011; however, the last entry is dated May 12, 2011, and there have been no further entries since. See http://vietremains.org/blog/

44. Joan M. Schwartz and Terry Cook, "Archives, Records, and Power: The Making of Modern Memory." *Archival Science* 2 (2002): 18.

45. Geoffrey Price, "Despatch to Senator D.R. Willesee on 15 August 1974." National Archives of Australia: Department of Foreign Affairs; A1838 2020/2/14 PART 11.

46. Price, "Despatch," A1838 2020/2/14 PART 11. Price's figure for Australian casualties refers to battle-related deaths and deaths in prisoner-of-war

camps. According to the Australian War Memorial, 20,194 Australian military deaths in the Second World War were nonbattle deaths. The overall total was 39,366.

47. Clarke, *Advice and Support*, 275.
48. Veith, *Black April*, 493–499.

CHAPTER 6

1. Nguyen Chi Thien, *Flowers from Hell (Hoa Dia-Nguc): Second Edition*. Huynh Sanh Thong ed. and trans. (New Haven: Council for Southeast Asia Studies, Yale Center for International and Area Studies, 1984), 133. Reprinted here by permission.

  Nguyen Chi Thien immigrated to the United States under the Humanitarian Operation program in 1995, and died in 2012.

2. Jean Libby, "Preface." In Nguyen Chi Thien, *Hoa Lo / Hanoi Hilton Stories* (New Haven: Yale University Southeast Asia Studies, 2007), xi.
3. See Nguyen, *Hoa Lo*, 248.
4. Nguyen, *Hoa Lo*, 2.
5. Nguyen, *Hoa Lo*, 2.
6. Nguyen, *Hoa Lo*, 2.
7. Nguyen Ngoc Bich, "Preface." Nguyen Chi Thien, *Hoa Dia Nguc / The Flowers of Hell: A Bilingual Selection* (Arlington, TX: To Hop Xuat Ban Mien Dong Hoa Ky, 1996), 20.
8. See Nguyen The Anh, "Phan Boi Chau's Memoirs and the Autobiographical Genre in Modern Vietnamese Literature." Seminar Paper (Oxford: Nissan Institute of Japanese Studies, 1990), 1–2.
9. Nguyen, "Preface," 20.
10. Nguyen, *Hoa Lo*, 9–13.
11. Libby, "Preface," xiii.
12. Nguyen, "Preface," 21.
13. Libby, "Preface," xiii–xiv.
14. Nguyen, *Hoa Lo*, 273.
15. Keegan and Holmes with Gau, *Soldiers*, 161.
16. Nancy Boyd Webb, "The Impact of Traumatic Stress and Loss on Children and Families." In Nancy Boyd Webb, ed. *Mass Trauma and Violence: Helping Families and Children Cope* (New York: The Guilford Press, 2004), 17.
17. See United Nations High Commissioner for Refugees, *Refugees*, 82; Desbarats, "Human Rights," 47–66; Hitchcox, *Vietnamese Refugees*, 36–68.

18. Nguyen, *Vietnam under Communism*, 190–191.

19. Nguyen, *Vietnam under Communism*, 192.

20. Terzani as quoted in Nguyen, *Vietnam under Communism*, 192. Nguyen writes that Terzani was in Saigon at the time, and was "at first favourably disposed towards the regime." Nguyen, *Vietnam under Communism*, 192, 197.

21. See Desbarats, "Human Rights," 54–55.

22. See Nguyen, *Vietnam under Communism*, 188; Vo, *Bamboo Gulag*, 59.

23. Nguyen, *Vietnam under Communism*, 188.

24. Nguyen, *Vietnam under Communism*, 198–199. Nguyen provides a map and list of prisons and reeducation camps in Vietnam by province.

25. Vo, *Bamboo Gulag*, 60.

26. Vo, *Bamboo Gulag*, 86–88.

27. Desbarats writes: "The practice of illegal arrest and detention is still common in the SRV [Socialist Republic of Vietnam], and includes cases of temporary detention exceeding the limits set by the law. In particular, there is much evidence of arbitrary arrest, and detention without trial in re-education camps and prisons. Arrests, which were particularly common in the post liberation period, have continued, though with decreasing frequency, over the past decade. In December 1985, for instance, the police security forces in the province of Long An 'searched and interrogated 180,000 families, arresting a total of 6,100 people who were then sent to concentration camps for re-education." Desbarats, "Human Rights," 54.

28. Kien Nguyen, *The Unwanted* (Sydney: Pan Macmillan, 2001), 245–249.

29. Nguyen, *Unwanted*, 245.

30. Nguyen, *Unwanted*, 245.

31. See, for example, Trong, *Enfer rouge*; Tran, *Lost Years*.

While the memoirs and poems by former male detainees have appeared in English and in French, and are therefore available to an international readership, no such writings by female detainees have as yet made their way into print. A recent memoir entitled *Doa Hong Gai* (Thorny Roses) by Nguyen Thanh Nga, for example, describes the author's ten years of internment in reeducation camps in Vietnam. However, it is only available in Vietnamese, which rather limits its readership.

32. For the experiences of South Vietnamese female veterans in postwar reeducation camps, see Nguyen, *Memory Is Another Country*, 75–82; Nguyen, "Women in Uniform," 20–33.

See also Linda Trinh Vo, "Managing Survival: Economic Realities for Vietnamese American Women." In Shirley Hune and Gail M. Nomura, eds.

Asian / Pacific Islander American Women (New York: New York University Press, 2003), 243. Vo refers briefly to South Vietnamese military women and to their imprisonment in postwar Vietnam.

33. "[A] 1985 UNHCR study revealed that 65 per cent of those apprehended by the authorities were imprisoned and of those 86 per cent were detained less than a year and 30 per cent less than a month." Robinson, *Terms of Refuge*, 179–180.

34. Perks and Thompson, "Introduction to the Second Edition," x.

35. Lynn Abrams, *Oral History Theory* (London: Routledge, 2010), 27.

36. Jay Winter, "Foreword: Remembrance as a Human Right." In Aleida Assmann and Linda Shortt, eds. *Memory and Political Change* (Houndmills: Palgrave Macmillan, 2012), xi.

37. Aleida Assmann and Linda Shortt, "Memory and Political Change: Introduction." In Assmann and Shortt, *Memory*, 4.

38. Nguyen Minh Tran, interview by Boitran Huynh-Beattie, August 29, 2010, Sydney.

39. The term *"nguy"* was used by the postwar communist regime to refer to all those who were associated with the former South Vietnamese government. The label extended to their families as well. See, for example, Hong's narrative and her description of *nguy* families in postwar Vietnam in Nguyen, *Voyage of Hope*, 97–115.

40. Veith, *Black April*, 278–279.

41. Truong Cong Hai, interview by Boitran Huynh-Beattie, November 3, 2010, Sydney.

42. Tran Nhu Hung, interview by author, September 19, 2013, Melbourne. NLA ORAL TRC 6525/35.

43. Nguyen, *Vietnam under Communism*, 196.

44. Joes, *War for South Viet Nam*, 59.

45. Lap, telephone interview by Boitran Huynh-Beattie, October 31, 2010.

46. Lua, telephone interview by Boitran Huynh-Beattie, October 26, 2010.

47. Ngoc, telephone interview by Boitran Huynh-Beattie, October 17, 2010.

48. Nguyen, *Nationalist in the Viet Nam Wars*, 330.

49. Nguyen, *Nationalist in the Viet Nam Wars*, 381.

50. Nguyen, *Nationalist in the Viet Nam Wars*, 381.

51. Nguyen, *Nationalist in the Viet Nam Wars*, 381–382.

52. Herman, *Trauma and Recovery*, 207.

53. Paul Ham, *Vietnam: The Australian War* (Sydney: HarperCollins, 2010), 685.

"The parade in Sydney on 3 October 1987 was the precursor to another Welcome Home parade and unveiling of the Australian Vietnam Forces National Memorial in Canberra on 3 October 1992. The Long Tan battle that was commemorated by some veterans on 18 August became a politically anointed national Vietnam Veterans Day to record the nation's apology and to acknowledge that the veterans deserved greater recognition." Bruce Davies with Gary McKay, *Vietnam: The Complete Story of the Australian War* (Crows Nest: Allen & Unwin, 2012), 584–585.

54. Selma Leydesdorff, Graham Dawson, Natasha Burchardt and T.G. Ashplant, "Introduction: Trauma and Life Stories." In Kim Lacy Rogers, Selma Leydesdorff and Graham Dawson, eds. *Trauma and Life Stories: International Perspectives* (London: Routledge, 1999), 1.

55. Kai Erikson quoted in Leydesdorff et al., "Introduction," 2.

56. Bessel A. van der Kolk and Alexander C. McFarlane, "The Black Hole of Trauma." In Bessel A. van der Kolk, Alexander C. McFarlane and Lars Weisaeth, eds. *Traumatic Stress: The Effects of Overwhelming Experience on Mind, Body, and Society* (New York: The Guilford Press, 1996), 9.

57. Sandra Soo-Jin Lee, "Aged Bodies as Sites of Remembrance: Colonial Memories in Diaspora." In Jill Bennett and Rosanne Kennedy, eds. *World Memory: Personal Trajectories in Global Time* (Houndmills: Palgrave Macmillan, 2003), 91.

58. Elie Wiesel, *Ethics and Memory* (Berlin: Walter de Gruyter, 1997), 17.

CHAPTER 7

1. Nguyen Huu An, interview by author, March 4, 2013, Melbourne. NLA ORAL TRC 6525/4.

2. Nguyen Huu An.

3. Christine McMurray, *Community Profiles 1996 Census: Viet Nam Born* (Belconnen: Department of Immigration and Multicultural Affairs, 1999), 1.

4. McMurray, *Community Profiles*, 1.

5. Mandy Thomas, "The Vietnamese in Australia." In James E. Coughlan and Deborah J. McNamara, eds. *Asians in Australia: Patterns of Migration and Settlement* (South Melbourne: Macmillan Education Australia, 1997), 275.

6. Australia, Department of Immigration and Multicultural and Indigenous Affairs, *The Viet Nam-born Community* (Canberra: Department of Immigration, Multicultural and Indigenous Affairs, 2003), 1.

7. Nancy Viviani, *The Indochinese in Australia: From Burnt Boats to Barbecues* (Melbourne: Oxford University Press, 1996), 104.

8. Thomas, "Vietnamese in Australia," 275.

9. Mandy Thomas, *Dreams in the Shadows: Vietnamese-Australian Lives in Transition* (St Leonards: Allen & Unwin, 1999), 6.

10. Australian Bureau of Statistics, *2011 Census of Population and Housing Basic Community Profile: B13 Language Spoken at Home by Sex* (Canberra: Commonwealth of Australia, 2012), B13 (b).

11. See Australia, Department of Immigration and Citizenship, *Community Information Summary: Viet Nam-born* (Canberra: Department of Immigration and Citizenship, 2011).

12. Nancy Viviani, *The Long Journey: Vietnamese Migration and Settlement in Australia* (Carlton: Melbourne University Press, 1984), 55.

13. Viviani, *Indochinese in Australia*, 1.

14. Australia, Senate, Senate Standing Committee on Foreign Affairs and Defence, *Report: Australia and the Refugee Problem: The Plight and Circumstances of Vietnamese and Other Refugees* (Canberra: Australian Government Publishing Service, 1976), 24.

15. NAA: Department of Foreign Affairs: South Vietnam—Australian representation—Evacuation of Australian personnel—Includes possible evacuation of refugees within Vietnam, 1975–1975. A1838 3014/10/6/1 PART 2: 108.

16. NAA A1838 3014/10/6/1 PART 2: 109.

17. Denis Warner, *Not Always on Horseback: An Australian Correspondent at War and Peace in Asia 1961–1993* (St Leonards: Allen & Unwin, 1997), 220–221.

18. See Christopher Price, "Last Days of Saigon Still Linger." *The Australian*, May 4, 2005, 14.

19. See Price, "Last Days," 14.

20. Australia, Senate, Senate Standing Committee on Foreign Affairs and Defence, *Report*, 18–24.

21. See NAA: Department of Foreign Affairs: Indo-Chinese refugees—Policies and programs—Staff at RVN [Republic of Vietnam] embassies, 1975–1975. A1838 1634/75/16 PART 1: 23, 38, 43–45 and 70–72.

22. Letter from Michael MacKellar to Tran Van Lam, February 18, 1976, as quoted in the Rymer Bayly Watson documentary film "All Points of the Compass," aired on ABC television in Australia, Sunday, May 1, 2005.

23. Peter Edwards, "The fall of Saigon, 1975." RG Neale Lecture Series (Canberra: The National Archives of Australia and the Department of Foreign Affairs and Trade, 2006), 15.

24. Jamie Mackie, "The Politics of Asian Immigration." In James E. Coughlan and Deborah J. McNamara, eds. *Asians in Australia: Patterns of Migration and Settlement* (South Melbourne: Macmillan Education Australia, 1997), 28.

25. Clem Lloyd and Jacqui Rees, *The Last Shilling: A History of Repatriation in Australia* (Melbourne: Melbourne University Press, 1994), 1.

26. Lloyd and Rees, *Last Shilling*, 419.

27. Australia, ComLaw, "Repatriation Acts Amendment Act (No. 2) 1979, No. 124, 1979 —Sect. 12." Canberra: ComLaw, 2012.
http://www.comlaw.gov.au/Details/C2004A02134

28. Albert Evan Adermann.

29. Australia, House of Representatives 1979, *Parliamentary Debates*, Vol H. of R. 116 (Canberra: The Commonwealth Government Printer, 1979), 1973.

30. Australia, House of Representatives 1979, *Debates*, 1973.

31. Australia, ComLaw, "Repatriation Acts Amendment Act (No. 2) 1979."

32. Australia, House of Representatives 1979, *Debates*, 1973.

33. Cabinet Submission 2596 1985 Attachment F. NAA Series A14039, 2596. My thanks to Peter Hamburger for providing me with copies of the relevant cabinet documents from the National Archives of Australia, and for his advice on cabinet procedures.

34. Cabinet Submission 2596 1985 Attachment F. NAA Series A14039, 2596.

35. Truong Cong Hai, interview by Boitran Huynh-Beattie, November 3, 2010, Sydney.

36. Tran Dang Vinh, interview by Boitran Huynh-Beattie, December 4, 2010, Sydney.

37. I made extensive enquiries with the Vietnam Veterans' and Veterans' Family Counselling Service as well as the Department of Veterans' Affairs in 2012. This information was confirmed in emails to the author from Letitia Hope, Assistant Secretary, Primary Health Care Branch, Department of Veterans' Affairs, Canberra, August 7, 2012, and Cathy Moss, Assistant Director Medical and Allied Health, Adelaide, June 27, 2012.

38. Nguyen Viet Long, interview by author, August 2, 2013, Melbourne. NLA ORAL TRC 6525/12.

39. Thien, interview by author, December 22, 2010, Melbourne.

40. See Andrew Lam, *Perfume Dreams: Reflections on the Vietnamese Diaspora* (Berkeley: Heyday Books, 2005), 1; Nguyen, *Memory Is Another Country*, 11–13.

41. See Australia, Department of Veterans' Affairs, "Service Details Questionnaire: (Pension or Qualifying Service Claim) Service with Forces in Vietnam" (Canberra: Department of Veterans' Affairs, 2012).

42. See Australia, Department of Veterans' Affairs, "Service Details Questionnaire."

43. See Nguyen-Marshall, "Oral History and Popular Memory," 159; Grey, "Review," 1–2.

44. See Tai, "Faces of Remembrance," 182; Nguyen, "War and Diaspora," 697–713.

45. Australia, House of Representatives 1985, *Parliamentary Debates*, Vols H. of R. 144–145 (Canberra: The Commonwealth Government Printer, 1985), 2178.

46. Australia, House of Representatives 1985, *Debates*, 2178.

47. Letter Gietzelt to Prime Minister, September 10, 1984, NAA Series 14039, 2596.

48. Cabinet Submission 3291 1985. Attachment D. Table 2. NAA Series A11116 CA2090 Part 1.

49. Cabinet Submission 3291 1985. Attachment D. Table 2. NAA Series A11116 CA2090 Part 1.

50. Cabinet Submission 2596 1985 Attachment D. NAA Series A14039, 2596.

51. Cabinet Submission 3291 1985. Attachment D. NAA Series A11116 CA2090 Part 1.

52. Australia, House of Representatives 1985, *Parliamentary Debates*. Vols H. of R. 144–145 (Canberra: The Commonwealth Government Printer, 1985), 2503.

53. Australia, Senate 1985, *Parliamentary Debates*, Vols S. 111–112 (Canberra: The Commonwealth Government Printer), 1985, 2459.

54. Australia, Senate 1985, *Debates*, 2459.

55. Australia, Senate 1985, *Debates*, 2460.

56. Australia, Senate 1985, *Debates*, 2460.

57. Australia, Senate 1985, *Debates*, 2474–2475.

58. Australia, Senate 1985, *Debates*, 2477.
59. Australia, Senate 1985, *Debates*, 2459.
60. Australia, Senate 1985, *Debates*, 2477–2478.
61. Australia, Senate 1985, *Debates*, 2478.
62. Australia, Senate 1985, *Debates*, 2479.
63. Australia, Senate 1985, *Debates*, 2479.
64. Australia, Senate 1985, *Debates*, 2480.
65. Australia, Senate 1985, *Debates*, 2481.
66. Australia, Senate 1985, *Debates*, 2481.
67. Australia, Senate 1985, *Debates*, 2591–2592.
68. Australia, House of Representatives 1985, *Debates*, 4044.
69. Australia, House of Representatives 1986, *Parliamentary Debates*, Vols H. of R. 147–149 (Canberra: The Commonwealth Government Printer, 1986), 2135.
70. Viviani, *Long Journey*, 55.
71. Don Peterson, "Our New Senator is a Man with a Mission." *The Courier Mail*, November 12, 1981, 5.
72. Fiona Jenkins, Mark Nolan and Kim Rubenstein, "Introduction: Allegiance and Identity in a Globalized World." In Fiona Jenkins, Mark Nolan and Kim Rubenstein, eds. *Allegiance and Identity in a Globalised World* (Cambridge: Cambridge University Press, 2015), 5.

CHAPTER 8

1. Oanh, telephone interview by Boitran Huynh-Beattie, May 9, 2011.
2. See Robinson, *Terms of Refuge*, 26–27.
3. See, for example, Robert S. McKelvey, *A Gift of Barbed Wire: America's Allies Abandoned in South Vietnam* (Seattle: University of Washington Press, 2002).
4. McKelvey, *Gift of Barbed Wire*, xix–xx.
5. Hai, interview by Boitran Huynh-Beattie, November 29, 2010, Sydney.
6. Nghiem, interview by Boitran Huynh-Beattie, April 25, 2011, Sydney.
7. Ngoc, interview by author, December 6, 2010, Melbourne.
8. Tuan, interview by author, December 4, 2014, Melbourne.
9. For further details of Ngoc's story, see Nguyen, *Memory Is Another Country*, 141–160.
10. See Nguyen Ngoc Bich, "From Facing Anti-War Crowds to Nation-building." In Taylor, *Voices*, 35.

11. Nguyen, "Anti-War Crowds," 35.

12. See, for example, Hong's story in Nguyen, *Voyage of Hope*, 109–110.

13. Desbarats, "Human Rights," 50.

14. Desbarats, "Human Rights," 50.

15. For further details of Thy's story, see Nguyen, *Voyage of Hope*, 2005, 13–14, 142–144; Nguyen, *Memory Is Another Country*, 2009, 154–160.

16. See, for example, John Sutton and Kellie Williamson, "Introduction: The Diversity of Embodied Remembering." In Lawrence Shapiro, ed. *The Routledge Handbook of Embodied Cognition* (London: Routledge, 2014), 315–320.

17. Marianne Hirsch and Leo Spitzer, "'We Would Never Have Come Without You': Generations of Nostalgia." In Katharine Hodgkin and Susannah Radstone eds. *Contested Pasts: The Politics of Memory* (London: Routledge, 2003), 85.

18. Thien, interview by author, December 22, 2010, Melbourne.

19. Eva Hoffman, "The Long Afterlife of Loss." In Susannah Radstone and Bill Schwartz, eds. *Memory: Histories, Theories, Debates* (New York: Fordham University Press, 2010), 406.

20. Hoffman, "Loss," 412.

21. Many South Vietnamese destroyed or burnt family papers and photographs in 1975. See Lam, *Perfume Dreams*, 1; Nguyen, *Memory Is Another Country*, 11–13.

22. See Nguyen, *Vietnam under Communism*; Hitchcox, *Vietnamese Refugees*; Freeman and Nguyen, *Voices from the Camps*; and Vo, *Bamboo Gulag*.

23. See, for example, Nguyen, *Unwanted*, 245–249.

24. Nicolas Argenti and Katharina Schramm, "Introduction: Remembering Violence: Anthropological Perspectives on Intergenerational Transmission." In Nicolas Argenti and Katharina Schramm, eds. *Remembering Violence: Anthropological Perspectives on Intergenerational Transmission* (New York: Berghahn Books, 2010), 1.

25. See Marilyn Lake and Joy Damousi, "Introduction: Warfare, History and Gender." In Joy Damousi and Marilyn Lake, eds. *Gender and War: Australians at War in the Twentieth Century* (Cambridge: Cambridge University Press, 1995), 3.

26. Denis Warner. "Witness Statement. The Senate Standing Committee on Foreign Affairs and Defence, Melbourne, 13 October 1975." Denis Warner Papers, NLA MS 9489/1/79. 243.

27. Warner, "Witness Statement," 240–301.

28. Vietnamese veterans in Australia have marched on Anzac Day since 1981.

29. For a detailed examination of side-by-side memorials featuring a South Vietnamese soldier statue standing or sitting next to the statue of an Australian soldier, see Christopher R. Linke, "Side-by-Side Memorials: Commemorating the Vietnam War in Australia." In Nathalie Huynh Chau Nguyen, ed. *New Perceptions of the Vietnam War: Essays on the War, the South Vietnamese Experience, the Diaspora and the Continuing Impact* (Jefferson: McFarland, 2015), 85–107.

30. Susannah Radstone and Bill Schwartz, "Introduction." In Susannah Radstone and Bill Schwartz, eds. *Memory: Histories, Theories, Debates* (New York: Fordham University Press, 2010), 3.

CONCLUSION

1. Thanh-Vân Tôn-Thât, *Le pays d'avant* (The Country from Before) (Rome: Portaparole, 2007), 9–10. Reprinted here by permission. Author's translation.

2. Veith, *Black April*, 7.

3. Cao Xuan Huy, *Thang Ba Gay Sung* (The March My Rifle Broke) (Westminster: Van Khoa, 1986). http://www.talawas.org/talaDB/showFile.php?res=435&rb=08. Translation by Quynh-Du Ton That.

4. Nguyen Viet Long, interview by author, August 2, 2013, Melbourne. NLA ORAL TRC 6525/12.

5. Michael Humphrey, *The Politics of Atrocity and Reconciliation: From Terror to Trauma* (London: Routledge, 2000), 52.

6. From "Em di trong chieu" (In the Evening You Walk) (1969) by Trinh Cong Son. Translation by Quynh-Du Ton That. Reprinted here by permission. http://www.tcs-home.org/songs-en/songs/in-the-evening-you-walk

7. For more details of Anh's story, see Nguyen, *Voyage of Hope*, 18–19, 90–95; Nguyen, *Memory Is Another Country*, 35–56.

8. Nguyen, *Voyage of Hope*, 93.

9. See Veith and Pribbenow, "'Fighting Is an Art,'" 163–213.

10. Veith and Pribbenow, "'Fighting Is an Art,'" 163.

11. Veith and Pribbenow, "'Fighting Is an Art,'" 213.

12. Dinh Soan, "Toi va Anh (He and I)." *Ly Tuong Uc Chau: Lien Hoi Ai Huu Khong Quan—QLVNCH—Uc Chau 2013* (Ideology Australia:

Magazine of the Republic of Vietnam Air Force Veteran Association in Australia 2013), 108–113. The events related occurred on April 16–17, 1975. Tinh Long 7 mission/821st Squadron/53rd Tactical Wing/5th Air Division. Translation by Tuan Bui.

13. Dinh Soan, "Toi va Anh," 108–119.

14. Nguyen, *Nationalist in the Viet Nam Wars*, 461.

15. Nguyen, *Nationalist in the Viet Nam Wars*, 461.

16. See, for example, Vieda Skultans, "Narratives of Displacement and Identity." In Brian Hurwitz, Trisha Greenhalgh and Vieda Skultans, eds. *Narrative Research in Health and Illness* (Malden: Blackwell Publishing, 2004), 292–308. Skultans, a child refugee from Latvia who moved to Britain in 1948, remembers the hostility that was directed towards East European refugees and writes, "the East Europeans might have seen themselves as political refugees but their host country saw them as economic migrants." Skultans, "Narratives of Displacement," 294. Many Vietnamese refugees were similarly labeled "economic migrants," especially in the 1980s.

17. See Returned Services League, Victorian Branch, "Minutes of Anzac Day Commemoration Council Meeting Held in the Board Room at Anzac House on Wednesday, 14 October, 1981 at 5.30pm," 3. My thanks to Keith Rossi for providing me with a copy of the Minutes.

18. Edwards, "Fall of Saigon," 15–16.

19. Selma Leydesdorff, Luisa Passerini and Paul Thompson, "Introduction." In Selma Leydesdorff, Luisa Passerini and Paul Thompson, eds. *Gender and Memory* (New Brunswick: Transaction Publishers, 2007), 6.

20. Nancy K. Miller and Jason Tougaw, "Introduction." In Nancy K. Miller and Jason Tougaw, eds. *Extremities: Trauma, Testimony, and Community* (Urbana: University of Illinois Press, 2002), 13.

BIBLIOGRAPHY

Abrams, Lynn. *Oral History Theory*. London: Routledge, 2010.
Andradé, Dale. *Trial by Fire: The 1972 Easter Offensive, America's Last Vietnam Battle*. New York: Hippocrene Books, 1995.
Ang Cheng Guan. *Ending the Vietnam War: The Vietnamese Communists' Perspective*. London: RoutledgeCurzon, 2004.
Antze, Paul and Michael Lambek. "Preface." In Paul Antze and Michael Lambek, eds. *Tense Past: Essays in Trauma and Memory*. New York: Routledge, 1996. vii–ix.
Argenti, Nicolas and Katharina Schramm. "Introduction: Remembering Violence: Anthropological Perspectives on Intergenerational Transmission." In Nicolas Argenti and Katharina Schramm, eds. *Remembering Violence: Anthropological Perspectives on Intergenerational Transmission*. New York: Berghahn Books, 2010. 1–39.
Arthur, Paige. "How 'Transitions' Reshaped Human Rights: A Conceptual History of Transitional Justice." *Human Rights Quarterly* 31 (2009): 321–367.
Asselin, Pierre. *Hanoi's Road to the Vietnam War, 1954–1965*. Berkeley: University of California Press, 2013.
Assmann, Aleida and Linda Shortt. "Memory and Political Change: Introduction." In Aleida Assmann and Linda Shortt, eds. *Memory and Political Change*. Houndmills: Palgrave Macmillan, 2012. 1–14.
Australia. Bureau of Statistics. *2011 Census of Population and Housing Basic Community Profile: B13 Language Spoken at Home by Sex*. Canberra: Commonwealth of Australia, 2012.

Australia. Cabinet Submission 2596 1985 Attachment D. National Archives of Australia Series A14039, 2596.

Australia. Cabinet Submission 2596 1985 Attachment F. National Archives of Australia Series A14039, 2596.

Australia. Cabinet Submission 3291 1985. Attachment D. National Archives of Australia Series A11116 CA2090 Part 1.

Australia. ComLaw. *Repatriation Acts Amendment Act (No. 2) 1979*. Canberra: ComLaw, 2012. http://www.comlaw.gov.au/Details/C2004A02134.

Australia. Department of Foreign Affairs; National Archives of Australia A1838 1634/75/16 PART 1, Indo-Chinese refugees—Policies and programs—Staff at RVN [Republic of Vietnam] embassies, 1975–1975; A1838 3014/10/6/1 PART 2, South Vietnam—Australian representation—Evacuation of Australian personnel—Includes possible evacuation of refugees within Vietnam, 1975–1975.

Australia. Department of Immigration and Citizenship. *Community Information Summary: Viet Nam-Born*. Canberra: Australian Government Publishing Service, 2011. http://www.immi.gov.au/media/publications/statistics/comm-summ/summary.htm.

Australia. Department of Immigration and Multicultural and Indigenous Affairs. *The Viet Nam-born Community*. Canberra: Department of Immigration, Multicultural and Indigenous Affairs, 2003.

Australia. House of Representatives 1979. *Parliamentary Debates*. Vol H. of R. 116. Canberra: The Commonwealth Government Printer, 1979.

Australia. House of Representatives 1985. *Parliamentary Debates*. Vols H. of R. 144–145. Canberra: The Commonwealth Government Printer, 1985.

Australia. House of Representatives 1986. *Parliamentary Debates*. Vols H. of R. 147–149. Canberra: The Commonwealth Government Printer, 1986.

Australia. Senate 1979. *Parliamentary Debates*. Vol S. 83. Canberra: The Commonwealth Government Printer, 1979.

Australia. Senate 1985. *Parliamentary Debates*. Vols S. 111–112. Canberra: The Commonwealth Government Printer, 1985.

Australia. Senate 1986. *Parliamentary Debates*. Vols S. 114–115. Canberra: The Commonwealth Government Printer, 1986.

Australia. Senate. Senate Standing Committee on Foreign Affairs and Defence. *Report: Australia and the Refugee Problem: The plight and circumstances of Vietnamese and other refugees*. Canberra: Australian Government Publishing Service, 1976.

Bonnano, George. "Loss, Trauma, and Human Resilience: Have We Underestimated the Human Capacity to Thrive After Extremely Aversive Events?" *American Psychologist* 59, no. 1 (2004): 20–28.

Brass, Alistair. *Medicine in South Vietnam Today*. Sydney: Australasian Medical Publishing, 1967.

Brigham, Robert K. *ARVN: Life and Death in the South Vietnamese Army*. Lawrence: University Press of Kansas, 2006.

Brigham, Robert K. "Dreaming Different Dreams: the United States and the Army of the Republic of Vietnam." In Marilyn B. Young and Robert Buzzanco, eds. *A Companion to the Vietnam War*. Malden: Blackwell, 2002. 146–161.

Brush, Peter. "The Vietnamese Marine Corps." *Viet Nam Generation: A Journal of Recent History and Contemporary Culture* 7, nos. 1–2 (1996): 73–78.

Bunker, Robert J. "Grenades, Launched: Allied and Democratic Republic of Vietnam." In Spencer C. Tucker, ed. *Encyclopedia of the Vietnam War: A Political, Social and Military History*. Vol. I. Santa Barbara, CA: ABC-CLIO, 1998. 252–253.

Cao Xuan Huy. *Thang Ba Gay Sung* (The March My Rifle Broke). Westminster: Van Khoa, 1986. http://www.talawas.org/talaDB/showFile.php?res=435&rb=08

Catton, Philip E. *Diem's Final Failure: Prelude to America's War in Vietnam*. Lawrence: University Press of Kansas, 2002.

Clarke, Jeffrey C. *Advice and Support: The Final Years, 1965–1973*. Washington D.C.: Center of Military History, United States Army, 1988.

Clendinnen, Inga. "The History Question: Who Owns the Past?" *Quarterly Essay* 23 (2006): 1–72.

Dang Phong, ed. *Lich Su Kinh Te Viet Nam 1945–2000* (Vietnamese Economic History 1945–2000), Vol II: 1955–1975. Hanoi: Social Sciences Publishing House, 2005.

Dang Thuy Tram. *Last Night I Dreamed of Peace: The Diary of Dang Thuy Tram*. Andrew X. Pham, trans. New York: Harmony Books, 2007.

Daum, Pierre. *Immigrés de force: Les travailleurs indochinois en France (1939–1952)* (Forced Migrants: Indochinese Workers in France (1939–1952)). Arles: Actes Sud, 2009.

Davies, Bruce with Gary McKay. *Vietnam: The Complete Story of the Australian War*. Crows Nest: Allen & Unwin, 2012.

DeBonis, Steven. *Children of the Enemy: Oral Histories of Vietnamese Amerasians and Their Mothers*. Jefferson, NC: McFarland, 1995.

DeGroot, Gerard J. "Introduction to Part 1: Arms and the Woman." In Gerard J. DeGroot and Corinna Peniston-Bird, eds. *A Soldier and a Woman: Sexual Integration in the Military.* Harlow: Longman, 2000. 3–17.

Desbarats, Jacqueline. "Human Rights: Two Steps Forward, One Step Backward?" In Thai Quang Trung, ed. *Vietnam Today: Assessing the New Trends.* New York: Crane Russak, 1990. 47–66.

Dinh Soan. "Toi va Anh (He and I)." *Ly Tuong Uc Chau: Lien Hoi Ai Huu Khong Quan—QLVNCH—Uc Chau 2013* (Ideology Australia: Magazine of the Republic of Vietnam Air Force Veteran Association in Australia 2013), 2013. 108–113.

Dong Van Khuyen. *The RVNAF.* Washington D.C.: U.S. Army Center of Military History, 1980.

Dorland, Gil. *Legacy of Discord: Voices of the Vietnam War Era.* Dulles: Brassey's, 2001.

Dunnigan, James F. and Albert A. Nofi. *Dirty Little Secrets of the Vietnam War: Military Information You're Not Supposed to Know.* New York: Thomas Dunne Books, 2000.

Dunstan, Simon. *The M113 Series.* London: Osprey Publishing, 1983.

Duthie, Roger. "Transitional Justice and Displacement." *The International Journal of Transitional Justice* 5 (2011): 241–261.

Eastwood, Terry. "Reflections on the Goal of Archival Appraisal in Democratic Societies." *Archivaria* 54 (2002): 59–71.

Edwards, Peter. "The fall of Saigon, 1975." RG Neale Lecture Series. Canberra: The National Archives of Australia and the Department of Foreign Affairs and Trade, 2006.

Fielding, Angela and Judi Anderson. "Working with Refugee Communities to Build Collective Resilience." AseTTS Occasional Paper 2008. Perth, WA: Association for Services to Torture and Trauma Survivors Inc., 2008.

Fraser, George MacDonald. *Quartered Safe out Here: A Recollection of the War in Burma.* London: Harvill, 1993.

Freeman, James M. and Nguyen Dinh Huu. *Voices from the Camps: Vietnamese Children Seeking Asylum.* Seattle: University of Washington Press, 2003.

Gaiduk, Ilya V. *Confronting Vietnam: Soviet Policy toward the Indochina Conflict, 1954–1963.* Stanford, CA: Stanford University Press, 2003.

Gaiduk, Ilya V. *The Soviet Union and the Vietnam War.* Chicago, IL: Ivan R. Dee, 1996.

Grey, Jeffrey. "Review of Lam Quang Thi, *The Twenty-Five Year Century: A South Vietnamese General Remembers the Indochina War to the Fall of Saigon.*" H-War, H-Net Reviews in the Humanities and Social Sciences, 2004. 1–2. http: //www.h-net.org/reviews/showrev.php?id=9193.

Guillemot, François. "Au cœur de la fracture vietnamienne: L'élimination de l'opposition nationaliste et anticolonialiste dans le Nord du Vietnam (1945–1946) (At the Heart of the Vietnamese Fracture: The Elimination of Nationalist and Anticolonial Opposition in Northern Vietnam (1945–1946))." In Christopher E. Goscha and Benoît De Tréglodé, eds. *Naissance d'un Etat-Parti: Le Viêt Nam depuis 1945 / The Birth of a Party-State: Vietnam since 1945.* Paris: Les Indes Savantes, 2004. 175–216.

Guillemot, François. "'Be Men!': Fighting and Dying for the State of Vietnam (1951–54)," *War & Society* 31, no. 2 (2012): 184–210.

Guillemot, François. *Dai Viêt, indépendance et révolution au Viêt-Nam: L'échec de la troisième voie (1938–1955)* (Dai Viet: Independence and Revolution in Vietnam: The Failure of the Third Path). Paris: Les Indes savantes, 2012.

Guillemot, François. *Des Vietnamiennes dans la guerre civile: L'autre moitié de la guerre 1945–1975* (Vietnamese Women in the Civil War: The Other Half of the War 1945–1975). Paris: Les Indes Savantes, 2014.

Gullett, Henry ('Jo'). *Not as a Duty Only: An Infantryman's War.* Melbourne: Melbourne University Press, 1976.

Ha Ma Viet. *Steel and Blood: South Vietnamese Armor and the War for Southeast Asia.* Annapolis: Naval Institute Press, 2008.

Hai Trieu. "Nguoi Nu Binh khong co So Quan tren khang tuyen Ba To (The Female Soldier without Military Number in Resistance Line Ba To)." *Guom Thieng: Vinh Danh Nu Quan Nhan QLVNCH* (Sacred Sword: Special Issue Glorifying the Women's Armed Forces Corps of the RVNAF), 2014. 86–88.

Ham, Paul. *Vietnam: The Australian War.* Sydney: HarperCollins, 2010.

Herman, Judith Lewis. *Trauma and Recovery.* New York: Basic Books, 1992.

Hirsch, Marianne and Leo Spitzer. "'We Would Never Have Come Without You': Generations of Nostalgia." In Katharine Hodgkin and Susannah Radstone, eds. *Contested Pasts: The Politics of Memory.* London: Routledge, 2003. 79–95.

Hitchcox, Linda. *Vietnamese Refugees in Southeast Asian Camps.* Basingstoke: Macmillan in association with St Antony's College, Oxford, 1990.

Ho Thi Ve. "Nu Quan Nhan" (Servicewomen). *Dac San Cuu Nu Quan Nhan QLVNCH: Ky Niem Ngay Hoi Ngo NQN 12 Thang 8 Nam 2001* (Magazine of the Servicewomen of the Republic of Vietnam Armed Forces: Special Bulletin of the Reunion of Servicewomen on August 12, 2001), 2001. 7–18.

Hoang Co Lan. "Etudiant et Médecin au Viet Nam (Student and Doctor in Vietnam)." In Tran Xuan Dung, Tran Quoc Dong, Vu Van Tung, Bui Khiet, eds. *Quan Y Quan Luc Viet Nam Cong Hoa: Le Corps de Santé des Forces Armées de la République du Viet Nam Nam* (The Medical Corps of the Republic of Vietnam Armed Forces). South Melbourne, Victoria: Tran Xuan Dung, 2000. 74–94.

Hodgkin, Katharine and Susannah Radstone. "Introduction: Contested pasts." In Katharine Hodgkin and Susannah Radstone, eds. *Contested Pasts: The Politics of Memory*. London: Routledge, 2003. 1–21.

Hoffman, Eva. "The Long Afterlife of Loss." In Susannah Radstone and Bill Schwartz, eds. *Memory: Histories, Theories, Debates*. New York: Fordham University Press, 2010. 406–415.

Hoi H.O. Cuu Tro Thuong Phe Binh va Qua Phu VNCH (Disabled Veterans and Widows Relief Association of the Republic of Vietnam). *Cam On Anh* (Thank You Brother), July 28, 2013.

Hukee, Brian E. *USAF and VNAF A-1 Skyraider Units of the Vietnam War*. Oxford: Osprey Publishing, 2013.

Humphrey, Michael. *The Politics of Atrocity and Reconciliation: From Terror to Trauma*. London: Routledge, 2000.

Jacobs, Seth. *Cold War Mandarin: Ngo Dinh Diem and the Origins of America's War in Vietnam, 1950–1963*. Lanham: Rowman & Littlefield, 2006.

Jamieson, Neil L. *Understanding Vietnam*. Berkeley: University of California Press, 1995.

Jenkins, Fiona, Mark Nolan and Kim Rubenstein. "Introduction: Allegiance and Identity in a Globalized World." In Fiona Jenkins, Mark Nolan and Kim Rubenstein, eds. *Allegiance and Identity in a Globalised World*. Cambridge: Cambridge University Press, 2015. 1–27.

Joes, Anthony James. *The War for South Viet Nam, 1954–1975*. Rev. ed. Westport: Praeger, 2001.

Keegan, John and Richard Holmes with John Gau. *Soldiers: A History of Men in Battle*. London: Hamish Hamilton, 1985.

Kelly, Francis John. *U.S. Army Special Forces 1961–1971*. Washington D.C.: Department of the Army, 1989.

Krall, Yung. *A Thousand Tears Falling: The True Story of a Vietnamese Family Torn Apart by War, Communism, and the CIA*. Atlanta, GA: Longstreet Press, 1995.

Kurylo, Elizabeth. "Honored patriot learned of liberty the hard way." *The Atlanta Journal—Constitution*, July 4, 1998, D10.

Kwon, Heonik. *Ghosts of War in Vietnam*. Cambridge: Cambridge University Press, 2008.

Lake, Marilyn and Joy Damousi. "Introduction: Warfare, History and Gender." In Joy Damousi and Marilyn Lake, eds. *Gender and War: Australians at War in the Twentieth Century*. Cambridge: Cambridge University Press, 1995. 1–20.

Lam, Andrew. *Perfume Dreams: Reflections on the Vietnamese Diaspora*. Berkeley, CA: Heyday Books, 2005.

Lam Quang Thi. *Hell in An Loc: The 1972 Easter Invasion and the Battle that Saved South Viet Nam*. Denton: University of North Texas Press, 2009.

Lam Quang Thi. *The Twenty-Five Year Century: A South Vietnamese General Remembers the Indochina War to the Fall of Saigon*. Denton: University of North Texas Press, 2001.

Le Thanh Y. "Pleime, Été 71 (Pleime, Summer 71)." In Tran Xuan Dung, Tran Quoc Dong, Vu Van Tung, Bui Khiet, eds. *Quan Y Quan Luc Viet Nam Cong Hoa: Le Corps de Santé des Forces Armées de la République du Viet Nam Nam* (The Medical Corps of the Republic of Vietnam Armed Forces). South Melbourne, Victoria: Tran Xuan Dung, 2000. 362–366.

Lee, Sandra Soo-Jin. "Aged Bodies as Sites of Remembrance: Colonial Memories in Diaspora." In Jill Bennett and Rosanne Kennedy, eds. *World Memory: Personal Trajectories in Global Time*. Houndmills: Palgrave Macmillan, 2003. 87–100.

Lewy, Guenter. *America in Vietnam*. New York: Oxford University Press, 1978.

Leydesdorff, Selma, Graham Dawson, Natasha Burchardt and T. G. Ashplant. "Introduction: Trauma and Life Stories." In Kim Lacy Rogers, Selma Leydesdorff, and Graham Dawson, eds. *Trauma and Life Stories: International Perspectives*. London: Routledge, 1999. 1–26.

Leydesdorff, Selma, Luisa Passerini, and Paul Thompson, "Introduction." In Selma Leydesdorff, Luisa Passerini and Paul Thompson, eds. *Gender and Memory*. New Brunswick: Transaction Publishers, 2006. 1–16.

Libby, Jean. "Preface." In Nguyen Chi Thien. *Hoa Lo / Hanoi Hilton Stories*. New Haven, CT: Yale University Southeast Asia Studies, 2007. xi–xiv.

Linke, Christopher R. "Side-by-Side Memorials: Commemorating the Vietnam War in Australia." In Nathalie Huynh Chau Nguyen, ed. *New Perceptions of the Vietnam War: Essays on the War, the South Vietnamese Experience, the Diaspora and the Continuing Impact*. Jefferson, NC: McFarland, 2015. 85–107.

Lloyd, Clem and Jacqui Rees. *The Last Shilling: A History of Repatriation in Australia*. Melbourne: Melbourne University Press, 1994.

Lu Tuan. "Nhung Phu Nu Dung Cam (The Brave Women)." *Dac San Cuu Nu Quan Nhan QLVNCH: Ky Niem Hoi Ngo NQN Ky IV 25–26 Thang 8 Nam 2007* (Magazine of the Servicewomen of the Republic of Vietnam Armed Forces: Special Bulletin of the 4th Reunion of Servicewomen on August 25–26, 2007). 28–30.

Luguern, Liêm-Khê. "Ni civil ni militaire: le travailleur indochinois inconnu de la Second Guerre mondiale (Neither civilian nor military: Unknown Indochinese Workers of the Second World War)." *Le Mouvement Social 2*, nos 219–220 (2007): 185–199.

Mackie, Jamie. "The Politics of Asian Immigration." In James E. Coughlan and Deborah J. McNamara, eds. *Asians in Australia: Patterns of Migration and Settlement*. South Melbourne: Macmillan Education Australia, 1997. 10–48.

Marolda, Edward J. "Vietnam, Republic of: Navy (VNN)." In Spencer C. Tucker, ed. *Encyclopedia of the Vietnam War: A Political, Social, and Military History*. Vol. II. Santa Barbara, CA: ABC-CLIO, 1998. 782–784.

Martin, Julie. "Excavations of Burial Sites at Vietnamese Re-Education Camps by The Returning Casualty." *The Southeast Asian Archeology Newsblog*. March 1, 2012. http://www.southeastasianarchaeology.com/2012/03/01/excavations-of-burial-sites-at-vietnamese-re-education-camps-by-the-returning-casualty/

Martin, Michael. "Introduction." In Michael N. Martin and McDonald Valentine Jr., eds. *The Black Tigers: Elite South Vietnamese Rangers and their American Advisors*. Louisville, KT: Harmony House Publishers, 1993. 13–19.

McKelvey, Robert S. *The Dust of Life: America's Children Abandoned in Vietnam*. Seattle: University of Washington Press, 1999.

McKelvey, Robert S. *A Gift of Barbed Wire: America's Allies Abandoned in South Vietnam*. Seattle: University of Washington Press, 2002.

McMurray, Christine. *Community Profiles 1996 Census: Viet Nam Born*. Belconnen: Department of Immigration and Multicultural Affairs, 1999.

Melson, Charles D. "Ripley at the Bridge: Dong Ha, South Vietnam, 2 April 1972." http://kbc3337design.tripod.com/ripley.htm

Military Institute of Vietnam. *Victory in Vietnam: The Official History of the People's Army of Vietnam 1954–1975*. Merle L. Pribbenow, trans. Lawrence: University Press of Kansas, 2002.

Miller, Nancy K. and Jason Tougaw, "Introduction." In Nancy K. Miller and Jason Tougaw, eds. *Extremities: Trauma, Testimony, and Community*. Urbana: University of Illinois Press, 2002. 1–21.

Momyer, William W. "The Vietnamese Air Force, 1951–1975: An Analysis of Its Role in Combat." In Major A.J.C. Lavalle, gen. ed. *The Vietnamese Air Force, 1951–1975: An Analysis of Its Role in Combat and Fourteen Hours at Koh Tang*. Washington, D.C.: Office of Air Force History, United States Air Force, 1985. v–xiv, 1–82.

Moyar, Mark. *Triumph Forsaken: The Vietnam War, 1954–1965*. Cambridge: Cambridge University Press, 2006.

Ngo Quang Truong. "Territorial Forces." In Lewis Sorley, ed. *The Vietnam War: An Assessment by South Vietnam's Generals*. Lubbock: Texas Tech University Press, 2010. 178–214.

Ngo Van Dinh. "Marine Brigade 258's Victory at Quang Tri." Tran Xuan Dung, ed. *History of the South Vietnamese Marine Corps Army of the Republic of Vietnam / Chien Su Thuy Quan Luc Chien Quan Luc Viet Nam Cong Hoa*. South Melbourne: Tran Xuan Dung, 2007. 896–912.

Nguyen, Cam. "East, West, and Vietnamese Women." *The Journal of Vietnamese Studies* 5 (1992): 44–50.

Nguyen Chi Thien. *Flowers from Hell (Hoa Dia-Nguc)*. Huynh Sanh Thong, ed. and trans. New Haven, CT: Council on Southeast Asia Studies, Yale Center for International and Area Studies, 1984.

Nguyen Chi Thien. *Hoa Dia Nguc / The Flowers of Hell: A Bilingual Selection*. Nguyen Ngoc Bich, ed. and trans. Arlington, TX: To Hop Xuat Ban Mien Dong Hoa Ky, 1996.

Nguyen Chi Thien. *Hoa Lo: Hanoi Hilton Stories*. Yale: Yale University Southeast Asia Studies, 2007.

Nguyen Cong Luan. *Nationalist in the Viet Nam Wars: Memoirs of a Victim Turned Soldier*. Bloomington: Indiana University Press, 2012.

Nguyen Huu An. "Con Cop Den Co 13 Cai Rang (The Black Tiger Has Thirteen Teeth)." *Nguyen Khap Noi* (Nguyen Everywhere), May 2, 2012. http://www.nguyenkhapnoi.com/2012/05/02/con-cop-den-co-13-cai-rang/

Nguyen Huu An. "No va Toi (He and I)." *Viet Luan* (Vietnamese Herald), August 14, 2009, 54–55; August 21, 2009, 54–55; and August 28, 2009, 54–55.

Nguyen Huu Hiep. "Souvenirs d'après Guerre (Postwar Memories)." In Tran Xuan Dung, Tran Quoc Dong, Vu Van Tung, Bui Khiet, eds. *Quan Y Quan Luc Viet Nam Cong Hoa: Le Corps de Santé des Forces Armées de la République du Viet Nam Nam* (The Medical Corps of the Republic of Vietnam Armed Forces). South Melbourne, Victoria: Tran Xuan Dung, 2000. 424–450.

Nguyen, Kien. *The Unwanted*. Sydney: Pan Macmillan, 2001.

Nguyen, Lien-Hang T. *Hanoi's War: An International History of the War for Peace in Vietnam*. Chapel Hill: The University of North Carolina Press, 2012.

Nguyen, Nathalie Huynh Chau. *Memory Is Another Country: Women of the Vietnamese Diaspora*. Santa Barbara, CA: Praeger, 2009.

Nguyen, Nathalie Huynh Chau. "South Vietnamese Women in Uniform: Narratives of Wartime and Post War Lives." *The Minerva Journal of Women and War* 3, no. 2 (2009): 8–33.

Nguyen, Nathalie Huynh Chau. *Vietnamese Voices: Gender and Cultural Identity in the Vietnamese Francophone Novel*. DeKalb: Southeast Asia Publications, Center for Southeast Asian Studies, Northern Illinois University, 2003.

Nguyen, Nathalie Huynh Chau. *Voyage of Hope: Vietnamese Australian Women's Narratives*. Altona: Common Ground Publishing, 2005.

Nguyen, Nathalie Huynh Chau. "War and Diaspora: The Memories of South Vietnamese Soldiers," *Journal of Intercultural Studies* 34, no. 6 (2013): 697–713.

Nguyen Ngoc Bich. "From Facing Anti-war Crowds to Nation-building." In K. W. Taylor, ed. *Voices from the Second Republic of South Vietnam (1967–1975)*. Ithaca: Southeast Asia Program Publications, Cornell University, 2015. 31–37.

Nguyen Ngoc Bich. "Preface." In Nguyen Chi Thien, *Hoa Dia Nguc / The Flowers of Hell: A Bilingual Selection*. Nguyen Ngoc Bich, ed. and trans. Arlington, TX: To Hop Xuat Ban Mien Dong Hoa Ky, 1996. 17–23.

Nguyen Phan. "Nhung Gio Phut Cuoi Cua Nhung Manh Ho (The Final Minutes of the Tigers)." *Que Huong Ngay Mai* (Homeland Tomorrow), May 9, 2013.

Nguyen The Anh. "Phan Boi Chau's Memoirs and the Autobiographical Genre in Modern Vietnamese Literature." Seminar Paper. Oxford: Nissan Institute of Japanese Studies, 1990. 1–10.

Nguyen Thi Hanh Nhon. "Phat bieu cua Dai dien Ban To Chuc Hoi Ngo Nu Quan Nhan Hai Ngoai Ky IV" (Speech of the WAFC Committee Representative delivered at the Fourth Overseas Reunion). *Dac San Cuu Nu Quan Nhan QLVNCH: Ky Niem Hoi Ngo NQN Ky IV 25–26 Thang 8 Nam 2007 Tai Nam California* (Magazine of the Servicewomen of the Republic of Vietnam Armed Forces: Special Bulletin to commemorate the Fourth Reunion of Servicewomen on August 25–26, 2007, in Southern California), 2007. 4–5.

Nguyen Thi Hanh Nhon. "Thu Moi Hop Mat Nu Quan Nhan Hai Ngoai" (Letter of Invitation to a Meeting of Overseas Servicewomen). *Dac San Cuu Nu Quan Nhan QLVNCH: Ky Niem Ngay Hoi Ngo NQN 12 Thang 8 Nam 2001* (Magazine of the Servicewomen of the Republic of Vietnam Armed Forces: Special Bulletin of the Reunion of Servicewomen on August 12, 2001), 2001. 5.

Nguyen Trieu Dan. *A Vietnamese Family Chronicle: Twelve Generations on the Banks of the Hat River*. Jefferson, NC: McFarland, 1991.

Nguyen Van Canh. *Vietnam under Communism 1975–1982*. Stanford: Hoover Institution Press, 1983.

Nguyen-Marshall, Van. "Oral History and Popular Memory in the Historiography of the Vietnam War." In Paul Budra and Michael Zeitlin, eds. *Soldier Talk: The Vietnam War in Oral Narrative*. Bloomington: Indiana University Press, 2004. 141–166.

Perks, Robert and Alistair Thomson. "Critical Developments: Introduction." In Robert Perks and Alistair Thomson, eds. *The Oral History Reader: Second Edition*. London: Routledge, 1998. 1–13.

Perks, Robert and Alistair Thomson. "Introduction to Second Edition." In Robert Perks and Alistair Thomson, eds. *The Oral History Reader: Second Edition*. London: Routledge, 1998. ix–xiv.

Peterson, Don. "Our new Senator is a Man with a Mission." *The Courier Mail*, November 12, 1981, 5.

Pham Duy Khiem. *La place d'un homme: De Hanoï à la Courtine* (A Man's Place: From Hanoi to La Courtine). Paris: Librairie Plon, 1958.

Pham Huu Trac. "Quelques Propos sur les Activités du Corps Médical Militaire (Some Reflections on the Activities of the Army Medical Corps)."

In Tran Xuan Dung, Tran Quoc Dong, Vu Van Tung, Bui Khiet, eds. *Quan Y Quan Luc Viet Nam Cong Hoa: Le Corps de Santé des Forces Armées de la République du Viet Nam Nam* (The Medical Corps of the Republic of Vietnam Armed Forces). South Melbourne, Victoria: Tran Xuan Dung, 2000. 32–44.

Pham Viet Tu. "Le Grand Hôpital Militaire Duy Tân dans la Guerre Contre l'Invasion Communiste (The Great Duy Tan Military Hospital in the War against the Communist Invasion)." In Tran Xuan Dung, Tran Quoc Dong, Vu Van Tung, Bui Khiet, eds. *Quan Y Quan Luc Viet Nam Cong Hoa: Le Corps de Santé des Forces Armées de la République du Viet Nam Nam* (The Medical Corps of the Republic of Vietnam Armed Forces). South Melbourne, Victoria: Tran Xuan Dung, 2000. 308–318.

Phung Thi Hanh. *South Vietnam's Women in Uniform.* Saigon: The Vietnam Council on Foreign Relations, c. 1970.

Pietrzak, Robert H. and Steven M. Southwick, "Psychological Resilience in OEF-OIF Veterans: Application of a Novel Classification Approach and Examination of Demographic and Psychosocial Correlates." *Journal of Affective Disorders* 133 (2011): 560–568.

Price, Christopher. "Last Days of Saigon Still Linger." *The Australian*, May 4, 2005, 14.

Price, Geoffrey. "Despatch to Senator D. R. Willesee on 15 August 1974." National Archives of Australia: Department of Foreign Affairs; A1838 2020/2/14 PART 11.

Radstone, Susannah and Bill Schwartz. "Introduction: Mapping Memory." In Susannah Radstone and Bill Schwartz, eds. *Memory: Histories, Theories, Debates.* New York: Fordham University Press, 2010. 1–9.

Returned Services League, Victorian Branch. "Minutes of Anzac Day Commemoration Council Meeting Held in the Board Room at Anzac House on Wednesday, 14 October, 1981 at 5.30 pm." 1–8.

Riessman, Catherine Kohler. *Narrative Methods for the Human Sciences.* Thousand Oaks, CA: Sage Publications, 2008.

Ríos, Lius, Almudena García-Rubio, Berta Martínez, Andrea Alonso, Jorge Puente. "Identification Process in Mass Graves from the Spanish Civil War II." *Forensic Science International* 219 (2012): e4–e9.

Ríos, Luis, José Ignacio Casado Ovejero, Jorge Puente Prieto. "Identification Process in Mass Graves from the Spanish Civil War I." *Forensic Science International* 199 (2010): e27–e36.

Robertson, Beth M. *Oral History Handbook: Fourth Edition*. Adelaide: Oral History Association of Australia, 2000.

Robinson, W. Courtland. *Terms of Refuge: The Indochinese Exodus and the International Response*. London: Zed Books Ltd, 1998.

Ruhe, C. H. William, Norman W. Hoover and Ira Singer. *Saigon Medical School: An Experiment in International Medical Education: An Account of the American Medical Association's Medical Education Project in South Viet Nam 1966–1975*. Chicago, IL: American Medical Association, 1988.

Schachter, Daniel L. *Searching for Memory: The Brain, the Mind, and the Past*. New York: BasicBooks, 1996.

Schafer, John C. *Vietnamese Perspectives on the War in Vietnam: Annotated Bibliography of Works in English*. New Haven, CT: Yale University Council on Southeast Asian Studies, 1996, 1. http://www.yale.edu/seas/bibliography/home.html

Schwartz, Joan M. and Terry Cook. "Archives, Records, and Power: The Making of Modern Memory." *Archival Science* 2 (2002): 1–19.

Siemon-Netto, Uwe. *Duc: A Reporter's Love for the Wounded People of Vietnam*. Uwe Siemon-Netto, 2013.

Skultans, Vieda. "Narratives of Displacement and Identity." In Brian Hurwitz, Trisha Greenhalgh and Vieda Skultans, eds. *Narrative Research in Health and Illness*. Malden, MA: Blackwell Publishing, 2004. 292–308.

Skultans, Vieda. *The Testimony of Lives: Narrative and Memory in Post-Soviet Latvia*. London: Routledge, 1998.

Sorley, Lewis. *A Better War: The Unexamined Victories and Final Tragedies of America's Last Years in Vietnam*. Orlando, FL: Harcourt, 1999.

Sorley, Lewis. "Could the War Have Been Won?" In John Norton Moore and Robert F. Turner, eds. *The Real Lessons of the Vietnam War: Reflections Twenty-Five Years after the Fall of Saigon*. Durham, NC: Carolina Academic Press, 2003. 403–420.

Stewart, Elizabeth, "Introduction." In Ashley Ekins and Elizabeth Stewart, eds. *War Wounds: Medicine and the Trauma of Conflict*. Wollombi, NSW: Exisle Publishing, 2011. 17–27.

Summerfield, Penny. *Reconstructing Women's Wartime Lives: Discourse and Subjectivity in Oral Histories of the Second World War*. Manchester: Manchester University Press, 1998.

Sutton, John and Kellie Williamson. "Introduction: The Diversity of Embodied Remembering." In Lawrence Shapiro, ed. *The Routledge Handbook of Embodied Cognition*. London: Routledge, 2014. 315–325.

Ta Van Tai. "The Status of Women in Traditional Vietnam: A Comparison of the Code of the Lê Dynasty (1428–1788) with the Chinese Code." *Journal of Asian History* 15 (1981): 97–145.

Tai, Hue-Tam Ho. "Faces of Remembrance and Forgetting." In Hue-Tam Ho Tai, ed. *The Country of Memory: Remaking the Past in Late Socialist Vietnam*. Berkeley: University of California Press, 2001. 167–195.

Taylor, Keith W. "Introduction: Voices from the South." In K. W. Taylor, ed. *Voices from the Second Republic of South Vietnam (1967–1975)*. Ithaca, NY: Southeast Asia Program Publications, Cornell University, 2015. 1–8.

Taylor, Sandra C. *Vietnamese Women at War: Fighting for Ho Chi Minh and the Revolution*. Lawrence: University Press of Kansas, 1999.

Thayer, Thomas C. *War without Fronts: The American Experience in Vietnam*. Boulder: Westview Press, 1985.

Thien Loi. "Su Tra Thu De Hen va Da Man (Despicable and Savage Reprisals)." *Tap San Biet Dong Quan So 2* (Ranger Magazine No. 2), 2000, 37–50.

Thomas, Mandy. *Dreams in the Shadows: Vietnamese-Australian Lives in Transition*. St Leonards: Allen & Unwin, 1999.

Thomas, Mandy. "The Vietnamese in Australia." In James E. Coughlan and Deborah J. McNamara, eds. *Asians in Australia: Patterns of Migration and Settlement*. South Melbourne: Macmillan Education Australia, 1997. 274–295.

Thompson, Virginia. *French Indo-China*. London: George Allen and Unwin, 1937.

Tôn-Thât, Thanh-Vân. *Le pays d'avant* (The Country from Before). Rome: Portaparole, 2007.

Tran Do Cam. "Giang Doan 26 Xung Phong tai Chien Truong Tan Chau—Hong Ngu (River Assault Group 26 at the Battle of Tan Chau—Hong Ngu)." *Ra Khoi* (Head to Open Sea) Giai Pham Xuan Quy Ty 2013 (Spring Year of the Snake 2013), 2013. 62–68.

Tran Duc Tuong. "Le Médecin Parachutiste (Paratrooper Doctor)." In Tran Xuan Dung, Tran Quoc Dong, Vu Van Tung, Bui Khiet, eds. *Quan Y Quan Luc Viet Nam Cong Hoa: Le Corps de Santé des Forces Armées de la République du Viet Nam Nam* (The Medical Corps of the Republic of Vietnam Armed Forces). South Melbourne, Victoria: Tran Xuan Dung, 2000. 114–138.

Tran Tri Vu. *Lost Years: My 1,632 Days in Vietnamese Reeducation Camps*. Berkeley: Institute of East Asian Studies, University of California, 1988.

Tran Quang Minh. "A Decade of Public Service: Nation Building during the Interregnum and Second Republic (1964–75)." In K. W. Taylor, ed. *Voices from the Second Republic of South Vietnam (1967–1975)*. Ithaca, NY: Southeast Asia Program Publications, Cornell University, 2015. 39–87.

Tran Van Nhut. "The Marine Corps at the beginning of its formation." In Tran Xuan Dung, ed. *History of the South Vietnamese Marine Corps Army of the Republic of Vietnam / Chien Su Thuy Quan Luc Chien Quan Luc Viet Nam Cong Hoa*. South Melbourne: Tran Xuan Dung, 2007. 70.

Tran Van Quan. "Hinh Anh Nguoi Linh Tiep-Van tai Chien Truong truoc Co-Quan Bao-Tro HOI VIET-MY (Image of the Logistics Soldier on the Battlefield for Sponsorship of the Vietnamese-American Association)." Vietnamese-American Association Auditorium, November 29, 1972.

Tran Xuan Dung. "A Bloody Battle, Albeit None Wounded." In Tran Xuan Dung, Tran Quoc Dong, Vu Van Tung, Bui Khiet, eds. *Quan Y Quan Luc Viet Nam Cong Hoa: Le Corps de Santé des Forces Armées de la République du Viet Nam Nam* (The Medical Corps of the Republic of Vietnam Armed Forces). South Melbourne, Victoria: Tran Xuan Dung, 2000. 165–171.

Tran Xuan Dung, ed. *History of the South Vietnamese Marine Corps Army of the Republic of Vietnam / Chien Su Thuy Quan Luc Chien Quan Luc Viet Nam Cong Hoa*. South Melbourne: Tran Xuan Dung, 2007.

Tran Xuan Dung, Tran Quoc Dong, Vu Van Tung and Bui Khiet, eds. *Quan Y Quan Luc Viet Nam Cong Hoa: Le Corps de Santé des Forces Armées de la République du Viet Nam Nam* (The Medical Corps of the Republic of Vietnam Armed Forces). South Melbourne, Victoria: Tran Xuan Dung, 2000.

Trong, Lucien. *Enfer rouge mon amour* (Red Hell My Love). Paris: Editions du Seuil, 1980.

Turley, Gerald H. *The Easter Offensive, Vietnam, 1972*. Novato: Presidio Press, 1985.

Turner, Karen Gottschang. *Even the Women Must Fight: Memories of War from North Vietnam*. With Phan Thanh Hao. New York: John Wiley & Sons, 1998.

United Nations High Commissioner for Refugees. *The State of the World's Refugees: Fifty Years of Humanitarian Action*. Oxford: Oxford University Press, 2000.

U.S. Department of the Army Headquarters, General Orders No. 24, Washington D.C., April 27, 1971.

U.S. Department of the Army Headquarters, General Orders No. 25, Washington D.C., June 8, 2001.

Valentine, McDonald. "Advisors to ARVN Rangers (Biet Dong Quan)." http://www.soft-vision.com/ranger/index2.html?http%3A//www.soft-vision.com/ranger/home.html

Valentine, McDonald. "The Vietnamese Rangers: An Overview." In Michael N. Martin and McDonald Valentine Jr., eds. *The Black Tigers: Elite South Vietnamese Rangers and their American Advisors*. Louisville: Harmony House Publishers, 1993. 20–22.

Valverde, Kieu-Linh Caroline. "From Dust to Gold: The Vietnamese Amerasian Experience." In P. P. Maria Root, ed. *Racially Mixed People in America*. Newbury Park, CA: Sage Publications, 1992. 144–161.

Van der Kolk, Bessel A. and Alexander C. McFarlane. "The Black Hole of Trauma." In Bessel A. van der Kolk, Alexander C. McFarlane and Lars Weisaeth, eds. *Traumatic Stress: The Effects of Overwhelming Experience on Mind, Body, and Society*. New York: The Guilford Press, 1996. 3–23.

Van Tan Thach. "Miracles." In Tran Xuan Dung, ed. *History of the South Vietnamese Marine Corps Army of the Republic of Vietnam / Chien Su Thuy Quan Luc Chien Quan Luc Viet Nam Cong Hoa*. South Melbourne: Tran Xuan Dung, 2007. 832–834.

Varas, Claudia Garrido, Marisol Intriago Leiva. "Managing commingled remains from mass graves: Considerations, implications and recommendations from a human rights case in Chile." *Forensic Science International* 219 (2012): e19–e24.

Veith, George J. *Black April: The Fall of South Vietnam 1973–1975*. New York: Encounter Books, 2012.

Veith, George J. and Merle L. Pribbenow II. "'Fighting is an Art': The Army of the Republic of Vietnam's Defense of Xuan Loc, 9–21 April 1975." *The Journal of Military History* 68, no. 1 (2004): 163–213.

Viviani, Nancy. *The Indochinese in Australia: From Burnt Boats to Barbecues*. Melbourne: Oxford University Press, 1996.

Viviani, Nancy. *The Long Journey: Vietnamese Migration and Settlement in Australia*. Carlton: Melbourne University Press, 1984.

Vo, Linda Trinh. "Managing Survival: Economic Realities for Vietnamese American Women." In Shirley Hune and Gail M. Nomura, eds. *Asian /*

Pacific Islander American Women. New York: New York University Press, 2003. 237–252.
Vo, Nghia M. The Bamboo Gulag: Political Imprisonment in Communist Vietnam. Jefferson, NC: McFarland, 2004.
Vo Thuong. "The Coup de Grâce." In Tran Xuan Dung, Tran Quoc Dong, Vu Van Tung, Bui Khiet, eds. Quan Y Quan Luc Viet Nam Cong Hoa: Le Corps de Santé des Forces Armées de la République du Viet Nam Nam (The Medical Corps of the Republic of Vietnam Armed Forces). South Melbourne, Victoria: Tran Xuan Dung, 2000. 290–294.
Vu Van Bao, "Phi Doan 237 Truc Thang Chinook CH 47-A (237th Helicopter Squadron Chinook CH-47A)." In Lien Hoi Ai Huu Khong Quan Australia (Republic of Vietnam Air Force Veteran Association in Australia), Quan Su Khong Quan Viet Nam Cong Hoa (Military History of the Republic of Vietnam Air Force). Melbourne: Van Luong, 2005. 272–277.
Vuong-Riddick, Thuong. Two Shores / Deux Rives. Vancouver: Ronsdale Press, 1995.
Warner, Denis. Not Always on Horseback: An Australian Correspondent at War and Peace in Asia 1961–1993. St Leonards: Allen & Unwin, 1997.
Warner, Denis. "Witness Statement. The Senate Standing Committee on Foreign Affairs and Defence, Melbourne, 13 October 1975." Denis Warner Papers, National Library of Australia MS 9489/1/79. 240–301.
Webb, Nancy Boyd. "The Impact of Traumatic Stress and Loss on Children and Families." In Nancy Boyd Webb, ed. Mass Trauma and Violence: Helping Families and Children Cope. New York: The Guilford Press, 2004. 3–22.
Wiesel, Elie. Ethics and Memory. Berlin: Walter de Gruyter, 1997.
Wiest, Andrew. Vietnam's Forgotten Army: Heroism and Betrayal in the ARVN. New York: New York University Press, 2008.
Willbanks, James H. The Battle of An Loc. Bloomington: Indiana University Press, 2005.
Winter, Jay. "Foreword: Remembrance as a Human Right." In Aleida Assmann and Linda Shortt, eds. Memory and Political Change. Houndmills: Palgrave Macmillan, 2012. vii–xi.
Winter, Jay. "Forms of Kinship and Remembrance in the Aftermath of the Great War." In Jay Winter and Emmanuel Sivan, eds. War and Remembrance in the Twentieth Century. Cambridge: Cambridge University Press, 1999. 40–60.

Yeager, Jack A. *The Vietnamese Novel in French: A Literary Response to Colonialism*. Hanover: University Press of New England, 1987.
Zhai, Qiang. *China and the Vietnam Wars 1950–1975*. Chapel Hill: The University of North Carolina Press, 2000.
Zumbro, Ralph. *The Iron Cavalry*. New York: Pocket Books, 1998.

INDEX

Airborne Division (RVNAF), xvi, 9, 19, 28, 52–54, 61, 70, 74–75, 83, 148, 156–57, 171, 183; Airborne Engineer Corps, 143–44; Airborne School course, 89; Bui Ngoc Thuy's service, 87–89, 134 (photo); casualty rates, 19, 67, 70; doctors at battalion level, 70, 74; 1st Airborne Brigade, An Loc, 28; 5th Airborne Battalion, 1975, 54–55; general reserve force, 67, 74, 146; Hoang Co Lan's medical service, 70; Lua's service, 153–55; medical evacuation procedures, 67; Nguyen Minh Tran's service, 143–45, 148–51, 157–62; Phan Cong Ly's service, 128 (photo); return to Saigon, March 1975, 144–45; supply missions to, 53; Tran Duc Tuong's medical service, 67–68; 2è Bataillon étranger de Parachutistes (2nd Foreign Airborne Battalion), 70

Air Force (RVNAF), xvi, 16, 19, 20, 44, 55, 74, 75, 156, 157; Air Force Headquarters, 51; Air Force nurse training, 92; battle of An Loc, 28–29; Bien Hoa Air Base, 51, 61; casualties, 52–54; Danang Air Base, 67; expansion, 52; 514th Fighter Squadron, 52; 516th Fighter Squadron, 52; history, 52; impact of cuts in U.S. aid, 10, 54; medical evacuation duties, 71; Nguyen Quoc Dat's service, 52; support for South Vietnamese forces, 28; Tan Son Nhat Air Base, 51, 73; training, 51; training accident death, 20; Tran Dang Vinh's service, 170; Trinh Tien Khang's service, 52; 219th Helicopter Squadron, 53; 237th Helicopter Squadron, 52–55; Vu Dinh Long's service, 209; Vu Van Bao's service, 50–55, 61–66

Amerasians: discrimination against, 12, 85–86. *See also* Nguyen, Kien

Amnesty International, 140

Anh, 209

An Loc battle, 12, 27–29, 38, 52, 53, 76, 78, 109, 235

Antiaircraft artillery (AAA) regiments (PAVN), 44, 54

Antze, Paul, 82–83, 124

Anzac Day participation (Australia): by Nguyen Huu An, 115; by Nguyen Manh Tien, 110; by Nguyen Thi Minh Nguyet, 101; by Nguyen Van Luyen, 50; by Nguyen Viet Long, 171; by Pham Van Chuong, xv; by Thanh, 102, 106; by Thuy, 106; by Tran Nhu Hung, 151;

by Tran Van Quan, 30; by Truong Cong Hai, 150, 151, 158–59, 169, 170; by Vu Van Bao, 55
Argenti, Nicolas, 204
Armor (PAVN), 9, 28, 43–44, 110, 209; key factor in North Vietnamese victory, 1975, 208; Soviet-built T54 tanks, 208–9
Armor Branch (RVNAF), 16, 44, 65; Armor School, 47, 62; battle of Bau Bang hamlet, 47–49; conversion of M113 armored personnel carriers, South Vietnamese innovation, 46; expansion, 47; history, 47; loyalty of armor trooper, 48; Nguyen Van Luyen's service, 45–50, 60, 62–66; number of personnel, 47; 3rd Armored Cavalry Squadron, 47; training at Long Thanh, 46; U.S. Presidential Unit Citation, 47, 220; veterans, 64
Army doctors. See Military doctors
Ashplant, T. G., 161
Assmann, Aleida, 143
Australia: acceptance of Vietnamese refugees, 166–67, 181; anti-Vietnamese veteran bill, 174–75; Department of Veterans' Affairs, 163, 169–74, 176; government policy and Vietnamese veterans, 167–74; MacKellar's apology to refugees, 166; 1976 report on the issue of refugees, 166; post-1975 Vietnamese refugees, 164; pre-1975 Vietnamese population, 164; recognition of formal status of RVNAF veterans, 16; refugee camps, 105; *Repatriation Acts Amendment Act (No. 2)*, 167–68, 174, 180, 181; veteran-related Senate controversies, 176–81; Veterans' Entitlements Amendment Bill, 179; Veterans' Entitlements Bill, 174–75, 176, 179–81; veterans' service pensions entitlements, 16–17, 167–69, 172–73, 180–81; Vietnamese Veterans' Association, 116, 171; Vietnam War Memorial, 116, 137 (photo), 204–5. See also Anzac Day participation; Returned and Services League of Australia

Australia, post-war resettlements: by Bui Ngoc Thuy, 88; by Nghiem, 189; by Nguyen Huu An, 116; by Nguyen Minh Tran, 145, 149–50, 151; by Nguyen Thi Minh Nguyet, 101, 102, 105; by Nguyen Van Luyen, 50; by Nguyen Viet Huy, 34–35, 42; by Thanh, 105; by Thuy, 106; by Tran Nhu Hung, 148; by Tran Van Giac, 59–60, 62; by Tran Van Quan, 30, 39; by Tran Xuan Dung, 80–81; by Tuan, 194; by Vu Hoai Duc, 26, 38; by Vu Van Bao, 55, 61
Australian Army, 15, 22, 36
Australian Department of Veterans' Affairs, 163
Australian Embassy (Saigon), 165–66, 180
Australian Task Force (Phuoc Tuy Province), 204
Australian Vietnamese Women's Association (AVWA), xviii

Bamboo Gulag, 17, 38, 85, 139–40, 157, 162, 209; famous detainee, 139; history, 141–42; number and size of camps, 141. See also Internment in communist reeducation camps
Battles: An Loc, 12, 27–29, 38–39, 52–53, 76, 78, 109, 235; Bau Bang hamlet, 46, 47–49, 60, 129 (photo); Dong Ha, 43–44; Long Tan, 50; Quang Tri, 12, 27, 28, 29, 94, 146, 152; Vinh Loc, 77–78; Xuan Loc, 30, 110, 209
Binh Thuan Province, 19, 31
Binh Xuyen, 6, 24
Bonnano, George, 62
Buddhism: Buddhists opposed to communism, 207; family background, 1,

3, 6, 26, 45, 55, 71, 74, 77, 88, 95, 112, 119, 192; fasting, 33; integrating backgrounds, 24; praying for soldiers, 33
Bui Ngoc Thuy: Airborne Division service, 87–88, 134 (photo); biographical background, 20, 87–89; four siblings in the military, 20; honored by her children for her service, 88–89; Medical Corps service, 88; military service, 87–89; parachute training and qualifications, 87–88; refugee from North Vietnam in 1954, 88; resettlement in Australia, 88; tension between career and demands of motherhood, 88
Burchardt, Natasha, 161
Burma, 45

Cao Dai religious sect, 6, 24, 36
Cao Van Vien, 7
Cao Xuan Huy, 208
Central Organizing Committee, 7
Cham, 24
Chieu Hoi program, 218
Children of veterans, 183–205; Hai, 185–87, 199, 205; Nghiem, 188–89, 199, 205; Ngoc, 189–91, 200–201, 205; Oanh, 183–84; Thien, 196–98, 202, 205; Thy, 194–96, 201–2, 205; Tuan, 191–94, 200–201, 205
China: support of North Vietnam, 9–10, 12, 29–30, 40, 63–64
Chinese Codes of the Ming, Qing Dynasties, 90
Chinh Luan (Opinion) newspaper, 7
Clem, David, 171
Clendinnen, Inga, 15
Code of the Le Dynasty (1428–1788), 90
Collective history, 15, 123
Collective memory, 15, 123
Collective narrative, 14
Collective resilience, 86
Combat casualties: Nguyen Manh Tien's narrative, 78, 79–80; Tran Xuan Dung's narrative, 77. *See also* Disabling injuries
Commemoration, 15, 59, 123, 210, 221
Communism: Buddhists opposed to, 207; common stance against, 164; divisiveness/destructiveness of, 2; fleeing of refugees from, 4, 59–60, 77, 88, 158, 210; North Vietnam's efforts at imposing, 4, 140. *See also* Internment in communist reeducation camps
Communist: "campaign of terror" in South Vietnamese countryside, 7, 143; massacre of civilians in Hue, 1968 Tet Offensive, 6, 214–15; murder or abduction of South Vietnamese civilians 1956–1965, 7, 215; murder or abduction of South Vietnamese civilians 1965–1972, 215; purges of 1945–1946, 11; targeting of village officials, medical personnel, social workers, schoolteachers, 7, 215; war memorials, 13. *See also* Internment in communist reeducation camps
Confucianism, 90
Confucian tenets, 90
Cong Hoa General Hospital, 69; Bui Ngoc Thuy's memories of, 101; Chau's broken leg treatment, 87; fund raising for, 96; Lua's memory of experience at, 154; Ngoc's memory of experience at, 155; Nguyen Van Luyen's evacuation to, 49; Trinh Tien Kang's evacuation to, 52
Convalescent centers, 69

Dawson, Graham, 161
Department of Veterans' Affairs (Australia), 163, 169–74, 176
Desertion: from the RVNAF, 11
Diem government (South Vietnam), 6–7, 22, 24, 30, 120
Dinh Minh Hung, 58–59

Disabled Veterans and Widows Relief Association (Vietnamese) (U.S.), 106–7
Disabling injuries: of Lap, 152–53, 159; of Lua, 153–55, 159; of Ngoc, 155–56, 159, 161
Doan Duong Kinh Hoang (Road of Horror), 70
Doan Thanh Nghiep, 60, 129 (photo)
Dong Ha Bridge, 43, 44
Dong Van Khuyen, 70; comment on female WAFC school enrollment, 92; on limited military doctors, 70; on medical evacuations, 71; on women/WAFC enrollments, 92

Easter Offensive. *See* 1972 Offensive
East Germany: support of North Vietnam, 63

Family Reunion program (Australia), 164
Famine, 11, 153
First Republic (1955–1963), 4
514th Fighter Squadron, 52
Flowers from Hell (Nguyen Chi Thien), 139
Four Virtues, 90
France, 2, 15, 22
Fraser, George MacDonald, 45
Fraser, Malcolm, 166–67, 178, 181
Free French Forces (North Africa), 22, 37

General Staff of the National Army of Vietnam, 69
Geneva Accords, 21, 69, 77
Gietzelt, Arthur, 175–77
Grey, Jeffrey, 12
Group 559, 7, 9
Guardian newspaper, 7
Guillemot, François, 24
Gulag. *See* Bamboo Gulag; Internment in communist reeducation camps
Gullet, Henry, 110

Hai (child of veteran), 185–87; enduring loyalty to Vietnamese past, 205; escape from Vietnam, refugee camp years, 186; expulsion from school, 199; migration to Australia, 186–87; return to Vietnam, 187; unclear memories of father's occupation, 185–86; witness to the suffering, postwar difficulties of family, 198
Ha Ma Viet, 47
Hanoi's War (Lien-Hang Nguyen), 7
Hell in An Loc (Lam Quang Thi), 29
Herget, Daniel J., 128 (photo)
Herman, Judith Lewis, 123, 158
The History of the August Revolution, 139
Hoa Hao religious sect, 6, 24, 36
Hoang Co Lan, 70
Ho Chi Minh, 2, 6, 191
Ho Chi Minh Trail, 8 (map); arms and matériel, tonnage, 10; Group 559, establishment of, 7; infiltration of arms, matériel and troops, 9–10; 1959 infiltration, 7
Hodgkin, Katharine, 14
Hoffman, Eva, 198
Holmes, Richard, 66, 140
Homesickness, 40
Hong Kong refugee camps, 85
Hospital facilities, 69–70; Cong Hoa General Hospital, 49, 52, 69, 87, 96, 101, 154, 155; Duy Tan General Hospital, 67, 69; Quang Tri Hospital, 69, 152; re-use of supplies, 10, 71
Ho Thi Ve: account of the WAC and WAFC, 90, 91; service as WAFC School Commander, 92, 97; Viet Binh Doan Trung Viet service, 90
Hue massacre, 124, 214–15
Hukee, Brian, 52
Humanitarian Operation program, 14, 140

Human rights violations, 4, 112, 125, 140. *See also* Internment in communist reeducation camps
Humphrey, Michael, 208
Hungarian Revolution, 6
Huynh Kim Buu, 109

India, 2
Indochina War (1946–1954), 15, 141
Indochinese Refugee Association, 30
Indonesia refugee camps, 100, 103, 105, 184
Injuries. *See* Disabling injuries
Internment in communist reeducation camps, 85, 112, 140–41; Amnesty International "prisoner of conscience," 140; blacklisting of former camp prisoners, 147; description by Kien Nguyen, 141–42; of military doctors, 71; of Nguyen Chi Thien, 139–40; of Nguyen Manh Tien, 81–82; of Nguyen Van Luyen, 47–48, 50; of Nguyen Viet Huy, 33–34, 35; origin of, 141–42; of Phan Cong Ly, 60, 128 (photo); "Reeducation Act No. 49," 139; of Tran Cam Huong, 91, 106; of Tran Nhu Hung, 146–47, 149; of Tran Van Giac, 59, 62; of Tran Van Quan, 30; of Tran Xuan Dung, 80–82; of Truong Cong Hai, 145–46, 149; of Vu Hoai Duc, 23, 25–26, 38; of Vu Van Bao, 55, 61. *See also* Bamboo Gulag
Interregnum Period (1963–1967), 4

Jamieson, Neil, 13
Jenkins, Fiona, 180
Joes, Anthony James, 4, 11

Keegan, John, 66, 140
Khanh Ly, 3
Kim Bai village, 1, 2

Krall, Yung, army radio journalist service, 93; *A Thousand Tears Falling*, 20
Kwon, Heonik, 13

Lambek, Michael, 82–83, 124
Lam Quang Phong, 21
Lam Quang Thi: acknowledgment of corruption, factionalism, 10–11; "Be men," General de Lattre, 21; effect of poverty, 10; father of writer Andrew Lam, 21; *Hell in An Loc*, 29; lieutenant general status, 21; not part of political faction, 11; South Vietnamese generals, 11; *The Twenty-Five Year Century*, 21; twenty-five years of service, 41
Land Reform campaign (North Vietnam), 6, 140; number of victims, 6
Lap: biographical background, 152; denial of war disability pension, 157; disabling injuries, 152–53, 159; fears of retribution in Vietnam, 160; personal dream of, 159; postwar year challenges, 153; Ranger service, 152; service in RVNAF elite units, 156
La place d'un homme: De Hanoï à La Courtine (A Man's Place: From Hanoi to La Courtine) (Pham Duy Khiem), 36–37
The Last Shilling: A History of Repatriation in Australia (Lloyd and Rees), 167
Le Cau, 13
Le Duan, 7–8, 9
Le Duc Tho, 7
Le Minh Dao, 110; battle of Xuan Loc, 110, 209; commander of the 18th Infantry Division, 27, 110, 209; friendship with Tran Van Quan, 39, 110; successes in battle, 39, 110, 209; Tran Van Quan's work with, 27; years in postwar gulag, 209

Le Thai To, 89–90
Le Thanh Y, military doctor service, 71
Le Van Tai, 122
Lewis, Austin, 177–80
Leydesdorff, Selma, 123, 161
Lloyd, Clem, 167
Logistics (RVNAF): battle of An Loc, 1972, 27–29, 37–39; disparity between RVNAF logistics and U.S. Army logistics, 27, 29–30, 38–39; Tran Van Quan, commander of 18th Logistics Battalion, 22, 27–30, 38–39, 109
Long Tan battle, 50
Long Tan Day, 55, 151
"Loss, Trauma, and Human Resilience" (Bonnano), 62
Lua: biographical background, 153; on consequences of damaging policies, 159; denial of war disability pension, 157; loss of legs in battle, 153–55, 159; pain in seeing family suffer during wartime, 161; pride in military service, 160; service in RVNAF elite units, 156, 160; youthful idealism of, 156
Lu Tuan, 93–94
Luu Thi Huynh Mai, 91

MacKellar, Michael, 166
Macklin, Michael, 176, 177–80
Mad dynasty, 1
Malaysian refugee camps, 103
Maoism, 24
Marine Corps (RVNAF), xvi, 9, 16, 68, 70–71, 126, 144; arms and equipment, 9; battle of Dong Ha, 43–44; doctors at battalion level, 74; general reserve force, 73–74; high casualties, 74; *History of the South Vietnamese Marine Corps*, 83–84; Marine Task Force B, 73; Ngoc's service, 155–57, 159–62; 1972 Offensive, 43–44, 67; number of personnel, 73; 3rd Battalion, 258th Marine Brigade, 43–44; Tran Nhu Hung's service, 146–48; Tran Xuan Dung's medical service, 73–74, 77–78, 80–81, 83–86; U.S. Presidential Unit Citations, 220; Van Tan Thach's medical service, 43–44; Vietnamese Marine Corps Association, 151; yearly anniversary, 151
Mass grave: Cu Chi, 117, 118–26, 136 (photo), 137 (photo); Hue, 124, 214–15
May Economic Statement (1985, Australia), 175
McFarlane, Alexander, 162
McKelvey, Robert, 184
Medical Corps (RVNAF), 68–71; convalescent centers, 69; founding, 69; hospital facilities, 69–70; impact of U.S. aid cutbacks, 71; personnel shortages, 70. *See also* Military doctors
Medical evacuations, 71
Mekong Delta, 19, 46
Memory: "agent of remembrance," 123; "bearing witness," 17; contest the past, 14–15; disjuncture between public or state-sanctioned memories, and private or bodily memory, 14; individual and collective, 15; interpretive reconstructions, 82; interrogate the ways in which the war has been remembered and memorialized, 14; memory and commemoration, 14–15; postwar remembrance, 82–86; problematic and contested memory, war, 14; reliance on, 15; role of memory in totalitarian societies, 17
Military cemeteries, 13–14
Military doctors: Hoang Co Lan, 70; Le Thanh Y, 71; Nguyen Manh Tien, 74–78, 81–83; Pham Viet Tu, 67; Tran Duc Tuong, 67–68; Tran Xuan Dung, 68, 71–74, 77, 80–84; Vo Thuong, 70–71

Momyer, William, 54
My Chanh Base, 43

Narrative, 16, 17, 21, 22, 26, 30, 35–36, 41, 45, 68, 83, 103, 106, 115, 160, 198, 205; collective narrative, 14; conventions, 83; counter narratives, 117, 160; emblematic of resilience, 86, founded on acts of witnessing, 123; national historical narrative, 13; oral, 15, silences in, 38; structured sequence of events, 77; trauma narratives, 105, 161
National Army of Vietnam, 10, 21, 22; armored units, 47; General Staff, 69; integration of Viet Binh Doan, 90; Lam Quang Phong's service, 21; reconnaissance platoon, 47; service by Nguyen Viet Huy's father, 19; service by Tran Nhu Hung's father, 146; Vu Hoai Duc's service, 23–24, 36, 41
National Liberation Front (NLF), 9
National Police (Republic of Vietnam), 93
National Rehabilitation Institute, Saigon, 69, 232
Navy (RVNAF): Dinh Minh Hung's service, 56; expansion, 56; history, 56; impact of cuts in U.S. aid, 10, 56, 64; Naval Academy, 56, 59, 60, 62, 65, 109–10, 231; number of personnel, 56; transport of South Korean troops, 57; Tran Van Giac's service, 55–60, 61–66, 138 (photo); Truong Cong Hai's service, 145–46, 169; U.S. support for, 56; zones, 56
New Economic Zones: forced deurbanization to, 11–12, 14; forced displacement to, 14, 85, 100, 104, 141, 147, 155, 184, 193–94, 222; Vu Van Bao's relocation to, 55
Nghiem (child of a veteran): enduring loyalty to Vietnamese past, 205; imprisonment, hard labor, 189; resettlement in Australia, 189; unclear memories of father's occupation, 188; visits with father in reeducation camp, 199; witness to the suffering, postwar difficulties of family, 198
Ngoc: absence of disability benefits, 155–56; biographical background, 155; on consequences of damaging policies, 159; denial of war disability pension, 157; loss of legs on the battlefield, 155–56, 159, 161; postwar posttraumatic stress disorder, 162; pride in military service, 160; service in RVNAF elite units, 156, 160; unwillingness to disclose postwar feelings, 159–60; youthful idealism of, 156
Ngoc (child of a veteran, sibling of Tuan): concerns for her Australian-born children, 200; enduring loyalty to Vietnamese past, 205; impact of postwar propaganda on, 191; postwar internment of grandfather, uncle, 190–91; thankfulness for intact family unit, 200–201; visits with RVNAF officer grandfather, 189–90; witness to the postwar difficulties of family, 198
Ngo Dinh Diem, 4, 24
Ngo Dinh Nhu, 24
Ngo Quang Truong, 32, 40–41, 144
Ngo Van Dinh, 44
Nguyen, Kien, 141–42
Nguyen, Lien-Hang, 7
Nguyen Chi Thien: adoption by Amnesty International, 140; internment in hard labor camps, 139–40; poetry of, 139–40; U.S. Congressional testimony, 140
Nguyen Code (19th century), 90
Nguyen Cong Luan: account of student resistance to communist forces, 209; description of refugee evacuation, 69–70, 156; on protests by disabled veterans, 156
Nguyen family of Kim Bai, 1–2

Nguyen Hanh Nhon, 106–7
Nguyen Hoang Hai, 133 (photo)
Nguyen Huu An, 111, 112–16, 119; as "agent of remembrance," 123; anger at lack of protection for friends at prisoner-of-war conventions, 124; application for allied veteran recognition, 163; biographical background, 112–13, 119; first battle, 114–15; friendship with, memories of Tran Dinh Tu, 111–12, 116–18, 119, 120, 125, 126; hospitalization for malaria, 115; march on Anzac Day, 115; Ranger Association (U.S.), 116; Ranger Association (Victoria, Australia), 116; Ranger Battalion service, 113–15; reconnaissance platoon leadership, 114–15; resettlement in Australia, 116, 163; Vietnam War Memorial of Victoria committee, 116; work at Saigon Supreme Court, 1974–1975, 115–16
Nguyen Manh Tien, 133 (photo); battlefield conditions narrative, 75–76; biographical background, 74–75; choice of unit to serve with, 83; combat casualties narrative, 78; form of memorializing the war, 85; internment in prison camps, 81–82; length of Ranger service, 83; limited say in military unit, 83; march on Anzac Day, 110; medical service, 68, 74–77; memories of the *esprit de corps*, 110; requalification as medical practitioner, 82; ruptured family life or, 77; survival of artillery bombardment, 79–80
Nguyen Minh Tran: Airborne Engineering Corps service, 143–44; biographical background, 143; guilt feelings of, 158; internment in reeducation camp, 143–44, 158; memories of atrocities, 148; postwar posttraumatic stress disorder, 161; resettlement in Australia, 145, 149–50, 151; role in aiding Vietnamese boat people, 151;
Nguyen Ngoc Phach: army duties, freelance journalist role, 6–7; RVNAF military service, 6–7; writing on North Vietnam's weapons, 9
Nguyen Phan, 121
Nguyen Thanh Chuan, 78
Nguyen Thi Minh Nguyet, 135 (photo); Armed Services Day parade in Saigon, 95; Army Social School work, 103; biographical background, 95–96; father and brothers in the military, 95; march on Anzac Day, 101; pivotal role of army service, 107; pride in the RVNAF women's corps, 98; relocation to New Economic Zone, hard labor, 100–102, 105; resettlement in Australia, 101, 102, 105; service as WAFC sergeant, 95–97, 103; top graduate of Noncommissioned Officer Course, 95; WAFC uniforms, 96; work in Bien Hoa Military Cemetery, 96–97
Nguyen Thi Nam, 93
Nguyen Trieu Dan, 1–4
Nguyen Tue, 1
Nguyen Uyen, 1
Nguyen Van Canh, 141
Nguyen Van Luyen, 128 (photo), 129 (photo); Armor Branch service, 46–47, 62–63; Bau Bang battle injury, 46–50, 60; biographical background, 45–46; Doan Thanh Nghiep saved by, 60, 129 (photo); internment in communist prisons, 47–48, 50; march on Anzac Day, 50; narrative of service, 48–49, 60; postwar meetings with friends, 64; resettlement in Australia, 50
Nguyen Van Thieu, 4, 6
Nguyen Viet Huy: biographical background, 19, 22, 30, 39–40; escape from Vietnam, 34; memoir of camp survivors, 38; military

college training narrative, 34–35; move to New Economic Zone, 35; prisoner-of-war experience, 33–34, 35; Regional Forces service, 19, 22, 30–32, 33, 35, 36, 40; resettlement in Australia, 34–35, 42; service in two armies, 41; Thu Duc Military Academy years, 31–32

Nguyen Viet Long: Navy service, 170–71; resettlement in Australia, 171; role in naval evacuation of soldiers, civilians, 208

1968 Tet Offensive: 21, 55, 67, 95, 98, 115, 143, 148; arms, 9; casualties, 143–44; increase in volunteers for the RVNAF, 216; Marine Task Force B, 73; massacre of civilians during North Vietnamese occupation of Hue, 124, 214–15; medical care to civilians, 73; rally to South Vietnamese government, 9

1972 Offensive: 28, 30, 40, 43–44, 67, 69, 76, 83, 98–99, 224, 227; across demilitarized zone into I Corps, 43–44, 227; An Loc, 76; enrollment in RVNAF combat units, 83; full-scale invasion, 9; *Mua He Do Lua* (Red Fire Summer), 30, 67, 98; multidivision, 21, 43; South Vietnamese military hospitals, 67, 69

1975 Offensive: 9–10, 21, 30, 208–9

Ninth Plenum, 9

Nolan, Mark, 180

North Africa, 15, 22, 23, 25, 26, 37

North Vietnam (Democratic Republic of Vietnam), 43; AAA regiments, 44, 54; abrogation of Paris Peace Accords, 10; atrocities committed by, 112, 117, 120, 122–24; China's support of, 9, 29–30, 40, 63–64; East Germany's support of, 63; foundation of National Liberation Front (NLF), 9; full-scale invasion of South Vietnam, 1972, 9; General Offensive and General Uprising, 9; Group 559, establishment of, 7; Ho Chi Minh Trail, 7–10; human rights violations, 4; imposition of communism by, 4; Land Reform campaign 1953–1956, 6; Le Duan's war strategy, 7–9; Le Duc Tho, 7; 1972 Great Offensive 9, 21; Ninth Plenum, 9; offensive against South Vietnam, 9–11, 27–29, 43–44, 54, 73, 99, 101–3, 110, 207–8; one million troops infiltrated into South Vietnam 1959–1975, 10, 217; Resolution 15 of January 1959, 7; SAM regiments, 44, 54; Soviet support of, 9, 12, 29–30, 40, 54, 63–64; supply of arms and matériel, Ho Chi Minh Trail, tonnage, 10; takeover of South Vietnam, 11; Third Party Congress, 9; total war, 9; troops stationed in South Vietnam, 1973, 10; Vietnam Workers' Party, 7. *See also* Internment in communist reeducation camps

North Vietnamese Army. *See* People's Army of Vietnam

Nung, 24; division of, 24

Oanh (child of veteran), 183–84

Oral history, xviii, xx, 4, 60; collection at the National Library of Australia, xvi; context of interview, 118; distinctive contribution, 12; "hidden from history," 12; historical record, 68; interviews, xvii, 164; personal experience of war, 64; purpose of, xvii; and testimonies, 17; use of, 142–43; validity of, 162

Parachute training: of Bui Ngoc Thuy, 87–88, 134 (photo); of Hoang Co Lan, 70; parachuting exhibitions (WAC), 91; of women working in military supplies (WAC), 91

Paris Peace Accords (1973), 2, 9, 10

Passerini, Luisa, 123

People's Army of Vietnam (PAVN): armor 44, 47; atrocities by, 112; branches of, 44; infiltration of one million troops into South Vietnam, 1959–1975, 9, 217; Le Minh Dao's stopping of, 110; repulsion of attacks by, 30
People's Republic of China, 10, 40
People's Self-Defense Forces (PSDF), 20, 93, 153, 154
Perks, Robert, 12, 68
Pham Bieu Tam, 69
Pham Duy Khiem, 36–37
Pham Viet Tu, 67, 69
Phan Cong Ly, 60, 128 (photo)
Phan Dong Bich, 11
Phan Thiet, 19
Phoi Pha (Passage of Time) (Trinh Cong Son), 3
Phung Thi Hanh, 92, 93
Pietrzak, Robert, 60
Popular Forces (RVNAF), xvi; Ngo Quan Truong's assessment, 40–41; part of territorial forces, 32; roles, 32; volunteers, 41; wives supporting husbands in the PF, 93–94
Postwar Vietnam (Socialist Republic of Vietnam): burning of books, 193–94; campaign to "exterminate decadent literature," 194; challenges of escaping from Vietnam, 158; communism in, 11; curtailment of individual and religious liberties, 12; disabling injuries and life in, 152–57, 169; discrimination against ethnic Chinese and Amerasians, 12, 85; discriminations against those associated with the South Vietnamese government, 12, 85, 222; erasing of family histories, 174; executions, 124; family separations, 61, 203; family tragedies, 161, 189; forced deurbanization, 11–2, 100, 103, 141; forced displacement, 85, 112, 184; forced labor, 85, 100, 103, 105, 112, 141, 184, 203, 208; forced migration, 15, 45, 143, 198, 201, 203, 207; hardship and poverty, 14, 183–84; human rights abuses, 112; identity and belonging issues, 205; illegal arrest and detention, 141, 245; internment of children, 141–42, 188–89; internment of women, 142; loss and trauma, 16; loyalty to the memory of the dead, 200, 211; mass departures, 11; military women's experiences, 99–105; nationalization of commerce and industries, 12; New Economic Zones, 12, 14, 55, 85, 100, 102, 104, 141, 147, 155, 184, 193–94, 222; propaganda, 191; razing of military cemeteries, 13–14; reeducation camps 11, 14, 25, 38, 45, 55, 60–1, 71, 81, 85, 91, 99, 100–2, 104–6, 112, 116, 141, 144, 146–47, 149–50, 184, 188, 190, 192–93, 195, 197, 201, 203, 243, 245; refugee exodus, 11–12, 180–81, 190, 200; remembrances, 82–86; reticence in relating experiences about, 160; "reunification" under communist regime, 140; secondary trauma, 195; state control of commemorative practices, 13; state repression, 11–2, 15; state violence and suppression, 66, 185; suffering by association, 199; wartime and lives during, 60–66, 143–49. *See also* Internment in communist reeducation camps
Pribbenow, Merle, xix; figures for North Vietnamese troop infiltration into South Vietnam, 1959–1975, 217; translation of North Vietnamese histories, 217, 227
Price, Christopher, 165–66
Price, Geoffrey, 125, 165
Prison camps. *See* Internment in communist reeducation camps
Prisoner, "cross the border" prisoners, 102; Amnesty International

Index

"prisoner of conscience," 1986, 140; communist propaganda coup, 1975, 81; deaths, 34–5; in Hanoi, 52; hard labor camps, 14, 26, 38, 59, 61, 64, 80, 85, 139–42, 189, 199, 203; numbers in reeducation camps, 141; political prisoner in North Vietnam, 139; prisoner-of-war camps, 31, 33–5, 125; prisoner-of-war conventions, 124; of the Viet Minh, 71–2; of war, 16, 19, 33, 80–81, 111, 117, 240–41; reeducation camps, xvi, 25–6, 38, 55, 81, 147, 187, 190, 192, 222; III Geneva Convention, Prisoners of War, 240–41
Psychological Warfare College, 22, 24, 37

Quang Tri battle, 12, 27–29, 94, 146
Quang Tri Hospital, 69, 152
Quang Trung Training Center, xv, 30, 51, 72, 97

Radstone, Susannah, 14
Ranger Association (U.S.), 116
Ranger Association (Victoria, Australia), 116
Rangers (RVNAF), xv–xvi, 16, 29, 68, 71, 155–57; *chot*, 76; deaths after battle of Vinh Loc, 77–78; decorations, 114; *esprit de corps*, 110; evacuation of An Loc, March 1975, 78; 44th Ranger Battalion, 113–14; 42nd Ranger Battalion, 113–14; Go Dau Ha, April 1975, 78–80; history, 76; impact of cuts in U.S. aid, 78; Lap's service, 152–53, 160; mass grave of Rangers, Cu Chi, 117, 120–26, 136–37 (photos); Nguyen Huu An's service, 111–26; Nguyen Manh Tien's medical service, 71, 74–76, 78–80, 83, 110; Pham Van Chuong's service, xv–xvi; prisoners of war, 111–12, 116–17; reconnaissance platoon, 114–15; roles, 76, 114; 3rd Ranger Group, battle of An Loc, 28; 38th Ranger Battalion, 111–12, 116–26; 32nd Ranger Group, 76, 118; Training Center at Duc My, 114; Tran Dinh Tu, commander of 38th Ranger Battalion, 111, 116–26; U.S. Presidential Unit Citations, 114
Reeducation camps. *See* Bamboo Gulag; Internment in communist reeducation camps
Rees, Jacqui, 167
Refugee, xviii, 14, 16, 41, 59, 72, 76, 82, 104, 144, 148, 151, 159, 163, 194, 200, 211; in Australia, 84, 164–68, 172–73, 177–81; boat, 50, 141, 169–70; from communism, 4, 77, 88, 125, 158, 210; community, 73; experience, xvii, 15, 45, 68, 86, 198, 204; 207; land, 141; memoirs, 192; North Vietnam to South Vietnam, 6, 11, 98, 112, 119–20, 123, 126; political refugees, 2; rape of refugee women and girls, 186, 197, 199; reception centers, 95; in Southeast Asia, 85; stress of exile and refugee state, 3; war refugees, 25, 28, 54, 69, 208
Refugee camps, 187, 197, 201; in Australia, 105; boat journeys to, 65; in Hong Kong, 85; in Indonesia, 100, 103, 105, 184; Kota Bharu, 82; in Malaysia, 103; in Southeast Asia, 85; in Thailand, 30, 102, 105, 186
Regional Forces (RVNAF): engagements, 33, 35; expansion, 32; First World War vintage weapons, 40; history, 32; lack of equipment, 33; Ngo Quang Truong's assessment, 40–41; Nguyen Viet Huy's service, 19, 22, 30–32, 33, 35, 36, 40; number of personnel, 32; part of territorial forces, 32; percentage of RVNAF strength, 32; proximity to home, 41; roles, 40; volunteers, 41; wives supporting husbands in the RF, 93

Repatriation Acts Amendment Act (No. 2) (Australia), 167–68, 174, 180, 181
Report of the Senate Standing Committee on Foreign Affairs and Defence (Australia), 166
Republic of Vietnam Armed Forces (RVNAF), 2, 9; armored personnel carriers, 46; Australia's recognition of veterans, 16; compulsory military service, 19–20; desertion problem, 11; disparity between RVNAF logistics and U.S. Army logistics, 27, 29–30, 38–39; impact of cutbacks in U.S. aid, 10; killed in action, 12–13, 98, 238; Lap's service, 156; Lua's elite unit service, 156, 160; Ngoc's elite unit service, 156, 160; Ngoc's visit with officer grandfather, 189–90; Nguyen Ngoc Phach's service, 6–7; Nguyen Viet Huy's service, 19; oral narratives of, 15, 16; postwar hardships of veterans, 14; Special Forces, 21; U.S. supplied medical supplies, 69; varied makeup of soldiers, 36; victories of, 12–13; women's military service in, 89; wounded in action, 13, 70, 98, 239
Resilience, 15, 26, 68, 86, 211; ability to adapt successfully to acute stress and trauma, 60; adjust to different country and culture, 161; collective, 86; core of, 85, 157; memories of subordinate groups, 123; pathways to, 62; personal, 86; physical and emotional, 38; pressures of combat, 45
Resolution 15 (of Le Duan), 7
Returned and Services League of Australia (RSL), 30, 170–71, 174, 176, 204–5; RSL Footscray, xviii; RSL Footscray president, xviii
Revolutionary Development cadres, 93
Riessman, Catherine Kohler, 15
Ripley, John, 44

Rubenstein, Kim, 180
RVNAF Servicewomen's Magazine, 106

Sacrifice, 45; of combat soldiers, 68; for their country, 13; friendship and, 16, 110–11, 126; service and, RVNAF, 4, 174; of 38th Ranger Battalion, 117, 122
Saigon Post newspaper, 7
SAM regiment. See Surface-to-air missile (SAM) regiment
Schramm, Katharina, 204
Second Republic (1967–1975), 4, 6
The Second World War, 15, 22, 36
Shortt, Linda, 143
Siemon-Netto, Uwe, 124
Skultans, Vieda, 17
Soon-Jin Lee, Sandra, 162
Sorley, Lewis, 10
Southeast Asian refugee camps, 85
South Vietnam (Republic of Vietnam), 2; alternative vision of Vietnam, 4; central participants in the war, 12; communist atrocities against civilians, 6–7, 143, 215; communist massacre of civilians in Hue, 1968, 6, 215; communist takeover in 1975, 11–12, 207–8; compulsory military service, 19–20; constitutional government, progress toward, 6; democratization, work on, 6; disabled veterans, 156; disadvantages in war, 10; distribution of rice-growing land, 6; effects of unrelenting war, 6; enrollments in combat units, 1972 Offensive, 83; fall to North Vietnamese forces, 11; First Republic, 4; general mobilization, 1968, 20; impact of Paris Peace Accords, 9–10; Interregnum Period, 4; judiciary, 6; militarized society, 15, 19–20; military cemeteries, 13–14; Mua He Do Lua (Red Fire Summer)—the 1972 Offensive, 30, 67, 98; National Liberation Front, 9; nation-building, work

on, 6; 1966–1967 map, 5; North Vietnam's offensive against, 9–10, 28–29, 43; rally to government, 1968 Tet Offensive, 9, 216; refugees from North Vietnam, 3, 6, 11, 50, 119, 126; representative government, 6; repulsion of 1972 Offensive, 83; resistance to communism, 4; role of Medical Corps, 68–71; RVNAF killed in action, 12–13, 21, 98, 238; RVNAF wounded in action, 13, 21, 70, 98, 239; Second Republic, 4, 6; soldier losses, 12, 21; support by United States, 9, 28–29; Tran Van Quan on loss by, 29–30; two central tasks, 5–6; U.S. Presidential Unit Citations, 13; volunteers, 1968 Tet Offensive, 216
Southwick, Steven, 60
Soviet Union: support of North Vietnam, 9, 12, 29–30, 40, 54, 63–64, 78
Special Broadcasting Service (Australia), 151
Special Forces of the RVNAF, 21
Standing Committee of the International Committee for Disabled Veterans, 156
Stewart, Elizabeth, 68–69
Surface-to-air missile (SAM) regiments (PAVN), 44, 54

Tai, Hue-Tam Ho, 14
Tap San Biet Dong Quan (Ranger Magazine), 120
Taylor, Keith, 6
Telegraph newspaper, 7
Temple of Literature (Hanoi), 1
The Testimony of Lives (Skultans), 17
Tet Offensive. *See* 1968 Tet Offensive
Thach Thi Dinh, 94
Thailand refugee camps, 30, 102, 105, 186
Thanh: assistance to disabled RVNAF veterans in Vietnam, 107–8; biographical background, 94–95; comment on strengths gained in the army, 104; march on Anzac Day, 102, 106; Noncommissioned Officer Course, 94; pivotal role of army service, 107; postwar experiences, 99–100, 104–5; refugee camp work, 102; Regiment 51, 95; resettlement in Australia, 105; war evacuees, 1968 Tet Offensive; 95; work and study in the military, 94
Thien (child of a veteran): childhood in Australia, 196–97; dissociation from Asian, Vietnamese identity, 202; enduring loyalty to Vietnamese past, 205; on father's military experiences, 197–98; on parent's escape from Vietnam, 197; witness to the suffering, postwar difficulties of family, 198
Third Party Congress, 9
Thompson, Paul, 123
Thomson, Alistair, 12, 68
A Thousand Tears Falling (Yung Krall), 20
Three Submissions, 90
Thu Duc Association (Australia), 50, 64
Thu Duc Military Academy xv, 7, 27, 31, 40, 46, 47, 51, 60, 64, 72, 75, 94, 109, 113, 119, 128 (photo), 131 (photo)
Thuy: biographical background, 97–98; educational qualifications, 103; father in the military, 97; incarceration of in postwar Vietnam, 102, 105; incarceration with son, 105; joined from high school, 97; march on Anzac Day, 106; military training, 97; Noncommissioned Officer Course, 97; North Vietnamese expulsion of South Vietnamese amputees from hospitals, 1975, 101; North Vietnamese looting of South Vietnamese hospitals, 1975, 101; postwar experiences, 101–2; Red Fire Summer (1972 Offensive)

Pleiku, 98; resettlement in Australia, 102; traumatized, 105
Thy (child of a veteran): belief in sharing traumatic histories across generations, 201–2; enduring loyalty to Vietnamese past, 205; escape by boat, with family, from Vietnam, 194–95; pain of father's physical, emotional distance, 196; portrayal of father's experiences, 195–96; witness to the suffering, postwar difficulties of family, 198
Tong Le Chan, 52–53
Tôn-Thât, Thanh-Vân, 207
Tran Cam Huong, 91, 106; first Chief of the WAFC, 91
Tran Dang Vinh: gratitude for Australia, 173–74; resettlement in Australia, 170; U.S.-based aerial photography training, 170
Tran Dinh Thai (pseudonym, son of Tran Dinh Tu): account regarding Tran Dinh Tu, 120–21; as "agent of remembrance," 123; record of excavation of mass grave in Cu Chi, 120–21, 122–23, 125
Tran Dinh Tu, 121–23; biographical background, 119; memories of Nguyen Huu An's friendship, 111–12, 116–18, 119, 120, 125, 126; Nguyen Phan's memories of, 121; Ranger Battalion service, 111, 119; *Tap San Biet Dong Quan* article on, 120; Tran Dinh Thai's memories of, 120–21
Tran Duc Tuong, 67–68
Tran Nhu Hung: biographical background, 146, 149; internment in reeducation camps, 146–47, 149; Long Tan Day participation, 151; march on Anzac Day, 151; radio programming in Australia, 151; receipt of help from former Marines, 147–48; resettlement in Australia, 148; social ostracism of, postwar Vietnam, 157; temporary work in Hong Kong, 151; Vietnamese Marine Corps service, 146; volunteer work in Australia's Vietnamese community, 159

Tran Van Giac, 131 (photo), 132 (photo); beheading of naval personnel by the communists, 58–59; biographical background, 55–56; internment in hard labor camps, 59, 62; memories about friends, 109; narrow escapes narrative, 58; postwar sentiments, 63; resettlement in Australia, 59–60, 62; transporting South Korean troops narrative, 57, 61; Vietnamese Navy service, 56–57, 61, 63
Tran Van Nhut, 29
Tran Van Quan, 128 (photo); advanced training in the U.S., 27, 36; biographical background, 22, 26–27; commander of 18th Logistics Battalion, 22, 27–30, 38–39; disparity between RVNAF logistics and U.S. Army logistics, 27, 29–30, 38–39; escape from Vietnam, 30; friendship with Le Minh Dao, 110; internment camp years, 30; internment in prison camps, 30; logistics at battle of An Loc, 27–29, 37–39; loss of friends at battle of An Loc, 109; march on Anzac Day, 30; memories of battle of An Loc, 27–28, 38–39, 109; military service, 27; Ordnance School co-founder, 27; resettlement in Australia, 30, 39; on South Vietnam's loss, 29–30
Transitional justice, 112; connotations of communist war crimes, 124; measures, 125
Tran Xuan Dung, 132 (photo); battalion responsibilities, 74; biographical background, 71–72, 77; combat casualties narrative, 77; form of memorializing the war, 83–84; internment in prison camps, 80–82; length of Marine Corps

service, 83; limited say in choice of military unit, 83; medical service in Vietnamese Marine Corps, 68, 72–74; requalification as medical practitioner, 81; resettlement in Australia, 80–81; ruptured family life of, 77; Tet Offensive narrative, 73–74

Trauma, 15, 60, 103, 105, 178, 202; accumulated traumas, 105, 199; basis for social action, 158; individual, 161; loss and, 16, 62, 68, 104, 157, 211; mass trauma, 85, 140, 161; physical trauma, 159, 160; posttraumatic stress disorder, 170; recovery, 86; secondary trauma, 195; survivor, 85, 158; survivor guilt, 158; traumatic history, 201; traumatic journey, 186; traumatic memory, 80, 162; traumatic stress, 141; traumatized minds and bodies, 142; war trauma, 110, 140, 181

Trinh Cong Son, 208–9

Trinh Tien Khang, 52

Truong Cong Hai: biographical background, 145, 169; gratitude for Australia, 173–74; internment in communist reeducation camps, 145–46, 149, 169; marching on Anzac Day, 150, 151, 158–59, 169; march on Anzac Day, 150, 151, 158–59, 169, 170; postwar posttraumatic stress disorder, 162; receipt of service pension in Australia, 170; social ostracism of, 157; U.S. Seventh Fleet service, 145, 169; Vietnamese Navy service, 148–49, 169

Tuan (child of a veteran, sibling of Ngoc): enduring loyalty to Vietnamese past, 205; extended family war connections, 191–92; resettlement in Australia, 194; thankfulness for intact family unit, 200–201; train journey to the north, 192–93; witnessing of violent bombing,
deaths, 192; witness to burning of books by communists, 193–94; witness to the suffering, postwar difficulties of family, 198

Tu Ve Thanh (Self-Defense Force), 23

The Twenty-Five Year Century (Lam Quang Thi), 21

219th Helicopter Squadron, 53

237th Helicopter Squadron, 52–53

U.N. High Commissioner for Refugees, 148

United States (U.S.): backing of South Vietnam, 9, 28–29, 47; effects of cutbacks to South Vietnam, 10, 56, 64, 71; female officer training in, 92; honoring of Vietnamese veterans in, 170; military advisory role to RVNAF, 11; Nguyen Chi Thien's Congressional testimony, 140; support for Armor Branch, 47; support for Vietnamese Air Force, 28, 52; support for Vietnamese Navy, 56; Thu Duc Association, 64; Tran Dang Vinh's aerial photography training, 170; Tran Van Quan's advanced training in, 27, 36; Truong Cong Hai's service with the Seventh Fleet, 145, 169; Vu Hoai Duc's visits to, 24; Vu Van Bao's aviator training in, 61

U.S. Army Aviation School, 61

U.S. Army Logistics: disparity between RVNAF logistics and U.S. Army logistics, 39–40

U.S. Army Ordnance School, 27

U.S. Army Primary Helicopter School, 61, 131 (photo)

U.S. Coast Guard, 56

U.S. Military Assistance Advisory Group, 76

U.S. Military Assistance Program, 40

U.S. Presidential Unit Citations: to 514th Fighter Squadron, 52; to South Vietnamese units, 13; to 3rd Armored Cavalry Squadron, 47; to

219th Helicopter Squadron, 53; to Vietnamese Marine Corps, 220; to Vietnamese Ranger Units, 114
U.S. Rangers, 76
U.S. Seventh Fleet (Japan), 145, 169
U.S. Special Forces Group, 114
U.S. Women's Army Corps, 89

Van der Kolk, Bessel, 162
Van Tan Thach, 43–44, 45
Veith, George, 9, 126
Veterans' Entitlements Amendment Bill (Australia), 179
Veterans' Entitlements Bill (Australia), 174–75, 176, 179–81
Veterans' service pensions entitlements (Australia), 16–17, 167–69, 172–73, 180–81
Viet Binh Doan Trung Viet (Army of the Center), 90
Viet Minh, 1, 21
Viet Minh People's Army, 24
Vietnam Enquirer newspaper, 7
Vietnamese Air Force. *See* Air Force (RVNAF)
Vietnamese-American Association, 128 (photo)
Vietnamese Australian Veteran Friendship Association, 55
Vietnamese boat people, 151, 194, 210
Vietnamese Marine Corps. *See* Marine Corps (RVNAF)
Vietnamese Marine Corps Association, 151
Vietnamese Navy. *See* Navy (RVNAF)
Vietnamese Rangers. *See* Rangers (RVNAF)
Vietnamese Veterans' Association (Australia), 116, 171
Viet Nam Quoc Dan Dang (National Party of Vietnam), 23
Vietnam Reports for the Vietnam Council on Foreign Relations, 7
Vietnam Veterans' Association, 116
Vietnam War Memorial (Victoria, Australia), 116, 137 (photo), 204–5

Vietnam Workers' Party, 7
Vo, Nghia, 26
Vo Thuong, 70–71
Vu Hoai Duc, 127 (photo); biographical background, 22–23; commander of Psychological Warfare College, 24–25; Free French Forces, North Africa, 23, 37; French Army service, Second World War, 23, 36; internment years, 23, 25–26, 38; military service in Vietnam, 23–24, 41; mistakes of Ngo Dinh Diem government, 24; Montpellier University, 23, 37; National Army of Vietnam, 23–25; *ouvriers non spécialisés* (ONS), 23, 37; postwar internment, 25–26, 38; press officer, 23–24; resettlement in Australia, 26, 38; travels to the United States, 24
Vuong-Riddick, Thuong, 1
Vu Van Bao, 130 (photo), 131 (photo); aviator training in the U.S., 61; biographical background, 50–52; interment in communist prison, 55, 61; Long Tan Day participation, 55; march on Anzac Day, 55; narrative of war service, 53, 54; postwar friendships, 64–65; postwar sentiments, 63, 64; resettlement in Australia, 55, 61; supply and transport missions, 53–54; 237th Helicopter Squadron service, 52–54; Vietnamese Air Force service, 50, 61, 64; writings on Vietnamese history, 64

War crime: Cu Chi, 111–12; 116–26
Warner, Denis, 165, 204
Webb, Nancy Boyd, 140
Whitlam, Gough, 166
Wiesel, Eli, 162
Women in the military: Bui Ngoc Thuy, 20, 87–89; Ho Thi Ve, 90–92, 97; Nguyen Thi Minh Nguyet, 95–98, 100, 102–3, 105,

107; Thanh, 99–100, 102–5, 107; Thuy, 97–98, 101–8

Women's Armed Forces Corps (WAFC) (RVNAF), 16, 89–94; basic military training in, 91–92; history, 89–94; recruitment of female troops, 92; societal resistance to, 92–93; specialized branches, 91, 92, 93; specialized military training in, 92; transition from the WAC, 89, 91; U.S.-based training, 92; WAFC School, 92; WAFC Training Center, 92; women's roles in Viet Binh Doan Trung Viet, 90

Women's Auxiliary Corps (WAC) (RVNAF), 89–91; women's roles in Nu Phu Ta, 90

Xuan Loc: battle of, 30, 110, 209; Le Minh Dao's defense of, 110, 209; unsuccessful attacks by PAVN, 30; Vu Hoai Duc's internment at, 25, 26

About the Author

NATHALIE HUYNH CHAU NGUYEN, PhD, is associate professor and Australian Research Council Future Fellow at the National Centre for Australian Studies at Monash University. Her published works include Praeger's *Memory Is Another Country: Women of the Vietnamese Diaspora*, 2010 *Choice* Outstanding Academic Title; *Voyage of Hope: Vietnamese Australian Women's Narratives*, shortlisted for the 2007 New South Wales Premier's Literary Awards; and *Vietnamese Voices: Gender and Cultural Identity in the Vietnamese Francophone Novel*. She is editor of *New Perceptions of the Vietnam War: Essays on the War, the South Vietnamese Experience, the Diaspora and the Continuing Impact*. Nguyen holds a doctorate from the University of Oxford. Her previous fellowships include an ARC Australian Research Fellowship at the University of Melbourne, a Harold White Fellowship at the National Library of Australia, and a Visiting Fellowship at the University of Oxford.

www.ingramcontent.com/pod-product-compliance
Lightning Source LLC
Chambersburg PA
CBHW050625300426
44112CB00012B/1656